THE POLITICAL ECONOMY
OF RISK AND CHOICE
IN SENEGAL

The Research Program in Development Studies of the Woodrow Wilson School of Public and International Affairs, Princeton University is a group of social scientists interested in developing countries. The program has previously published a series of books, *The Political Economy of Income Distribution in Developing Countries*, under the general editorship of Henry Bienen:

I. TURKEY
Ergun Ozbudun and Aydin Ulusan, editors

II. NIGERIA
Henry Bienen and V.P. Diejomaoh, editors

III. EGYPT
Gouda Abdel-Khalek and Robert Tignor, editors

IV. MEXICO
Pedro Aspe and Paul E. Sigmund, editors

THE
POLITICAL ECONOMY
OF
RISK AND CHOICE
IN
SENEGAL

Edited by
Mark Gersovitz and John Waterbury
Princeton University

Routledge
Taylor & Francis Group

LONDON AND NEW YORK

First published 1987 by
FRANK CASS & CO. LTD.

Published 2004 by Routledge
2 Park Square, Milton Park, Abingdon, Oxon OX14 4RN
605 Third Avenue, New York, NY 10017

Routledge is an imprint of the Taylor & Francis Group,
an informa business

This collection Copyright © 1987 Taylor & Francis

British Library Cataloguing in Publication Data

The Political economy of risk and choice in
  Senegal.
  1. Senegal — Economic conditions
  I. Gersovitz, Mark   II. Waterbury, John
  330.996'305   HC1045

Library of Congress Cataloging-in-Publication Data

The Political economy of risk and choice in Senegal.

  Bibliography: p
  Includes index.
  1. Senegal— Economic conditions.   2. Senegal—Economic
policy.   I. Gersovitz, Mark.   II. Waterbury, John.
HC1045.P65 1987   338.966'3   86–26859
ISBN 0-7146-3297-X

ISBN 13: 978-0-7146-3297-1 (pbk)

Contents

MAP

Preface

The Political Economy of Risk and Choice in Senegal grows out of the efforts and concerns of many people and institutions. The Ministry of Plan in the Government of Senegal and the United States Agency for International Development Dakar called on the Research Program in Development Studies of the Woodrow Wilson School to address Senegal's rural development problems in the light of RPDS experience doing policy relevant research in African countries. RPDS worked closely with the Ministry of Plan and USAID, Dakar on this effort from 1982 to 1984. In particular, we are grateful to the following people for their interest, ideas, and support for our work.

In Dakar, David Shear, Director of USAID was the driving force behind the research from the start. He has been surely one of the most innovative USAID officials in the field. The Ministry of Planning and Cooperation of the Government of Senegal was our principal interlocutor in the elaboration and execution of the project. We are particularly grateful for the support we received from the Director of Planning, Malick Sow, Technical Counselor Abdou Laye Mar Dieye, and our project managers Mademba Ndiaye and Badara Sy. Also in USAID, Norman Rifkin and Donald Rassekh, David Kingsberry and Sam Re especially, helped with complicated financial and administrative problems. In Washington, Francis Johnson, who was desk officer for Senegal when we began the project, was instrumental in helping us to get off the ground. Jacqueline Damon of USAID Dakar was most helpful as was Kathryn Craven.

Also Edouard Benjamin, IBRD Dakar and Johann de Leede at IBRD, Washington, were excellent colleagues. François Simon of the CCEE, Hadj Oumar Touré, Director of SODEVA, Tidiane Sy, Director of ENEA, Jacques Faye of ISRA, James Bingen of Michigan State University, all made important contributions to our work. Also in the Government of Senegal, Mamadou Dieye at the Ministry of Plan, and Alain Marais, in the Office of the Prime Minister, were a source of great support. At the Ministry of Finance, we received help from Idrissa Thiam — now with the World Bank — and Ousmane Sane. At the BCEAO Senegal Agency, we wish to thank Mamadou Niang. Alassane Ouattara, director of Research at the BCEAO – now at the IMF – gave advice and support.

Our academic colleagues in Senegal made our task very pleasant and rewarding. Moustapha Kasse, chairman of the Department of Economics at the University of Dakar-Fann, and his colleagues heard our ideas from the start and provided enthusiastic support. We also thank Marc Raffinot of the University of Paris-IX (Dauphine) then visiting the Ecole Supérieure de Gestion des Entreprises, and Jean-Claude Nascimento of ESGE. Patrick and Sylviane Guillaumont of the University of Clermont I in France and their colleagues shared with us their insights and experience about African monetary issues.

Papa Assane Diouf, former director of the Senegalese Co-operative Service and his successor Mansour Seck gave generous assistance to Sheldon Gellar, giving him access to their Service and to the Senegalese cooperative movement. Thanks also go to Matar Ndiouga N'Diaye, Papa Sene, Ibrahima Baby, Momar Seck, Sidaty Diagne, Abdoulaye Diagne, and Abdoulaye Gueye, Issa N'Diaye, Ibrahima Ba, Bassirou Agne, Ibrahima Sarr, and Moussa N'Diaye, officials with the Cooperative Service and Lutz Sackniess and Hubert Schillinger of the Frederick Ebert Foundation who all provided an insider's view of the cooperative movement.

We are grateful to the commentators who participated in a USAID/Ministry of Plan/RPDS Conference in Dakar, which helped us to refine our work. We are also grateful to a number of Princeton people for their efforts. Our colleagues Mark Montgomery and Joseph Stiglitz made important contributions to our thinking. David Spiro worked valiantly with the manuscript and bibliography. Ellen Goldstein helped in the field. Laura Tuck has written her own excellent contribution to the volume. She also handled many administrative tasks in the field. Agnes Pearson was, as always a helpful and cheerful business manager in the Woodrow Wilson School. Dean of the Woodrow Wilson School, Donald Stokes supported our research. Jerri Kavanagh was, once again, administrative secretary, budget officer, travel agent. At the Office of Research and Projects Administration Glen Davis was most helpful.

I am appreciative of the work of my colleagues who have contributed to the volume and especially to the two editors, Mark Gersovitz and John Waterbury.

We benefitted from the hospitality and warmth of many Senegalese friends and colleagues. We hope the volume will be of some use to the Government of Senegal and to USAID, who supported the research.

HENRY BIENEN
Princeton University

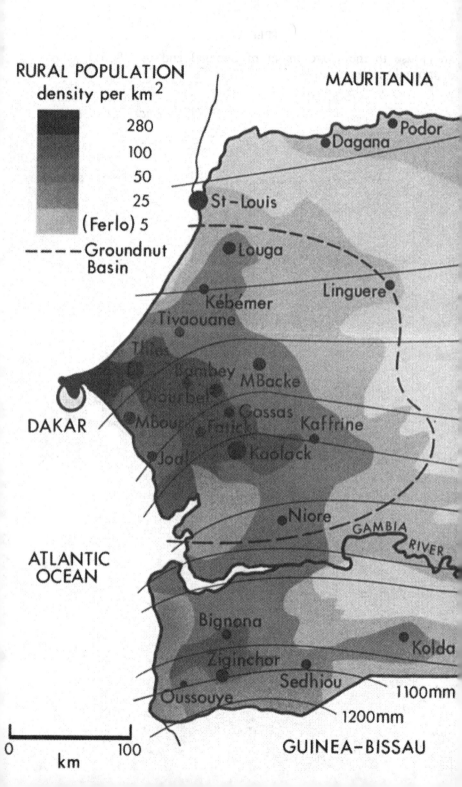

RURAL POPULATION
density per km²

280
100
50
25
(Ferlo) 5
——— Groundnut
Basin

MAURITANIA

Podor
Dagana

St-Louis

Louga

Kébémer

Linguere

Tivaouane

Thies

Bambey

MBacke

Diourbel

Gossas

MBour

Fatick

Kaffrine

DAKAR

Joal

Kaolack

Niore

GAMBIA

RIVER

ATLANTIC
OCEAN

Bignona

Kolda

Ziginchor

Sedhiou

1100mm

Oussouye

1200mm

GUINEA-BISSAU

0   100
      km

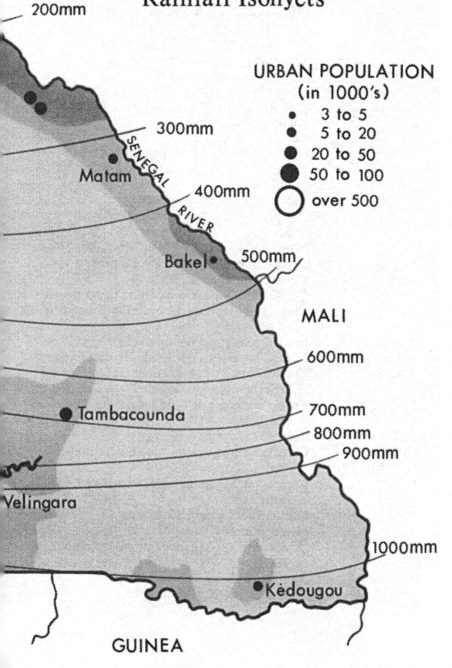

SENEGAL: Population Densities and Rainfall Isohyets

200mm

URBAN POPULATION
(in 1000's)
- 3 to 5
- 5 to 20
- 20 to 50
- 50 to 100
- over 500

300mm

SENEGAL

Matam

RIVER

400mm

Bakel

500mm

MALI

600mm

Tambacounda

700mm

800mm

900mm

Velingara

1000mm

Kėdougou

GUINEA

Glossary

ACP	African, Caribbean, Pacific countries party to the Lomé Agreement
ADB	African Development Bank
Animateur	Community development cadre
AOF	Afrique Occidentale Française
ATCR	agent technique de la communauté rurale
assakas	portion of crop given to religious leaders
aval	endorsement, guarantee
bana–bana	rural petty trade
barème	overhead charge on producer price
BCEAO	Banque Centrale des Etats de l'Afrique de l'Ouest
BDS	Bloc Démocratique Sénégallais
BNDS	Banque Nationale de Développement du Sénégal
BOM	Bureau d'Organisation et de Méthodes
BSD	Banque Sénégalaise de Développement
carré	extended household
CCCE	Caisse Centrale de Coopération Economique
CFA	Currency of UMOA (Coopération Financière en Afrique)
chef de carré	head of communal household unit
CIEH	Comité Interafricain d'Etudes Hydrauliques
CILSS	Comité Permanent Inter-Etats de Lutte contre la Sécheresse dans le Sahel
CNCAS	Caisse Nationale de Crédit Agricole Sénégalaise
cotisation	dues
CPSP	Caisse de Péréquation et de Stabilisation des Prix
CSPT	Compagnie Sénégalaise des Phosphates de Taiba
CSS	Compagnie Sucrière Sénégalaise
daara	Murid pioneer villages of unmarried males
DAC	Development Assistance Committee of the OECD
démariage	thinning of plants
DS	Direction de la Statistique

désenclavement	reducing regional isolation
EB	encadreur de base
économie de traite	colonial economic trading system based on groundnuts
EEC	European Economic Community
EFF	Extended Funding Facility of the IMF
EMS	European Monetary System
ENEA	Ecole Nationale d'Economie Appliquée
escale	trading post
exploitations	farming units
FAC	Fonds d'Assistance et de Coopération
FAO	Food and Agriculture Organization
Ferlo	pastoral transhumant zone
filière arachide	groundnut production and marketing system
GOPEC	Groupement Opérational Permanent d'Etudes et de Concentration
GOS	Government of Senegal
Groupexar	Consortium of groundnut buying houses
hivernage	rainy season
houe	plough, harrow
IBRD	International Bank for Reconstruction and Development
ICS	Industries Chimiques du Sénégal
IDA	International Development Association
IFAD	International Fund for Agricultural Development
IFC	International Finance Corporation
IMF	International Monetary Fund
IRAM	Institut de Recherches et d'Application des Méthodes de Développement
ISRA	Institut Sénégalais de Recherches Agronomiques
jom	sense of honor
LDC	Less Developed Country
marabout	leader or noble of religious order
ménage	household
Murid	follower of Muslim religious order
navetane	immigrant rural worker
NGO	Non-Governmental Organization
OCA	Office de Commercialisation Agricole
ODA	Official development assistance

OECD	Organisation for Economic Cooperation and Development
OMVS	Organisation pour la Mise en Valeur du Fleuve Sénégal (Senegal River Basin Development Organization)
ONCAD	Office National de Coopération et d'Assistance pour le Développement
Organismes Stockeurs	private merchant groups in groundnut marketing
PIDAC	Project Intégré de Développement Agricole de la Casamance
prêts de soudure	loans for hungry season
RDA	Rural Development Associations (SAED, SODEVA, etc.)
RFM	Rural financial markets
ristourne	rebate system on groundnut purchases
SAED	Société d'Aménagement et d'Exploitation des Terres de Delta et de la Vallée du Sénégal et de la Falemé
SAL	World Bank Structural Adjustment Loan
SATEC	Société d'Aide Technique et de Coopération
secco	cooperative collection station for groundnuts
SEIB	Société Electrique et Industrielle du Baol
SFIO	Section Française de l'Internationale Ouvrière
SIES	Société Industrielle des Engrais Sénégalaise
SIP	Société Indigène de Prévoyance (pre-independence coops)
SM	Service Météorologique
SMDR	Société Mutuelle du Développement Rural
SODEFITEX	Société de Développement des Fibres Textiles
SODEVA	Société de Développement et de Vulgarisation Agricole
SOFISEDIT	Société Financière Sénégalaise pour le Développement de l'Industrie et du Tourisme
SOMIVAC	Société pour la Mise en Valeur de la Casamance
SONADIS	Société National de Distribution
SONAR	Société Nationale d'Approvisionnement du Monde Rural
SONED	Société Nationale des Etudes de Développement

SONEPI	Société Nationale d'Etudes et de Promotion Industrielle
SONOCOS	Société Nationale de Commercialisation des Oléaginaux du Sénégal
soudure	hungry season (May–November)
souleveuse	groundnut lifter
sourga	unmarried male
SPIA	Société des Produits Industriels et Agricoles
SSPT	Société Sénégalaise des Phosphates de Thiès
Stabex	Stabilisation of export revenues, part of Lomé Agreement
taalibe	followers of Marabout (literally 'students')
terres neuves	new lands; unexploited agricultural zones
thème	technical package
tieboudienne	Senegalese national dish of fish in sauce on broken rice
toll diatti	cash fields
toll gor	bush fields
toll keur	fields of the carré
tontine	rotating savings association
UMOA	Union Monétaire Ouest Africaine (West African Monetary Union)
UNTS	Union Nationale des Travailleurs Sénégalais
UPS	Union Progressiste Sénégalaise

Introduction

Mark Gersovitz and John Waterbury

I. THE STRUCTURE OF THE STUDY

The chapters in this study take as their common theme the analysis of risk in agricultural production, management, and policy implementation in Senegal. Because the agricultural sector occupies such an important, if not preponderant, place in the Senegalese economy, our study often borders on an analysis of that economy as a whole. In the course of what follows, we hope to shed light on formal economic approaches to risk analysis and on policy-specific applications in Senegal. In both senses our findings will be of broader comparative usefulness, particularly as regards Sahelian agriculture.

The undertaking is inter-disciplinary, combining the concerns of economists, political scientists and what might best be called policy analysts. We focus on three sorts of actors in Senegal; the cultivators themselves, the agencies of state intervention in agriculture, and the state, taken here for the sake of convenience as embodying a unified set of interests, and which is the most powerful force in determining new directions for Senegalese agriculture. Each of these actors corresponds crudely to a hierarchy of power in the Senegalese polity, and each warrants some further elaboration here.

The cultivators bear the greatest risks in the process of agricultural production and marketing. They are responsible for their own subsistence production, centered on millet, and in the event of failure must rely on their personal grain reserves to survive. Internal markets and imported rice may alleviate subsistence crises but not obviate them. Cultivators also bear the principal risks in the production of Senegal's major cash crop, groundnuts (peanuts). Because of the importance of groundnuts to Senegal's exports and the economy as a whole, the state has made a greater effort to share risks with the cultivator, especially through the national seed stock, rural credit, provision of fertilizers on credit, and extension services. The cultivator, however, depends on groundnuts for much of his or her cash income, and in the event of production failures there is no immediate compensatory mechanism for lost revenue.

1

The greatest unknown facing Senegalese cultivators is rainfall. Since the middle 1960s rainfall has been below norms established earlier in the century, with periods of severe drought producing disastrous conditions in the periods 1968–72 and 1981–85.

In the chapters by Gellar, Gersovitz, Tignor, Tuck and Waterbury, an attempt is made to delineate the major elements of risk confronting peasant cultivators and the strategies they have developed to balance subsistence and cash production, credit and debt, state and private actors in marketing and the provision of inputs, and off-farm and on-farm revenues. What becomes clear in these contributions is that the Senegalese peasantry has become habituated to and skilled in dealing with markets and state agents. Adversarial relations inevitably emerge, with the state seeking to extract a surplus from the agrarian sector through administered prices while the peasant resorts to parallel private markets and debt default. In the present year, 1985, the government put through a thinly-veiled reduction in the groundnut producer price by increasing the proportion withheld to pay for the national seed stock and for fertilizers from 10 to 20 cfa/kg. Inasmuch as the quality of the seed is mediocre, total supply inadequate, and fertilizers available to only a very few cultivators, the withheld 20 cfa meant a defacto reduction in the purchase price from 70 cfa to 50 cfa/kg. The response of the peasants was dramatic. Of the middling harvest estimated at 700,000 metric tons, only 168,000 tons were marketed through official channels. The rest was sold on parallel markets in Senegal or smuggled to Gambia and Mali. The Senegalese state was left with only enough groundnuts to reconstitute the national seed stock, generally maintained at 120,000 tons, with another 50,000 tons left over for the crushing factories whose capacity is about 900,000 tons per annum. Numerous examples of a similar nature have accumulated over the quarter century since Senegal became independent.

At the upper level of the power hierarchy, the Senegalese state bears considerable risks of a macro-economic variety. These pertain mainly to the country's balance of payments and its ability to import vital commodities such as petroleum and rice. The export of groundnut products (groundnut oil and feed cake) has diminished over the years as a proportion of total exports but still accounts for about a third of all Senegal's export earnings. Fish products, phosphates, and tourist receipts account for most of the rest. Still, production short-falls of groundnuts and food staples may cause a general contraction in domestic demand, lead to idle capacity in processing industries, and oblige the state to increase its imports of rice and wheat. In this sense the impact of poor agricultural performance is far greater than its weight in Senegal's exports.

The larger picture of how the agricultural sector fits into the Senegalese economy as a whole is developed by Mark Gersovitz in Chapter 1. Macro-economic policy is not developed in a political vacuum, either domestically or internationally. John Lewis analyses the process of 'policy dialogue' between Senegal and its major providers of concessional aid. Aid has been important in offsetting shocks to the Senegalese economy. Maintaining these flows is clearly another sort of risk that the state must face. The dialogue has become increasingly intense since 1979 and the launching in that year of a stabilization program (plan de redressement). It has focussed on a range of policy issues from government deficits and consumer subsidies to how best to organize rural producers and agricultural credit. In a related analysis, Gersovitz uses information on uncertainty to discuss one part of the aid Senegal receives, the European Community's Stabex payments. This scheme is designed to stabilize the export earnings of the Community's associated members among the developing countries. Finally, at the macro level, Jorge de Macedo assesses the implications for Senegal's foreign trade and balance of payments of its membership in the West African monetary union and its fixed exchange rate with the French franc. He pays special attention to the way in which this system allows Senegal to absorb shocks.

Between the cultivator and the state are a host of agencies and institutions that are designed to carry out public policy, or which directly affect the ability of public agencies to perform their tasks. Since 1960 such agencies have proliferated. Rural cooperatives have been established to handle primary marketing of agricultural produce, monitor peasant debt, and provide production inputs to members. Both Robert Tignor and Sheldon Gellar look closely at the history and performance of the cooperative system. The provision of public short term credit for seed and fertilizers and medium term credit for equipment and draft animals has been an essential element in promoting increased agricultural production. Laura Tuck examines the functioning of rural financial markets and the combinations of public and private credit to which peasants have access. She speculates about the possibility of promoting rural savings programs to avoid the periodic mass defaults on peasant debt that have become common since 1968.

Nearly all facets of groundnut, cotton, and rice marketing and processing are in the hands of the state. Referred to as *filières* in French, these 'chains' from cultivator to final consumer are buttressed by several kinds of state intermediaries. The national groundnut seed stock, for example, has been managed by parastatal organizations, first by the Office National de Coopération et d'Assistance pour le Développement (ONCAD) up to 1980, and since then by the Société Nationale d'Approvisionnement du Monde Rural (SONAR).[1] In each of Senegal's major regions rural development associations (Sociétés rurales de développement) were established to provide inputs such as fertilizers and fungicides, agricultural equipment, and crop-specific extension services. Finally, ONCAD and SONAR handled the official purchases of the groundnut crop, while the Société d'Aménagement et d'Exploitation des Terres de Delta et de la Vallée du Sénégal et de la Falemé (SAED) and the Société de Développement des Fibres Textiles (SODEFITEX) took on most purchases of locally produced rice and cotton. They then sold these commodities to state-owned crushing plants and to mills and textile plants, both public and private, for processing.

The intent of all these intermediate organizations was and is to sustain predictable levels of production and to reduce risks for the cultivators, the processors, and ultimately the state. In a general sense, however, public policies and public intervention in the agricultural production process, in marketing, the provision of inputs and credit, in debt recovery and in agricultural processing introduced new elements of risk and uncertainty without alleviating the old. Waterbury looks at these issues in his chapter on state intervention with particular attention to the groundnut basin. In addition the very important groundnut processing industry is analysed by Gersovitz and conclusions drawn as to the relationship between producer prices offered peasants and the variable and fixed costs of operating the crushing plants.

Unavoidably certain important issues of an analytic and policy-relevant variety have been ignored in our analysis. Ours is not a study of the entire political economy of Senegal nor even a complete overview of the agrarian economy. For example, various of the authors touch upon some of the institutional underpinnings of production in the Delta of the Senegal river and in its upstream portions, the Fleuve, as well. But relatively little is said about rice production in the Casamance, cotton production in Sénégal Oriental, maize production in the Sine-Saloum or animal husbandry anywhere. The very important question of the trade-offs between using scarce public and private sources to sustain or increase production in the heavily-populated rainfed areas (see Map 1) and costly projects to expand agriculture in the Senegal, Gambia, and Casamance river valleys is not squarely addressed. Our basic assumption is that no matter how the Senegalese authorities assess these trade-offs, for the next fifteen years or so the rainfed areas will continue to bear the major burden of agricultural production.

II. AN OVERVIEW OF SENEGALESE AGRICULTURAL POLICY SINCE 1960

In its broad outlines, the story in Senegal will sound familiar to observers of the agrarian crisis in Africa and in other LDCs. Long-term economic viability appears constantly sacrificed to short-term political expediency. Scarce resources are 'wasted' in patronage and corruption, over-staffed and inefficient bureaucracies are saddled with complicated tasks better left to markets, and the agrarian sector is skimmed in order to pay for the bureaucrats and for capital-intensive industries. Michael Lipton (1977), Goran Hyden (1980) and Robert Bates (1981) have all told variants of this story for the developing world in general and for Africa in particular, and all have focussed upon the public policy issues involved.

Since the late 1960s, Senegal's economy has been in crisis. With a few exceptions agricultural production, percapita and per hectare, has stagnated or declined as has the general standard of living for the bulk of the population. At the same time the civil service wage bill has grown substantially while public sector enterprises have incurred large operating losses, the two factors combining to generate high levels of deficit financing. All of these problems are susceptible to public policy remedies, but it is moot whether or not Senegal could have avoided economic stagnation, punctuated by periodic crisis, under any set of policies. At best agriculture and animal husbandry in this part of the Sahel are a high-stake poker game.

The Senegalese countryside has been put under severe stress, as a result of a human population growth rate of about 2.8 percent per annum and a saw-toothed but parallel growth of the animal population. The stripping of ground cover for fuel, the clearing of bush land for new fields or pasture, over-grazing everywhere, soil erosion and soil depletion in the absence of fallows or fertilizers, contributed to this situation. Crop diversification and hybrid seeds offer at best palliatives to the basic crisis. Given Senegal's level and distribution of rainfall in most areas, only a limited number of crops can be grown; millet, manioc and cowpeas for basic food, and groundnuts for cash. Rainfall in many parts of the country is too sparse to allow peasants to profit from chemical fertilizers, and, in the last decade, the cost of fertilizers has tended to rise against the value of Senegal's major field crops. Maize may offer an alternative for a limited number of farmers in the better-watered areas of southern and south-eastern Senegal, but the bulk of the rural population lies north of these zones. Despite the fact that 70 percent of the work-force is engaged in agriculture and that nearly all peasants rely to a significant extent on marketing their produce for cash (groundnuts, rice, cotton, millet, maize), in recent years the agricultural sector has contributed only about 15 percent of GDP.

Senegal does have rivers with year-round, but highly uneven, discharge: the Senegal, the Gambia, and the Casamance. Since the great drought of the early 1970s it became a national priority to harness these rivers. They were and are seen as the key to lowering the stakes in Senegal's agricultural game. Experts as diverse as Paul Pélissier (1966) and Samir Amin (1973) saw Senegal's agricultural future as lying in the river valleys and zones benefitting from regular rainfall. Some of Senegal's major donors, especially the IBRD, have been skeptical that large-scale water-storage projects on these rivers, and the introduction of irrigated agriculture to hundreds of thousands of hectares heretofore farmed, if at all, under recessional flood conditions, would be financially profitable or socially feasible. For our purposes here that question will be left entirely open. What should be retained, however, is that the thinly-veiled despair generated by the decline of Senegal's central groundnut basin has been matched by the hopes engendered by harnessing the rivers. From a purely economic point of view, there may have been and may still be among some of Senegal's policy-makers a temptation to write off rainfed agriculture in the groundnut basin, or at least in the northern two-thirds of it, and to use scarce financial resources to develop the river basins as quickly as possible.

Politically a policy of benign neglect of the agricultural heartland would be impracticable. About 70 percent of Senegal's six million inhabitants are rural.[2] About one half of these live in the regions of Thiès, Diourbel, Louga and the northern Sine-Saloum. In such areas successful production is either impossible or highly uncertain. In another twenty years' time the river valleys may be able to take over from the heartland the basic tasks of feeding the population and earning foreign exchange. But what does the government do with the heartland in the meantime? The question is momentous because it is precisely in these north central regions of the ground-nut basin that the *marabouts*, leaders of the powerful religious orders, and their followers are the most heavily concentrated and where, presumably, their economic interests are most at stake. Leaving these regions to their own devices while the State shifts resources into geographically, economically, and politically peripheral regions (Fleuve, Sénégal Oriental, Casamance) is not, in the medium term, a real option.

What we may expect then is a political and economic holding operation in the heartland. A review of the major policy initiatives toward the agricultural sector over the last twenty-five years may help us grasp how this operation will be conducted.

The agricultural lot of the groundnut basin and attendant government policies have gone through three fairly distinct phases and have entered a fourth. In the first seven years of independence, from 1960–67, agricultural conditions were good, French preferential prices for groundnut products above world prices, and Senegal's policy-makers intent on strengthening the country's role as a primary-produce exporter. The French, well before their departure, had launched Senegal's groundnut processing industry. Independent Senegal did not immediately embark on any further import-substituting industrialization. The seven-year period is, however, divided into two sub-periods. The first lasted from 1960–63 and witnessed a major effort at rural institution-building in the name of African socialism. The effort hinged on the implantation of a nationwide system of agricultural cooperatives to provide credit and inputs, market crops (almost exclusively groundnuts) and provide basic food goods during the 'hungry season'. An explicit goal of the effort was to displace the private money-lenders and crop purchasers (mainly Lebanese) who were judged to be exploitative, and, implicitly, by giving peasants 'democratic' control over the coops, to erode rural patronage systems in the hands of *notables* and *marabouts*. The new coops were to be paralleled by a more pronounced penetration of the countryside by the then-single party, the Union Progressiste Sénégalaise (UPS). The standard bearer of these policies was the Prime Minister, Mamadou Dia, unlike President Léopold Senghor, a Muslim with solid links to some of the *marabouts*, and yet a man fully committed to the reforms he was undertaking. It is not so clear if Senghor shared his commitment, but however that may be, both found enthusiastic support from

French proponents of *animation rurale* (see esp. Belloncle, 1964; Camboulives, 1967; and Gellar, 1980 and in this volume).

During this brief period, the government saw rural problems largely in terms of social organization, i.e., helping the producers to assume direct responsibility for their own production, so as to become real citizens. Both the ideology and the goals were not far different from Tanzania's *ujamaa* movement. Even as the initial impetus lost momentum after 1963, the State issued the National Domain Law in 1964 that linked access to agricultural land to proof of having cultivated it in the past. Private rural property in the conventional sense was abolished; the land was for those who worked it, and could be taken away, by rural councils, from those who were derelict in their cultivation.

Mamadou Dia fell into disgrace in the wake of the dissolution of the Mali Federation (Foltz, 1965) and his efforts at rural institution-building were quietly abandoned. A new approach soon became evident, and it was shaped by internal and external factors. Senghor, as Blanchet has shown, was as taken by Galbraith's view of the new industrial state as he was by an African socialism rooted in the parochial solidarities of pre-colonial African rural society. His faith in the ability of a small group of highly-trained managers and technocrats to master-mind the development process became stronger after 1963. In an address to the 7th UPS Congress of December 1969 he went so far as to say 'the principal obstacle to development is the lack of a sufficient number of technicians, managers and trained administrators' (Blanchet, 1983: 137). Significantly, Abdou Diouf, later to become President, Habib Thiam, Abdou Diouf's Prime Minister until 1984, and other young Senegalese technocrats began their ascent in the middle and late 1960s.

President Senghor's inclinations were re-enforced by two external factors. First, because of the position of France in the EEC (specifically as a result of commitments made under the Treaty of Yaoundé in 1963), French preferential prices for agricultural produce from its former African colonies were to be phased out by 1968. In order to uphold rural revenues the French recommended a major effort to increase agricultural productivity: selling more groundnuts even at a lower price would protect the cash income of the peasants. The French approach, entrusted to SATEC (Société d'Aide Technique et de Coopération), had little to do with institutions or citizen–peasants, and a great deal to do with improved cultivator techniques (draught animals, early sowing, proper weeding), improved seed adapted to rainfall zones, and extensive use of chemical fertilizers. This productionist approach corresponded in time to a general emphasis on the part of the donors to promote seed–water–fertilizer packages first developed for Mexico, the Philippines and India. With respect to Senegal, SATEC must have assumed that rainfall or water supply would not be a critical problem and devoted its attention to tools, techniques, seed and fertilizers. In this new mode the coops simply became the main transmission centers for supplying the inputs on credit and collecting the produce for the payment of debt and for marketing. A new parastatal entity was created in 1966 to handle provision of credit to the coops, to manage the national groundnut seed stock, to purchase groundnuts for resale to the crushing plants, and to recover peasant debt. The new entity, soon to become a monster in the groundnut basin, was ONCAD.

Perhaps, had average rainfall been sustained, pundits would have been writing in the early 1970s of 'the Senegalese miracle.' Instead rainfall declined just as preferential French groundnut prices came to an end. The two 'shocks' produced what has been euphemistically termed the 'malaise paysan', including massive default on debt, and introduced the second major period in agricultural policy-making.

No clear policy line emerged between 1968 and 1973. There was no return to institution-building in the countryside, and the cooperatives became more than ever simple extractive devices. Even in that task they failed, and in the wake of the drought the government forgave 2.6 billion cfa in accumulated short term debt (Laura Tuck, in this volume). The technical approach of the SATEC program did not fare well either, and while production increased when rainfall was adequate, the increase depended more on acreage expansion at the expense of fallows than upon more intensive cultivator techniques. Still the State persisted along these lines even after the SATEC mission came to an end in 1968. In the groundnut basin SODEVA (Société de Développement et de Vulgarisation Agricole) picked up where SATEC had left off, and other parastatal entities were created: in the irrigated areas of the lower Senegal river basin (SAED), the cotton growing areas of southeastern Senegal (SODEFITEX), and the rice growing areas of the Casamance (SOMIVAC, Société pour la Mise en Valeur de la Casamance). These entities, along with ONCAD, took on the provision of inputs and credit extension services, marketing and debt recovery. They epitomized the elitist-managerial approach to sustaining production that Senghor had come to favor. It was premised on the idea that intelligent planners and diligent managers could handle basic problems of production and distribution more efficiently than markets. The premise, it is important to note, was shared to varying degrees by the major international donors. They were willing to promote policy solutions to development challenges that were technicist, elitist, and dependent upon state intervention.

Despite the impressive investment of human and financial resources into the effort to upgrade production, the results were disappointing. The trends in groundnut production and marketing, the priority area for the Senegalese government, are indicative of the general problems. Gross production peaked in the decade 1960–70 on the strength of increased acreage. Yields however showed no improvement over those established in the 1930s, a period in which the use of chemical fertilizers was virtually unknown. After 1970 the impact of diminishing and variable rainfall, deteriorating soil quality, non-incentive pricing policies, and inefficiencies and corruption in parastatal marketing agencies combined to lower gross production and yields. Moreover since the late 1960s peasants have diverted more than a quarter of their harvest into parallel markets, a proportion that rose dramatically in the early 1980s (see Table 1). The 'malaise paysan', that was first identified around 1967, has become a quasi-permanent feature in the agrarian sector ever since.

The rural world was not alone in its malaise after 1968. While it may be true that Senegal maintained an out-sized bureaucracy that had once had all of French West Africa as its field of action, it was

TABLE 1

Production, Yield and Marketing Trends
for Senegalese Groundnuts 1930–1985

Periods	Average Total Production M.Ts	Average Yield in kg/ha	Average Tonnage Mkted	% of Prod. Mkted
1930/31–1939/40	529,000	869	426,200	81
1940/41–1949/50	443,000	790	309,920	70
1950/51–1959/60	699,000	880	452,200	65
1960/61–1969/70	937,000	879	684,200	73
1970/71–1979/80	867,000	767	660,000	76
1980/81–1984/85	756,000	704	417,200	55

Sources: for the periods 1930–1960, Bernard Founou-Tchuigoua, 1981 pp.130 and 154–55; for the period since 1960 the Bulletin of the BCEAO, various numbers, Ministry of Rural Development, La Nouvelle Politique Agricole, 1984, and African Economic Digest, various numbers.

not particularly spoiled. Nor were fully-employed formal sector workers. Between 1960 and 1967 salaries and wages declined in real terms by about 25 percent (George Martens, 1983). In May–June 1968, perhaps inspired by similar events in Paris, extensive student–worker demonstrations and riots broke out in Dakar. It was the most profound political crisis the Senghor regime had yet faced.

With his urban constituencies in disarray, Senghor had to make sure his rural alliances were in order. Given the drought, such order could be seen only in relative terms, but the forgiving of rural debt and a small increase in the producer price of groundnuts should be viewed as part of the fencemending process. Sometime in the period after 1968 the goal of eroding local patronage networks and the power of the *marabouts* was abandoned. Indeed, in conjunction with local party ward-heelers, they were allowed to take over the State's various distributive agencies at the local level.

The year 1973 is the terminal date for this second period because, on the one hand, rainfall had begun to recover, and, on the other, the first great OPEC oil shock was accompanied in Senegal by a dramatic surge in the world price of one of its major exports, phosphates. The third period was initiated in relative optimism. Groundnut production began to recover, achieving record levels in the middle 1970s. Groundnut producer prices in 1974 were more than twice their 1970 level although in constant terms the increase was considerably less. The retail price of rice, raised in 1974 in order to reduce government subsidies, was dropped again in 1976. In 1973 the value of Senegal's exports was only 54 percent of that of its imports but rose steadily thereafter, on the strength of groundnuts and phosphates, to 82 percent in 1977.

As in the early years of independence, the Senegalese state had room for policy maneuver. This time it set its sights in unambiguous fashion on import-substituting industrialization but with significant emphasis upon exporting its products. Its strategy was to be founded on the transformation of agricultural and other primary products. The lesson of the drought had been learned: simple reliance on agricultural production and exports could not guarantee the health of the Senegalese economy. In the official view the future lay then in improved agricultural productivity, expansion of irrigated acreage, and in industrial transformation. The principal chains were to include expanded transformation of groundnuts into oil products and feed cakes;[3] cotton into textiles, sugar cane into refined sugar; phosphates into fertilizers, maritime fish into fish meal, off-season vegetables and fruits into high-price exports to European winter markets. The State was to take the lead in financing and controlling all these sectors in collaboration, where appropriate, with multinational enterprises. The Fourth Plan aimed at achieving an annual growth rate of 9 percent. At the same time all sectors of the economy were to be brought under increasing Senegalese control through the displacement of foreign entrepreneurs and technicians in both the private and public sectors.

This period witnessed a rapid growth in public sector enterprise and in the government's wage bill, but the country's external accounts were healthy, foreign assistance was substantial, and the high investment levels of the Fourth Plan were, it was hoped, sure to give a powerful boost to domestic productivity. By 1977 however, the donor community had begun to become alarmed at growing government deficits and parastatals expanding prodigiously without adequate auditing or follow up. As these fears began to crystallize, the rains once again failed; world phosphate prices tumbled, and the second oil shock of 1979 left the Senegalese economy prostrate.

This second crisis, beginning in 1977/78, is more profound than the first of 1968–72, and Senegal has in no way yet emerged from it. All major economic indicators became unfavorable; by 1980 the value of exports covered only 45 percent of the import bill, the external debt grew rapidly, the investment program became almost totally dependent on external assistance, and the government deficit, fueled by heavy borrowing on the part of unprofitable parastatals, grew rapidly. After 1981 world market prices for groundnut products fell. To make matters worse, it was found that Senegalese groundnut feed cakes contained dangerous levels of aflotoxin, a carcinogen, and feed cake exports gave ground in European markets to soy cake and other substitutes. Senegal was obliged under these circumstances to move hesitatingly toward structural adjustment loans negotiated through the IBRD, the IMF and the major creditors.

The reforms sought included the obvious measures of reducing government spending through a deceleration in salary and hiring increases, whittling away at consumer subsidies; reorganizing the parastatals and bringing them under tighter financial control; reorganizing the rural credit system and the cooperatives. Declarations of intent were embodied in the country's Plan de Redressement (1979), and a spectacular step was taken toward implementation with the dissolution in 1980 of ONCAD, an organization that left behind 100 billion cfa in debts. In the midst of all this, President

Senghor, as he had long predicted, left the Presidency to his Prime Minister, Abdou Diouf, on 31 December, 1980.

The new President, despite his long experience as Prime Minister, occupied his office through designation not through election. Without a popular mandate, President Diouf had to proceed cautiously in implementing the SAP/SAL. Some of his first steps ran directly counter to the spirit of the SAL. As had occurred a decade earlier, all short term peasant debt was forgiven while medium and long term debt, held mainly by prosperous farmers and *marabouts* was to be rescheduled. In fact it too was simply canceled. The President temporized on all the major reforms sought by the donors, hoping that declarations of intent and limited initiatives on prices would be enough to hold the donors at bay and to keep open the channels of external assistance. His election to the Presidency was scheduled for February 1983, and there were hopes that once he had a popular mandate, he could take on the reform package with greater determination.

The elections have come and gone, and Abdou Diouf now has his mandate. Unfortunately his election preceded what became one of the worst agricultural years in memory. Nonetheless there are signs that he is moving in directions the donors want, and although the structural adjustment program was scrapped, some of the same reforms are being carried out in the context of an IMF stand-by agreement.

In August of 1983 President Abdou Diouf pushed though major consumer price increases, and followed that with increases in electricity and public transport rates. In compliance with the stabilization program, a cap was placed on public sector wage increases and a hiring freeze was initiated. Further price increases were imposed in 1985. In the space of three years the retail price of rice had doubled.

Moreover the President agreed to begin the process of dismantling a number of parastatal entities. All of the rural development associations were slated for dissolution except SAED. SONAR, in charge of the national seed stock, was also scheduled to be abolished. The oil crushing plants are to take over management of a reduced stock of 60,000 tons, available on credit only to farmers who use official marketing channels, while another 40,000 tons will be held for direct cash purchase. It was announced that after an absence of twenty years, private traders would be allowed back into the marketing process. This was merely acknowledgement of a fait accompli. Finally an across-the-board increase in produce prices was announced for 1985/86. The groundnut price had been 70 cfa/kg with 20 cfa withheld to cover the costs of seed storage and fertilizers. The new announced price was 90 cfa/kg with none withheld.

If all these measures are implemented and maintained, Abdou Diouf's government will have brought about a real policy revolution in Senegal. It could easily be overwhelmed by poor rainfall as well as the need to dilute austerity measures to service important political clienteles. Nonetheless, Abdou Diouf has shown great courage in promoting reforms whose benefits will not be felt for some time to come.

NOTES

1. To be done away with in 1986.
2. This is not to be taken very strictly. In years of poor rainfall and low production, many rural dwellers migrate to the cities in the dry season, December–May, in search of post-harvest, pre-planting work. Even in good years this kind of migration is substantial. Neat divisions between rural and non-rural work force or inhabitants misrepresent the true situation.
3. In 1974/75 and 1975/76 groundnut production reached 1 million and 1.4 million tons. These high levels may have seemed to justify the expansion of local crushing and refining capacity to 900,000 tons.

CHAPTER ONE

Some Sources and Implications of Uncertainty in the Senegalese Economy

Mark Gersovitz

I. INTRODUCTION

Fluctuations in climatic conditions and in international prices are important determinants of the well-being and behavior of participants in Senegal's economy. Climatic uncertainty is perhaps the most apparent feature of this economy. Indeed, it is the country's misfortune to provide the prototype for a poor economy reliant on a rainfed agriculture that is subject to significant climatic variation. In addition, Senegal is a small country that obtains many goods through international trade. It consequently faces additional uncertainty about the terms on which it can exchange its exports for foreign goods. Furthermore, Senegal receives transfers from various foreign sources, and these fluctuate from year to year (see also chapter 9 by John Lewis).

A simple framework for thinking about uncertainty is the sequence of anticipatory action–realization–reaction. It is easiest to cut into this sequence at the middle stage. Some economically-relevant variable, say rainfall, takes one of many possible values. The process determining which value is realized can be various, but it includes some fundamentally random component. In addition, the particular value that is realized is exogenous to the behavior of economic agents; rainfall affects economic outcomes, but economic choices do not affect rainfall.

The study of economic behavior under uncertainty best begins with a description of the characteristics of these random variables, most especially a description of their possible values and associated probabilities of occurrence. In the case of climatic and international price uncertainties, this task is possible because these variables are observable after the fact. From the information on their past realizations, I construct a picture of these uncertainties.

Economic agents take two sorts of decisions in an economy that is affected by random variables. First, they make choices before a random event occurs, using knowledge about what outcomes are possible and about their associated probabilities. Examples of such anticipatory actions include: choosing crops or crop combinations that are resistant to fluctuations in rainfall, or stockpiling food reserves or moving out of agriculture altogether. Second, they make choices after uncertainty is resolved when a random variable has taken a particular value. For instance, individuals may react to bad weather by drawing down food stockpiles, or migrating out of the rural sector to seek temporary work or sustenance elsewhere. Of course, the options that are possible after the uncertainty is resolved affect the type of decisions made beforehand, just as choices made beforehand constrain the ability to react afterwards. In this chapter, I document some of the scope available for various types of actions, both in reaction to uncertainty, i.e., in anticipation of the realization of a random variable, and in reaction to the actual realization.

II. CLIMATIC SHOCKS

Year-to-year climatic variation translates into fluctuations in agricultural outputs, given the levels of inputs under peasants' control, such as labor, seeds and fertilizers. This relationship is particularly notable in the Groundnut Basin, the mainstay of Senegal's traditional rainfed agriculture. The total rainfall during the growing season (June to September) at Diourbel at the center of the Groundnut Basin, r, is illustrated in Chart 1 for the years 1919–1980. The mean of this series is 573 mm. and its standard deviation is 160 mm.

There is much debate over whether current rainfall depends on its own past levels from one season to the next, i.e. the intertemporal dependence or autocorrelation of rainfall.[1] On the one hand, if rainfall is strongly positively related to its past values, there is an increased probability of sequences of bad years. Their cumulative effect may be worse than if bad years were separated by good years, as might be expected if rainfall were temporally independent. For instance, a stock of grain of a given size would tend to be exhausted by a succession of bad harvests. On the other hand, temporal autocorrelation means that next year's rainfall can be predicted by using the realization of the rainfall in this and past years. If this is true, it will be possible to anticipate bad weather, thereby mitigating

CHART 1

Rain During the Agricultural Season, mm.

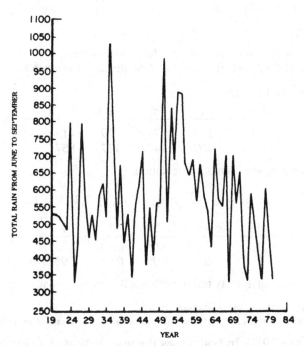

Source: Table 1

its effects. In principle, labor could be shifted from agricultural work to non-agricultural work in the rural sector, or conceivably even to work outside the rural sector. Animals could be moved to less affected areas or exported while still in good condition.

For these reasons, it is useful to examine the relationship between current rainfall and its values in past years. Table 1 gives the F statistics to test the joint significance of all coefficients for regressions of rainfall in June and July, r_1, on itself and lags of up to five years ($r_{1,t-i}$, $i = 1..5$), and for the same regressions of r_2, rainfall in August and September. There is no evidence at conventional levels of statistical significance of autocorrelation in the series. Based on these regressions, rainfall appears to be temporally independent; knowing last year's, or two years', up to at least five years' ago rainfall is of no use in predicting this year's rainfall.

As a second test of autocorrelation in rainfall, I calculated the Box-Pierce (1970) portmanteau test for r_1 and r_2 using the series

TABLE 1
Rainfall Regressions at Diourbel

Sample Period: 1924–1980

Variable Definitions

r_1: rainfall at Diourbel in June and July, millimeters
r_2: rainfall at Diourbel in August and September, millimeters

Statistics on the Variables

	x	x̄	σ	min x	max x
r_1	170	77	29	413
r_2	409	140	177	857

where x̄ = mean, σ = standard deviation.

Values of $F_{k,56-k}$: $r_{j,t} = \gamma_0 + \sum_{i=1}^{k} \gamma_i \, r_{j,t-i} + u_t$; j=1,2; k = 1,...5

j	k = 1	2	3	4	5
1	0.09	0.05	0.03	0.03	0.02
2	0.76	1.25	0.95	0.95	0.79

N.B. The value of F tests the hypothesis that $\gamma_1 = ... = \gamma_k = 0$.

Source: CIEH (1976) and SM worksheets.
Note: Time period for this and all tables refers to period of the dependent variable.

from 1919 to 1980. In both cases the tests indicated no evidence of any autoregressive moving average process, with significance levels of the B.P. statistic up to 6, 12, 18 and 24 autocorrelations being 0.99, 0.83, 0.83 and 0.94 for r_1, and 0.23, 0.49, 0.19 and 0.17 for r_2.

A related question is whether rainfall later in the growing season can be predicted from weather earlier in the year. Even if it could be done, this type of prediction would be much less useful than prediction based on the rainfall of past years since the time available for acting would be much less. Table 2 presents a regression of rainfall in the second half of the growing season, r_2, on the value of rainfall in the first half, r_1. This relationship is not statistically significant, and so short-run prediction of this type does not seem to be feasible.

The rains in West Africa move from south to north. It therefore makes sense to base short-run predictions of rainfall in one place on the early rainfall at stations further south, rather than on the place one is interested in. Table 3 presents correlation coefficients among four weather stations. Moving from south to north, these are:

18

TABLE 2
Within Year Rainfall at Diourbel

Sample Period: 1924–1980

Regression: $r_{2,t} = \gamma_0 + \gamma_1 r_{1,t} + u_t$

Coefficient	Estimate	Standard Error	t-Ratio
γ_0	$3.78 : 10^2$	$4.51 : 10^1$	8.38
γ_1	$1.81 : 10^{-1}$	$2.43 : 10^{-1}$	0.74
$R^2 = 0.01$	D W = 1.77		

Source: See Table 1.

Kolda, Kaolack, Diourbel and Linguere. The three more northern are all in the Groundnut Basin. The correlations within the two triangles are contemporaneous, but at different places. Looking at these correlations one sees that all are positive, moderately high, and all but one are statistically significant. Good and bad years tend to occur together at all four places. This phenomenon is particularly marked in the comparison between Diourbel and Kaolack, suggesting that it makes sense to speak of the rainfall in the Basin, rather than rainfall at different places. It is less so in the relationship between either of these stations and Linguere, already in a distinctly more marginal climatic zone.

In the square of Table 3 are the correlations between early rainfall and later rainfall. There does appear to be a pattern of early rainfall at stations to the south helping to predict later weather to the north as evidenced by the six correlations above the diagonal of the square, four of which are significant statistically and moderate in magnitude. By contrast, the correlations between early weather to the north and late weather to the south are negligible and insignificant statistically, as evidenced by the six correlations below the diagonal. In terms of predicting late weather from early weather at the same station (the diagonal elements of the square), only the correlation at Kaolack is significant. Thus there is some evidence that early weather to the south of the Groundnut Basin can be used to make short-run predictions of prospects in the Basin. Whether such predictions are of use depends very much on the accuracy with which they can be made, and the actions that can be made conditional on these predictions. Since I have no information on the costs and benefits of such short-run adjustments, these issues are not pursued further here.[2]

TABLE 3
Spatial Correlation of Rainfall

Sample Period: 1951–1980

Variable Definitions

r_1: rainfall in June and July in millimeters at the stations indicated
r_2: rainfall in August and September in millimeters at the stations indicated

Statistics on the Variables

	r_1		r_2	
at	x̄	σ	x̄	σ
Kolda	394	142	642	191
Kaolack	196	84	441	145
Diourbel	170	72	408	132
Linguere	125	63	271	83

Spatial and Temporal Correlation Coefficients

	r_1			r_2			
r_1	Kk	D	L	Ka	Kk	D	L
Kolda (Ka)	0.50**	0.37*	0.20	0.33	0.45*	0.35	0.27
Kaolack (Kk)		0.65**	0.43*	0.33	0.40*	0.42*	0.45*
Diourbel (D)			0.47**	0.19	0.06	0.13	0.44*
Linguere (L)				0.14	0.16	0.22	0.27

r_2		Kk	D	L
Ka		0.53**	0.49**	0.54**
Kk			0.76**	0.47**
D				0.55**

Source: As Table 1.
Note: * significant at the 0.05 level
** significant at the 0.01 level

III. EFFECTS OF WEATHER ON CROP YIELDS

In an economy such as Senegal's, the primary effect of fluctuations in weather is on the yields of crops. From here, the effects of weather spread to influence other aspects of agriculture and the economy as a whole. Individuals take actions based on the possible types of weather that may occur (and the associated probabilities of occurrence), and they react to the actual realizations of weather in any period. What then are the characteristics of the uncertainty in crop yields induced by fluctuations in weather?

Charts 2a, 2b and 2c plot the time-series of yields from 1951 to 1980 for three important Senegalese crops, groundnuts, millet and rice. Table 4 reports the means and standard deviations of these series.

CHART 2A
Yield of Groundnut, Tonnes per ha.

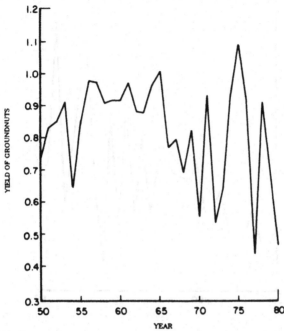

Source: Table 4

Crop yields fluctuate for several reasons. Variations in weather conditions relevant to production are one cause. There are also year-to-year differences in the quantities and qualities of inputs (labor, seeds, fertilizers, among others) that peasants apply to a unit of land. As well, there may be annual differences in the average suitability of the land used to produce the crops. Some of the apparent variability in crop yields may result from error in measuring outputs and areas planted. Finally, there may be any number of residual sources of variation not encompassed in these traditional categories.

For many purposes, it is important to decompose the variation in crop yields into parts that can be attributed to these different sources. Lack of data, however, especially on the important category of labor inputs and wages, makes impossible a fully specified production or cost function approach to the decomposition of the random and systematic influences on crop yields.

Instead, I have focussed on estimating the effects of climatic

21

CHART 2B
Yield of Millet, Tonnes per ha.

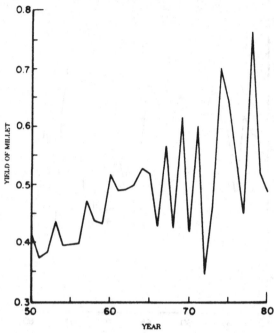

Source: Table 4

uncertainty on yield, largely neglecting the role of inputs. This procedure seems justified because climatic and input variables are likely to be unrelated, so that omission of the input variables should not bias the estimates of the climate–yield relationships, the classic result on bias from omitted variables. Since I have argued in the preceding section that rainfall is largely unpredictable, there may be little scope for peasants to adjust many inputs in response to rainfall, so that these two sets of variables would be independent. Statistical evidence on the relationships between rainfall and the application of inputs discussed in succeeding sections provide some limited support for this view. On the other hand, inputs of labor at harvest time certainly depend on realized rainfall, and if rains are poor early in the season, peasants may be able to replant. To capture one important influence on the use of inputs in the Groundnut Basin, where the main trade-off is between groundnuts and millet, the estimating equations for these crops do include the one-year lag of the ratio of the groundnut price to the millet price (ρ_{-1}).[3]

22

CHART 2C
Yield of Rice, Tonnes per ha.

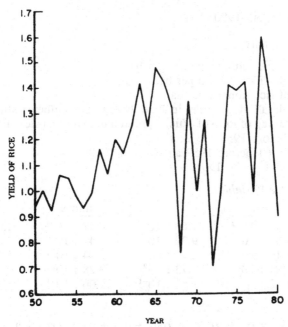

Source: Table 4

The influence of weather on agricultural yields has many dimensions, including but not limited to rainfall and temperature. One way these different phenomena affect crop yields is through their impact on moisture availability, with rainfall adding to it while factors increasing evaporation subtract from it (FAO, 1979). Here again data limitations pose problems. I tried a measure of evapotranspiration using the method of Linacre (1977), modified for the fact that I had only monthly average of daily means of high and low temperatures, rather than separate monthly averages for the highs and lows. This approximation did not seem useful in practice, however, so I present results based only on rainfall data.

Table 4 contains estimated yield equations for groundnuts, millet and rice. The results show that the rainfall variables are highly statistically significant. The negative coefficients on the squared terms mean that yields are relatively more sensitive to changes in rainfall at low levels of rainfall, as is to be expected. The trends in all yields are positive, but significant only for millet and rice. The R^2's

TABLE 4
Crop Yield Equations

Time Period: 1950–1980

Variable Definitions

y_G: yield of groundnuts, tonnes per ha.
y_M: yield of millet, tonnes per ha.
y_R: yield of rice, tonnes per ha.
r: total rainfall at Diourbel in June through September, millimeters
ρ_{-1}: one-year lag of ratio of official groundnut to millet prices from 1959, and 0 before 1959
D: dummy = 1 before 1959 and 0 from 1959
t: time trend = 1 in 1901.

Statistics on the Variables

x	$\bar{x}$	σ	min x	max x
y_G	$8.18 : 10^{-1}$	$1.66 : 10^{-1}$	$4.37 : 10^{-1}$	1.09
y_M	$4.87 : 10^{-1}$	$9.72 : 10^{-2}$	$3.43 : 10^{-1}$	$7.60 : 10^{-1}$
y_R	1.15	$2.28 : 10^{-1}$	$7.04 : 10^{-1}$	1.60
r	$5.91 : 10^2$	$1.73 : 10^2$	$3.28 : 10^2$	$9.92 : 10^2$
ρ_{-1}^*	1.18	$1.53 : 10^{-1}$	$9.00 : 10^{-1}$	1.39

*1959–80

Regression: $y_G = \alpha_0 + \alpha_1 \rho_{-1} + \alpha_2 D + \alpha_3 r + \alpha_4 r^2 + \alpha_5 t + u$

Coefficient	Estimate	Std. Error	t-Ratio	Joint F
α_0	$-6.30 : 10^{-1}$	$5.19 : 10^{-1}$	1.21	
α_1	$3.77 : 10^{-1}$	$1.69 : 10^{-1}$	2.23	
α_2	$4.28 : 10^{-1}$	$2.21 : 10^{-1}$	1.94	
α_3	$3.77 : 10^{-3}$	$7.61 : 10^{-4}$	4.96	
α_4	$-2.81 : 10^{-6}$	$6.09 : 10^{-7}$	4.62	12.69
α_5	$-2.45 : 10^{-3}$	$4.30 : 10^{-3}$	0.57	

$R^2 = 0.59$ SSE = 0.3383   DW = 2.02

Regression: $y_M = \beta_0 + \beta_1 \rho_{-1} + \beta_2 D + \beta_3 r + \beta_4 r^2 + \beta_5 t + u$

Coefficient	Estimate	Std. Error	t-Ratio	Joint F
β_0	$-7.21 : 10^{-1}$	$2.75 : 10^{-1}$	2.62	
β_1	$4.73 : 10^{-2}$	$8.94 : 10^{-2}$	0.53	
β_2	$2.94 : 10^{-2}$	$1.17 : 10^{-1}$	0.25	
β_3	$1.55 : 10^{-3}$	$4.04 : 10^{-4}$	3.83	
β_4	$-9.77 : 10^{-7}$	$3.23 : 10^{-7}$	3.03	12.02
β_5	$9.45 : 10^{-3}$	$2.28 : 10^{-3}$	4.15	

$R^2 = 0.66$ SSE = 0.0952   DW = 2.11

Table 4 (cont'd)

Regression: $y_R = \gamma_0 + \gamma_1 r_1 + \gamma_2 r_2 + \gamma_3 r_1 r_2 + \gamma_4 r_1^2 + \gamma_5 r_2^2 + \gamma_6 t + u$

Coefficient	Estimate	Std. Error	t-Ratio	Joint F
γ_0	-1.64	$5.36 : 10^{-1}$	3.06	
γ_1	$5.77 : 10^{-3}$	$2.14 : 10^{-3}$	2.70	
γ_2	$5.51 : 10^{-3}$	$1.20 : 10^{-3}$	4.59	$\gamma_1 - \gamma_5$
γ_3	$-1.15 : 10^{-5}$	$3.64 : 10^{-6}$	3.15	5.02
γ_4	$-2.08 : 10^{-5}$	$4.68 : 10^{-5}$	0.44	
γ_5	$-3.26 : 10^{-6}$	$9.22 : 10^{-7}$	3.53	
γ_6	1.61	$4.81 : 10^{-1}$	3.34	
$R^2 = 0.57$	SSE = 0.6681		DW = 1.71	

Source: Table 1, BCEAO, Department of Agriculture worksheets and Daniel (n.d.).

indicate that a relatively high proportion of the total variation in yields can be explained with the help of only a limited number of rainfall variables that represent climatic conditions in a rather crude way at only one weather station in the whole groundnut area. Correspondingly, the implied role of variation in inputs (omitted for lack of data) must be limited.[4]

Agrometeorological sources suggest that it may be important to distinguish between moisture needs at different times in the growing season.[5] To capture these effects I substituted r_1 and r_2, their squares and cross-product for r and its square in the groundnut and millet equations of Table 4. The sums of squared errors from these regressions were 0.3011 for groundnuts and 0.0902 for millet, which do not reject restriction to the simpler formulation of Table 4. For rice, however, the restricted form produced a sum of squared errors of 0.7495 which rejects the simpler form at 5% (but not at 1%) significance, so the unrestricted specification is reported.

Rice, of course, is not grown in the Groundnut Basin. In 1979, for instance, 63% was grown in the Casamance and 16% in the Fleuve. The weather station at Kolda is in the Casamance. The same equation for rice yields as in Table 4, but with rainfall at Kolda instead of Diourbel, produced a sum of squared errors of 0.8165. This specification is, therefore, inferior since, although non-nested, it has the same number of regressors. The result may reflect the superiority of rainfall at Diourbel as an indicator of the flow in the Senegal and Gambia rivers available for irrigation, as well as rainfall in the north and east where some rice is grown.

One important issue is the extent of the correlation between rainfall-induced variation in groundnut, millet and rice yields, and the relative resistance of these crops to variation in rainfall. These two aspects are conceptually distinct attributes of the two crops. For instance millet yields could be very stable, yet what little variation there was might be highly correlated with variation in groundnut yields.

To obtain evidence on these phenomena, define the rainfall related component of yields as

(1) $y_G^r = \alpha_0 + \alpha_1 \rho_{-1} + \alpha_2 D + \alpha_3 r + \alpha_4 r^2 + \alpha_5 t$

(2) $y_M^r = \beta_0 + \beta_1 \rho_{-1} + \beta_2 D + \beta_3 r + \beta_4 r^2 + \beta_5 t$

(3) $y_R^r = \gamma_0 + \gamma_1 r_1 + \gamma_2 r_2 + \gamma_3 r_1 r_2 + \gamma_4 r_1^2 + \gamma_5 r_2^2 + \gamma_6 t$

where the numerical values of all coefficients are from Table 4. Assuming ρ_{-1}, D and t are constant and generating 62 values by substituting the values of rainfall from 1919 to 1980, the correlations are: y_G, y_M 0.82; y_G, y_R 0.94; y_M, y_R 0.83. There is therefore very little opportunity to reduce risk of this type by diversifying among these crops. In fact, since the price of groundnuts is traditionally higher than that of millet, while the yield of millet per hectare is lower, there would be little reason based on diversification against rainfall risk to grow millet, except to the extent that the millet market may not function in some areas or at the (official) prices.

In general, uncertainty is something that individuals dislike and wish to avoid; they are risk averse. For an individual with a utility of consumption given by the function U(:), the expected value of utility can be used to compute the relative valuation of consumption prospects of varying riskiness. For instance, if a dam is under consideration to reduce fluctuations in crop yields, one can use the expected utility criterion to value this benefit.

Several important gaps in knowledge about Senegal stand in the way of a complete operationalization of these ideas. First, there are no estimates of people's attitudes toward risk, i.e., their utility functions. Second, while something is known about fluctuations in income from crop yields, little is known about other sources of income fluctuations. The prices of crops vary, as does income from nonagricultural activities. Further, the effects of these and other types of uncertainty are not generally additive with those that I can measure. Third, fluctuations in income are unlikely to translate into equivalent fluctuations in consumption, for the very reason that risk averse individuals take actions to ensure that this does not happen. For instance, peasants store grain in good years for consumption in bad. Assuming that fluctuations in income do show up in equivalent variations in consumption tends to overstate the risk faced by peasants. Instead, as in the grain storage example, one needs to know both the unrecorded costs of stabilizing consumption (such as loss through storage) and the success achieved in stabilizing consumption.

On balance, these factors suggest that assuming consumption fluctuates as much as income probably overstates the riskiness of consumption. Keeping this in mind, an upper bound on the riskiness of consumption can be derived by assuming that an agriculturalist in the Groundnut Basin consumes the value of income from ground-nuts and millet. In 1980 the groundnut to millet relative price was $\rho_{-1} = 1.25$, the allocation of land was 49 percent to groundnuts, and the time trend was $t = 80$. Under these assumptions, income in terms of millet from a hectare of land is given by

(4) $Y_i = (1.25) (0.49) y_{G,i} + (0.51) y_{M,i}$

where y_G and y_M are evaluated using eqs. (1) and (2) at rainfall values in each year from 1919 to 1980. Expected income ($\bar{Y}$) and expected utility ($\bar{U}$) are

(5) $\bar{Y} = \Sigma\, Y_i/62$

and

(6) $\bar{U} = \Sigma\, U\,(Y_i)/62$

for $i = 1919$ to 1980.

The certainty equivalent value (Y^c) of a random income prospect with expected utility of $\bar{U}$ is that income which if received with certainty would be equally desirable, i.e., Y^c is the solution to the equation $U\,(Y^c) = \bar{U}$. If individuals are risk averse the certainty equivalent income is always less than the expected utility of the risky prospect. How much less depends on attitudes toward risk and the nature of the risk. Specifying a functional form for the utility of consumption (of income for the upper-bound calculation) allows one to compare different risks. The constant relative risk aversion function is $U = -Y_i^\gamma/\gamma$. In this case, the number of hectares of land a peasant owns does not influence his attitude toward risk. Risk can therefore be evaluated as though income from one hectare is at issue.

The results for two values of γ are given in Table 5. The premium applied to riskless income relative to income that has the risk characteristics of income generated by eq. (4) is

$$(7) \quad P = (\bar{Y} - Y^c)/Y^c,$$

so that $(1 + P) Y^c = \bar{Y}$. For instance, the results of Table 5 state that of two projects of equal cost, the one providing income with certainty when $\gamma = -1$ would still be worth doing even if it had a 1.2 percent lower return than the mean return of land planted to groundnuts and millet in the proportions of 1980, 0.49 to 0.51. The values of γ taken for illustration are broadly consistent with the values Binswanger (1980, Tables 1 and 3) found in his studies in India, and if anything would seem to embody more risk aversion. These results are based on a series of rather crude calculations, as noted above. They do suggest, however, that low risk projects cannot have average returns very much lower than those of the traditional alternatives of the Groundnut Basin if they are to be worth doing.[6]

TABLE 5

Expected Utilities and Certainty Equivalents

γ	$\bar{Y}$	$\bar{U}$	Y^c	P
−1	0.823	−1.233	0.813	0.012
−2	0.823	−0.773	0.804	0.022

Source: Calculations described in text.

Another important question is the persistence of the effects of bad weather. Are yields affected in years following bad weather? There are a number of reasons for such a relationship. Subsequent yields may be affected positively by bad weather because the failure of the crops puts lower nutrient demands on the soil, in effect acting similarly to a fallowing. This is a structural effect, in that it operates given the levels of all relevant inputs under the control of peasants. Alternatively, bad weather in a preceding year may encourage peasants to work harder in the next year to recoup their losses. This is a reduced form effect, in that if the data to control for other inputs were available it would be seen to operate through increases in these other inputs. On the other hand, peasants may transfer inputs between the crops, so that while the yield on one increases, that on the other falls. For instance, it is said that, following a bad year, risk-averse peasants will transfer their efforts from groundnuts to millet to rebuild their food stocks. In this case, millet yields rise while groundnut yields fall. Finally, it is possible that the government's reaction to past poor rainfall will be to change groundnut prices or alter the level of inputs supplied to agriculture by the parastatals.

Table 6 presents evidence on the net effect of these different influences via the parameters α_6 and β_6 which multiply the variables representing last year's rainfall. For groundnuts, the parameter α_6 is negative indicating that poor rainfall in the preceding year raises yields in the subsequent year. The parameter is not, however, statistically different from zero. For millet, by contrast, the parameter β_6 is negative *and* statistically significant. Thus, bad rainfall in the previous year is associated with higher millet yields in the subsequent year.[7] Of course, this analysis does not allow the different effects to be disentangled. But it suggests that

TABLE 6
Tests of Persistence

Regression: $y_G = \alpha_0 + \alpha_1\rho_{-1} + \alpha_2 D + \alpha_3 r + \alpha_4 r^2 + \alpha_5 t + \alpha_6 (\alpha_3 r_{-1} + \alpha_4 r^2_{-1}) + u$

A "−1" subscript indicates a one-period lag.

Coefficient	Estimate	Std. Error	t-Ratio
α_0	$-4.64 : 10^{-1}$	$6.22 : ^{-1}$	0.75
α_1	$3.86 : ^{-1}$	$1.71 : ^{-1}$	2.26
α_2	$4.31 : ^{-1}$	$2.24 : ^{-1}$	1.92
α_3	$3.74 : ^{-3}$	$7.73 : ^{-4}$	4.80
α_4	$-2.79 : ^{-6}$	$6.10 : ^{-7}$	4.57
α_5	$-3.11 : ^{-3}$	$4.51 : ^{-3}$	0.69
α_6	$-1.05 : ^{-1}$	$2.15 : ^{-1}$	0.49
Total sum of squares = 21.5754		SSE = 0.3349	

Regression: $y_M = \beta_0 + \beta_1\rho_{-1} + \beta_2 D + \beta_3 r + \beta_4 r^2 + \beta_5 t + \beta_6 (\beta_3 r_{-1} + \beta_4 r^2_{-1}) + u$

Coefficient	Estimate	Std. Error	t-Ratio
β_0	$-2.17 : ^{-1}$	$2.93 : ^{-1}$	0.74
β_1	$5.43 : ^{-2}$	$7.78 : ^{-2}$	0.70
β_2	$3.39 : ^{-2}$	$1.02 : ^{-1}$	0.33
β_3	$1.52 : ^{-3}$	$3.32 : ^{-4}$	4.58
β_4	$1.00 : ^{-6}$	$2.50 : ^{-7}$	4.00
β_5	$6.80 : ^{-3}$	$2.14 : ^{-3}$	3.18
β_6	$-5.98 : ^{-1}$	$2.46 : ^{-1}$	2.43
Total sum of squares = 7.6386		SSE = 0.0695	

the desire of peasants to rebuild their millet stocks is dominant, although they do not seem to do this at the expense of groundnut yields. Where possible, some of the subsequent sections address this question; lack of data, however, means that it is impossible to distinguish precisely the mechanisms at work.[8] Rice yields show no statistically significant persistence effects (the estimated equation is not shown).

IV. THE EFFECT OF WEATHER ON AGRICULTURAL DECISIONS

Both the government of Senegal and individual agriculturalists may react to the actual realization of rainfall. The scope for these reactions depends very much on whether the actual value of rainfall can be anticipated and on the amount of time that has passed since a particular realization of rainfall.

In section 2, evidence suggests that it is very difficult to predict rainfall much, if at all, in advance of its occurrence. If there are to be responses to the level of rain in the year when it falls, such reactions will therefore have to be very rapid. In general, it seems likely that meaningful reaction to rainfall within the same agricultural season will be limited. Peasants may find it difficult to shift land between crops after the rains come, since the growing season will be in progress. Similarly, the government has to supply fertilizer and peasants have to apply it before rainfall is known. The government may establish official prices for crops before the rains, although it need not do so.

Over the period 1961–80, these conjectures were confirmed for the following dependent variables: the price of groundnuts relative to the price of millet, the total amount of fertilizer and the per ha. amount of fertilizer applied to groundnut land. These dependent variables were regressed on a time trend and the following groups of rainfall variables and their squares and cross-product in the case of r_1 and r_2: (r, r_{-1}), (r_1, r_2, r_{-1}), $(r_1, r_2, r_{1,-1}, r_{2,-1})$, (r), (r_{-1}). In no case were any of the rainfall variables in the year in which they occurred jointly significant at the 5% level or better. Some specifications for each dependent variable did, however, produce results significant at the 10% but not the 5% level for the effect of rainfall in the current but not the previous year. There is thus no strong evidence that these variables respond to contemporary or lagged rainfall.

The evidence is somewhat different in the case of the ratio of land

30

under groundnuts to land under both millet and groundnuts, x_G. Regressions of x_G on the same sets of rainfall variables just discussed for the period of 1960-80 yield insignificant results for the contemporary rainfall variables, and only in the cases of (r, r_{-1}) and (r_{-1}) are the lagged rainfall variables significant (at better than the 10% and the 5% levels respectively).[9] For the longer period, however, there were some significant results. These did not occur when groups based on r_1, r_2, their squares and cross-products, or the corresponding lags, were tested jointly, but rather when the variables r and its square, and/or their lagged values were used. Furthermore, the restrictions on r_1 and r_2, their squares and cross-product necessary to produce a specification based on r and its square could not be rejected.

Because this last equation has residuals that were autocorrelated, I added the lagged dependent variable to the equation to produce the equation of Table 7. To test the assumption of independent errors in this equation, I regressed the residuals on their one-period lagged values and the variables included in the equation. The coefficient of the lagged residual was insignificant.

The results of Table 7 suggest that land allocation responds both to contemporaneous and to one-period lagged rainfall, as well as to its own lagged value. (Longer lags of these variables were not, however, significant.) These variables suggest that there are persistence effects that arise through land allocation rather than through yields. Good rainfall, in both the contemporary year and the preceding one, tends to increase the allocation of land to groundnuts.

V. TRANSMISSION OF RAINFALL SHOCKS TO OTHER SECTORS

The level of rainfall affects yields and therefore agricultural output directly via plant physiology. But these shocks may then be transmitted to the rest of the economy in various ways by the actions of individual Senegalese and of the government. There are four main channels by which this transmission can take place:

(1) Other sectors provide inputs to the agricultural sector, inputs that are demanded in relation to the actual output rather than the planned output of the sector. Transportation of the crop is a good example.
(2) Other sectors use the output of the agricultural sector as an input. The most prominent example is the groundnut processing industry.
(3) Rainfall affects the demand for harvest labor. In years of bad rainfall individuals may migrate to the cities where they seek employment in other sectors.

31

TABLE 7

Determinants of the Land Ratio

Sample Period: 1951–1980

Variable Definitions

x_G: ratio of land planted to groundnuts to that under both millet and groundnuts

Statistics on the Variables (1950–1980)

	x	x̄	σ	min x	max x
x_G	0.516	0.35	0.445	0.577	

Regression: $x_G = \gamma_0 + \gamma_1\, \rho_{-1} + r_2\, D + \gamma_3\, r + \gamma_4\, r^2 + \gamma_5\, r_{-1} + \gamma_6\, r^2_{-1} + \gamma_7\, t + \gamma_8\, x_{G,-1} + u$

Coefficient	Estimate	Std. Error	t-Ratio	Joint F
γ_0	$-1.84 : 10^{-1}$	$1.33 : 10^{-1}$	1.38	
γ_1	$5.82 : 10^{-2}$	$2.89 : 10^{-2}$	2.01	
γ_2	$7.12 : 10^{-2}$	$3.63 : 10^{-2}$	1.96	
γ_3	$4.13 : 10^{-4}$	$1.53 : 10^{-4}$	2.70	
γ_4	$-3.51 : 10^{-7}$	$1.32 : 10^{-7}$	2.67	3.66
γ_5	$4.41 : 10^{-4}$	$1.32 : 10^{-4}$	3.33	
γ_6	$-2.77 : 10^{-7}$	$1.10 : 10^{-7}$	2.52	9.40
γ_7	$1.61 : 10^{-3}$	$8.15 : 10^{-4}$	1.98	
γ_8	$4.98 : 10^{-1}$	$1.47 : 10^{-1}$	3.39	

$R^2 = 0.77$ SSE = 0.00747

Source: Table 4.

(4) There may be general demand influences of a Keynesian sort. Rainfall affects rural incomes and therefore the demand for goods and services produced by the other sectors. If wages and prices do not adjust rapidly, a fall in demand may cause a loss of output and unemployment in other sectors.

The first, second and fourth factors suggest that the output of other sectors will be low when agricultural output is low. Only the third factor acts to increase the output of other sectors when agricultural output is low. The actual paths of real output in the secondary (inclusive of groundnut products) and tertiary sectors are plotted in Charts 3a and 3b, based on data from Daniel (n.d.). These data are constructed so that agricultural output is attributed to the year following the rainfall that would have affected it. Thus the marked trough in both series in 1978 was roughly contemporaneous with the very bad rains of 1977 and similarly with 1973 (see Chart 1). Despite these two correspondences, indicating a negative relation between output in these sectors and in the agricultural sector, regressions of output in these sectors on rainfall do not produce

CHART 3A

Real Output of the Secondary Sector, bns. of 1971 cfa.

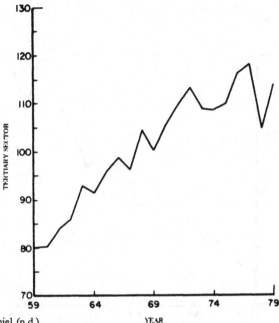

Source: Daniel (n.d.)

statistically significant results.[10] Thus there is no strong statistical
evidence for any transmission between agriculture and the other
sectors; this result may stem from government policies that shelter
these sectors.

While evidence on factors three and four is especially difficult to
obtain, an input–output table, given in Table 8 makes clear why the
first and second factors do not operate. Most industries purchase
very few inputs from agriculture, as can be seen by comparing the
entries of row 1 with the entries of row 9. The only exception is
industry 3, the oil mills, with large purchases from agriculture but
few sales to other industries. Further, agriculture purchases relatively little of the output of the other sectors to use as inputs, as can
be seen by comparing the entries of column 1 with the entries of
column 9. The linkages between agriculture and the other industries
are quite weak even in a year of good rainfall, 1974 when the
input–output table was constructed. The only exception is the
linkage from agriculture through the oil mills which in turn have
large purchases from the service industries, 6–8.

33

CHART 3B

Real Output of the Tertiary Sector, bns. of 1971 cfa.

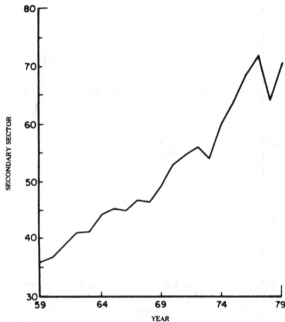

Source: Daniel (n.d.)

It therefore makes good sense to focus additional attention on how climatic variability impacts the oil mills. The processing of groundnuts requires both processing capacity and variable inputs. The costs of capacity are incurred whether groundnuts are processed or not, while variable costs arise only to the extent that groundnuts are processed. The profit made in any year on groundnut processing, π_p, is

$$\text{(8a)} \quad \pi_p = (P_O - v - p_F)G_m - rK \qquad \text{if } G_m \leq K$$

and

$$\text{(8b)} \quad \pi_p = (P_O - v - p_F)K - rK \qquad \text{if } G_m \geq K,$$

where p_O is the value of the products (oil and cake) in a kg. of unshelled groundnuts, v is the variable cost of processing a kg. of unshelled groundnuts, p_F is the price paid to peasants for a kg. of unshelled groundnuts, G_m is the size of the crop available for

34

TABLE 8

An Aggregated Input–Output Table for 1974

Purchases by col. from row

Sales by row to col.	1	2	3	4	5	6	7	8	9
1	10260	0	11638	566	1117	185	0	0	23766
2	18	5513	0	35	0	40	0	0	5606
3	0	122	20	1	0	0	0	0	143
4	160	275	0	1801	0	242	0	0	2478
5	980	3137	303	1600	13712	2114	3352	1551	26745
6	168	2036	855	865	4328	3396	2227	4270	18059
7	190	1595	2089	1337	5612	1389	1229	4414	17855
8	210	475	4399	195	1964	490	553	155	8541
9	11986	13153	19304	6400	26733	7956	7361	10390	103283
10	930	1873	684	13463	35816	2575	1018	845	57204
11	12916	15026	19988	19863	62549	10531	8379	11235	160487
12	69591	40219	45231	28518	115555	29349	26132	49908	404503
13	56675	25193	25243	8655	53006	18818	17753	38673	244016
14	320	5948	2042	4422	12982	7052	9207	9712	51685
15	0	769	864	1176	3888	2106	1859	2649	13311
16	0	754	377	726	1882	444	607	3150	7932
17	80	702	18352	2068	8959	2971	2598	16293	52023
18	56275	17789	4472	1447	29183	8351	5341	9518	132376

Definitions of Industries 1–8 (cols. & rows)

1. agriculture and husbandry
2. fishing and forestry
3. oil mills
4. other agro-industry, various food, grain and flour, sugar, tobacco, matches, confectionery
5. textiles, wood, paper, printing, chemicals, extractive industries, construction materials, mechanical industries, energy, building
6. hotels, financial and misc. services
7. transportation and telecommunication
8. commerce

Definition of rows 9–18

9. sum of 1–8
10. imported inputs
11. total inputs
12. production
13. value added
14. salaries
15. expatriate salaries
16. interest and insurance
17. indirect taxes
18. sum of 13–18

Definition of col. 9: Sum of 1–8

Source: J. Daniel (1977)   *Units:* FCFA millions

processing in kg., K is processing capacity in kg., and r is the fixed cost of capacity to process one kg. Equation (8a) states that capacity can only be used to the extent groundnuts are available, while (8b) states that groundnuts in excess of capacity cannot be processed.

Year-to-year variations in weather influence the amount of

groundnuts available for processing, as documented in preceding sections. Allocations of agricultural inputs and investments in processing capacity must be made before the actual realization of weather is known to decision-makers. The criterion for these decisions must, therefore, be based on the distribution of weather possibilities and on the expected consequences of different input allocations and investment strategies. The expected profit from processing is therefore

$$(9) \quad E\pi_p = \int_0^K (p_o - v - p_F)G_m \, f(G)_m)dG_m + \int_K^\infty (p_o - v \, p_F)K \, f(G_m)dG_m - rK$$

where G_m is a random variable because rainfall is random, with probability density function $f(G_m)$, and cumulative density $F(G_m) \equiv \int_0^{G_m} f(x)dx$. The first part of eq. (9) corresponds to (8a), and the second part to eq. (8b).

The expected profit of processing is one component of the expected (net) benefits from activity in the Groundnut Basin. The other components are: (1) the value of the income earned by peasants from selling their groundnuts for processing or export at price p_F; (2) the value of exports of unprocessed groundnuts at international price p_G, net of payments to peasants; (3) the value to them of the groundnuts they do not market, $G - G_m$ where G is the size of the crop; (4) the value of the millet harvest. There is little information on peasants' decisions about how much of any crop to market, although the BCEAO does publish some data in its annual *La Campagne Arachidière*.[11] The amount of the crop that is marketed depends not only on peasant decisions but also on marketing institutions that have often been the product of government policy, as discussed in subsequent chapters. Neglecting the marketing question, and assuming $G_m = G$, eliminates the third component just discussed.[12] The value of the expected income of activities in the Groundnut Basin is then

$$(10) \quad EY = E\pi_p + \int_0^\infty p_f \, G \, f(G) \, dG + \int_K^\infty (p_G - p_F) \, (G - K) \, f(G) \, dG + \int_0^\infty p_M \, M \, h(M) \, dM$$

where the components have been enumerated above, and the millet crop, M, which depends on weather, has p.d.f. $h(M)$ and sells at price p_M.

Under certain assumptions, the maximization of eq. (10) provides the appropriate criterion for making two important decisions that concern the Senegalese government.[13] These are: (1) the optimal groundnut capacity to install (K); and (2) the price of groundnuts to offer peasants (p_F) relative to the price of millet (p_M). These problems are discussed in more detail in Gersovitz (1986). There, I showed that if international prices and the size of the groundnut crop are independent, the first-order conditions for optimal decision-making imply

(11a) $(p_O - v - p_G)[1 - F(K)] = r$

and

(11b) $\dfrac{p_F}{p_M} = \dfrac{(p_O - v)\,w + p_G(1 - w)}{p_M}$

in which situations of excess processing capacity account for the proportion w of the expected groundnut crop.

The left-hand side of eq.(11a) states that the expected benefit of increasing capacity by one unit is the probability of the increase resulting in additional utilized capacity, $(1 - F)$, times the benefit net of both variable costs and the return from exporting un-processed groundnuts. The marginal cost of the capacity is the right-hand side, r. From eq.(11a), $p_O - v - p_G$ must exceed r otherwise it would never be profitable to install capacity. The right-hand side of eq.(11b) is the ratio of a weighted average of $(p_O - v)$, the benefit of oil processing net of variable costs and p_G, the international price of groundnuts, to the price of millet. Eq.(11b) applies even if the available processing capacity is not optimal, say because there has been over-investment. In this case, eq.(11a) is dropped since K is no longer a choice variable, and the given K is substituted into eq. (11b), via the definition of w.

Gersovitz (1986) operationalized eqs.(11a) and (11b) to test for the optimality of Senegalese decisions on K and p_F/p_M as of 1981 using data on crop yields and acreages, cost figures for groundnut processing and international prices. These calculations suggest some *tentative* conclusions on the situation in 1981: (1) Given prices paid to farmers, the probability of excess capacity in groundnut processing, F, was a very high 0.9. (2) Given assumptions on processing costs and international prices, however, investment in groundnut processing was only profitable if the probability of excess capacity was a much lower 0.175. (3) These two points, in turn, suggest that at the prices paid to peasants in 1981, there had been excess investment in processing capacity. (4) The prices paid to peasants were, however, estimated to be too low relative to their optimal value since with so much capacity the weight, w, took a high value of 0.89. (5) Raising the price paid to peasants for their groundnuts might increase the availability of groundnuts sufficiently to justify past investments in processing capacity, since it would then be less likely to be idle.

The central point of this approach to the determination of agro-industrial processing capacity and agricultural pricing is that the two decisions are interdependent. In particular, when the bulk of groundnuts will be processed since processing capacity is likely to be in surplus (w near one), the opportunity cost of sacrificing groundnut production is not primarily the international price of unprocessed groundnuts (p_G), but rather the value of the products, oil and cake, contained in the groundnuts (p_O) minus the variable costs of obtaining these products (v), without adjustment for the fixed cost, r.

VI. INTERNATIONAL PRICE VARIABILITY

To this point, I have focused on the uncertainties in economic well-being that arise because variations in climatic conditions imply variations in production. But individuals and the Senegalese government also are concerned with variations in international prices. The price variation that arises from international markets is at least potentially exogenous to events in Senegal, since Senegal is a relatively small participant in international markets. It therefore makes sense to focus on international price variability as an additional source of uncertainty.

At the most aggregate level, the international price variation that Senegal faces can be summarized by the terms of trade, the ratio of export to import prices. Chart 4 plots Senegal's terms of trade over the last two decades. The perspective of the entire post-independence period is valuable in underscoring that Senegal was a net gainer during the middle 1970s. Despite not having any petroleum reserves, Senegal benefitted sufficiently from the general commodity boom of this period that the terms of trade actually improved. Even after the second oil shock, Senegal's terms of trade were no worse than during the 1960s. With 1975 as a base of 100, the mean value of the terms of trade was 75.6 with a standard deviation of 13.2. Thus the variation as a percentage of the mean is of the same order of magnitude as the variations in the yields of groundnut and millet.

CHART 4

The Terms of Trade Index, 1975 = 100

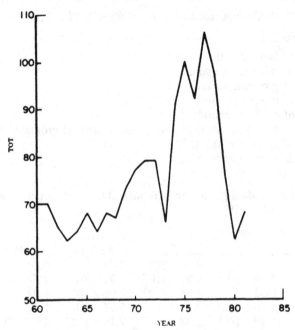

Source: UNCTAD *Handbook of International Trade and Development* computer tape.

Relatively few individual commodities account for the bulk of Senegal's exports. For instance from 1976–1980, the average of the annual percentages of total exports comprised by the three largest product groups were: groundnut products (37.2%), phosphate products (15.6%) and fish products (14.8%). Thus, these three together accounted for an average of 67.6% of exports in these years, while petroleum product exports and re-exports accounted for an additional 13%, on average.

Tables 9 and 10 provide information on the behavior of the export prices of certain narrowly defined commodities divided by the price of imports, the denominator of the terms of trade. The proportionate variation in the command over imports of these exports is quite large, as given by the standard deviation divided by the mean. Furthermore, Table 10 indicates that the correlations among these price relatives are quite high and statistically significant. They are not, however, so high as to preclude the degree of diversification that is found in practice from reducing the overall

39

TABLE 9

Export Prices: Definitions and Statistics

Time Period: 1962–1980 for F, C, and 1966–1980 for S, P, M, T, O.

Variable Definitions

q_F: price of canned fish
q_C: price of calcium phosphate
q_T: price of groundnut cake
q_O: price of groundnut oil
q_S; price of shelled groundnuts
q_T: price of groundnut products in a unit of shelled groundnuts
$[= (0.42\ q_T + 0.34\ q_O)/0.76]$
q_M: groundnut processing margin $[=q_p - q_s]$
q_I: import price index

All prices of individual goods are in thousand CFA per tonne. The import price index = 100 in 1975.

Statistics on the Variables

$q_i/q_{I,i=}$	$\bar{x}$	σ	min x	max x
F	3.93	$9.80 : 10^{-1}$	2.64	6.80
C	$7.13 : 10^{-2}$	$3.81 : 10^{-2}$	$3.71 : 10^{-2}$	$1.61 : 10^{-1}$
S	1.02	$4.56 : 10^{-1}$	$4.90 : 10^{-1}$	1.92
P	$8.76 : 10^{-1}$	$2.59 : 10^{-1}$	$5.71 : 10^{-1}$	1.41
M	$-1.48 : 10^{-1}$	$2.78 : 10^{-1}$	$7.19 : 10^{-1}$	$1.17 : 10^{-1}$

Source: For individual goods, the data were derived by dividing the value series in thousand CFA by the quantity series in tonnes as published in various issues of the Direction de la Statistique, BCEAOa and BCEAOb. For the import index, see Figure 4. For S and P, the data were multiplied by the ratio of the average world price to the guaranteed price as given in IMF (1970, p.507, Table 7) for 1965–1967 to adjust for the French subsidy.

TABLE 10

Export Price Correlations

Time Period and Variable Definitions: 1966–1980

Correlations		$q_i/q_I,i=$		
$q_i/q_I,J=$	C	S	P	M
F	0.58**	0.88***	0.73***	−0.77***
C		0.67***	0.66***	−0.49**
S			0.84***	−0.87***
P				−0.46**

Source: Table 9.
Note: ** denotes significance at a minimum of 5%; *** at a minimum of 1%.

variability of the terms of trade, as remarked above. The margin on groundnut processing has been negative on average, calling into question the value of investment in the oil mills.[14] Table 11 records the results of regressing these export price relatives on their own lagged value and, in the case of groundnuts and groundnut products, on rainfall in the preceding year, when the groundnuts were grown. The significant coefficients on the lagged value of the dependent variable indicates the persistence of shocks over time. Second and third order lags of the dependent variables were insignificant. I also tested for omitted autocorrelation by regressing the residuals on the right-hand-side variables in each equation and on the lagged residuals without any jointly significant results on the lagged residuals up to three lags of the residuals.

The evidence on the relation between the groundnut and groundnut product price relatives and rainfall is mixed. In both cases, the signs of the rainfall variables are the reverse of their signs in the yield and land allocation equations; large harvests reduce prices. But the coefficients on the rainfall variables are insignificant in one equation and only marginally so in the other. Thus there is only very mild evidence that prices and quantities of these exports are negatively correlated so that production shocks are automatically offset by price movements.

TABLE 11

Export Price Equations

Time Period: 1963–1980 for F and C, and 1966–1980 for S and P.

Regression: $(q_i/q_I) = \gamma_0 + \gamma_1 (q_i/q_I)_{-1} + \gamma_2 r_{-1} + \gamma_3 r^2_{-1} + u$

$i=$

	F	C	S	P
γ_0	$3.84 : 10^{-1}$	$3.08 : 10^{-2}$	1.97	1.65
	(0.42)	(1.86)	(1.47)	(1.79)
γ_1	$9.22 : 10^{-1}$	$6.08 : 10^{-1}$	1.01	$6.09 : 10^{-1}$
	(3.76)	(2.82)	(4.85)	(2.66)
γ_2	–	–	$-7.35 : 10^{-3}$	$-4.24 : 10^{-3}$
			(1.24)	(1.04)
γ_3	–	–	$6.69 : 10^{-6}$	$3.12 : 10^{-6}$
			(1.14)	(0.79)
$\gamma_2 \& \gamma_3$	–	–	0.31	0.05
R^2	0.47	0.33	0.72	0.55
SSE	8.27	$1.72 : 10^{-2}$	$8.11 : 10^{-1}$	$4.22 : 10^{-1}$

Source: See Tables 1 and 9.
Note: Numbers in brackets are t-statistics. The value denoted $\gamma_2 \& \gamma_3$ is the joint significance of the two coefficients.

Table 12 presents a regression in which the dependent variable is the official price for groundnuts.[15] This equation indicates that this price is set with reference to international prices (γ_4 is significant) but with a lag (γ_1 is also significant). Because γ_0, the constant, is insignificant, there is no money illusion in this price setting equation. Taking into account that the official price is for unshelled groundnuts containing 24% shells, the point estimate of the proportion of the international price that is turned over to peasants, in the long-run, is $(0.0827 + 0.0561)/[(1 - 0.402) 0.76] = 0.305$, while in the same year, only $0.0872/0.76 = 0.109$ is turned over, so the government stabilizes domestic prices.

TABLE 12

Official Price of Groundnuts

Time Period: 1963–1980
Variable Definitions
q_G: price to peasants of unshelled groundnuts, thousands CFA per tonne

Regression: $q_G = \gamma_0 + \gamma_1 q_{G,-1} + \gamma_2 r_{-1} + \gamma_3 r^2_{-2}$
$+ \gamma_4 q_s + \gamma_5 q_{s,-1} + u$

	G
γ_0	$1.46 : 10$
	(1.09)
γ_1	$4.02 : 10^{-1}$
	(2.08)
γ_2	$-2.28 : 10^{-2}$
	(0.41)
γ_3	$1.43 : 10^{-5}$
	(0.27)
γ_4	$8.27 : 10^{-2}$
	(2.51)
γ_5	$5.61 : 10^{-2}$
	(1.26)
$\gamma_2 \& \gamma_3$	0.40

$R^2 = 0.95$ $SSE = 1.08.10^2$

Source: See Tables 4 and 9. The value of q_s was not adjusted during the year of the French subsidy.

VII. STABEX

The Stabex scheme of the European Economic Community (EEC) seeks to stabilize the export earnings of its associated members among the developing countries, of which Senegal is one. This program provides transfers to less developed members under certain conditions.[16] First, Stabex defines a reference level of the (nominal) value of earnings from the export of a particular commodity to the EEC equal to the average of earnings in the preceding four years from the same source. Subject to a number of conditions, the transfer is then calculated as the excess of the reference value over the actual value of exports of the commodity to the EEC, if positive.

Among the most important conditions for a member to receive a Stabex payment are: (1) The actual level must be at least 6.5% below the reference level. (2) In the preceding year earnings from the export of the commodity to all destinations must have been at least 6.5% of total export earnings. (3) There must not be any evidence that the shortfall in export earnings from the EEC was under the control of the exporting country. This last provision introduces an important discretionary element into the operation of Stabex. On the one hand, when exports to non-EEC countries increase while those to the EEC fall, the transfer is typically reduced. On the other hand, the administrators of Stabex weigh situations such as increases in domestic consumption or in domestic processing, or transportation problems, in reducing the transfer, but without a clear formula.[17] Finally the funds available for payment to countries over the period of a Stabex agreement are limited, and when they are exhausted, further payments cannot be made. In practice this feature means that transfers have been pro-rated in the early 1980s.

The mechanics of applying for a transfer and its disbursement take time. In particular, there are problems of statistical cross-checking that arise in measuring the actual and reference levels of export earnings. Delays are important because they divorce the occurrence of an adverse shock from the offsetting effect of the transfer. There is, however, an option whereby countries can obtain an advance against the transfer based on a *prima facie* case that they have suffered an adverse shock. At least part of the transfer can then be paid in a timely fashion.

Recipient countries can spend the transfer in any way they wish. There is no requirement that their expenditure compensates the affected sector.

There is a replenishment provision in Stabex whereby the recipient may be obliged to repay the transfer without interest over a period of up to seven years. For a repayment to be due in any year, the quantity, price and value of earnings from exports to the EEC must exceed certain reference levels. In practice, repayments have been limited, and it is unclear to what extent repayments are automatic.

The Senegalese exports covered by Stabex are groundnuts and groundnut products. From 1975–82, Senegal received payments of 168.6 million European units of account (EUA). In 1979, Senegal apparently agreed to waive a transfer of 16.6 million EUA for which she was eligible, illustrating the negotiated nature of the scheme.

A full assessment of the expected benefits that Senegal obtains from Stabex is beyond the scope of this paper. For one thing, the scheme's discretionary nature raises considerable doubt about how changes in domestic consumption and quantities that are marketed will affect the transfer. Furthermore, since other countries also apply for transfers, the aggregate of these requests may exceed the Stabex funds, and transfers to Senegal will be correspondingly reduced. Projections of likely requests by all member countries is, however, a large undertaking. Finally, conditions that require repayment seem vaguely defined and ambiguous. Despite these difficulties, some useful benchmark calculations can be made from the analysis developed in previous sections. Because Stabex insures earnings, its assessment requires information on both climatic and price uncertainty.

One of the most important characteristics of Stabex is that transfers are based on the comparison of two nominal quantities. Because nominal prices are generally trending upward, there is a tendency for actual export earnings to exceed the reference level. For instance, from 1966–80, a regression of the natural logarithm of the export price of groundnuts (as defined in Table 9) on a constant and time produced a coefficient of 0.128, implying an average increase in this nominal price of 13.7% per year. Using this value in the formula for the reference price, while assuming that all other factors influencing earnings are constant, implies a current value of earnings 36% above the reference level.[18] Adding to this 36% the 6.5% by which the reference value must exceed the actual value for a transfer to be made, means that there is a built-in cushion of 42.5% before Stabex is triggered. Under this assumption about trends in prices, a payout requires a very particular sequence of yields over five years.

For instance, if the only variations in earnings were due to yields, payments would be made in very few years. In this case, the reference level in period t is $\Sigma (1+\alpha)^i y_{t-4}$ while the actual value is $(1+\alpha)^4 y_t$ where the y_t's are the yields, and α is the growth rate in the (nominal) price of groundnuts. Using the actual yields

(Table 4) in this formula produces only two years from 1954 to 1980 in which payments would have been made. Oddly enough, these years are 1977 and 1980, when the scheme was actually in operation. Using instead the y_G^r of equation (1), with ρ_{-1}, D and t at their 1980 values, predicts transfers in only three of fifty-eight years, 1925, 1935, and 1968. With a lower α, of course, payouts are more frequent.

VIII. CONCLUSIONS

Uncertainties of various sorts affect the well-being and behavior of Senegalese in many ways. This paper documents some of the sources of uncertainty and their implications. I provide various examples of the consequences of uncertainty for welfare and decision making. These include: the risk discount applicable to millet–groundnut culture in the Groundnut Basin; the effect of climate–yield uncertainty on agricultural prices and agro-industrial capacity; and the operation of the Stabex scheme. The description of the sources of uncertainty is background for the studies that follow, for example John Lewis on aid, when aid is a response to adverse shocks, and Laura Tuck on the forgiving of debt. This analysis may also be of help in other studies of the Senegalese economy, such as cost–benefit assessment of irrigation or climatic stress on fuelwood plantations.

NOTES

* Laura Tuck assembled many of the materials that made this paper possible. Mansour Seck, Directeur, Météorologie Nationale du Sénégal kindly cooperated in making available meteorological data. Hans P. Binswanger influenced my early thoughts on some of the issues I discuss, and Henry S. Bienen, Angus Deaton, Cheikh Sene and John Waterbury made valuable comments on various drafts. I thank all these people.

1. Nicholson (1979) provides a discussion and references on long cycles in Sahelian weather.
2. Whether rainfall earlier in the year at places south of Senegal can be used to increase the reliability of predictions about rainfall in Senegal is something I have not looked at. Winstanley (1976, p. 196) has suggested that not only may this be feasible, but that rainfall sufficiently south of Senegal is negatively correlated with rainfall in Senegal. The idea is that the Sahelian rains fail when the rain system does not move far enough north, but instead releases its moisture over the southern regions. If this effect were sufficiently strong, and if crop yields in southern regions responded favorably to the extra rainfall, there is the potential for risk-sharing between the Sahelian and southern states. This is a vast topic, since it involves the simultaneous study of weather and crop yields in many different areas of West Africa. The existence of such phenomena could have implications for such institutions as the BCEAO. For instance, it implies scope for pooling of foreign exchange reserves among its geographically dispersed members, if their export performances are negatively correlated for these climatic reasons.
3. Lack of data precluded incorporation of a price variable in the rice-yield equation.

4. The correlations among the residuals from the regressions of Table 4 are: y_G, y_M 0.68; y_G, y_R 0.52; and y_M, y_R 0.55, all significant at a minimum of the 0.01 level. Since all correlations are positive, it seems that the omitted variables largely represent other weather conditions not captured by the rainfall variables and omitted measures of the aggregate availability of inputs that would be spread over all crops, including labor. By contrast, omitted factors that reflect the transfer of inputs among crops seem less important, since this type of omission should lead to at least some negative correlations.

5. On the Groundnut Basin crops, see Cochemé and Franquin (1967, pp. 90–92, 109–11).

6. An alternative to the calculation based on the y_G^t and y_M^t of equations (1) and (2) of the text uses the actual y_G and y_M in equation (4). This latter calculation incorporates aspects of weather–yield relationships lost because the rainfall variables do not represent all weather-related influences. Further, the actual yields incorporate the effects of other random variables not related to weather. On the other hand, the actual series vary because input and other variables vary and these are not random from a peasant's perspective. As well, there may be considerable errors in measurement. Given the data problems there is no completely satisfactory solution; the y_G^t and y_M^t probably contain too little variation and the actual series, too much. By way of comparison, the P of Table 5 recalculated using the actual yield series for 1950–1980 are 0.032 and 0.049 for $\gamma = -1$ and -2. These results reflect the additional variation in the actual series.

7. Since this is a reduced form effect, I have not used the millet equation of Table 6 to perform simulations of the sort presented in Table 5.

8. For some further tests of persistence in groundnut yields, also all negative, see Gersovitz (1986).

9. It was on these results, available before I obtained a longer series on millet areas, that I based the discussion in Gersovitz (1986). Despite the difference between results based on the periods 1950–1980 and 1960–1980, there does not appear to be a statistically significant difference in behavior across the two periods.

10. Regressions of secondary sector output and tertiary sector output on total rainfall and its square and a time trend produced joint significance levels for the rainfall variables of 0.22 and 0.31 respectively.

11. There are some apparent anomalies in this information. For instance, it is usually thought that land planted to groundnuts should be seeded at the rate of 100 kg. per ha. The ratio of the BCEAO series on seeds to the land planted to groundnuts in the next year, however, rises almost continuously from about 70 kg. per ha. in 1966 to about 170 kg. per ha. in 1979.

12. In fact, it does not alter the argument if some fixed amount of G is set aside, for instance, to provide next year's seed. What is an important assumption is that the amount of a crop of a given size that is marketed does not depend on the price of groundnuts. If it does, as is surely true to some extent, it is sub-optimal to offer peasants a price for groundnuts set before the size of the harvest is known. Instead, the price should depend on the size of the crop relative to processing capacity. In this way, the price can be used to encourage marketing when processing capacity is underutilized.

13. The assumptions include the risk neutrality of peasants and the absence of certain types of dynamic considerations. These and other assumptions are discussed in Gersovitz (1986).

14. I have not, however, been able to ascertain whether there are anomalies in the data that produce these results.

15. This equation was subjected to the same diagnostic tests for lagged dependent variables and autocorrelation discussed in connection with the equations of Table 9, with the same results.

16. For this account of Stabex I rely on the Commission of the European Communities (1981), Hewitt (1983), and Ravenhill (1984).

17. See the Commission of the European Communities (1981, pp. 53-56) for a non-exhaustive list of forty-two causes of changes in export earnings and their impacts on the transfers.

18. The formulae used are: actual value = $(1+\alpha)^4$; reference value $[1+(1-\alpha) + (1+\alpha)^2 + (1+\alpha)^3]/4$ where α is the assumed growth rate.

CHAPTER TWO

The Senegalese Peasant: How Good is our Conventional Wisdom?

John Waterbury

In this chapter we shall be concerned with peasant behavior, or more accurately, the behavior of the rural-dweller. He, and to a much lesser extent, she is the object of great concern on the part of policy-makers, international aid donors, extension services, credit banks, groundnut oil refiners and so on down a long list. But the peasant is scarcely passive in the face of this concern, and while eschewing direct confrontation with 'the authorities,' whoever they may be, he has devised ways of thwarting, manipulating and occasionally turning to his advantage the public policies of which he is the target (see especially Gellar and Tuck in this volume). In turn policies are formulated on the basis of assumptions about how peasants act and react. What are these assumptions and how good are they? To answer this question we shall focus upon peasants in the groundnut basin.

I. SENEGALESE PEASANTS AND MARKETS

Senegalese rural dwellers have not only been long familiar with market systems but deal with them fairly comfortably and eagerly. We are not then confronted with African peasants of the kind analysed by Goran Hyden for Tanzania, pulled reluctantly into commercial agriculture and prepared to retreat into subsistence farming and auto-consumption at the first opportunity. There are very old commercial and market traditions in which many West African societies have shared and that predate extensive contact with Europe (Hart, 1982). But even contact with the world economy is not very recent, and in Senegal the groundnut trade, for instance, is a century and a half old.

There are in Senegal virtually no regions that have been isolated from market forces. The only partial exceptions would be the pastoral transhumant zone, known as the Ferlo, lying between the Senegal River Basin and the eastern edge of the groundnut basin (but even here systems of bartering cattle for grain and consumer goods are very old), eastern Senegal (where today the *terres neuves* projects are concentrated), and the lower Casamance, long a region of relatively self-sufficient Diola and Mandinke rice-cultivators. Although Senegalese officials often talk of reducing regional isolation (*désenclavement*), the river, roads, and the railroad to Bamako have already taken care of most of the challenge.

The Wolof–Serer core of the old and new groundnut growing areas[1] has long been woven into the fabric of commercial agricultural markets and the cash economy. It would not occur to these populations to escape the market; rather, it is a question of manipulating the public agencies and private entrepreneurs that determine the terms of trade. Cultivators respond to deteriorating or unfavorable terms of trade, primarily in groundnut production, by emphasizing other forms of activity: millet cultivation, petty trade, or migration. They de-emphasize, without by any means abandoning, groundnut production by reducing the surface cultivated, the amount of labor applied, or the amount of inputs used in their cultivation. The groundnut peasant thus has some cards to play, but it would be a great error to assume that all peasants have roughly the same hand. They do not. Sex, age, marital status, effective power within the extended family, the organization of production and consumption units, come together in different combinations to determine a range of cultivator strategies.

II. PRODUCTION UNITS AND CONSUMPTION UNITS

Much of the micro-economic literature of rural households will miss the mark in Senegal because the locus of decision-making varies according to crop and to contact with public authorities. Over the years it has become something of a convention to treat the extended household, the *carré* (from the Wolof word, *keur*), comprising at least two and perhaps as many as five nuclear families, unmarried males (*sourgas*), migrant laborers (*navetane* or *firdu*), and occasionally religious disciples (*taalibe*), as the basic unit of production and decision-making. The head of the *carré* (known as the *chef de carré* in French and henceforth referred to as such)[2] has, in theory, the authority to allocate land among the households, *sourgas*, women, and *navetanes* in the *carré*. Likewise he can influence or directly determine the proportions of land under groundnuts, millet, and garden plots. When the first large-scale efforts were undertaken in the 1960s to improve cultivator practices and stimulate production, it was assumed that the *carré* and the *chef de carré* were the appropriate unit and person to fasten upon. The SATEC (*Société d'Aide Technique et de Coopération*) technical package of 1964–1968 (see chapter 6) designed its programs according to that assumption, and it was bolstered by the analyses of a number of competent observers (among others, Kleene, 1976).

There is by now, however, a substantial body of literature that calls these assumptions into question. First, it is noted that the *carré* is more a consumption than a production unit. It is at this level that marriages are contracted, collective cultivation of millet takes place, meals in common are shared, and ceremonies celebrated. The *chef de carré* remains a powerful figure, sanctioning marriages, attributing land when a son marries, redistributing it if any male dies without heirs or abandons the land. Redistribution is thus a relatively rare occurrence:

A peasant, once he is allocated a field, tends to cultivate it year after year, and upon his death it passes to his eldest son. (O'Brien, 1971: 201).

In addition the *chef de carré* is responsible for the production of security stocks of millet, and other members of the *carré* owe him labor on his fields to ensure that such production is attained. The millet so produced is held at the disposal of all the households in the *carré* and cannot be disposed of freely by the *chef de carré*. Often the *chef de carré* will be the only member of the local cooperative from amongst people of the *carré*, but this is by no means always the case. As the principal interlocutor with various state authorities, he may establish within the *carré* a relative monopoly over fertilizers, agricultural equipment, and access to public credit. In this sense he retains considerable influence over the production decisions of other actors within the *carré* (Sarr, 1980). And, as indicated in Table 1, the *chef de carré* has maintained control, at least until a decade ago, of significant amounts of land within the *carré*.

It is now widely recognized, however, that the household (*ménage* in French) and the household head (*chef de ménage*) have become the meaningful operative production units in the groundnut basin[3] (Pélissier, 1966: 131; Hopkins, 1975: 40; Benoit-Cattin, 1982). With the spread and intensification of groundnut cultivation and marketing, the *ménage* has attained considerable autonomy. Often

TABLE 1

The Division of Land and Production within the Carré
(260 Carrés in the Sine Saloum: 1971)

Status in the Carré	Groundnuts		Millet	
	Percentage of Groundnut Plots	Average Yield Size ha kg/ha	Percentage of Millet Plots	Average Yield Size ha kg/ha
Chef de Carré	25	2.4 1292	73	1.6 1165
Chef de Menage	8	1.6 1078	13	.9 1196
Women	29	.7 985	8	.8 551
Sourgas	24	1.3 1067	5	.9 781
Navetanes	13	1.3 1071	1	.3 504

Source: SODEVA, 1973.

sourgas and women now owe their labor to the *chef de ménage* and whereas twenty years ago these same actors might have provided five mornings of labor per week to the *chef de carré*, by the mid-70s those obligations had been reduced to at most three (Barnett, 1979). Furthermore, all labor exchanges tend to take place among members of the same *ménage*, and seldom among the *ménages* that make up the *carré*.

So long as he continues to farm, the *chef de ménage* maintains stable rights to household land; he shares responsibility with the *chef de carré* for millet production and storage, he is owed labor by his family members, and frequently he will be a member of the local cooperative. He will therefore have independent access to credit, equipment, and fertilizer, and he can follow his own production strategy. There is, then, a trend toward the break-up of the *carré* into household units for purposes of production.

The *carré* is centrifugal both in spatial and in production terms. In a very general sense the land of the *carré* (perhaps 15–30 ha) is organized in concentric circles. Close around the dwellings are the millet fields (*champs de carré* or *toll keur*) under the supervision of the *chef de carré*, or perhaps the *chefs de ménage*, drawing upon collective labor and producing for collective ends. The arrangements for mobilizing labor vary temporally and by location. These fields normally receive the most animal manure and household waste. They constitute the subsistence core of the *carré*. They may be partially used for vegetable production as well (*champs de case*).

Lying further away are the cash fields (*toll diatti*), used primarily for the groundnut production of the *chefs de carré* and the *chefs de ménage.* No collective labor is used on these fields unless the 'owners' are *marabouts*, but *navetanes* and *sourgas* may owe the *chefs de ménage* and *chef de carré* a certain amount of weekly labor on these fields. The produce becomes the 'owners'' private property. Over time these fields have been subject to increasing soil depletion. They do not receive the same amounts of organic nutrients as the *toll keur* and nowhere in the groundnut basin have these been sufficient to offset the nutrients lost through plant production.

Finally there are the most distant fields, the bush fields (*toll gor*), so named because as groundnut cultivation spread into virgin areas these were the last fields conquered from the bush by the pioneering *carré*. It was these fields in general that were given over for cultivation to *sourgas*, women and *navetanes*. For considerable periods of time these fields remained relatively fertile because fallows were more extensively practised upon them and cultivation techniques were less intense than those utilized on the *toll keur* and the *toll diatti*. But those factors have been attenuated in the last few decades: fallows have tended to disappear everywhere, the *toll gor* receive virtually no fertilizers of any kind, and their cultivators have a strong incentive to mine the soil.

These are the cash fields for the three groups of producers mentioned above. They are rarely used for millet production. *Sourgas*, or bachelors, want to accumulate as much cash as quickly as possible in order to marry and to head their own household. The *sourgas* therefore strive to reduce their labor obligations to the *chefs de carré* and the *chefs de ménage*, to achieve maximum groundnut production without financial commitments to fertilizer and agricultural equipment, and to lengthen their dry-season, off-farm migration to other sources of employment. In short, the *sourgas* tend to show up with the first rains and leave once they have marketed their groundnuts. Indeed they may wish to market before the official opening of the marketing season even if the price they receive for groundnuts is below the official price. There is thus an especially high opportunity cost for *sourga* labor, determined by off-farm, off-season employment.

The *navetanes* are long distance labor migrants, generally from Guinea and Guinea Bissau who have helped meet labor shortages in the groundnut basin during the peak periods of the growing season. They attach themselves contractually to individual *carrés*, in which they are assigned fields for their personal cultivation in exchange for labor on the millet and groundnut fields of the *chefs de carré* and the *chefs de ménage.* Like the *sourgas* they mine the soil, using no other inputs but seed, and thereby maximizing their cash returns. In the decade or so after the Second World War the *navetanat* involved perhaps 50,000 migrants each year. Today, however, there are relatively few of them as rapid population growth in the groundnut basin has reduced demand for outside labor as well as surplus land within the *carré* that could be allocated to strangers (David, 1980: throughout).

Married women have a right to their own independent sources of cash and thus are allocated their own fields in the *toll gor.* They may also draw revenue from the vegetable plots lying close in to the dwellings. Insofar as groundnut cultivation is concerned, they are no kinder to the soil than the *sourgas* and the *navetanes* – but the reasons for this are quite different. First, there are heavy conflicting labor demands placed on women: hauling water, pounding millet, and working the fields of the *chefs de carré* and *chefs de ménage.* Secondly they will be the last to have use of the agricultural equipment available to the *carré*, and they are allotted minimal amounts of fertilizer. Consequently, their productivity is very low, but, unlike the *sourgas* and the *navetanes*, there is reason to believe that it could be greatly increased by reducing competing labor demands (millet mills could revolutionize the groundnut basin as could deep wells and mechanical pumps) and by more equitable access to fertilizers and equipment. Women, after all, are already married, do not generally migrate in the off-season, and have a long term interest in maintaining the production of the *carré*. One can speculate that women would be willing to incur some production costs through fertilizer use that *sourgas* and *navetanes* shun and that they would be responsive to labor-intensive techniques (for better thinning, weeding, and post harvest handling) and dry-season activities for improving soil quality (composting, manure and crop residue gathering, etc.).

There are, of course, great variations in the internal structuring of the *carré*. These variations are a function of time (increasing autonomy of the *ménage*, increasingly contractual labor relations, reduction in the incidence of land loans, etc.), of ethnicity (for example, Wolof vs. Serer) and of location (for example, *terres neuves* vs. the old groundnut basin). In the same vein, cropping and yield patterns are not consistent over time and across space. That should cause no surprise, as rainfall, relative prices, seed quality, and other exogenous factors strongly influence production decisions and performance.

It should be emphasized, however, that local variations in the millet/groundnut proportions of cultivated acreage are not reflected in aggregate national statistics (see Table 2). There the evidence indicates that despite irregular rainfall, mounting peasant indebtedness, and discouraging producer prices, peasants continued to demonstrate a preference for groundnut cultivation. In general, over the twenty year period represented in Table 2 total cultivated acreage increased by about a quarter while the proportion devoted to groundnuts did not vary in any significant sense. The Senegalese peasant of the groundnut basin appears as strongly wedded to his cash crop as ever. Perhaps Serer more than Wolof exhibit a concern for millet production, but neither will retreat willingly from the market except under the most adverse conditions.

TABLE 2

Groundnut and Millet Acreage and the Proportion of Groundnuts to Total Acreage in Senegal: 1960/61–1980/81

	Ha Millet	Ha Groundnuts	Total ha	Ha Groundnuts/ Total ha
1960/61	762,211	976,994	1,739,205	56.1%
1961/62	830,800	1,025,500	1,856,300	55.2%
1962/63	864,622	1,031,129	1,877,751	54.0%
1963/64	959,373	1,084,215	2,043,588	52.8%
1964/65	1,010,818	1,054,901	2,065,719	51.0%
1965/66	1,069,390	1,112,100	2,181,490	51.0%
1966/67	996,666	1,114,065	2,110,731	52.8%
1967/68	1,155,365	1,163,846	2,319,211	52.4%
1968/69	1,053,687	1,191,027	2,244,714	53.0%
1969/70	1,037,260	963,050	2,000,310	48.2%
1970/71	966,553	1,049,751	2,016,304	52.1%
1971/72	973,450	1,060,344	2,033,794	52.4%
1972/73	935,941	1,071,444	2,007,385	53.6%
1973/74	1,102,829	1,024,947	2,127,776	48.2%
1974/75	1,144,758	1,052,113	2,196,871	48.0%
1975/76	964,688	1,311,562	2,276,250	57.5%
1976/77	948,839	1,294,963	2,243,802	57.8%
1977/78	942,796	1,161,098	2,103,894	55.5%
1978/79	1,054,800	1,154,365	2,209,165	52.4%
1979/80	954,800	1,096,800	2,051,600	53.5%
1980/81	1,150,000	1,050,376	2,200,376	49.2%

Source: BCEAO Bulletin, various years.

A second generalization that emerges from aggregate statistics and micro-studies is that the *chefs de carré* enjoy a relative advantage in the amount of equipment they own and through its allocation are able to establish a hierarchy of users within the *carré*. The *chefs de ménage* may frequently enjoy the same privileges. The difference is one of degree of credit-worthiness and the amount of equipment owned. The *chef de carré* may be the only one to own a cart, or he may have more than one yoke of oxen, or he may own a veritable flotilla of seeders. If he is the sole member of the coop, he may control the distribution of seed and fertilizer. In some ways, distribution of these inputs has supplanted the older role of the *chef de carré* as allocator of the *carré*'s land.

All *chefs de carré* and *chefs de ménage* receive more labor from the adult members of the *carré* than they provide. However they do provide inputs in the form of loans of equipment and traction animals (horses or oxen). Because they can use equipment and fertilizers to their own maximum advantage, yields on their land tend to be higher than on the land of *sourgas* and women. If however they were unconcerned about the subsistence floor of the *carré* one would expect them to abandon millet cultivation for which they are largely responsible (see Table 1) and utilize their privileged access to inputs to increase their personal groundnut production to the greatest extent possible. The fairly consistent proportions of land given over to millet cultivation, as indicated in Table 2, show that they have not done so. They have accepted, if not enjoyed, the familial obligations placed upon them by the *carré* to bear chief responsibility for the group's subsistence needs.

These kinds of concerns have been subsumed by Edgar Ariza-Nino (in CRED, (Center for Research in Economic Development), 1982: 281–303) under the label of the 'prosumer' farmer whose production decisions must be analysed in terms of both production and consumption preferences. Decisions are not driven purely by profit and less than minimum production of the cash crop will be accepted in order to protect consumption needs. This is a continent-wide phenomenon (Development Alternatives Inc., 1975: 162–63; Cleave, 1974: 137; Levi and Havinden, 1982: Chap. 4) and perhaps one common to most peasant economies participating in rural markets (Ortiz, 1980).

What practical conclusions might one draw from this schematic presentation of the *carré*, and the motivations of rural producers? First we see that the concentric spatial and production circles have groundnuts or cash crops on the periphery pulling at food crops in the center. This reflects the continued importance of protecting the subsistence floor of the *carré*. As long as the *carré* remains an important component of rural social and production organization, this process will place special weight upon the leadership and foresight of the *chef de carré* and to a lesser extent the *chef de ménage*.

In seeking this balance, the head of the unit of family production must take measures to prevent the centrifugal forces (the excessive growth of satellites) from jeopardizing the very existence of the unit, which is held together, so to speak by its nucleus. A pronounced disequilibrium between the nucleus and its satellites would keep the unit from assuring the subsistence of its members and thus its reproduction. (SONED, 1977)

In this sense the frequently-criticized policy of SODEVA in the early 1970s to target extension programs on the so-called '*paysan de pointe*' is not necessarily flawed. The *paysan de pointe* has nearly always been a *chef de carré* or a *chef de ménage*. The real mistake of earlier extension efforts in fastening upon him lay in the fact that he was seen as the catalyst to increased groundnut production rather than as the patriarchal manager of differentially-motivated producers within the *carré*.

Second, extension programs concerned with increased millet production should address themselves primarily to *chefs de ménage* and *chefs de carré*. Those that aim at increased groundnut production should aim at women, who may, with the proper structuring of competitive labor demands, bring about relatively large production increases, and because of their availability in the dry season act as the catalysts to diversification. The *sourgas* appear to be a sort of necessary evil whose mining instincts can only be curbed through marriage. It should be obvious that to suggest selected targets within the *carré* is a far cry from suggesting how to reach them.

III. OFF-FARM REVENUES

In LDCs with weak statistical reporting mechanisms rural incomes have been traditionally estimated by dividing the number of rural inhabitants into the estimated gross agricultural product. It is as if everyone in the countryside farmed and that the value of their production, both marketed and auto-consumed, gave an accurate measure of their well-being. In some instances this approach, *faute de mieux*, may do little violence to reality. However, it is increasingly clear in Africa and elsewhere that what we are dealing with are part-time peasants with important sources of off-farm income as well as rural-dwellers that conduct no farming activity at all. If we do not measure this phenomenon with greater accuracy, we will be unable to assess the peasant's portfolio; that combination of assets and revenue streams that ensures his survival and on occasion his prosperity. We may, for instance, over-estimate the spread between rural and urban incomes, or seriously over-estimate the amount of leverage on peasant behavior that can be exerted through agricultural price signals and the presumed returns to technological innovation.

Senegalese data reflect the general disparity in LDCs between urban and rural average incomes, although the claim put forth by some (Chambas, 1980; FAO, 1976) that the spread is five or six to one, appears high. The figures in Table 3 were obtained from sectoral contributions to GDP as estimated in the Sixth Development Plan (1981–1985), divided by sectoral population estimates for 1976 and 1980. Figures from the FAO (1976:16) reveal a similar decline in national and agricultural per capita income for the decade 1960–70. However in that earlier period the decline in national per capita income was accounted for entirely by the decline in rural incomes. In the 1970s, by contrast, we see that all sectors suffered declines in income. In both periods the picture is one of the absolute impoverishment of the bulk of the Senegalese population.

TABLE 3

National, Agricultural, and Non-Agricultural Per Capita
Income in Senegal: 1976 and 1980 (CFA in constant 1971 prices)

	National Income per capita	Agricultural Income per capita	Non-Agricultural Income per capita	Agricultural over Non-Agri. Income
1976	58,416	20,439	144,568	7
1980	47,989	17,276	112,585	6.5

Source: GOS, Sixth Plan.

The general decline, due to the *malaise paysan* in 1968 and the beginning of the Sahelian drought shortly thereafter, is undeniable, but one suspects that many rural activities, on-farm and off-farm, as well as seasonal migration toward the urban informal sector, have not been captured by national statistics. It may be that the diversification of revenue-generating activities cushioned the impact of the *agricultural* depression for the Senegalese peasant and that that depression in fact promoted further diversification in the 1970s.

Various studies have for some time signaled the importance of off-farm revenue. At the time of independence, the Conseil Economique et Social estimated the aggregate value of all marketed produce at approximately 26 billion CFA, and the value of all rural income at 38 billion CFA, net of the value of auto-consumption. That would mean that about 31 percent of all monetary revenue was generated off-farm, a level that corresponds to what we know to be the case in other LDCs (see Anderson and Leiserson, 1980).

At about the same time, I. de Garine (1960 as cited in Brochier, 1968: 119) produced the following results of a mini survey at Khombol, lying between Thiés and Diourbel (see Table 4 below).

TABLE 4

Estimation of Per Capita Income in CFA: Khombol

	Rural Serer		Rural Wolof		Urban Wolof	
	CFA	%	CFA	%	CFA	%
I. Monetary Revenue						
Groundnuts	3012	50	4887	37	2119	12
Animals	137	2	285	2	281	2
Coop rebates	–	–	38	–	2	–
Occasional revenue*	855	14	6012	46	8033	46
Regular revenue	–	–	–	–	5443	34
Gifts	241	4	432	3	495	3
Sub Total	4245	70	11654	88	16873	97
II. Auto Consumption	1795	30ᵗ	1476	12ᵗ	463	3
Total	6040	100	13130	100	17336	100

*Refers to rural commerce, services (healers, barbers, etc.) or informal sector labor in the cities.
ᵗ Bears out the image of the Serer being more subsistence oriented than the Wolof.

Several important propositions emerge from this table. First the urban/rural per capital income ratio calculated in this manner is about 3:1, again in line with what we know from other countries. Second, non-farm income accounts for 18–49 percent of all revenues, and if one excludes the value of auto-consumption, 26–55 percent of *monetary* revenue. Third, urban Wolof generate more income from 'occasional' sources than from the formal sector and salaried work which is exactly what one would expect. Mini-surveys may pick this up, but formal statistical reporting probably does not. To that extent remittances to the countryside will be underestimated.

Nearly twenty years later, Stormal-Weigal carried out her own mini-survey in two villages and came up with the figures shown in Table 5.

TABLE 5

Structure and Level of Revenues
(CFA per capita, per year)

	Neourane (Serer)		Keur Makhaly (Wolof)	
	CFA	%	CFA	%
Agricultural Production Sales	4558	19.8	10485	26.6
Animal Production Sales	6117	26.8	11521	29.2
Artisanry	600	2.6	1855	4.7
Trade, Services	1785	7.8	6220	15.7
Marabout-healer	4059	17.7	439	1.1
Gifts, Ceremonies	2310	10.1	2135	5.4
Remittances, Salaries, Pensions	1457	6.4	1127	2.8
Loan, debt repayments	1982	8.6	5668	14.4
Total	22848	100	39450	100

Source: Stormal-Weigal, 1981.

Although Table 5 includes no valuation of auto-consumption, the structure of monetary revenues parallels that of Table 4. We see that non-farm sources generate between 44 and 53 percent of all monetary revenue, and, as in the earlier period the Serer are less involved than the Wolof in off-farm activities and in market transactions in a more general sense. Conversely, as conventional wisdom suggests, Serer emphasize millet cultivation and auto-consumption more than the Wolof.

Over time, however, these cultural contrasts appear to be diminishing. We should also note that we are not confronted in any obvious way with the phenomenon, common in Asia, of the poorest rural dwellers having the highest proportion of off-farm income. That phenomenon in essence consists in 'distress sales' of labor, but in Senegal high levels of off-farm income seem to be linked to the greater commercial proclivities of the Wolof.

Let us look finally at the survey of three villages in the Diourbel region carried out by Josserand and Ross in 1980/81 (CRED, 1982). Their findings confirm several of the tentative conclusions already advanced. The value of non-farm activities as a proportion of total income, including auto-consumption, ranged from 13 percent to 52 percent. As in the other surveys, the Serer village turned out to be the least involved in off-farm work and derived most of its revenue from cattle sales. The poorest village was Wolof and was plagued with poor quality soils. Its poverty, however, had not propelled its members into pervasive and recurrent off-farm 'distress sales' of labor; only 25 percent of the village's revenue was so derived. The village did engage, however, in distress sales of horses, perhaps because 1980/81 was a year of very poor rainfall and this village was particularly hard hit. By contrast, the most prosperous village, also Wolof, was the most heavily engaged in off-farm activities, generating 52 percent of its income through them. The authors point out that this village was the best endowed with agricultural equipment which was used to free up time and labor for non-agricultural pursuits.

These surveys reveal wide disparities in household incomes. The mean for the three villages studied by Josserand and Ross was about 120,000 CFA/household/year, but the *median* was only 64,000 CFA/household/year (ca. $318). That is half of all households earned less than that figure, although the authors made no estimate of migrant remittances. It would appear from this and other surveys that the levels of rural income have about doubled in nominal terms over the last two decades. However, as indicated in Table 3, in real terms there has probably been absolute decline in rural revenues. The price of subsidized items, such as rice and fertilizers, doubled over the same period, while in most instances the prices of agricultural equipment and draught animals have trebled. If we take 60,000 CFA in the mid-1970s as giving a rough approximation of gross revenue per *active adult* in the rural areas, we may juxtapose that figure to estimated incomes in the urban areas (BIT, 1980; Chambas, 1980):

minimum legal industrial wage, 1975:   290,000 CFA/yr.
informal sector workers' average wage: 160,000 CFA/yr.
informal sector apprentices' average wage: 54,000 CFA/yr.

The 60,000 CFA figure mentioned above probably comprises some income generated in the urban sector and therefore double counting may be involved. We may nonetheless conclude that while formal wage employment exercises a strong economic pull on rural dwellers, the attraction of the urban informal sector may be less than expected, except during the agricultural off-season.

All surveys are unanimous in emphasizing the seasonality of off-farm activities. The primary actors are males, generally unmarried, in their 20s and 30s perhaps in quest of the $500–$800 needed to pay brideprice in 1980. Frequently they will engage in rural petty trade (*bana-bana*), using their proceeds from the sale of groundnuts to buy merchandise (cloth, notions, soaps, jewelry, etc.) that they then sell in rural markets.

An alternative is temporary migration to the cities. It was found in Dakar in 1971, for example, that the number of temporary residents increased during the dry season from 33,000 to 87,000 (Van Chi-Bonnardel, 1978: 232). Dry season out-migration for all purposes may involve between 15 and 20 percent of the total population or 30–40 percent of the active population (Josserand and Ross in CRED, 1982; Faye, 1981; and Sarr, 1980).[4] There are a number of policy trade-offs that must be examined in light of what has been presented above. Public agencies may try to encourage or rationalize these off-season activities. One avenue is to try to build up the service and petty manufacturing sectors of small rural centers. One can see evidence all over Senegal – at Louga or Mback, at Kaffrine or Fatick – that this process is well under way spontaneously (in general see Anderson and Leiserson, 1980; Hart, 1982: 55–80). But if it is the goal of the state to promote the agricultural *mise en valeur* of the groundnut basin, and to exploit the availability of off-season labor for that purpose, it will find itself in direct competition with very powerful economic forces. Its incentives would have to be commensurately great.

To examine this question, let us take an example that may be reflective of conditions prevailing in the groundnut basin. The GOS could respond to its own cultivators and to occasional pressure from international donors by raising the producer price for groundnuts. Assume a household that produces 3 tons of groundnuts. At the 1982 producer price, we find:

$$3000 \text{ kg at } 60 \text{ CFA/kg} = 180,000 \text{ CFA.}$$

Assume that this represents 40 percent of all monetary revenues for the household which then total 450,000 CFA. Monetary revenues are 70 percent of total revenues which include the value of auto-consumption: i.e., 645,000 CFA. The State then raises the producer price of groundnuts by 10 percent to 66 CFA/kg. The household may maintain production or, in response to the new price, raise it by, say, 15 percent. In both cases we obtain:

3000 kg/groundnuts at 66 CFA/kg =	198,000 CFA
Gross gain due to price increase	18,000 CFA
Gain as percent of monetary revenue	4%
Gain as percent of total revenue	2.8%
15 percent production increase	450 kg
earnings on additional production due to price increase	450 kg at 66 CFA/kg – 29,700 CFA
earnings resulting from production increase as percent of monetary revenue	6% (29,700/468,000)
earnings resulting from production increase as percent of total revenues	4.4% (29,700/663,000)

Given the overall diversification of this household's revenue sources, we would have to conclude that a 10 percent producer price increase might yield real income gains of marginal interest to the household. If a price increase is designed to engineer a major transfer of income to the rural areas it may fall well short of its goal. If, however, the object of the price increase is to stimulate production, the likely response is difficult to predict. One would have to know the opportunity costs for labor at crucial points in the growing season in order to gauge whether or not a part-time peasant will sacrifice off-farm revenue to devote more time to farming or use resources to acquire fertilizers and equipment in an effort to boost production (see Helleiner, 1975: 29–30). It is not clear if price signals can be made loud enough to engineer a reallocation of labor and capital toward increased production.

IV. THE MILLET–RICE–GROUNDNUT TRIANGLE

Beginning in the 1920s, Senegalese peasants were encouraged to favor groundnut cultivation in their allocation of land, and to rely upon cheap broken rice from Indochina to make up for deficits in millet production (Founou–Tchuigoua, 1981). In the 1930s one kg of broken rice sold for less than one of groundnuts. Senegal was doubly entrapped: first sacrificing food crops to groundnuts, and, second, deepening its dependence upon foreign sources of staple foods. Since the Second World War Senegal has imported in most years over 150,000 tons of rice. By the late 1970s, as domestic production stagnated below 100,000 tons, imports exceeded 300,000 tons. The bulk of the imported rice is consumed in urban areas, but the remainder has become an important element in rural consumption habits.

Millet, of course, has traditionally been and remains the staple food item for Senegal's rural population: per capita consumption is on the order of 120 to 170 kg per year as opposed to 20–80 kg per capita in urban areas (SONED, 1979: 119). On the other hand per capita rice consumption in the rural sector is on the order of 15 to 40 kg per year (Ross, 1979) and in recent years has averaged about 30 kg per cap. But rice must be purchased whereas millet is grown for auto-consumption.

The most interesting and most vexing question is whether or not millet is perfectly substitutable for rice, especially in Senegalese rural diets. There is a general presumption that demand for rice throughout Senegal is fairly elastic, and that if the retail price of rice is allowed to rise, rural consumers in particular will prefer to buy (and perhaps to grow) millet. This, with prudent reservations, is the argument of Josserand and Ross (CRED, 1982), and Ross (1979) observed that during the 'hungry season,' when millet reserves are low, rice purchases did not increase. If food self-sufficiency is Senegal's goal, then under this assumption a major increase in the retail price of rice would stimulate the production and consumption of millet. If increased millet production entailed some loss in groundnut export earnings, that loss might be off-set by foreign exchange savings due to reduced rice imports.

The available evidence however is not entirely clear. Although less nutritious than millet, rice is prized both for its convenience and its prestige value. Rice is bought milled and ready to pre-pare. It stores fairly well and is readily available through the institutionalized retail distribution system of the country. By con-trast, millet flour does not store well and must be prepared daily through an elaborate and gruelling ritual, carried out entirely by women, of soaking, drying, pounding, and cooking the millet grain. Leaving aside the wealthiest city dwellers, who can afford servants, urban Senegalese cannot readily substitute millet for rice because of the difficulties in preparation. This may account partially for the peculiar income elasticities uncovered by Josserand and Ross that show that while rice consumption rises with income, millet con-sumption rises more than twice as fast (a 10 percent increase in income leads to a 2.6 percent increase in rice consumption as opposed to a 6 percent increase in millet consumption).

Second, rice is an essential part of Senegalese festive or ceremonial cuisine; the national dish, *tieboudieunne*, requires broken rice and large quantities of cooking oil. Indeed, rice consumption entails oil consumption. The frequency with which such dishes are consumed may be reduced (Van Chi-Bonnardel claims that in the 1930s and 1940s rice was consumed daily in rural areas whereas by the 1970s twice a week was more the norm), but millet cannot replace rice in them.

Stormal-Weigel found in her micro-survey of two villages, both of which produced more millet than they consumed, that about 20 percent of all household expenditures went to the purchase of rice and 9 percent to oil (1981: 130–35). In villages of the Bakel region surveyed by Weigel (1982: 87) 24 percent of all *food* outlays went to rice and oil, and another 8 percent to fish. Josserand and Ross, studying one Serer and two Wolof villages (CRED, 1982) found that outlays on rice and oil ranged from 11 percent of total food outlays in the Serer village (predictably the most self-sufficient of the three villages in food consumption) to 26 percent in the most prosperous village, to 40 percent in the poorest village.

Since 1968 the retail price of rice has been about double the producer price of groundnuts and more than two times that of unprocessed millet. Yet despite this, rice imports continued to rise, albeit in saw-tooth fashion. It is true that because Senegal has subsidized the retail price of rice, some portion of the imported rice has been smuggled into neighboring countries where the price is substantially higher (*Le Soleil*, 11/15/82). Still, as Table 6 shows, imports of rice grew by leaps and bounds in the mid and late 1970s although the ratio of rice retail prices to millet and groundnut producer prices remained basically unchanged.[5]

The rice import figures cannot be broken down into urban and rural consumption per capita, but Hopkins, Van Chi-Bonnardel, and others believe that rural consumption of rice has declined since the late 1960s. That may be the case, but it will take more empirical investigation to prove it. It is, however, a prudent assumption that even in those years when millet granaries are full, there will still be substantial demand for imported rice in the Senegalese countryside.

Since independence there has been a modest, although uneven, increase in the acreage given over to millet and a similar modest increase in average yields and total production. Some have seen in

TABLE 6

Relative Prices for Rice (retail), Millet (producer),
and Groundnuts (producer) and Rice Imports
1970/71 — 1980/81

Year	Rice Retail Price: CFA/kg	Millet Producer Price: CFA/kg	Groundnut Producer Price: CFA/kg	Rice Imports: Tons
1970/71	40	18	24.1	131,200
1971/72	40	18	23.1	
1972/73	40	18	23.1	
1973/74	60	25	25.5	
1974/75	100	30	41.5	102,126
1975/76	90	30	41.5	244,508
1976/77	80	35	41.5	248,018
1977/78	80	35	41.5	238,996
1978/79	80	40	41.5	351,860
1979/80	80	40	45.5	302,536
1980/81	105	50	60	306,000
1981/82	105	55	70	321,800

Source: BCEAO publications and figures provided by the CPSP. Between 1980 and 1982 the CPSP allotted on average 87,000 tons of rice to the rural areas or about 30% of the total amounts distributed annually.

this (among others, Van Chi-Bonnardel, 1978: 69) evidence of a retreat into subsistence or a flight from markets. The argument is that the absolute decline in groundnut prices after 1967 and their relative decline vis-à-vis rice and other consumer goods produced this retreat. But as we have seen in Table 2, the evidence of the last two decades does not bear this out. Peasants have increased both millet *and* groundnut acreage. They have been trying to maximize both food security and market returns.

There are a number of factors that would lead one to predict, over time, a fairly even balance between millet and groundnut acreage. There is some tendency for one crop to follow the other on the same acreage, at least on land close to the *carré*, in order to obtain maximum effects of residual fertilizer in the soil.[6] Beyond this, millet serves several unique functions that no other agricultural product can fully match. Not only does it act as a subsistence cushion for families and *carrés*, it has become increasingly a source of savings and of cash. It is difficult to know how much millet is traded annually in non-official markets. The amounts will clearly vary with the size of the harvest and amounts available above subsistence needs. Total millet production over the first twenty years of independence averaged about 530,000 tons a year. With the exception of one year, in which state procurement agencies purchased 100,000 tons, official markets have handled at most 5 percent of the total harvest. Yet it may be the case that a quarter or more of the harvest is marketed through cash sales or barter. It is usually cash. Because it is harvested earlier than groundnuts and is available for sale up to two months before the official opening of the groundnut marketing season, millet may constitute the *only* source of cash at the end of the hungry season (*soudure*). Moreover, as private traders have been legally excluded from groundnut trade, they have increasingly turned to millet as collateral for loans made to peasants during the *soudure*. Finally, millet can be stored over-year as a hedge against a bad agricultural season or against poor groundnut prices. So powerful have the advantages or the imperatives of millet production become, that women and even *sourgas* have sacrificed groundnut acreage to it.

The only other rural activity that fulfills some of these functions is animal husbandry, especially cattle. However it is only among the peoples of the Ferlo and the Sine Saloum that the tradition is firmly rooted, and even then cattle (aside from production of milk) are not a major source of nourishment. Thus one may conclude that millet will not be sacrificed in contemporary Senegalese agriculture unless very large amounts of rice are available at highly subsidized prices in the countryside, combined with high groundnut producer prices. To some extent that was the situation prevailing in the halcyon days of groundnut production from 1955 to 1965. It is hard to conceive of a set of circumstances in which the same relative prices could prevail in the 1980s.

V. PEASANT: UNDER-WORKED OR OVER-EXPLOITED?

René Dumont has argued more than once that if rural African men would work as hard as rural African women, the continent's agricultural problems could be solved. If one looks only at agricultural activities it appears that the Senegalese peasant is hardly the 'over-exploited' (*sur-exploité*) victim depicted by Founou-Tchuigoua (1981), part of a stratum that may not have at its disposal the means of its own biological reproduction.[7] Even within Senegal, Paul Pélissier has remarked on the great contrast in work habits, especially during the off-season, between the Diola of Casamance and the rest of Senegal (Pélissier, 1966: 759).[8]

Estimates of labor inputs for various crops and rural activities vary widely. Part of the variation is a function of the level of equipment on the farming unit, but by and large the use of seeders, plows, lifters, bullocks, etc., is not so much labor-saving per unit of production as it is surface expanding. SONED (1979) measured average labor time in man hours equivalent for millet to be 573 per ha (or about 95 days of labor at 6 hours per day) and, surprisingly, 330 per ha (or about 55 days) for groundnuts. The relative shares here are the reverse of what one would normally expect. Josserand and Ross came up with 56 days per ha of millet and 80 days per ha of groundnuts which conforms more to our general sense of the greater demand for labor exerted by groundnuts. On a five hectare exploitation, with acreage divided equally between millet and groundnuts, and with the equivalent of five male adults farming it, the average labor requirement of each would be about 68 days – this in pre-planting, growing and post-harvest periods running from June through October (120-150 days).

Stormal-Weigel found that during the peak season in the Wolof village she investigated the average daily work load was 4.8 hours for women and 2.2 for men, and in the Serer village 5.6 hours for women and 3.1 hours for men. She also notes, however, that Serer men and boys spend an average 2.5 hours a day *year round* tending livestock while for the the Wolof about an hour a day is so spent. In sum, even under the most labor intensive conditions, agriculture and associated activities do not command the bulk of the Senegalese peasants' time. These findings are fully consistent with general patterns of African labor utilization of ca. 600–900 hours of agricultural labor annually spread over 140 to 160 days. The more intense the labor, the shorter the working day (see Cleave, 1974; Levi and Havinden, 1982). Whatever the claims on labor time, peak season agricultural activity puts very heavy demands on the energy and health of the peasant. Maximum physical energy is expended at a time when food reserves are low or non-existent and cash available only from the money-lender. Seasonal charting of caloric intake shows marked deficiencies during the hungry season – May, June, July – and during the harvest in September (Weiner, 1980). Dumont and Mottin (1982), referring to recent surveys in the Thiès region assert that caloric in-take drops from 2700 per day in the off-season to 1500 per day in the *soudure*.

The caloric deficits of these months are paralleled by an increased incidence of disease, especially malaria, as a result of the proliferation of disease vectors during the rainy months. Thus, even the relatively low number of peak season labor hours devoted to agriculture recorded by Stormal-Weigel may represent the maximum possible under prevailing health and nutritional circumstances. The non-expenditure of labor time for agricultural purposes in the off season is, however, altogether a different matter and is taken up in Chapter 6.

VI. THE IMPROVIDENT PEASANT

> It is no exaggeration to say, then, that the 'imprudent
> peasant-monopsonized market' model is at best
> unproved, at worst pure myth. (CILSS, 1977:93)

What is this model that the CILSS authors seek to debunk? It is premised on the induced change in economic behavior as peasants are drawn away from subsistence production and into the market economy. To understand it, we must cut arbitrarily into the agricultural cycle. When peasants are paid for their groundnut crop, they immediately pay out their cash returns in a splurge of consumer buying and ceremonial display. Before the state nationalized groundnut marketing, the private traders that bought the crop in turn sold the peasants the consumer goods they coveted. When the peasants ran out of cash and faced their own now-inadequate millet reserves, the trader would lend them money to buy rice or millet during the *soudure*, claiming repayment at harvest time, in cash or kind, at usurious interest rates. The traders then had stocks of grain and cash with which to initiate the next season's sales of food, consumer goods and credit. That, in essence, is the model, and so widely held was it in Senegal (and elsewhere), that the colonial authorities initiated the *Sociétés Indigènes de Prévoyance* to undermine the private traders and to provide credit in kind during the hungry season (the so-called *prêts de soudure*; see Chapter 3).

This model is still widely held in Senegal today (among others, Sene, I, 1982) and there are those like Van Chi-Bonnardel who argue that those subjected to it are on the increase. By the late 1960s, with the 19 percent decline in the producer price for groundnuts and a slight increase in the price of fertilizers, peasants found themselves increasingly indebted to the coops, for purchase of seed, fertilizers, and equipment, and increasingly pressed for cash during the *soudure*. The *prêts de soudure* by the coops, mainly in the form of millet, were inadequate to cover peasant needs. The private traders, excluded from the groundnut markets, were only too willing to step in to offer cash during the *soudure* against sales of millet or groundnuts at harvest time at prices well below the official floor, that represented effective interest rates of 50-150 percent. For instance a peasant might borrow 3000 CFA in July and agree to pay back 500 kg of millet at the end of September valued at 10 CFA/kg for a total repayment of 5000 CFA. In this manner Van Chi-Bonnardel argues that while about 15 percent of total agricultural income represented debt to the coops, another 15 percent represented debt to private traders (1978: 488), and that only the private traders could exercise effective claims for repayment. Whereas 'village solidarity' or collective responsibility for debt represented the cooperatives' basic collateral, leading in the late 1960s to collective default, the private traders took liens on crops and agricultural equipment.

Peasants exacerbated this situation by depleting food reserves after poor harvests, a factor enormously aggravated by the Sahelian drought, and by maintaining high levels of sumptuary outlays. Seen from outside the culture such expenditures appear at best non-productive and at worst frivolous and wasteful. Nonetheless nearly everywhere in Africa they are an integral element in honoring social obligations and maintaining familial prestige. Some obligations, such as baptismal gifts or amassing wedding expenses, are highly institutionalized, but there are also constant outlays in small gifts, interest free loans, emergency aid and so forth that put a heavy drain on resources (see Ware, 1977).

It is normally in the winter, after groundnut marketing, that these ceremonial expenditures are undertaken, and they may well leave the peasant's cash reserves totally depleted. Only drop-by-drop millet sales, city-ward migration, or *bana-bana* retailing in the countryside will stand between the peasant and the money-lender. As Laura Tuck found in her nation-wide survey (see appendix to this chapter), 22 percent of all borrowing was for ceremonial expenses: funerals, baptisms, marriages, and Tabaski (Muslim feast of Abraham).

Elliot Berg, CILSS, Ross (1979), and Josserand and Ross (1982), among others, are highly skeptical that this model describes reality. Berg (1980) offers a different model, that of an experienced peasant who plants as much grain as it will take to feed his family on the assumption of normal rains and with some safety margin. He has storage capacity up to one year's consumption of millet. He knows he will have need of cash prior to harvest and prepares for it by migration during the dry season and by growing cash crops. Entry into local markets for labor or trade is relatively easy, and they are competitive rather than monopsonistic.[9]

The policy implication that can be drawn from this is that rural marketing and credit systems in which the state plays a minor role need not be and in fact probably are not exploitative. They may be fairly efficient, and are therefore to be encouraged. The idea is appealing, but one may doubt that it is yet well anchored empirically.

We should first distinguish between agricultural sales that constitute repayment of *soudure* loans at possibly usurious rates, and distress sales after harvest whereby peasants gain a little desperately needed cash and traders acquire grain at well below official floor prices which they hold for sale, at high prices, during the next *soudure*. Ross observed two phenomena in this context in 1977 and 1978. The frequency of millet sales was not greater immediately following the harvest than in the ensuing four months, but 28 percent of all sales for the year took place in October–December (the groundnut marketing season generally opened on December 15). He also recorded that the average price received fell to about 4 CFA below the official price (35 CFA/kg) in December. For the entire year the average price received was slightly above the official price. Thus there is no *direct reported* evidence of usurious debt acquittals and only weak evidence of distress sales. Nonetheless it seems significant that in tabulating the frequency of sales according to the buyer, Ross came up with the following distribution (1979: 34) (Table 7).

TABLE 7

Village-Level Marketing Data

	No. of Sales	% of Total Sales
village store	51	30
rural trader	81	47
rural market	26	15
neighbors	11	6
ONCAD	4	2
Total	173	100

Parallel private markets thus absorbed 92 percent of all sales which certainly piques one's curiosity as to profit margins when millet is resold, as well as to *unreported* repayment of debt.

Other sources, while not focussing explicitly on this problem, yield evidence that can only urge caution in accepting the 'provident peasant' model (e.g., Camboulives, 1967: 68). Before the state take-over of groundnut trading and the elimination of nearly 7000 traders from that market, there is no question that the 'improvident peasant' model was anything but myth. The massive COGERAF study of groundnut marketing in Senegal, published in 1963, emphasizes the extent of hungry season borrowing from traders with repayment in kind (groundnuts) after harvest at usurious rates. In a given year, COGERAF estimated, *half* of the groundnut harvest could be tied up in such repayments (1963: I, 113). Even as the cooperative system spread throughout Senegal along with the generalization of the *prêts de soudure*, the problem was only altered, not eliminated. SODEVA (1971) estimated the grain deficit for the groundnut basin during the *soudure*, and after a good agricultural year, at 50–60,000 tons. Over the period 1963–1970, *prêts de soudure* (rice and millet) averaged 12,000 tons per year, but over the period steadily declined from 23,500 tons at the beginning to 5200 tons at the end. Coops practiced a self-defeating policy of determining the level of such loans so as not to exceed 25 percent of the value of the groundnuts marketed at the coop in the preceding season (18 percent of the authorized level of lending to go to equipment and only 7 percent to grain). In other words, peasants were encouraged to grow less millet to market more groundnuts so as to borrow more millet in the *soudure*. As groundnut prices tumbled after 1967 so too did the amounts marketed and hence the levels of *prêts de soudure*. Millet production did not increase substantially. By a process of elimination, the peasant could survive only by pulling in his belt or by borrowing cash and grain from traders, or both.[10]

The same kinds of constraints are operative today, with the added factor that *prêts de soudure* have been pretty much suspended since the dissolution of ONCAD. A SONED study in 1976 (cited by Sene, I, 1982) found four-month interest rates on private *soudure* loans of 55 percent, paid in kind. However the study apparently did not estimate the volume of such loans. Sene himself, looking primarily at Sine–Saloum, emphasizes the intense need for cash in October and November that forces peasants into millet sales at prices 30 percent below the official floor. This observation is confirmed by SONED

(1979: 123). Finally A. Dione (1980) found in a survey of 321 *exploitations* in Sine-Saloum in 1980/81 that 63 percent had *some* millet in storage at the beginning of the *soudure* but that only 26 percent had enough to provide 60 kg per capita over the following three months of heavy labor. Laura Tuck's data do not directly address the question of forward or tied sales, but they do confirm (a) that most borrowing takes place during the *soudure*; (b) that most borrowing is for food; (c) that merchants and villagers are the major source of such loans; (d) the loans are substantial, and (e) annualized interest rates range from 40–90 percent.

In sum, there is good circumstantial evidence to indicate that the old model of the 'improvident peasant' is not yet obsolete. The adjective may be misleading. The peasant's need to borrow is not the result of poor planning or hedonistic consumption, but rather has structural causes with which he is ill-equipped to grapple. He is both urged and wants to grow millet and groundnuts, but he can seldom grow enough of the former to cover his food needs nor market enough of the latter to buy the food he is lacking. The state has so far been incapable of making grain loans to him during the hungry season or of upholding its floor price in the post harvest season. Finally the peasant is socially obliged to divert cash income into ceremonial expenses and familial obligations. He cannot flee these responsibilities. The situation virtually cries out for consumption credit provided by the private merchant *cum* money lender and better-off villagers.

VII. CONCLUSION

The aspects of peasant organization and economic behavior emphasized in this paper are by no means exhaustive but rather represent areas of debate as well as areas of opportunity for policy intervention. The conclusions offered here are very tentative but their implications could have considerable medium term policy significance.

First, the Senegalese peasant is fully if not happily integrated into the market system. He will only abandon it under the duress of severe price disincentives, and then only partially. Conversely the peasant will sacrifice basic grain production only if groundnut prices are very high relative to rice, millet, edible oils, etc. Either way the *maximum* swing in acreage would be 60/40. Given that groundnut prices are not likely to rise significantly in the near future and that rice prices will probably remain 2 times those of groundnuts and 2+

times those of millet, we can expect swings between groundnut and millet acreage on the order of 53/47 one way or the other.[11] The availability of quality groundnut seed may have more influence on these swings than official producer prices.

Second, the *carré* comprises diverse production interests that have seldom been targeted by policy makers and extension agents. Perhaps they should not be, for penetrating the *carré* to hand tailor programs to women, or *sourgas*, or *chefs de ménage*, may be beyond the capacity of the RDAs and socially disruptive.

Senegalese cultivators are increasingly part-time peasants whose most important revenue streams may come from non-farm sources. On the one hand this means that agricultural price signals will have diminished resonance especially for *sourgas*; on the other hand it means the extent of diversification and the standard of living of rural dwellers are greater and higher than conventional accounting methods would indicate. The state may have many opportunities for promoting productive use of off-farm income for rural modernization.

The Sixth Plan declared food self-sufficiency as a major objective. It is unlikely, however, even if millet production increases substantially and rice retail prices remain high, that millet will be completely substituted for rice in rural diets let alone in urban diets.

The Senegalese peasant is not overworked, but if the state seeks to capture his labor power it will have to be during the dry season at a time when the opportunity cost for farm labor is very high. Relieving certain kinds of labor demands on women – hauling water, pounding millet, gathering firewood, etc. – may allow them to reallocate labor to agriculture, collective vegetable plots, off-season diversification, in short upgrading agricultural assets at a time when most able-bodied men are away from the *carré*.

Finally, the Senegalese groundnut peasant cannot consistently make ends meet. Failure to do so in one bad agricultural season may lock him into debt obligations that subvert his recovery in average or good agricultural seasons. Off-farm revenues mitigate this spiral, as do periodic *épongements* of the debts owed the coops, but the present system does not provide him any sure means of escape from debt, distress sales, and usurious loans. Should the state let private markets take their course and their toll, or put together new instruments of intervention?

NOTES

1. The old coastal areas, mainly north of Dakar, were given over to groundnut cultivation prior to the construction of the railroad to Mali. The new areas, east and south of Thiès, followed the line of the railroad and were developed principally through Murid colonization in the inter-war years.
2. In Wolof this person is called the *borum keur* and in Serer, the *yal mbind*. Both figures derive from that ancestor that burned off, cleared, and farmed the land, thus establishing title to its usufruct for himself and his descendants.
3. The *chef de ménage* is known as the *borom ndiel* in Wolof and the *yal ngak* in Serer.
4. Migration, seasonal and otherwise, also includes 'migrants for education,' high school or university level students, as well as *navetanes*, now migrating during the wet season from the more crowded parts of the groundnut basin to the *terres neuves*. The best overview is in Faye (1981).
5. By 1985 the retail price of rice had been raised to 160 CFA/kg while the millet purchase price was increased to 70 CFA/kg and groundnuts to 90 CFA/kg.
6. It is not clear how this alternation works out on the fields of the *sourgas* who are generally depicted as exclusively involved in groundnut cultivation. Alternation on the better-fertilized, more intensively farmed soils closer to the *carré* is probably the norm.
7. If one combines the analyses of Founou-Tchuigoua emphasizing the *sur-exploitation* of the groundnut peasant and that of Chris Gerry (1979:1154) who writes of Dakar's informal sector in these terms:

   > [It is] able only to reproduce its conditions of existence ... the continued impoverishment of the mass of the population is inevitable.

   One has an image of the rural and urban populations living in grinding and systemic squalor. Neither of the two parts nor their sum are accurately represented.
8. The Diola spend much of the off-season in the maintenance of dikes, field ridges, canals, etc. The only slack period comes in January–February which is devoted to ceremonies and celebrations.
9. Two other revisionists are Bauer (1954), and Jones (1982).
10. Gatin (1968: 18) speculated that a large part of the high demands expressed by peasants for equipment loans can be explained by the fact that the equipment was used for collateral on loans from private traders. The peasants would then default on the equipment loans.
11. At the time of writing it is impossible to know how peasants will respond to the 1985 announced increase in the groundnut producer price from 70 to 90 CFA/kg.

Appendix

Laura Tuck

I. BORROWING

It is generally accepted that there is an active market in informal credit in rural Senegal. However, little is known about its impor'tance in relation to the economy as a whole. Christin (1982) estimates that the amount of informal credit transacted in the rural economy is roughly equal to 1.5 percent of the value added in the primary sector. In 1983, this would amount to approximately three billion CFA.

A survey on informal rural financial markets (hereafter referred to as the RFM-survey) was done for the present study during the Spring of 1983. It was carried out in five of the seven agricultural regions of Senegal. Most of the information presented in this section is based on these results. The findings were fairly consistent with the above conclusions as to the size of informal markets and the prevalence of borrowing. The survey found that 67 percent of the households studied borrowed at least once during the course of the year. The average amount borrowed per household was 23,000 CFA. Work done by the Aménagement du Territoire based on the 1976 census data shows that there are 284,586 households in rural Senegal (this includes only those outside of the communes or cities). A rough estimate, then, of the order of magnitude of rural credit suggested by this study would be in the 4.4 billion CFA range.

It is likely however, that this estimate is biased downwards. Recall methods were used in the survey to calculate the value of borrowing. It is probable that in some cases the person speaking for the household either forgot or was not aware of certain transactions during the year. It is also possible that some households simply did not wish to discuss their financial situation and intentionally neglected to mention past loans they had received. Moreover, it is doubtful that farmers exaggerated the amount of borrowing they had done. Therefore, this 4.4 billion CFA can probably be taken as the minimum size of the informal credit market in rural Senegal in 1982–1983.

A. *Types of Loans*

A little over half (54 percent) of the borrowing was undertaken in the form of cash. All cash loans were also repaid in cash. The use of funds can be broken out as shown in Table 1.

TABLE 1

Uses of Cash Borrowing
(in % of loans)

food	53.0%
funerals	9.4%
baptisms	6.3%
daily expenditures	6.3%
trips to Dakar	6.3%
construction of homes	6.3%
marriages	3.1%
sheep for Tabaski	3.1%
clothes for children	3.1%
taxes	3.1%

n=37

Forty six percent of the borrowing was done in-kind but only one-third of that was repaid in-kind. The items borrowed are broken out in Table 2.

TABLE 2

Type of Borrowing in-Kind
(in % of loans)

millet	47%
rice	34%
corn	9%
sheep	9%

n=32

It should be noted that no informal borrowing was done for 'productive' purposes. Certainly none of the farmers surveyed borrowed specifically for agricultural activities. Of course, the cash and kind resources listed above are fungible and, to the extent that farmers did buy agricultural inputs, these loans helped to free up the cash they used for these transactions. However, no farmers included in the survey bought either fertilizer or farm equipment for the 1982–83 growing season.

Not surprisingly, most households borrowed during the *soudure* or hungry season (May–November). One hundred percent of the farmers interviewed said this was when their credit needs were the greatest. Seventy one percent of their actual borrowing took place between June and October alone (see Figure 1).

FIGURE 1

Seasonality of Borrowing

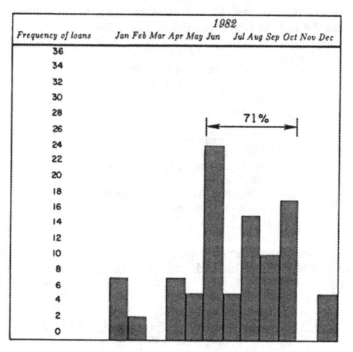

The average amount borrowed in a single transaction for all types of loans was 12,321 CFA (approximately $35). The average in-kind transaction for all types of loans was valued at 9,053 CFA or 40 percent less than the average cash transaction of 15,068 CFA.

For cash and in-kind borrowing, the largest loans came from merchants, mid-sized loans came from other villagers and family members while sources outside of these principal categories provided funds in the smallest denominations (see Table 3).

B. Interest Rates

Less than half of the loans (44 percent) carried interest charges. There was a large difference in this respect between cash and in-kind loans. Only 26 percent if the former were repaid with interest while the figure was 66 percent for the latter (see Table 5). The reasons for this phenomenon are not obvious. For loans in-kind that are repaid in cash (two-thirds of the in-kind loans fall into this category), the

TABLE 3

Average Value of Borrowing Transaction
By Source (in CFA)

Source	All Types	Source	Cash	Source	In-Kind
Merchants	22,750	Merchants	45,000	Merchants	14,659
Villagers	11,827	Villagers	13,675	Family	8,465
Family	8,833	Family	8,818	Villagers	8,193
Other*	1,227	Other	3,500	Other	469

*'Other' includes all lenders who do not fall into the category of family, villagers or merchants except it also includes all religious leaders, even if they could also be classified in one of the above groupings. Other examples would include individuals residing outside the village who are not either family or merchants, and government organized cooperatives.

TABLE 4

Average Duration of Borrowing
By Source (in months)

Source	All Types	Source	Cash	Source	In-Kind
Other	5.8	Villagers	5.4	Other	7.0
Villagers	4.7	Family	3.9	Merchants	4.5
Merchants	4.0	Merchants	2.8	Villagers	3.6
Family	3.3	Other	2.3	Family	2.3
	n=69		n=37		n=32

interest cost is not explicit. It is possible that this makes it easier, in a Moslem country, to impose such charges.

Interest costs have been broken out in several ways. First, a simple average was calculated, including all the loans bearing zero interest. Second, an average rate was calculated for only those rates carrying an interest charge.

The reason there is such a substantial difference between the average interest rates on cash loans is because such a large percentage of them do not bear interest (76 percent). Interest rates on those that do, however, are high. A much larger percentage of the borrowings made in-kind do require interest payments, but on average the rates are lower. Nonetheless, it turns out that the low percentage of cash loans exacting interest charges, on balance, makes it cheaper to borrow in cash than in kind. In terms of total

TABLE 5

Percent of Loans Bearing Interest
By Source

All Loans	%	Cash	%	In-Kind	%
Other	75	Villagers	35	Other	100
Merchants	53	Merchants	25	Merchants	64
Villagers	42	Family	9	Villagers	55
Family	20	Other	0	Family	50
All Sources	44	All Sources	24	All Sources	66
	n=69		n=37		n=32

TABLE 6

Average Annual Interest Rates

	All Loans	Cash	In-Kind
Average Rate (including zeros)	34.2%	22.9%	47.2%
Average Rate (interest bearing only)	78.6%	94.2%	71.9%
	n=69	n=37	n=32

TABLE 7

Average Annual Interest Rates
By Source

	R	R*
Villagers	39.8%	94.9%
Merchants	30.8%	57.8%
Family	29.7%	148.5%
Other	26.7%	35.6%
	n=69	

R = Average interest rates including loans with zero interest.
R* = Average interest rates on interest bearing loans only.

value, farmers borrowed almost twice as much in cash as they did in kind.

Interest bearing loans (R*) from other family members were more costly than those from any other source (see Table 7). This can be partially explained by the fact that all sheep loans for ceremonies came from other family members, and these loans carried the highest annual interest rates. However, due to the short-term nature of the loans, the absolute interest cost was actually less than for many other types of loans.

Another noteworthy observation is that merchants did not charge the highest interest rates. In fact, other villagers charged, on average, one-third again as much, while the average cost of a loan from a merchant was almost identical to that of one from a family member. This contradicts the common argument that merchants' monopoly position for lending capital allows them to charge the most 'usurious' rates.

C. Borrowing by Source

Only 22 percent of all loans came from merchants although the loans they provided were larger, on average, than those from any other source (approximately twice the size of those from the source extending the next largest loans). Merchants supplied 42 percent of the total capital borrowed from informal sources.

Twenty six percent of the households surveyed were found to have actually borrowed from merchants in amounts ranging from 2,000 CFA to 100,000 CFA. Thirty seven percent felt they could borrow at least 5,000 CFA if they needed it, 21 percent felt they could borrow at least 25,000 CFA and 43 percent contended that merchants would never lend them anything.

Other villagers furnished 45 percent of the total loans extended or twice the number made by either merchants or family members. This was one surprising result of the survey since merchants and family members are often considered to be the traditional sources of informal credit. It should be noted, however, that in terms of total amount borrowed, the value of loans provided by other villagers was only 7 percent larger than that supplied by merchants. This means that they furnish many more loans than their counterparts but for much smaller amounts.

Twenty six percent of the households reported instances of intra-familial borrowing (the same number that borrowed from merchants). However, the average value of loans was only 40 percent of the average amount borrowed from commercial sources. This was true even though farmers felt that the same amount of resources would be available from within the family if they needed them.

While 52 percent of the respondents felt that they could not borrow anything from sources outside the village, the other half felt that they could. Nonetheless, only 1.4 percent of the total loans actually did come from outside the village. This category did not include merchants or family members residing outside the village as they were categorized separately. These loans came primarily from farmers in neighboring villages or acquaintances in nearby towns.

Less than 2 percent of the households were documented as having borrowed from a religious leader. This was a somewhat surprising result as they are traditionally considered to be an important source of funds for farmers in time of need.

D. Regional and Ethnic Contrasts

1. *Casamance*: Van Chi-Bonnardel argues that the Diola are one of the ethnic groups least likely to become indebted. Both villages surveyed in the Casamance for this study were Diola, and the data seem to support this conclusion.

The size of loans in the Casamance were, on average, the smallest of all regions (cash loans in the region with the next highest average were more than twice the size, and in-kind loans were almost 20 times as large). Furthermore, the only interest-bearing loans were those organized by the PIDAC cooperative. No loans, cash or in-kind, came from local merchants. The much less commercialized nature of informal financial activity in the Casamance would appear to be a result of (a) the attitudes of the Diola and (b) the lesser degree of integration into the cash economy. This latter can be attributed to the importance of subsistence crop production (rice) relative to cash crop production in the Casamance.

2. *Diourbel*: In contrast to the results from the Casamance, the data from Diourbel show that this is the region with the most informal credit activity. Again, this is not surprising. Van Chi-Bonnardel claims that the Wolof are the most indebted of the rural Senegalese because of the greater importance they attach to ceremonies and ostentation. All of the villages surveyed in the Diourbel region were Wolof. Furthermore, as the heart of the groundnut basin, this is an area where farmers are heavily integrated into the cash economy. In addition, the Diourbel region is the home of the richest and best organized Moslem brotherhood (the Mourides) and is hence a region of relatively high cash flow.

The data show that, on average, cash loans in Diourbel are 73 percent greater in value than those in the next most important region and 41 percent greater in value for in-kind loans. The interest rates in Diourbel are by far the highest for both cash and in-kind loans. The largest percentage of all loans come from local merchants, again indicating the more commercialized nature of economic activity in the groundnut basin.

3. *Other Regions*: The data from other regions indicate conditions ranging between the two extreme cases described above. Louga and the Sine-Saloum exhibit characteristics which resemble those of Diourbel on a more moderate scale. This is attributed to their similar integration into the cash economy from the groundnut trade, and their large Wolof populations. The averages from the Sine-Saloum, however, show that loans there are smaller, have a shorter duration and carry lower interest charges. This reflects the influence of the Serer who tend to use credit much less than their Wolof counterparts (Van Chi-Bonnardel).

The farmers surveyed in the Fleuve were half Wolof and half Toucouleur. The data show that 98 percent of the loans carried no interest charges. These results are probably due more to the fact that farming in the Fleuve is not highly commercialized (the bulk of the primary crops, rice and corn, is consumed on farm) than to its ethnic composition.

E. Income classes

The baseline survey data were adequate to calculate for each household (a) the economic value of crop production and total production (including livestock), (b) the net monetary revenues from agricultural income, (c) the value of farm assets (equipment and livestock), (d) the weight of cereals production, and (e) the per capita equivalents for each of these variables.

Analyses show that there is no demonstrable relationship between the value of household borrowings and any of these variables. This is not surprising. The amount of funds actually borrowed is fundamentally a function of both the supply and demand schedules for resources. There is no *a priori* motivation for the assumption that farmers demand more or less borrowed capital as any of these variables increase. Both rich and poor farmers may borrow to smooth their income over the course of the year. It is not clear whether richer farmers would therefore borrow more because the magnitude of their finances is greater or whether they would borrow less because they have greater internally generated resources. On the supply side, higher values of these variables probably make a farmer more credit-worthy. Greater access to capital may increase the amount he actually borrows.

II. LENDING

Since two-thirds of all loans came from other villagers or family members, it is not surprising that the RFM survey would uncover households involved in lending. In fact, one-third of all households did lend at least once during the year. Averaging across households, the mean loan size was 15,865 CFA. However, among only households that lent, the mean number of transactions was two, for a total of 33,111 CFA. One-quarter of the households that lent also borrowed at some point during the year.

A. Interest

None of the farm households that lent admitted receiving interest payments on their loans. Because of Moslem principles against charging interest, there is reason to suspect that farmers would be reluctant to disclose that they exacted such payments. Consequently, these results are probably somewhat inaccurate.

Merchants, on the other hand, in a separate series of interviews, did admit to charging interest. They claimed that the rate charged on any given loan is a function of how good a customer the borrower is and how much the merchant likes the client. Presumably these closer ties reduced the credit risk of lending. The interest rates, merchants claim, can range from 0 to 400 percent per annum, although loans carrying interest above 100 percent are usually very short term (so when the rate is annualized, it becomes quite high). These loans are very common but account for very little value in absolute terms.

More important are the cereals transactions which were found in the survey to range up to 40,000 CFA in value. Associated loans last, on average, four to five months and their interest costs rarely exceed 100 percent.

B. Repayment

It is commonly believed that default is not a problem in the informal system. It is true that it is significantly less problematic than for the formal credit programs described in Chapter 5. This phenomenon is usually explained by the fact that social pressure can be brought to bear on a delinquent borrower. It is said that vicious talk by the village women at the common well is to be avoided at all cost.

Default, however, does occur from time to time. In fact, social pressure can even work in the opposite direction. Farmers that lent cited instances where repayment, especially from family members, could not be forced. When asked what was done if a loan was not reimbursed, a common response was: 'drop it.' It is estimated that default occurs on at least 15 percent of total loans between family members and villagers. Merchants were even less sanguine about their own success in fully recouping loans. The repayment rate, they say, is about 80 percent, but can fall well below that in years of bad harvests. Most default comes on very small purchases.

In the case of default, little effort is made to pursue repayment actively although social pressure can be exercised. Few merchants admitted to exacting guarantees, though some of the literature on the subject suggests that this is not an uncommon procedure. According to *Evaluations de la Filière Arachide* (République Française, 1982), posting land as collateral, though now illegal, is a frequently practiced tradition. If the loan is not repaid, the fields become the 'property' of the lender. Historically, this practice has rendered some farmers landless while enabling some lenders to build up sizeable land holdings. It appears however, that repayment rates have been sufficiently high and/or these transactions sufficiently few that the basic land tenure system has not been affected.

Some claim that, with the exception of particularly severe drought years, land is no longer used as collateral. This phenomenon has been attributed to the availability of large quantities of farm equipment under the government credit programs. Through these programs, farmers have acquired a large variety of implements which they prefer to use as guarantees. This custom was particularly common during the years of the *Programme Agricole* (see Chapter 5 for a description of this program). A farmer, defaulting on a loan to a local merchant, could always contract a loan for more equipment from the government, knowing that this too was likely to go unpaid. (See Van Chi-Bonnardel, 1978; Diarasouba, 1968; République Française, 1982). It is probable that this practice has lapsed since the end of this program, though it is not clear what effect it has had. Perhaps collateral in the form of land is regaining popularity. Perhaps the amount of capital available for borrowing has been reduced. Or perhaps lenders have raised their interest rates to cover increased risk.

Merchants seem to feel fairly free in their ability to deny additional credit to farmers whose lack of repayment was not due to circumstances beyond their control. Indeed, many of the farmers surveyed who did not borrow claimed to have no sources of credit, even in emergencies. While it was considered polite not to request elaboration, it was generally indicated that lending can be selective and informal credit can be denied those who do not repay.

C. Gift-Giving

In this paper, the sections on credit have included only credit transactions in the European sense of the word. However, in Senegal, gift-giving may be an extremely important factor in describing the amount of resources a rural household has available at any given time. While the survey did not concern itself specifically with gifts, such transactions have been documented in some of the literature (see Vercambre, 1974; and Van Chi-Bonnardel, 1978).

The most important gifts in value terms are the *assakas* or portion of the crop given by *chefs de carré* (heads of communal household units) to religious leaders or nobles. *Chefs de carré* are supposed to give one-tenth of both their millet and their groundnut crops. A sample taken from the SODEVA agroeconomic data for the groundnut basin show that during the 1982/83 growing season, households gave away an average of 8.5 percent of their groundnut crop and 16.1 percent of their millet crop as *assakas*.

D. Cash savings

The results of the RFM survey undertaken for this study showed that for 93 percent of men in the rural sector, currency is their only form of liquid savings. Contrary to the popular expression 'under the mattress,' the Senegalese farmer usually keeps his money on his person at all times.

E. Deposits

Among men, 7.4 percent keep some part of their cash on deposit with merchants (no interest is earned) and 3.7 percent deposit cash with their parents. Another 3.7 percent have deposits in a bank (Fleuve region only), and 1.85 percent have deposits at a Post office (also in the Fleuve region only). (These percentages total to more than 100 percent because some farmers have more than one form of deposit.) Although remittances were not covered in this survey, it is known that the Fleuve is a region of heavy out-migration and also the recipient of substantial remittances flowing back from its absent workers (see Aprin, 1980). As a consequence, it is likely that households using the banks and post office for savings have much more cash at their disposal than the average Senegalese rural household.

F. Savings Clubs

Another common form of cash savings in LDCs is the rotating savings associations. In Senegal, these are called *tontines*. They are extremely prevalent in urban areas among both sexes. Often clubs are composed of members that work in the same office, but social relationships can also serve as a basis for such organizations. In cities, any number of people can join together to create a *tontine*. They agree upon a sum of money to be deposited on a regular basis (monthly, weekly, etc.). For salaried workers, the deposits are usually made to coincide with their monthly pay-checks and can often involve rather large sums.

All members place their names in a common pool and one is drawn at random. This person receives the deposits from each member for that period. Each time period, another name is drawn from those remaining to determine the next recipient until every member has had a turn. The result, in essence, is that the first one to take possession of the cash gets an interest free loan which is paid off in installments over the duration of the rotation. The last one to receive the money is, instead, making an interest free loan in installments for the same time period. Those in between earn or pay implicit interest depending on how soon their name is drawn. In major cities, especially in Dakar, there is an obvious alternative: everyone could deposit their money in a bank and earn interest. The expectation of earnings is identical. The probability of earning more than a savings account by participating in a *tontine* is exactly the same as the probability of earning less. However, if the individual is risk averse (meaning the gain in utility he would feel from earning the additional interest is less than the loss in utility he would experience if he got less interest) then he is worse off by participating in the *tontine*. Nonetheless, they are widespread. The most common explanation by members is that they value the forced savings aspect of the process. Without some kind of pressure to make deposits, they would not be able to save enough over the year to make a large-scale purchase.

The situation is somewhat different in the rural communities.

Tontines are still quite popular (34 percent of all households interviewed had members while 70 percent of all households in the groundnut basin did), although only women belong.

Two types of *tontines* were documented by the survey. The first is different in concept from the urban rotating savings club described above. Fifty five percent of the households had a member in this form of *tontine*. Its purpose is to generate funds for ceremonies such as weddings, baptisms and funerals. The amount of money required for such occasions is substantial relative to rural incomes and would have to be saved over long periods of time and held in reserve until needed. Instead, a large group of women (the average for the survey was 87 members) will form a *tontine* that collects funds on an as-needed basis. The average amount collected per member is 136 CFA, though in 91 percent of the cases, it was only 100 CFA. With this form of *tontine*, women can be assured access to large sums of cash when needed, without being subject to the risk of loss, theft or social pressure to spend their savings.

The second form of *tontine* is almost identical to its urban counterpart. However, deposits are made on a weekly basis, while those in the cities are generally monthly. Only women belong. These weekly *tontines* average 22 members. The mean deposit is 283 CFA although two-thirds only collect 100 CFA.

As in the cities, the funds rotate to each member selected in random order. Seventy eight percent of these weekly *tontines* were found in the survey to allow members to 'borrow' the money if it was not their turn. Forty three percent charge the borrower for this privilege. The average interest rate is flat 25 percent of the amount borrowed.

One woman is responsible for collecting the money each week, though the survey did not find any instances where she was paid for these efforts.

The use of the funds from these rotating savings clubs is allocated as follows:

ceremonies	70%
purchase of clothes	20%
purchase of general merchandise	10%

It does occur from time to time that a woman will fail to make her deposit. Survey responses indicated that if this happens before the woman has had her turn to receive the funds, the rest of the group will not collect money for her. If it happens after the woman has had her turn at taking the money, she will be 'sanctioned' by a general assembly of the women in the village and given a lengthy sermon for her wrong-doings. She is also barred from further participation in the *tontine* until she makes amends.

G. Small Durables

Purchases of small durables which can be sold as cash needs arise are a common form of savings in less developed countries. While this survey only investigated livestock, other commodities such as gold or jewelry also fall into this category. In the Senegalese rural economy, jewelry is valued immensely by women for its intrinsic value. It is bought primarily for the purpose of personal adornment as this is thought to reflect the economic status of the family. Such investments are not made explicitly as a means to store capital until liquidity needs arise. However, they can and do serve this concomitant function and clearly represent a store of wealth available for use in hard times.

H. Livestock

Livestock on the other hand, is the most common form of investment used to store wealth. Every single household surveyed had some capital invested in livestock. Periodic sales during the year are made explicitly for liquidity purposes. This means of saving is practiced primarily by men however. Marketing takes place at itinerant markets and, since women are generally responsible for all of the household chores, they are usually not able to invest the amount of time that commercial livestock transactions require.

As a form of savings, investment in livestock has both advantages and disadvantages. Some farmers do generate profits on their livestock activity. However, it is a risky form of investment and many farmers lose money. As SODEVA points out, the lack of understanding of animal husbandry techniques can result in losses farmers are not aware of. For example, farmers are often unable to calculate the optimal time to sell in order to maximize the profit on their investments. Sometimes they sell too early in order to meet pressing cash needs. Sometimes the farmer will keep an animal as a store of wealth for so long that a substantial loss is incurred once it is finally sold. This can occur in several ways. First, the value of the animal begins to decline after it reaches a certain age. Second, the farmer will generally run out of his own fodder during the rainy season and resort to purchases on the retail market, raising his livestock maintenance costs considerably. Finally, livestock mortality is high and while many farmers will earn respectable rates of return on the livestock they maintain, the overall margin can be quite low or negative due to these high mortality rates (SODEVA, 1981/82).

I. Cereals

Another means of saving is in the form of cereal grains. Farmers rarely sell such production. Instead, they stock it in graineries and withdraw it over the course of the year as the family's consumption needs arise. On occasion, a pressing need for cash will provoke a sale of cereals. In a study of grain transactions in the groundnut basin, Ross found that, on average, only 11 percent of millet production was sold (Ross, 1979). In the Fleuve and the Casamance, farmers produce little or no groundnuts and thus have a very limited cash income. However, they only sell cereals (in this case, rice) if their production is substantial. The data from the RFM survey showed that rice sales took place in only one-quarter of the households that produced it. Furthermore, these sales occurred only when more than three tons per household were harvested and no cash crop was produced.

J. Seed

Despite the fact that seed is available to farmers from national stocks, farmers save a great deal of their own. Traditionally, farmers have saved all of their seed. It has only been during the last 30 years or so when government programs have made seeds available virtually cost-free (especially after years of bad harvest) that farmers have reduced their saving in this form.

III. SUMMARY – INFORMAL MARKETS

A substantial amount of borrowing for consumption purposes takes place during the hungry season. Two-thirds of the households surveyed borrowed resources equivalent to 23,000 CFA. Resources (cash and in-kind) appear to be available on credit from merchants, other villagers and family members for an average of 4.4 months. Less than half of the loans documented by the survey carried interest charges. The average interest rate on all loans (including zeros) is 34.2 percent. One-third of all farmers surveyed lent resources. Almost all farmers give away, on average, 8 to 16 percent of their groundnut and millet crops, primarily to religious leaders. Land loans have been documented by other surveys primarily as a means to reduce disparities in land/labor allocations which have arisen due to restrictions on land transactions. Savings is either held in currency or in items such as livestock, small durables, cereals and seed. Few farmers hold liquid deposits although rotating savings associations are prevalent among the women.

Methodological Note: A survey on informal credit and savings was carried out during the spring of 1983 using as a reference period the year between harvest 1982 and harvest 1983. Fifty-four producer units were surveyed in eleven villages; two villages each in the Casamance, Diourbel, Fleuve and Louga regions and three villages in the Sine-Saloum. Additional information about the methodology can be obtained from the author.

CHAPTER THREE

Senegal's Cooperative Experience, 1907–1960

Robert L. Tignor

In 1960–61, as Senegal achieved its independence, the state embarked upon a bold and imaginative reform of the cooperative system. Local village coops were refashioned. Rural animators endeavored to inculcate new values in the peasantry and to establish a cooperative ethos. The central government founded a group of institutions to support the financial, technical, and marketing functions of the village bodies. The movement was championed by an energetic and high-ranking *UPS* politician, Mamadou Dia. The new coops, it was predicted, would inspire peasant enthusiasm, promote agricultural diversification and productivity, and retain the profits of Senegal's still lucrative export trade (Belloncle, 1978; Brochier, 1968; Camboulives, 1967; and Diarassouba, 1968).

Senegalese cooperatism, however, foundered in the following two decades, failing to live up to its high promise. Some of the reasons for failure were specific to the 1960s and 1970s. The incorporation of Francophone Africa into the European Common Market cost the Senegalese preferential groundnut export prices. A series of exceptionally severe droughts in the late 1960s and early 1970s produced poor harvests and immense human suffering. But many of the problems that afflicted the new coops were the same as those that had beset the old *Sociétés Indigènes de Prévoyance* (*SIPs*) and the voluntary organizations created briefly after World War II. Not unlike the *SIPs*, the new coops were notorious for autocracy, hierarchy, and fiscal instability. Just as the voluntary organizations of the 1950s were corrupt and dominated by local religious and political leaders and technical experts so too were the new coops.

A historical analysis of the cooperative movement, tracing its development from inception up to 1960, can provide insight into the problems that plagued not just these Senegalese bodies but cooperative groups throughout Africa. Historical reconstruction reveals how much the new leaders in Senegal owed to the French colonial experience, how much peasant attitudes toward coops had already been shaped by the earlier experience, and how intractable certain structural and financial problems proved to be. The analysis offered here does not imply a kind of historical determinism. It does suggest, however, that African cooperatives have revealed certain systemic problems and that these appeared from the outset in Senegal.

Risk and ways to contain it were central features of Senegalese agriculture well before the modern colonial era. In the subsistence economy the Senegalese farmer had to conserve enough food to last through the hungry season (the *soudure*) and enough seed for the next planting period. Risk and vulnerability became more pressing as Senegal was steadily integrated into the world economy. To the traditional worries of variable climate and periodic droughts were added the risks of fluctuating world demand and world prices for Senegalese exports. The traditional practices designed to protect against these risks (communal labor and hierarchical forms of labor allocation) no longer sufficed.

The groundnut trade with France originated in the middle of the nineteenth century. The first exports of groundnuts in the shell commenced in the 1840s. By the end of the nineteenth century groundnuts had assumed the first position in Senegal's exports. The first cultivating areas, located near the port cities of St. Louis and Rufisque, gave way, as the French extended their authority, to the region later known as the groundnut basin. Groundnut growing also followed the lines of railway construction first from Dakar to St. Louis and then into the interior, and also spread with the French armies of conquest into Sine-Saloum where Kaolack became the leading port.

By the end of the nineteenth century an important division had occurred in groundnut imports to France. Two main exporting centers (Senegal and Coromondel in British India) were linked to two major importing and manufacturing cities in France (Marseilles and Bordeaux). The bulk of Marseilles groundnuts, originating in India and decorticated there, were used for the manufacture of soap and livestock feed. Senegalese groundnuts, on the other hand, were shipped to Bordeaux, arrived in their shells, and, because they had few impurities, were used for salad and cooking oil (Giraud, 1937: 13 and 34). This difference was to prove significant when in the 1930s the French metropolitan government endeavored to assist Senegalese farmers and exporters by allowing their groundnuts to enter the French market duty free while charging a duty on non-colonial oleaginous imports.

Although at first groundnut cultivation may have been an unmitigated economic gain for the Senegalese farmer (since land was plentiful and food cultivation was not yet jeopardized), in time a rise in population, expanded consumer wants, and increased monetary demands challenged the peasant farmer with difficult agricultural choices. He had to decide how much of his land to plant in the main export crop (groundnuts) prior to knowing the price it would fetch. Decisions had to be made on what proportion of the land to reserve for foodstuffs (millet, beans, and so forth). Extensive debt obligations compelled cultivators to plant an increasing amount of the land in export crops, regardless of world prices.

In the French colonial system the major rural institution designed to cope with agricultural risk (and therefore to free colonial peasants to cultivate cash crops of interest to the metropole) was the *Société Indigène de Prévoyance* (*SIP*). This institution was first established in Indo-China and North Africa and then introduced into black Africa; it differentiated the French economic experience from the British. The British had more capital invested in their African colonies, and they were ideologically more disposed toward free markets and peasant initiative. The French, on the other hand, looked to the power of colonial administrators, and in the agricultural sphere they channeled this power through the *SIPs*. Even later in the economic history of British and French colonies, this difference remained significant. During the Second World War, for example, when the British were creating all-powerful marketing boards to regulate African economies, the French continued to rely on the *SIPs* to direct local economic activity. Not surprisingly, then, at independence, although all former colonial territories created independent cooperative structures, these movements tended to be more significant in territories like Senegal where the colonial experience had been profound.

The creation of *SIPs* in Senegal owed much to the reactions of French administrators to local conditions. But these local officials carried to Africa a set of metropolitan ideas and assumptions. Among these influences was an evolving French cooperative tradition, which French colonial officials endeavored to implant in African societies.

By the end of the nineteenth century cooperatives enjoyed an important niche within French society. Although they were indebted to the French socialist tradition – in particular the ideas of Proudhon, Fourier, Saint Simon, and Louis Blanc – their institutionalization was largely the result of left radicalism and social Catholicism. In the fragile Third Republic – challenged by the socialist left and the monarchist right – the prevailing ideology of the middle classes was radicalism. Left radicalism or solidarism as enunciated by its most energetic parliamentary leader, Léon Bourgeois, sought to merge support from middle classes, workers, and peasants through programs of state economic intervention. The left radicals extolled the cooperative as a shield against unregulated and exploitative capitalism (see Hayward, 1959, 1961, and 1963). On the right clerics and landed nobles sponsored peasant cooperatives. They were inspired by the organizing and corporatist ideals of social Catholicism (for these two cooperative traditions in France, one should consult Berger, 1972; and Wright, 1964). By the outbreak of the First World War these two traditions had created a significant cooperative movement in France.

In our present state of knowledge it is not possible to know which of the two traditions was more relevant for the creation of coops in Indo-China, Algeria, Tunisia, and Senegal. On the face of things, the solidarist influence was probably more significant since French colonial administrators tended to be drawn from the middle and lower middle classes and to be resolutely anti-clerical and anti-aristocratic (Cohen, 1971).

The history of the foundation and early development of the *SIPs* in Senegal reveals how metropolitan traditions mixed with local innovation. The first *SIPs* were established in 1907. They were founded in response to a series of local problems, but they aspired to deal with broad local concerns. Of course, by the time these coops were founded, Provident Societies had already become commonplace in other overseas French territories. In 1905 there were 173 such cooperatives in Algeria, with 462,682 members and a total participating capital of 13,921,317 francs, or $2,687,513 (Minister of Colonies to Governor General AOF, 1910). The first Senegalese *SIP* was established in Sine-Saloum where famine and a perceived rapacious mercantile class prompted the French commandant there (Le Filliatre) to create a local cooperative. A second body was established at Baol by Theveniault. Its primary purpose was to dig deep wells and thus expand the area in which groundnuts could be cultivated (AOF, 1909; Ly, 1958: 32ff; and Boyer, 1935: 44). Sine-Saloum and Baol, in fact, were the two most important areas in

Senegal's expanding groundnut cultivation zone, accounting for 50 percent of the groundnuts grown in the country at the outbreak of World War I (see Table 1).

Shortly thereafter other *SIPs* were created in groundnut-growing centers of Senegal (see Table 2). But after this flurry of activity further expansion ceased. Provident Societies in Senegal remained confined to the groundnut region until the 1930s.

TABLE 1

Groundnut Production, 1885–1930 (1000 metric tons)

Years (5 year average)	Total Production	Total from Baol and Sine-Saloum	%
1885/86–1889/90	31		
1902/03–1906/07	125		
1910/11–1914/15	232	115	50
1925/26–1929/30	458	244	53

Source: Vanhaeverbeke, 1970: 16.

TABLE 2

Foundation of *Sociétés Indigènes de Prévoyance* in Senegal

Baol	1907	Thiès	1911
Sine-Saloum	1907	Makel	1911
Cayor	1910	Matam	1911
Louga	1911	Dagana	1912
Kedougou	1911	Tambacounda	1912
Podor	1911		

Source: Boyer, 1935: 85.

Although the first Provident Societies were inspired by the French cooperative tradition, they also owed much to pressures from Senegalese farmers. The Sine-Saloum *SIP* founded by Le Filliatre appeared in response to farmer agitation against mercantile demands and the peasants' constant need for seed stock. By placing 279 tons of seed in collective granaries the French administration assumed its first responsibility for distributing seed to cultivators (Giraud, 1937:51).

In the first period of development (1905–1929), *SIPs* assumed long-lasting traits. To begin with, French administrators displayed boundless faith in what these organizations could accomplish.

Their founders wrote glowingly about protecting cultivators from exploitation, inculcating a new ethos of industry in the countryside, and transforming standards of life. In their minds the coop became the symbol of a new rural order, and no matter how obdurate rural reality proved to be local officials clung to their beliefs. In subsequent *SIP* history the disjuncture between the ideals and the realities of coop performance remained striking.

The title of these bodies (*Sociétés Indigènes de Prévoyance*) revealed a dominant French worry – the peasantry's reputed lack of foresight. Although the first organizations arose out of specific economic problems, their pre-World War I founders described ambitious long-range goals. In Sine-Saloum the *commandant* envisioned a body offering assistance to needy families during bad years and distributing grain during the *soudure*. At Baol the *commandant du cercle*, while seeking to minimize government bureaucracy and affirming faith in the peasant as an efficient and rational cultivator, wanted coops to play a central role in seed provision, in organizing the distribution of foodstuffs during the *soudure*, in carrying out development projects beyond the capacities of individual families (such as digging deep wells and making modern agricultural equipment available), and in promoting agricultural education in the villages.

The early administrative experiments revealed another persistent trait: a powerful anti-mercantile bias. The originators of the *SIPs* in Senegal, like colonial administrators elsewhere, portrayed the African peasants at the mercy of rapacious moneylenders and wanted to shield peasants from merchants. By providing cultivators with critical resources (seed, foodstuffs, and agricultural equipment), the coops could break the ties of indebtedness which bound peasants to merchants. Dreyfus, *commandant* at Thiès, expressed this sentiment well: 'The black shall cease to be unhappy the day he is no longer at the mercy of the merchants for procuring the seeds necessary for sowing' (Dreyfus to Lieutenant-Governor of Senegal, 1911).

It is clear, then, that Provident Societies were not set up originally to work in harness with commercial agents. Although administrators believed in the value of cash crop cultivation and were confident that African peasants would benefit, under the right circumstances, from being more closely integrated into the world economy, they were anxious for peasants to draw the maximum profit from overseas trade and to be independent of local merchants.

Most of the far-reaching suggestions put forward by local administrators were spurned by the colony's central administration. When confronted with these proposals, the Chief Economic Officer, based in Dakar, opposed them on the grounds that they would transform the Societies into 'charitable' organizations, causing them to lose sight of what the central administration believed to be their primary goal, that of instilling an ethos of work among African peasants who were by nature 'nonchalant and lazy,' prepared always to accept gifts and little worried about the future (see Office des Affaires Economiques to Lieutenant-Governor of Senegal, 1907).

Nonetheless, Provident Societies quickly lost the voluntarist and democratic impulses intended by their founders. The President of the *SIP*, originally an elected official, became by a 1915 decree the *Commandant de cercle*. All persons living in a circle were compelled to become members and to pay annual dues (*cotisation*). Provident Societies were dominated by their officers: president, vice-president, local African chiefs, and later, from the 1930s, secretary-treasurer, all of whom were administrative appointees. Increasingly these organs were viewed by the population not as bodies that sprang from their own needs and wishes, but as an arm of the state. The *cotisation* became a colonial tax. The General Assembly, which had delegates chosen from the villages, met only twice a year, mainly to oversee the budget (see Robinson, 1950; and the revealing debate in Conseil de la République, 1947).

The size of the Provident Societies precluded genuine grass-roots involvement and magnified the powers of the administration. *SIP* jurisdiction extended to an entire circle and meant that the total membership in a populous groundnut-growing area could be over 200,000 or 300,000 persons. That the administration regarded *SIPs* as just another administrative body was evidenced by the regularity with which *SIP* powers were delegated to *chefs de canton* and *chefs de village*. The tasks of distributing and collecting seeds and collecting the *cotisation* were discharged by African chiefs and were not carefully differentiated from tax collecting and labor recruitment. Not surprisingly, *SIPs* were subject to the same abuse of power and even outright corruption which characterized local French administration during the twentieth century.

It is no doubt misleading to refer to *SIPs* as cooperatives. I do so, however, because they owed their existence and rapid development in Senegal (and other French territories) to the French cooperative tradition. Additionally, Provident Societies remained a fecund example for French colonial nationalists as they endeavored to create truly popular cooperatives after World War II.

While it is true that *SIPs* were created in all of the main groundnut cultivating regions of Senegal, they made but a limited contribution to the expansion of the crop in the period before the depression. In certain areas energetic administrators worked in close consultation with *Murid* leaders and used the *SIP* to facilitate the migration of peasant cultivators to new lands. As a tax, albeit not a large one, the *cotisation* compelled African families to devote some portion of their fields to cash crops. Finally, the provision of seed for the next growing season was an important prop in the groundnut economy. Even so, as Table 3 demonstrates, the *SIPs'* importance was for a long time not substantial. As late as 1930 they distributed only 40 percent of seed stock, the rest being provided by far-sighted farmers themselves and local merchants (Fouquet, 1958:88).

TABLE 3

SIP Provision of Groundnut Seed Stock, 1909–1930

Year	Quantity Provided (tons)	Proportion of seed stock (%)	Year	Quantity Provided (tons)	Proportion of seed stock (%)
1909	279	1.1	1925	5636	11.3
1920	1940	6.5	1926	6747	16.9
1921	2362	7.9	1927	8480	20.5
1922	4260	14.2	1928	10549	26.0
1923	4601	15.3	1929	13203	25.9
1924	5085	11.3	1930	18830	41.2

Source: Giraud, 1937: 56.

In reality, the peasant farmers themselves and merchants, small and large, were the prime movers in the spectacular expansion of groundnut production. In particular, the *Murid* brotherhoods, using a work ethic and strong religious and charismatic devotion to *marabout* leaders, organized pioneer colonies that expanded into the interior into the so-called *terres neuves*. The leaders founded special work villages (*daara*) and mobilized dedicated and hard-working followers (*taalibe*) to bring unutilized or little utilized lands under cultivation (see Pélissier, 1966; Copans, 1980; and O'Brien, 1975).

In some of the administrative reports one has the distinct impression that the commercial impact was, if anything, negative.

Especially in describing the small-scale local merchants, adminis-trators tended to offer up the classical portrait of the parasitical moneylender. While administators extolled the economic contri-butions of the large export–import houses (and naturally, albeit wrongly, expected these firms to join with the administration in undercutting small merchants), they depicted the village money-lender and merchant, often a Syrian or a Lebanese, as creating a web of indebtedness with cultivators. Local merchants, it was said, squeezed surplus profits out of helpless peasants, thus inhibiting the peasant drive to increase production and to be rational cultivators.

There is some value in considering these charges, for they have remained a standard argument of administrators through-out Senegal's twentieth century economic history, whether the administrators were French or Senegalese. Senegalese nationalists, in fact, broadened their attack to include the entire foreign commercial community – the export–import firms as well – and endeavored to supplant them with parastatal organizations. To what extent then did the private sector inhibit agricultural expan-sion and increase the vulnerability and risks of Senegalese peasants?

Although, given the rudimentary state of our present information and the dearth of local studies, these questions cannot be answered in a definitive way, some insights can be gleaned from general works and hints to be found in archival sources.

French commercial relations with Senegal stretched far back in time. The groundnut trade originated in the nineteenth century through the work of small commercial firms, having their seat of business in Bordeaux. By the 1920s and increasingly in the 1930s, these trading arrangements changed and assumed a form very similar to those prevailing in other export-oriented economies in West Africa, notably the Gold Coast and Nigeria (Charbonneau, 1961; and Bauer, 1954). At the apex of the commercial system was a small number of large, relatively heavily capitalized export–import firms that had taken over the dominant role in the trading economy from the old Bordeaux firms. Two of the biggest houses were French (la Compagnie Française de l'Afrique Occidentale and la Société Commerciale de l'Ouest Africain) while the third firm, the Compagnie du Niger (known in Senegal as la Nouvelle Société Commerciale Africaine) was a branch of Unilever, a multinational giant.

The new firms introduced new economic principles into West Africa, thus differentiating themselves from their smaller, less capitalized predecessors. In particular, they accelerated the substitution of monetary transactions for barter. They also curbed the local merchants' penchant to charge exorbitant interest rates in the interior arguing that heavy indebtedness was injurious to trade. They paid relatively high prices for cash crops as an incentive to expand cultivation and to increase the amount of money African farmers could expend on European-manufactured commodities which their firms supplied (see 'Les Grandes Sociétés' in Charbonneau, 1961; and an opposing view in Suret-Canale, 1971). In these very tangible ways (but only in comparison with their predecessors) they fostered the expansion of groundnut cultivation. By returning more of the profits of the groundnut trade to African cultivators than had the earlier firms, they drew the peasantry into the market and money economy.

Beneath the great export–import houses, with their offices in the ports, major buying centers, and railway points in West Africa, came the traders. Customarily they had at their disposal the financial resources to purchase upwards of twenty tons of groundnuts. They usually purchased groundnuts from smaller merchants who were themselves in contact with the growers. The traders bagged groundnuts and sent them off to depots. Syrians and Lebanese predominated among the smaller merchants (Batude, 1941: 53ff). As Table 4 indicates, in the 1920s and 1930s, Syrian and Lebanese merchants began to move into the interior of Senegal, spreading the monetized, Western-oriented economy.

TABLE 4

Lebanese and Syrians in Senegal, 1897–1936

	Dakar	Senegal
1897	–	10
1904	–	101
1909	173	211
1923	578	651
1930	1388	1599
1936	1269	2560

Source: Desbordes, 1938: 17–20.

The host of merchants operating in the groundnut regions of Senegal did the same things as those merchants described in the classic accounts of the Gold Coast and Nigeria. By providing money loans they helped to tide the farmer over during the non-cultivating season. They collected seeds and stored them for sale for the next planting season. If new agricultural equipment was required, the merchants were more likely to be the distributing agents than the state. They sold foodstuffs to the farmers during the hungry season and supplied them with European manufactures and rice.

If the Gold Coast and Nigerian materials can be used as guides, local merchants endeavored to bind cultivators to them and to those firms for whom they worked. When merchant competition was keen and the prices for primary products were high, as was the case during the 1920s, loans were granted freely at relatively low rates. Profound problems occurred in farmer–merchant relations, however, when world prices turned down, as they did in the late 1920s and 1930s, and when under these pressures, the great export–import houses conspired to fix prices paid to local cultivators. If the prices offered to the cultivator dropped, often precipitously, while the debt payments remained high, suffering could be acute. In the Gold Coast, cocoa farmers, in alliance with similarly devastated small moneylenders, organized a boycott, but in Senegal no such concerted action took place (see House of Commons, 1937–38). Discontent existed, but an effort to organize cultivators did not materialize, perhaps because of the increasing activities of the *SIPs* during the depression.

One of the salient features of French colonial activity in black Africa – especially in contrast with the British – and perhaps one of the reasons that the Provident Societies were expected to play such a decisive role in the economic life of Senegal (while having no real functional equivalent in British Africa) was the small amount of private French investment in tropical Africa. Although the amount of private French capital in French West Africa rose some threefold in nominal terms between 1910 and 1920, French investment remained weak (Sow, 1976–77: 23). In 1938, for example, the French West African territories had attracted the smallest amount of capital invested in Africa (£30,426,000) as well as the smallest proportion of investment per person (£2.1 compared to £3.9 in Nigeria, £6.8 in Kenya and Uganda, £13.0 in the Belgian Congo, and £9.8 in Angola and Mozambique). The capital invested in French colonies in black Africa represented only 5.76 percent of the total invested in all of Africa (excluding Egypt and North Africa). The British territories, in contrast, enjoyed 77 percent of the total (Frankel, 1938: 160–170). Economic programs in Francophone Africa thus required a strong push from the public sector.

I. PROVIDENT SOCIETIES AND THE DEPRESSION

The rather limited agenda of the *SIPs* changed radically with the onset of the depression. During the decade of the 1930s the *Sociétés* assumed more varied responsibilities. While many of their new functions helped to solve agricultural and peasant problems, their work also created a new cluster of longlived difficulties.

The decline in the price of groundnuts was sharp; nor did the first response of groundnut cultivators – to increase the amount of land devoted to groundnuts and the tonnage exported – stem Senegal's declining return from the trade. The value of groundnut exports fell steadily from its high point in 1926 (when groundnut exports were worth 752,643,000 francs [$28,305,490]). In 1931 the value of Senegal's groundnut exports was only 306,731,000 francs ($11,962,988) despite the fact that the tonnage exported had been exceeded only in 1930 and the record year of 1926 (see Table 5). This reduction in the cultivation and marketing of groundnuts challenged the vital economic interests of many groups. Beyond the cultivating community itself, the most immediately affected were the export–import firms, the groundnut-crushing factories based in France, and the smaller merchants. Equally concerned – though from a different perspective – was the French colonial administration of AOF (Afrique Occidentale Française) which drew half of its revenues from custom duties. The export duty return on groundnuts fell by 80 percent between 1930 and 1932; other key revenue items of Senegal and AOF declined (see Table 6). Moreover, many of the other revenue items in the Senegalese budget (such as *cotisations*, head tax, and so forth) derived from the sale of the cash crop. The government's equally strong desire to revive the colonial economy caused the administration to convoke a summit conference of leading administrators and businessmen in June, 1932, following the disastrous harvest of that year (Fouquet, 1958: 87–91).

As the price for groundnuts plummeted, Senegalese farmers responded by planting foodstuffs rather than groundnuts. Between 1930 and 1931 they increased millet cultivation by 150,000 hectares and again by a smaller area in 1932. Unfortunately, the millet harvest was relatively small because of adverse weather conditions. Administrators noted a remarkable extension in manioc growing and commented on the greater attention being devoted to food-stuffs (AOF, 1931: 191). The administration had good reason to fear the diminution of groundnuts in favor of subsistence agriculture,

TABLE 5

Value and Quantity of Groundnut Exports from Senegal, 1926–1936

	Quantities (tons)	Value (francs)		Quantities (tons)	Value (francs)
1926	494,416	752,643,000	1931	453,811	306,731,000
1927	405,608	616,623,000	1932	191,469	162,340,000
1928	413,356	593,310,000	1933	388,010	188,276,000
1929	406,760	554,936,000	1934	494,264	234,090,000
1930	508,195	501,841,000	1935	392,308	347,334,000
			1936	487,340	351,675,000

Source: Giraud, 1937: 37

TABLE 6

Impact of the Depression on Senegal and AOF Revenues
Francs 000,000

	Groundnut Export Tax Revenues*	Export Tax Revenues from all AOF Commodities*	Total AOF Budget**	Total Budget of Senegal**	Customs Duties, Senegal**	Customs Duties, AOF
1928					103.2	218.9
1929					108.6	214.2
1930	21.7	35.6			110.5	210.6
1931	10.1	20.6	290.2	157.3	58.0	123.7
1932	4.3	13.2	185.5	121.6	62.7	120.8
1933	7.9	14.8	179.7	99.1	82.8	

Sources: *Sow, 1976–77: 48   **AOF, 1928–1933

particularly in light of the disastrous harvest of 1932 (191,469 tons exported worth only 162,340,000 francs).

The French administration decided on economic intervention; a comprehensive program, involving both Senegalese supports and metropolitan assistance, was put forward. The main architect of the new economic arrangements was Governor-General Jules Brevie (1930–1936), though he was ably aided by the Senegalese delegate to the French parliament, Blaise Diagne, and the French Minister of Colonies, Albert Sarraut. Brevie's chief goal was to ensure that reasonable profits from groundnuts could be made by Senegalese cultivators. In his mind this would only become feasible when the price per kilo reached 90 francs in France and between 67 and 70 francs in Kaolack (Giraud, 1937: 177ff). To this end he suppressed the Senegalese export tax on groundnuts (until 1937) and lowered railway rates (Brevie to Minister of Colonies, 1935). In France where the major thrust of his program took place, the Minister of Colonies, Sarraut, succeeded, despite acrimonious debate in the French Chamber of Deputies and Senate, in enacting a tariff reform on oleaginous fruits and grains entering France. The law of August, 1933 established a duty of approximately 10 percent on all oleaginous imports originating in foreign countries, while permitting Senegal's groundnut imports to enter the country duty-free. The tariff program evoked strong protest from Marseilles soap and oil industrialists who depended on groundnut imports from India. They were joined in protest by textile manufacturers, especially woolen industrialists, who used imported oils to wash their woolens, and by livestock owners who fed groundnut cakes made in Marseilles and industrial cities in the north of France to their livestock (France, Chambre des Députés, 1933: 3522–561).

In Senegal the chief obstacle to reviving the groundnut trade was the lack of available seed. Following the harvest of 1930 the state acquired 18,650 tons of groundnuts itself and estimated that individual farmers themselves had another 7500 tons. It still anticipated a short-fall of about 20,000 tons if Senegal was to achieve its export target of 450,000 tons. As the farmers had no money to purchase seed from local merchants, Governor-General Brevie called upon the state to purchase and distribute seed to cultivators. State-purchased grains were distributed to the farmers through the Provident Societies. Fifteen thousand tons alone were purchased and distributed by the most powerful of the *Sociétés* – that in Sine-Saloum (Fouquet, 1958: 87–91). The debt was owed to the French West African federation and was to be retired by charging cultivators a 25 percent interest rate in kind on the loaned seed. The interest was payable in seed to the Provident Societies at the conclusion of the harvest season. From this moment onwards, *SIPs*, taking the place of merchants, assumed full responsibility for the provision of planting seed.

The financial transactions associated with the purchase of seed from local merchants proved to be onerous financially. They saddled the Senegalese Provident Societies with a large debt. At the time that the state drew up its plans for seed purchase, the price of a kilo was hovering between 45 and 50 francs. By the time the state entered the market, however, groundnuts were selling from 100 to 150 francs. The purchase of seed cost the state 29 million francs (over $1 million) rather than the 10 million originally budgetted and forced the Provident Societies into taking out a 50-year loan for repayment (Boyer, 1935: 129).

Another aspect of the state effort to revive and improve groundnut cultivation was the increased role given to the experimental agricultural station at Bambey. Though it had been founded in 1913, it did not assume prominence in Senegalese agriculture until the 1930s. The government turned to Bambey to realize its goal of distributing specially-selected and high-yielding seed stock to the *SIPs* in the primary groundnut producing districts of Sine-Saloum, Baol, and Thiès. Although Bambey began in a small way, distributing only 27 tons of its seed to farmers working in the Sine-Saloum region in 1934, it had reached many of its goals by the outbreak of World War II (Société Indigène de Prévoyance, 1933).

The provision of seed for planting had always been the main responsibility of the Provident Societies. But colonial officials deduced from peasant reactions to the impact of the depression that other, more substantial incentives were required to stem peasant withdrawal from groundnut cultivation. *SIPs* began to be more determined in encouraging the expansion of Serer and Wolof populations into the *terres neuves* of the eastern part of the colony (Société Indigène de Prévoyance, 1933). The alliance between the administration and *Murid* brotherhoods was hardened in the 1930s. The former dug wells in districts south and east of the main Wolof population concentrations in preparation for the movement of pioneer colonies.

French colonial administrators also realized that uncertainty about foodstuff provisioning was a cause for peasant retreat into subsistence. The government looked to the *SIPs* to take a more active part in storing and distributing food during the hungry season. It also encouraged the import of rice from Indochina. To be sure, *SIP* activity in food distribution was still on a small scale, but it reflected an understanding of this deep-seated peasant dilemma and was a harbinger of future administrative actions. The Provident Society at Sine-Saloum, as befitted its size and general importance, led the way by collecting maize and millet reserves (*Rapport de Présentation à la Commission Centrale,* 1937–38). By the beginning of 1937 Senegalese *SIPs* had stored substantial amounts of food (Table 7) for distribution during the hungry season. The administration hoped that a reassured peasantry would increase its cultivation of groundnuts.

The bias among government officials and *SIP* leaders against the merchant community, especially small moneylenders, deepened in the 1930s. In the view of many administrators, rural merchants braked the expansion of groundnut cultivation. The state supported a series of administrative measures, designed to increase mercantile competition in the countryside. In the administration's view pre-World War I trading arrangements served farmers better than the

TABLE 7

Senegalese *SIP* Storage of Foodstuffs and Groundnuts, 1937
(metric tons)

Groundnuts	*Millet*	*Rice*	*Maize*	*Niebes*
53,775	236	68	12	2

Source: Cavaille, 1937.

innovations introduced in the 1920s. Before 1914 farmers had brought groundnuts to a few major trading posts (*escales*) where, in the opinion of the administration, merchant competition had bid up the selling price. Since then, though, merchants had gone out into the bush in search of clients and sales and succeeded in capturing an increased proportion of the trade profits. In an effort to restore the old trading conditions the state shrank the buying period by legislating the dates for its opening and closing, hoping thereby to intensify mercantile competition and the selling price. For the same reason the state reduced the number of authorized buying centers (Fouquet, 1958: 87–91; Sow, 1976–77: 70ff; and Cavaille, 1937).

As a second part of its marketing reform, Provident Societies themselves began to enter the marketing arena, encouraging cultivators through chiefs and religious leaders to sell groundnuts directly to them. By a decree passed on November 9, 1933 the *SIPs* were allowed to organize the sale of the products of their adherents. That this action was likely to threaten the interests of the Syrio-Lebanese community did not worry Brevie who submitted a terse view of the situation: 'The colony has nothing to lose from the diminution of the Syrian element' (Brevie to Minister of Colonies, 1935). The *SIPs* sold directly to the export–import houses. The marketing function began in an exceedingly small way, with only 600 tons being collected in 1933–34 out of a total harvest of 613,000 tons. Even as late as 1938–39 the *SIPs* were marketing only 20,000 tons out of 677,000 (see Table 8).

The difficulties were transparent. The administration did not have enough staff to move far into the countryside. The administrative buying centers generally had an effective radius of not more than 2 or 3 kilometers (Cercle de Kaolack, 1934). Also administrators were quick to admit that they were novices as purchasing agents, not able to understand the mentality of the African peasant as well as local merchants (Société Indigène de Prévoyance, 1933). Perhaps, in fact, the largest deterrent to the *SIPs* was the tie of

TABLE 8

SIPs as Marketing Depots for Groundnuts, 1933/34–1938/39
(metric tons)

1933–34	600	1936–37	19,054
1934–35	1683	1937–38	19,088
1935–36	7635	1938–39	20,101

Source: Annual reports of Senegalese *SIPs* in Senegalese National Archives.

indebtedness which bound peasant to local merchant. Another difficulty was the *ristourne* or rebate system introduced by the state. *SIPs* offered to pay the farmer three-quarters of the purchase price when taking the crop on the understanding that the remainder of the price (the *ristourne*) would be paid after the crop had been sold and administrative and transportation expenses paid. The peasants were suspicious of this arrangement, fearing, quite rightly, that they might never receive the *ristourne* (Sow, 1976–77: 70ff).

Given these problems, it was hardly surprising that the *SIPs* were unsuccessful marketing agents. What is remarkable, however, was the strong reaction that rose within the commercial community. While administrators anticipated opposition from smaller merchants, whose sphere of operations they were challenging, they were astonished at the antagonism of larger merchants, even the great export–import houses. In fact their surprise revealed how little they understood Senegalese commerce. Export–import firms feared administrative intrusion as the leading edge of the wedge. They also favored indebtedness arrangements as a way to bind individual cultivators to their firms and to make the conduct of the trade relatively predictable. All of the business groups banded together under the aegis of the Senegalese Chambers of Commerce and organized a *Syndicat Corporatif Economique du Sénégal* to register their discontent.

Commercial groups used a variety of techniques to thwart the administration. Employing their hold over local notables, they spread rumors that farmers would be unlikely to receive their *ristournes*. Local buyers also used their ties with donkey drivers to deny peasants transport to *SIP* buying centers. By paying commissions, they rewarded drivers for delivering the crops to them rather than to the administration. At the same time they lodged vehement complaints at the Governor General's Office that the administration had unfair advantages in local buying since it was able to use ordinary tax revenues to create a staff in competition with merchants. In parts of Sine-Saloum there were open clashes between administrators and merchants. Much to the dismay of the administration these confrontations – which usually involved the pilfering of the state's weighing equipment – entailed incidents between French colonial agents and European merchants (Beurnier, 1935).

Although the Provident Societies gained only a toehold in marketing (and their agents admitted that the only groups who sold to them on a consistent basis were individuals beholden to the administration), the 1930s witnessed a large expansion, especially following the severe decline in groundnut exports in 1931 and 1932. Increased activities at the local level required larger economic and financial structures at the center. The new financial bodies established at Dakar in the 1930s served as embryos for the much more elaborate national institutions created in the 1950s and early 1960s. The first body to be created was the Crédit Agricole Mutuel, established in June 1931. Modelled after the Crédit Agricole de France, it operated as an agricultural bank. It received funds from different sources, especially, however, loans from the central government. It then lent out these monies to individuals and organizations like the *SIPs*. Between 1932 and 1940 it contracted 6,337,000F in loans from the central government. The Crédit Agricole worked in harness with leading *Murid* cultivators and hence supported the advance of Wolof groundnut cultivators into new lands (Caisse Centrale de Crédit Agricole Mutuel, 1941).

Far more important, however, was the organ called the *Fonds Commun des Sociétés de Prévoyance*, established by decree in October, 1936. The Fonds served as an intermediary for the loans contracted by the individual Provident Societies and helped these bodies to purchase agricultural materials (especially sacks and scales) and agricultural equipment for distribution to individual farmers (Fonds Commun des Sociétés de Prévoyance, 1937–38).

The increased activities of Provident Societies placed greater financial burdens upon them and brought them face-to-face with financial insolvency. Their purchase of 20,000 tons of seed in 1932 had encumbered them with what one administrator described as 'a heavy charge of indebtedness' right from the outset (Cavaille, 1937). Increased responsibilities required larger staffs, but the *SIPs* were unable to expand their revenue sources to keep up with the growth in staff. In the groundnut basin, where the *SIPs* had already achieved nearly 100 percent membership, and where the *cotisation* could not be increased without causing acute distress, the Provident Societies began to slip into serious debt. Moreover, one of the main revenue-earning items other than the *cotisation* – the seed lent at a 25 percent interest rate – was beginning to fall into arrears by the outbreak of the Second World War (*Rapport de Présentation à la Commission Centrale*, 1937–38).

The administration hoped that the increased powers accorded to the *SIPs* would enable them to serve the small farmer better. No doubt the provision of seed and the enlarged role of the Provident Societies as purchasers of grain and sellers of agricultural machinery helped the farmer. But the *SIPs'* already pronounced traits of autocracy, oppression, and corruption were also strengthened. Peasant resentment against them and their illegal use of power was solidified. The chiefs' abuses of powers, including those they exercised as agents of Provident Societies, became so pronounced in the 1930s that the French administration delegated one of its inspectors to report on their activities. De la Rocca, French inspector of administrative affairs, found *chefs de canton* and *chefs de village* in Baol and Sine-Saloum circles living 'a sumptious life,' largely based on the exploitation of the local population, who were too intimidated to raise a complaining voice. In Sine-Saloum he found chiefs commonly using a small bushel when distributing grain to the peasants and a large bushel when collecting repayments. Also, de la Rocca found that unless granaries of the Provident Societies (*seccos*) were put under lock and key, held by the French administrators themselves, the chiefs stole from them for their personal enrichment.

In comparing chiefs in Baol with those in Sine-Saloum, de la Rocca wrote:

They are neither worse nor better than those in Sine-Saloum. As is the case there the complaints against them abound. Their cupidity is as great and their appetites as voracious. They endeavor to establish their authority for the purpose of increasing their privileges. Toward this secret end nothing is neglected. All profitable occasions are seized and all sacrifices are made. One must add that in Baol also the *chefs de canton* try to assure powerful alliances. (De la Rocca, 1934)

Under Brevie, in an effort to make the *SIPs* more efficient and less corrupt, the government introduced new bureaucratic procedures. Unfortunately, their well-intentioned reforms had the opposite effect. The administration believed that *SIPs* were inefficient and corrupt because African chiefs exercised wide and unchecked powers. The state sought to replace them with educated officers, recruited by means of an examination system. These bureaucrats, who would fill the newly created positions of secretary, would bring more order and stamp out corruption. In reality, the new secretaries who began to replace chiefs as local agents of the *SIPs* in the 1930s were as corrupt and oppressive as their predecessors. They had the added disadvantage of not being locally based and lacked traditional legitimation. As a consequence, *SIPs* became even more distant, alien, and colonial institutions.

World War II

The Second World War strained the resources of the *SIPs* even more than the depression; financial problems became more pronounced. In the early war years, with French West Africa cut off from the rest of the world, the primary concern of the administration took the form of provisioning the local population. Cultivators retreated once again into the cultivation of foodstuffs, in which Senegal was no longer self-sufficient, since even before the war it had come to rely heavily on the import of Indo-Chinese rice (Founou-Tchuigoua, 1981; and Chambre de Commerce de Dakar, 1944). With the marked decrease in groundnut cultivation and export, the *SIPs* assumed increased responsibilities for collecting and distributing foodstuffs to local cultivators. The state imported rice, maize, and millet from the French Sudan, Dahomey, and Guinea and entrusted the *SIPs* with their distribution to needy areas. In the first years of the war, the *SIPs* purchased about three times as much food as they had before the outbreak of hostilities, and by 1943–44 they were distributing about half of the foodstuffs required during the hungry season (*Rapport sur l'Activité des Sociétés de Prévoyance*, 1940; and *Rapport Moral et Financier*, 1943–44).

The administrative emphasis on food self-sufficiency gave way in the latter stages of the war once again to the export of groundnuts. Renewed pressure for groundnut cultivation was apparent in the state's goal for the 1943–44 season for an export of 400,000 tons (Boisson to Governor at Conakry, 1943). The government also demanded that local communities maintain a high level of foodstuff cultivation since imports still remained in short supply and large numbers of immigrant rural workers (*navetanes*) had to be fed on Senegalese resources (Geismar to Governor General, 1943).

Increasingly, the financial capabilities of the *SIPs* were insufficient for the heavy demands made upon them. Before the outbreak of the war, when the activities of the *SIPs* were still restricted, receipts exceeded expenses, and *SIPs* made some headway in repaying the large loan contracted in 1932. But by the middle years, a rapid expansion of the *SIPs* put their budgets far in arrears (see Tables 9, 10, and 11). Deficits had occurred because of large increases in administrative expenses – which in 1938–39 had constituted 34 percent of receipts but had risen by 1942–43 to 107 per cent of receipts. Also the *SIPs* experienced a sharp reduction in the revenue realized from the sale of excess grains. Farmers failed to repay the Provident Societies at the rate required for the seed furnished to them (25 percent) and were also in arrears in repayment of foodstuffs (see Tables 12 and 13).

TABLE 9

SIP Activities during World War II

Year	Adherents of SIPs	Total Groundnut Production Marketed from Senegal	Groundnut Seeds Distributed by SIPs	Foodstuffs Distributed by SIPs (metric tons)	Groundnuts Marketed by SIPs
1939–40	1,140,734	560,078	48,460	7,566	34,403
1940–41	1,115,006	419,218	50,640	7,364	41,734
1941–42	1,140,661	199,412	48,162	9,069	37,243
1942–43	1,124,715	114,122	55,663	59,555	–
1943–44	1,085,453	274,482	56,402	52,411	–
1944–45	1,108,602	234,202	62,184	35,709	–
1945–46	1,072,203	354,404	55,736	32,610	–

Source: Annual reports of *SIPs* in Senegalese National Archives

By the end of the Second World War, the *Sociétés* had revealed themselves to be financially unstable. But because they were now fully connected with larger nation-wide structures through the *Fonds Commun* and the *Crédit Agricole Mutuelle*, their deficits were less important because they could be made up at higher levels.[1]

Financial pressures were not the only factors drawing the *SIPs* into closer alignment with the central administration. The French colonial government, like the British administration in West Africa, wanted to regulate local economies so that the populations could

TABLE 10

Receipts and Expenses of *SIPs* in Senegal, 1938/39–1942/43

Receipts – Francs

	1938–39	% of Total	1939–40	%	1940–41	%	1941–42	%	1942–43	%
Cotisation	3,707,333	19	3,749,684	18	4,249,027	23	4,619,663	33	9,468,307	49
Sale of Groundnuts	14,950,459	78	12,811,021	62	12,036,959	66	8,121,596	58	8,160,613	43
Total	19,198,186	100	20,769,125	100	18,249,863	100	14,087,589	100	19,138,050	100

Expenses – Francs

	1938–39	%	1939–40	%	1940–41	%	1941–42	%	1942–43	%
Administrative Expenses	6,467,535	38	8,755,997	40	9,230,194	54	11,026,322	50	18,955,101	42
Total	17,025,299	100	22,153,375	100	17,177,707	100	22,186,068	100	45,409,634	100
Balance	+2,172,887		−1,384,250		−1,072,156		−8,098,479		−26,271,584	
Administrative Expenses as % of Receipts	34		53		56		86		107	

Compiled from annual reports of *SIPs* found in Senegalese National Archives.

TABLE 11

SIP Indebtedness at the End of Fiscal Year 1942–43

Kaolack	10,000,000F
Kolda	1,300,000
Thiès	6,000,000
Ziguinchor	1,800,000
Louga	3,000,000

Source: Annual Reports of *SIPs* in Senegalese National Archives.

TABLE 12

SIP Seed Distribution, Repayment, and Arrears
1937/38–1946/47 (metric tons)

1937–38	45,469	44,616	12,220
1938–39	48,748	59,828	13,327
1939–40	48,474	57,940	15,980
1940–41	50,639	59,806	19,473
1941–42	44,614	51,278	23,963
1942–43	49,025	58,020	27,224
1943–44	55,165	63,088	33,092
1944–45	56,329	58,646	44,857
1945–46	61,616	72,616	49,261
1946–47	56,981	63,209	57,278

Source: Reports in Senegalese National Archives.

feed themselves and also contribute surpluses to the war effort. The French created their own counterpart of the British marketing boards, although in the French version the *SIPs* were assigned a dominant role in local affairs. Responsibility for collecting, storing, and transporting groundnuts once again reverted to the mercantile establishment, and *SIP* competition was done away with. Nonetheless, the state's supervisory powers were greatly enhanced. The state fixed the price to be paid for groundnuts (based on the world price and adjusted from week to week) and allocated the tonnage to be purchased among a consortium of buying houses, called the *Groupexar*. In reality, the great export–import houses became

112

TABLE 13

Foodstuff Distribution and Sums Remaining to be Repaid to the
SIPs, 1946–49 (Current Francs)

Year	Total Advances	Sum Outstanding	Percent Outstanding
1946	122,920,621	39,022,265	32
1947	103,809,578	19,627,743	18
1948	120,374,000	17,385,858	14
1949	185,491,742	86,150,095	46

Source: Rapport Economique Annuel, 1949.

mere state purchasing agents (though, of course, their sale of European manufactures was not regulated by the state). Mercantile profits from the groundnut trade were determined by the state and included in the buying price (Fouquet, 1958:130ff).

These arrangements enabled the state to capture the lion's share of profits from groundnut exports, and in 1946, with the creation of a special government account – the *Compte d'Arachide* – it used these funds to support groundnut production in general and to make good the deficits in *SIP* finances.

II. THE LIBERAL ERA, 1947–1960

By the end of World War II, Provident Societies had become an administrative and economic fixture in Senegal, albeit a fiscally troubled one. It is not surprising, therefore, that in the decade and a half before independence these cooperative organizations were in the forefront of French planning and nationalist ambitions. Significantly the institutions and the debate in official circles and in the nationalist press about cooperatives laid the foundations for the reforms carried out immediately after Senegal achieved its independence.

Agricultural cooperatives were an integral part of African nationalist demands. They were viewed as the most effective instrument for wresting economic power from overseas business groups and establishing local control over the profits of the export–import trade. In Senegal, where the indigenous cooperative movement was an active one, nationalists were eager to replace the old coops (the Provident Societies) with democratic, nationalist, and populist institutions. Yet the new bodies that emerged in the 1950s and early

1960s were beset by the same problems that had plagued the *SIPs* in earlier decades.

Post-war experimentation with coops flowed firstly from impulses transmitted from the metropole to the colonies. In the enthusiasm of the post-war years and the impulse toward colonial assimilation a resolution was passed in the Conseil de la République in August, 1947, calling upon the French government to replace the *SIPs* with genuine agricultural cooperatives, run by directors elected by members and responsible to them. The debate provided an occasion for two Senegalese delegates – Ousmane Socé and Fodé Mamadou Touré – to excoriate the colonial Provident Societies as undemocratic and autocratic (Conseil de la République, 1947:1855–56). Nonetheless, the important cooperative law of September 10, 1947, which stressed democracy and restricted interest rates, was clearly meant for the metropole. While its introduction into the colonies resulted in a veritable outburst of new cooperatives, its impact overseas was quickly curtailed.

In 1947 four new, independent Senegalese cooperatives came into being, their financing of 59,000,000F ($500,000) being provided and guaranteed by the French colonial government (see Table 14). Although in their first year of existence they marketed only a small proportion of the total groundnut crop (a mere 6540 tons), they aspired to a larger role.

TABLE 14
Private Cooperatives in Senegal, 1947

	Government-guaranteed loan (francs)	Groundnuts Marketed (metric tons)
1. Coopérative Mutuelle Agricole Sénégalaise	16,000,000	1600
2. Coopérative de Kahone-Diakhao	17,000,000	1900
3. Coopérative Agricole de Diourbel	11,000,000	1000
4. Coopérative Agricole de M'Backe	15,500,000	2040
Total	59,500,000	6540

Source: Rapport Economique Annuel, 1947, SNA 2G47-26(1).

These first indigenous cooperatives had been created by influential religious and political figures. Three of the new bodies were headed by powerful *marabouts*; the fourth by a political chief.[2] They

114

were also patronized by leading political figures and enjoyed close connections with the Senegalese Socialist party, the SFIO (Section française de l'Internationale ouvrière).

Inevitably, the SFIO tie provoked a reaction from Senegal's newer and more populist party, the BDS (Bloc démocratique Sénégalais), rising under the leadership of Leopold Senghor and Mamadou Dia. It is perhaps not accurate to say that the BDS had a more authentic cooperative thrust, but one of its leading spokesmen – Mamadou Dia – was a committed advocate of cooperativism. From the beginning of his career, Dia had stressed its importance (see Dia's own publications, especially Dia, 1952; also see Gellar, 1967). He insisted that indigenous coops, unlike the *SIPs*, would spring from the people and would encourage peasant enterprise and reward peasant initiative. Under BDS sponsorship, Dia created cooperatives at Fatick, la Petite Côte, and Kougheul Bambouk (Jalin, 1951).

The new, indigenous cooperatives enjoyed a spectacular, albeit short-lived flourishing. Though they had multiple functions, they stressed groundnut marketing and allowed the *SIPs* to maintain responsibility for seed and foodstuff distribution. Within 5 years there were 214 of them; their government-backed loans had increased to 500,000,000F ($1,400,000), and they were marketing 80,000 tons of groundnuts yearly (see Table 15). Even so (and perhaps because of their very rapid expansion) they fell consistently short of their goals. Despite Dia's hope that they would be peasant-run, they were dominated by big men – political and religious grandees. Increasingly, they became embroiled in political and nationalist disputes, with one cooperative being favored at the expense of another because of political affiliations. Although Dia and others intended indigenous cooperatives to supplant 'le commerce,' many of the local bodies came to be dominated by merchants who paid large commissions to themselves and other mercantile agents (Wibaux, 1953: 120ff).

The new cooperatives found themselves in the same financial straits as the *SIPs*. Their fiscal problems were even more intractable because of widespread corruption (at least if one can rely on the French reports – a useful report can be found in Gaye, 1963). At the outset the government's loan was turned over to the cooperatives, and in far too many cases cooperative directors used these funds for personal enrichment. By 1950, the French administrators had come to the conclusion that cooperative directors were incompetent, that coops were dominated by merchants and politicized, and that

TABLE 15

Private Senegalese Coops, 1947/48–1955/56

Year	Number of Cooperatives	Government-Backed Loan (francs)	Groundnuts Purchased (metric tons)
1947–48	4	30,000,000	4,000
1948–49	27	230,000,000	14,400
1949–50	43	568,000,000	63,000
1950–51	77	307,000,000	80,000
1951–52	214	500,000,000	45,000
1952–53	104	–	45,000
1953–54	20	–	23,000
1954–55	–	–	–
1955–56	–	–	10,216

Source: Compiled from annual economic reports in the Senegalese National Archives.

they degenerated into veritable '*sociétés de commerce* which often ignored the interests of producers' (Wibaux, 1953: 122ff). Most of the coops failed to pay *ristournes* while turning over exorbitant sums to cooperative administrators, many of whom were clients of the founders.

Perhaps not surprisingly, peasants increasingly regarded both the state-run and the privately-administered coops as distant financial organizations whose debts were the last call on their own resources. One colonial administrator wrote:

It is useful once again to mention the fact that in spite of the instructions and efforts made by the cooperatives for recovering the debts of their adherents, the return is not what one would be able to expect. A certain *état d'esprit*, a certain propaganda circulated that all that which is lent must be considered as a gift so that each year a part of the arrears held as unrecoverable must be passed along to the profits and losses and constitutes a mass of several million definitely lost to the groundnut account which advances funds to the cooperatives. (*Rapport Moral et Financier*, 1950–51)

Although this statement described the Provident Societies, it applied with equal force to the indigenous cooperatives, the financing of which was in a dreadful condition in the early 1950s. By the end of the 1950–51 growing season private coops had debts totalling nearly 400,000,000 francs divided as follows:

172,438,000F to the banks
56,878,333F to the public treasury
34,572,318F to *Groupexar*
120,000,000F to oil crushing mills (Goujon, 1951)

This heavy indebtedness posed the vexing problem to the French of what to do about the proliferation of these local bodies, each demanding state-guaranteed financing. In previous decades French administrators would simply have used the heavy hand of coercion. But with nationalist sentiment on the rise and power-sharing and assimilation the order of the day, colonial administrators were hesitant to embark upon a campaign of suppression. To be sure, the state did prosecute the most blatantly corrupt directors; Louis Dienen Faye at Koungheul and Moussa Faye at Saloum Oriental were brought before the tribunals (Jalin, 1951). But it preferred to adopt a regulative approach, gradually withdrawing funds and technical support from poorly run branches while building up the few that were efficient. To this end the state created *Secteurs Coopératifs Pilotes*, under the jurisdiction of a new oversight body – the Entente Coopérative – which was administered by a council of 12 members, designated by the *conseil d'administration* of the *Sociétés* themselves. Attached to the *Entente Coopérative* was an *Inspection des Coopératives*, created in July 1949 to report on local coops and offer recommendations for their development.[3]

Nonetheless, the indigenous cooperatives expanded, and the state found itself unable and unwilling to provide state financing for all. Gradually the inspectorate reduced the number of coops which it deemed suitable for state financial assistance. In 1949–50 only 40 coops qualified for state financing; the numbers fell sharply in succeeding years. As the state withdrew its financial support, it attempted to place the better-run bodies in contact with local oil-crushing mills which as of 1949 and under pressure from the state assumed a large role in financing and marketing the groundnut crop (Jalin, 1951). Although the state's financial obligations were reduced, its role as an intermediary between coop and business firms created considerable tension. The oil-crushing plants claimed financial support when the coops failed to repay their loans (Goujon, 1951). By 1953–54 the experiment in privately-organized coops had virtually run its course. With state financial backing nearly non-existent and oil-crushing firms suspicious, many of the private coops went out of existence. The twenty that remained in that year marketed only 23,000 tons of groundnuts.

These local cooperatives had arisen in opposition to the autocracy of the Provident Society and its imperial bias. Although the *SIPs* did not immediately disappear, their days were numbered. The drive to create indigenous organizations representative of peasant interests was strong, fueled, as it was, by nationalist sentiments.

Equally significant was an infusion of metropolitan technical and humanitarian ideas. In the agricultural sphere the impact of French technical advice was palpable in the Portères mission to Senegal in 1952. The Portères report called attention to a growing imbalance between urban and rural incomes, a rural exodus, declining agricultural productivity, and the decreased capacity of the Senegalese to feed themselves. The mission was particularly critical of the traditional expansionist groundnut policies which, it argued, had brought short-run gains at the expense of rational long-term agricultural improvement. In particular the mission condemned the government policy of 'caressing *muridism* to extend its agriculture of rapine' and roundly castigated the old *SIPs* for allowing Senegalese tillers to overwork the soil (Portères, 1952:I, 13). Portères' new policies envisioned an increase in food production, the practical education of the peasantry, which had been neglected in favor of powerful religious and political magnates, and a reinvigorated program of 'mutualism and cooperation' drawing its strength from small holders (Portères, 1952:II, 302).

A second metropolitan influence stemmed from a renewed interest in the poor in the 1950s and was provided by French liberal Catholicism, especially under the aegis of an extraordinarily talented and dynamic Dominican priest, Father L. J. Lebret. Born in 1897 in Brittany and interested at first in the less developed parts of France, Lebret founded a society, called Economie et Humanisme, a study group and intellectual movement. For Lebret an important instrument for realizing his goals was the cooperative which he believed would be as effective in the Third World as in backward parts of France. Lebret was invited to Brazil, Columbia, and Vietnam. Since his work was well known to Mamadou Dia, he and a number of his followers also worked in Senegal during the 1960s (see especially Lebret, 1961 – particularly his *avant propos* to the volume; and Malley, 1969).

In the 1950s and early 1960s Senegal's cooperative movement reflected these indigenous and metropolitan influences, with the result that the overarching administrative framework was gradually reorganized. Responding to nationalist pressures, French colonial administrators began to replace the Provident Societies with new cooperatives, known as *Sociétés Mutuelles du Développement Rural*. The first of these bodies was created in 1955. Though the much-resented *cotisation* and obligatory peasant membership remained in place, the SMDRs were mainly elected bodies (two-thirds of the members of the *conseil* being elected, the other one-third being appointed by the government). As for the presidents, they were no longer *commandants du cercle*. Instead, though still designated by the government, they were now chosen from among nominees presented by the *conseil* itself. Another administrative change was that the *Fonds Commun* and the *Crédit Agricole*, the national financial bodies of the rural sector, were merged into the *Banque Sénégalaise du Développement* (Camboulives, 1967).

CONCLUSION

Major reforms took place in the cooperative structure after independence. Though these changes were based on precedents from the colonial period, they were intended to overcome traditional problems and to reflect the new spirit of independence and grassroots support. With Mamadou Dia as the guide a group of rural animators was sent out into the countryside to energize the new organs. Inspired by Dia's vision of a new world consecrated by political independence, the new village coops enjoyed some spectacular early successes. They made big gains in undercutting the power of the local merchant in groundnut marketing. By 1963–64, the *SMDRs* which had marketed only 15 percent of the groundnut crop before independence were able to dispose of 70 percent of the crop.

But it was not long before the old problems began to reappear. That the same problems cropped up in the post-independence period suggests that these difficulties were systematically connected with each other and were related to problems of initiating economic development with limited resources.

The unfolding of the history of the Senegalese cooperative movement displayed these difficulties graphically. As hard as the administration might try, it was not able to eradicate them.

1. In the first place, Provident Societies as precursors of coops and coops themselves tended to be dominated by a few people, either those with political power (*commandants*, chiefs, and religious and political leaders) or those with technical expertise (rural *animateurs*, government bureaucrats, and even weighers). Given

the lack of education and political powerlessness of the rural populace, it was difficult for ordinary villagers to compel coop directors to be responsive to their wishes.

2. The cooperative movement was characterized by ideological inflation. There was a tendency to see in the coops a panacea for a host of rural problems. Inevitably a disjuncture arose between ideals and reality, goals and accomplishments.

3. Considerable ideological continuity existed from the foundation of the Provident Societies before World War I to the present-day cooperatives. While early advocates of *SIPs* favored integration of Senegal into the international economy and later exponents sought greater economic autonomy, the proponents of cooperatives strove (albeit often in a paternalistic and sometimes wholly rhetorical way) to safeguard and elevate the peasantry, to make them more efficient cultivators, and to enable them to draw greater profit from their agricultural efforts.

4. Tensions existed between center and periphery. In the early French colonial period this tension manifested itself in the grandiose ambitions of the local administrators and the more circumscribed view of coops held by French administrators in Dakar. Later, local village officials (cooperators, rural animators, and so forth) fought with Dakar-based bureaucrats from the central secretariat or from the Senegalese development bank for control over cooperative activities.

5. Almost from the first days of its existence cooperative leaders displayed a marked anti-mercantile bias. In the 1930s the French commandants held local merchants largely responsible for the farmers' retreat into auto-consumption. Merchants had their day of glory during the early 1950s when they dominated many of the local voluntary cooperatives. But Mamadou Dia's followers effectively drove merchants from the field of groundnut marketing, though they continued to dominate the import trade. It is not altogether clear that the anti-mercantile bias of the cooperative leaders was entirely justified, since the contribution that local merchants and large-scale import–export houses made to economic growth and the improvement of the material well being of the peasantry was at many times considerable.

6. Corruption became a marked feature of the cooperatives from the early 1950s onward and remained a problem after inde-

pendence. The coops were politicized during the 1950s. They received political and even financial support from political parties, and they were not averse to funnelling resources to parties in return. Also, the leaders of these organizations were in a position of little accountability. Their inflated powers enabled them to siphon off resources for themselves and their immediate followers.

7. The cooperative experience seems to have taught the peasantry that government organs had the last call on their resources. Coops came to their rescue during harsh economic times – when stock seed needed replenishing or families were desperately seeking to survive the hungry season – and yet peasants tended to repay advances only after loans to moneylenders were discharged and other financial obligations removed.

8. Perhaps underlying all of the difficulties were the mounting financial imbalances of the cooperatives. These first became palpable during the depression years, and they grew to even more serious proportions as the demands on the cooperatives multiplied. In a poor country like Senegal where so much was expected of any organization established in the countryside – whether it was administered by the French or by independent Senegalese bureaucrats – and where peasants shunned their financial obligations the cooperatives were destined to be run at a deficit.

I have tried to highlight institutional continuities. The purpose was to identify bed-rock realities which remained, sometimes because administrators sought to preserve them, more often in spite of administrative efforts to eradicate them. Nonetheless, important variations occurred during Senegal's long cooperative experience.

1. *SIPs* as organs of the French colonial administration and supervised by *commandants de cercle* were not politicized the way independent coops were in the post-World War II and post-independence periods. Still, at local levels where *chefs de canton* and *chefs de village* were involved, local clan and client rivalries impinged on *SIP* activities. Also the widespread corruption of post-World War II and post-independence coops was not a prominent feature of the *SIPs*, although, here too, at local levels African chiefs engaged in petty and sometimes large-scale corruption. The French administrators usually turned a blind eye.

2. Although *SIPs* and private coops were beset by financial instability, even insolvency, the nature of their problem was

different. From the depression onwards the *SIPs* had to discharge a wide range of responsibilities (seed and foodstuff distribution and, for a short while, groundnut marketing). They could not collect enough revenue from the local population to pay for these diverse activities. The new privately-run cooperatives which appeared in the late 1940s stressed groundnut marketing; their financial troubles occurred largely because of inexperience, politicization, and gross corruption.

NOTES

1. The French administration estimated that the Provident Societies' deficit in 1945 was 26,500,000 francs. Dagain to Governor of Senegal, January 23, 1945, SNA 2G 43–121.
2. Shaykh M'Backe was President of the M'Backe coop; Bassiron M'Backe at Diourbel; Ibrahim Naisse at Comas; and Fode Diouf at Kahone Diakho (Jalin, 1951).
3. The best description of these changes can be found in Camboulives (1967). Mamadou Dia was critical of state regulation, claiming that the government adopted short-sighted and narrowly technical criteria when evaluating the coops. He also argued that the state used its regulative powers for political ends (*Condition Humaine*, December 29, 1951).

CHAPTER FOUR

Circulaire 32 Revisited: Prospects for Revitalizing the Senegalese Cooperative Movement in the 1980s

Sheldon Gellar

Senegalese cooperatives have little in common with those found in Europe and North America. Historically, Western cooperatives were initiated by groups of individual farmers banding together to pool their resources to improve their bargaining positions in the marketplace.[1] In Senegal, what came to be known as the cooperative movement had its roots in the *Sociétés de Prévoyance*, a colonial institution designed to provide food and seed security for so-called improvident peasants and insure the smooth functioning of the peanut economy. In contrast with cooperatives in Europe and North America which emerged from the collective efforts of private individuals, the cooperative movement in Senegal was largely the creature of the state. The Senegalese government launched the post-independence Cooperative Movement to mobilize the rural populations to implement national rural development policies and a communitarian socialist ideology.

Rather than constituting a popular movement, the cooperatives in Senegal were, in reality, a vehicle through which different groups and institutions accomplished different goals. The state used cooperatives to regulate the peanut economy, promote its agricultural modernization programs, and extract surpluses from the rural economy; politicians used the cooperatives to build political support by rewarding their followers and allies with easy access to credit and other resources (D.C. O'Brien, 1975); and rural notables and religious leaders used the cooperatives to reinforce their authority and enhance their prestige (D.C. O'Brien, 1977; Copans, 1980; and Sy, 1969).

123

The peasantry for whom the Cooperative Movement had been created tended to regard the cooperatives primarily as a vehicle used by the state to collect groundnuts rather than a peasant-controlled organization to promote their economic welfare. As long as the cooperatives provided services and benefits which peasants needed or found useful, the peasants supported them. When the cooperatives became a burden, the peasants tended to withdraw their support and to look elsewhere to satisfy their most pressing needs.

This paper traces the rise and fall of the Cooperative Movement during the first twenty years of independence (1960–1980); discusses national cooperative policy and structural changes in the Cooperative Movement in the 1980s; and identifies the main issues and obstacles currently confronting it. Much of the analysis revolves around three central issues: (1) the Cooperative Movement as an instrument of state rural development policy; (2) the forms and degree of state intervention needed to make Senegalese co-operatives work effectively; and (3) the extent to which Senegalese peasants participate, manage, and control their cooperatives in accordance with the principles and guidelines laid out in *Circulaire 32* of 21 May 1962 which remains the cornerstone of Senegalese cooperative doctrine.

I. THE RISE AND FALL OF THE SENEGALESE COOPERATIVE MOVEMENT: 1960–1980

A. *African Socialism,* Circulaire 32, *and the Cooperative Movement*

The establishment of a nation-wide network of rural cooperatives in Senegal in 1960 was one of the national leadership's top priorities for several reasons. First, the Cooperative Movement was to be the main instrument for implementing African Socialism, the official ideology of the regime. Second, the Cooperative Movement provided the Senegalese government with a lever for nationalizing the groundnut trade and gaining control over a key sector of the economy. Third, the Cooperative Movement was to serve as the main motor for modernizing and diversifying Senegal's rural economy which had been overly dependent upon the groundnut. Fourth, the Cooperative Movement could be used to maintain the political support of the rural populations by distributing patronage and other material benefits to the rural populations.

The ideological foundations of the post-independence Cooperative Movement lie in the national leadership's commitment to African Socialism (Dia, 1952; Dia, 1976; Senghor, 1961). Senghor and Dia regarded cooperatives as the key institution in constructing African Socialism. Village-based cooperatives were to be the basic economic units of a communitarian socialist society and combine traditional African solidarity values and Rochdalian democratic principles (Camboulives, 1967).[2]

Mamadou Dia, the theoretician of Senegalese cooperative ideology, defined the basic goals of the Cooperative Movement and guidelines for its future evolution in *Circulaire 32* issued on May 21, 1962. Three main themes permeated *Circulaire 32* which constituted the cornerstone of Senegalese cooperative doctrine throughout the post-independence era: (1) the withering away of the state's tutelage over the Cooperative Movement as cooperatives became capable of managing their own affairs; (2) the evolution of groundnut marketing cooperatives into multifunctional, multisectoral development cooperatives; and (3) the vertical integration of the Cooperative Movement through the creation of local, regional, and national cooperative unions.

Ideally, the Cooperative Movement was to be a village-based grassroots movement run by and for the benefit of the rural populations. To make this possible, however, the government had taken the initiative by establishing the legal and institutional framework for a national system and providing it with technical assistance and financial support. The tutelage of the state was to be temporary. As peasants gained the skills needed to manage the cooperatives efficiently, the state would withdraw and transfer full responsibility to them. During the transition period, government agents would be the humble servants of the Cooperative Movement and work to make their role unnecessary in the future.

Senegalese doctrine also regarded the Cooperative Movement as an instrument for liberating Senegalese peasants from moneylenders and middlemen and providing producers with a larger share of the profits generated by the groundnut trade. In theory, the nationalization of the groundnut trade and the assumption of the functions of groundnut marketing by cooperatives would reduce peasant indebtedness and dependency on middlemen and moneylenders and make available additional income which could be used to raise living standards and finance investments to improve agricultural productivity.

Senegalese doctrine insisted that the Cooperative Movement

should not remain primarily an institution built around groundnut marketing. On the contrary, cooperatives should evolve rapidly into multisectoral and multifunctional organizations capable of spearheading the drive to modernize and diversify the rural economy. Multisectoral and specialized cooperatives would produce and market a wide variety of products – cereals, vegetables, fish, meat and dairy products, etc. – and help Senegal break out of its excessive dependency on the groundnut. Multifunctional cooperatives would eventually permit the movement to meet most, if not all, of its members' needs for credit, basic consumer commodities, transportation, investment goods, and other economic services. It was thus envisaged that the cooperatives rather than the state or the private sector would eventually become the principal economic force and motor for development in the countryside.

Village cooperatives would combine to form self-governing rural communes which would constitute the primary units of local government in the countryside and the main locus of economic and social services for the villages within their jursidiction. The rural cooperatives would also form local, regional, and national unions which would represent the Cooperative Movement and eventually take over the management and control of equipment and services provided by the state during the tutelage period.

The official ideology which inspired Senegalese cooperative doctrine, however, often clashed with Senegalese political and social realities and the heritage of past cooperative experiences. Ideology had its greatest influence on the movement during the early years of independence. During the mid-1960s, cooperative doctrine was downplayed as the government increased its tutelage over the movement and the rural economy. With the rural economy in decline, *Circulaire 32* was resurrected as a guide to cooperative reform during the late 1970s and early 1980s.

B. The Big Push: 1960-1962

The most dynamic period of expansion for the Cooperative Movement came during the early years of independence when the Senegalese government was under the direction of Mamadou Dia. The Cooperative Movement developed rapidly for several important reasons: (1) it had the full support of Senegal's national leaders; (2) it was an integral component of sweeping institutional reforms aimed at nationalizing the groundnut trade and creating a post-colonial development administration capable of modernizing

Senegal's rural economy; and (3) it was received favorably by the peasantry because of the material advantages coop membership offered over the former system.

Despite its initial successes, the Cooperative Movement did not evolve according to the ideological blueprint laid out in *Circulaire 32*. Conservative political and social forces generally captured control of the newly created cooperatives and resisted efforts to create modern cooperatives based on egalitarian principles; the Cooperative Movement became highly politicized and a funnel for political patronage rather than a unified grassroots movement for economic change; the commitment of the peasantry to the Cooperative Movement was shallow and based more on immediate material advantages than acceptance of cooperative principles and government development priorities; and decisions concerning the organization of the Cooperative Movement continued to be imposed from above with little input from the rural populations themselves.

The establishment of a nation-wide network of cooperatives in 1960 was closely linked to the government's nationalization of the groundnut trade. Before building the new socialist society, the old colonial system – the *économie de traite* – dominated by French trading companies and banks had to be dismantled (Gellar, 1967; Schumacher, 1975). Nationalization of the groundnut trade required the creation of new financial institutions to take over the roles previously played by the French colonial banks, groundnut processing factories, and import-export companies providing the credit that greased the wheels of the groundnut trade. In 1960 the government established the *Banque Sénégalaise de Développement* (BDS), which financed much of the groundnut trade, and the *Office de Commercialisation Agricole* (OCA), which assumed a monopoly over the marketing of the groundnut crop. Henceforth, the groundnut crop had to be marketed either through cooperatives or private merchant groups – *Organismes Stockeurs* – licensed by the state. Having 'nationalized' the groundnut trade, the Senegalese government moved to 'socialize' the groundnut trade by encouraging the cooperatives to market an ever larger share of the groundnut crop.

During the early 1960s, Senegalese groundnut farmers eagerly joined the new cooperatives organized by the state because of the advantages offered to their members (Gellar, 1983a; Schumacher, 1975). By selling their groundnuts through the cooperatives, producers would be assured of getting the full official price for their crops during the regular trading season and rebates (*ristournes*) in

May and June when the peasants were usually short of cash and food. The combination of guaranteed groundnut prices, timely rebates, and low interest food loans (*crédits de soudure*) provided by the government was aimed at freeing Senegalese peasants from the allegedly usurious practices of rich farmers and unscrupulous merchants. Moreover, since each cooperative served as a collecting station, groundnut farmers welcomed new cooperatives in their villages because it reduced their transport costs.[3]

The Cooperative Service was part of a triad of rural development agencies which also included *Animation Rurale* and the *Centres d'Expansion Rurales* (CERs) bearing the main responsibility for organizing and mobilizing the rural populations to implement national rural development policy (Gellar, 1980). The Cooperative Service worked closely with *Animation Rurale* to promote the Cooperative Movement throughout the country. The main tasks of the Cooperative Service were to organize new cooperatives and educate the peasantry in cooperative matters. Coop agents explained coop statutes and regulations to the rural populations and how to set up a cooperative, elect coop officials, run meetings, and keep records. *Animation Rurale* officials encouraged peasants to join cooperatives and also worked to promote dialogue between the peasantry and the post-colonial state and to overcome peasant mistrust of the state and state policies. Most extension efforts were channeled through the CERs which were established in January 1960 to implement the Dia government's integrated rural development strategy.[4] In principle, the CERs were designed to meet the total needs of the rural populations in their districts (*arrondissements*). Thus, they were expected to provide technical assistance in the areas of farming, livestock, fishing, and forestry; stimulate the adoption of new technologies; and to help organize and supervise cooperatives.

Another important state agency directly linked with the Cooperative Movement were the *Centres Régionaux d'Assistance au Développement* (CRADs), which assumed responsibility for seed management, running the *Programme Agricole*, distributing food credits, and collecting the crops marketed by the cooperatives. CRAD agents also directly administered and managed the *Associations d'Intérêt Rural* or pre-cooperatives, kept track of coop accounts and retrieved coop debts for the OCA and BSD. In theory the functions of the CRADs eventually were to be taken over by regional cooperative unions.

CRAD officials showed little interest in training Senegalese coop members to manage their own accounts. On the contrary, some agents took advantage of peasant illiteracy to shortchange them and embezzle cooperative funds. The CRADs soon acquired a reputation for corruption and subservience to the wishes of powerful politicians, rural notables, and religious leaders seeking to divert credit and other resources their way. While at odds with cooperative ideals, the highly politicized CRADs permitted the ruling party to establish a formidable patronage network in the countryside.

Dia's decision to expand the role of the cooperatives at the expense of the private sector in mid-1962 was accompanied by a drive to strengthen Dia's position in the party vis-à-vis Senghor, thus touching off a bitter power struggle within the *Union Progressiste Sénégalaise* (UPS). Most of the conservative forces in the ruling party lined up with Senghor while many of the younger reform oriented development officials supported Dia or remained neutral (Gellar, 1980). Dia lost the power struggle and his political demise in December 1962 marked the end of the Big Push phase in the evolution of the Senegalese Cooperative Movement.

C. Consolidation, Stagnation, and Reorientation: 1963-1966

During the Big Push phase, the number of Senegalese cooperatives and pre-cooperatives jumped from little more than one hundred in 1959 to more than 1100 by the middle of 1962. After the 1962-63 season, the Cooperative Movement began to stagnate even though groundnut cooperatives steadily increased their share of total quantity of groundnuts marketed.

TABLE 1

Evolution of Associations d'Intérêt Rural and Groundnut Cooperatives
1960/61–1965/66

Marketing Season	Number of Coops	Number of Organismes Stockeurs	Percent Total Marketed By Coops	Groundnuts Marketed in Metric Tons
1960/61	668	3,000	20	786,000
1961/62	1,123	1,210	49	883,000
1962/63	1,415	778	58	765,000
1963/64	1,424	606	63	782,000
1964/65	1,416	585	66	849,000
1965/66	1,467	510	75	999,000

Source: Schumacher, 1975: 163.

The mid-1960s were characterised by a downgrading of the role of the Cooperative Movement as the vanguard of a communitarian socialist society, the consolidation of the Cooperative Movement around the groundnut cooperatives, and a shift towards a more technocratic approach to rural development which stressed increasing productivity through technological innovation.

During this period, little was done to implement the principles laid down in *Circulaire 32*. In 1963, the government closed down many of the rural consumer cooperative sections that had been launched with great enthusiasm in 1962 as a major step towards creating multifunctional cooperatives (Camboulives, 1967: 214–223; Brochier, 1968). Most had been hastily set up without preliminary feasibility studies. Infrastructure was often inadequate, and the managers chosen to run the consumer sections frequently knew little about running a modern business or keeping good accounts.

While the momentum to create specialized and multifunctional cooperatives along the lines called for in *Circulaire 32* was fizzling out during the mid-1960s, the Cooperative Movement was expanding and consolidating its position as the dominant marketing mechanism in the groundnut trade. But like the middlemen who had been dependent upon and subordinate to the French trading companies and colonial banks before the nationalization of the groundnut trade in 1960, the groundnut cooperatives now found themselves in a similar position vis-à-vis the state. Instead of evolving towards independent, self-managing economic development cells, they remained under the tutelage of the state which set groundnut prices, distributed seed, provided credit for the *Programme Agricole*, collected the crop, supervised cooperative accounts, and determined local development priorities.

In 1964 the Cooperative Service was formally absorbed by the CRADs thereby losing its autonomy and vanguard role. Reduced to an appendage of the CRADs which were primarily concerned with assuring the smooth functioning of the groundnut trade and the agricultural credit program, the Cooperative Service had little opportunity to fulfill its original mission of training coop members to manage their own affairs.

An important reorientation of rural development policy took place in 1964 when the government called upon the *Société d'Aide Technique et de Coopération* (SATEC), a French-based development agency to increase groundnut and millet productivity in the groundnut basin within three years. The arrival of SATEC to take charge of agricultural extension activities in the groundnut basin marked the beginning of the ascendancy of the 'productionist' approach to rural development over the integrated rural development approach represented by the multifunctional CERs. It also signified a return to the groundnut bias in rural development policy. SATEC was the forerunner of the Regional Development Agencies (RDAs), which assumed primary responsibility for developing the rural economy within areas under their jursidiction.

The 1965–66 season marked the beginning of the end of a period (1958–65) in which government policy had clearly attempted to improve rural living conditions by extending and subsidizing services in the countryside while maintaining groundnut prices above those justified by world market levels. At that time the government began to react to the fact that French subsidies on Senegalese groundnut exports to France would end in 1967 which meant that the government would no longer be able to afford to subsidize groundnut producer prices. In late 1965 the government made important changes in its marketing regulations which shifted operating costs previously assumed by the OCA to groundnut farmers (Schumacher, 1975: 175–78). Groundnut farmers resented these measures and saw the new regulations as a roundabout way to reduce groundnut prices. While the record 1965–66 crop in which a million tons of groundnuts were marketed softened the impact, it did not prevent the beginning of a breach between the government and groundnut producers. The Cooperative Movement became increasingly less attractive to the peasants because membership no longer brought them the additional material benefits they had enjoyed during the early independence years.

D. The ONCAD Era, 1966–1980

The establishment of the *Office National de Coopération et d'Assistance au Développement* (ONCAD) in 1966 coincided with the 1966 drought which ended what had generally been a long period of good weather beginning in the early 1950s. ONCAD was created in mid-1966 to rationalize and consolidate the operations of the various state agencies involved in groundnut transactions. ONCAD absorbed both the CRADs and the Cooperative Service, and took control over most of the marketing functions previously exercised by the OCA. Shortly after ONCAD's creation, the state suppressed the *Organismes Stockeurs* and declared that all groundnuts had to be marketed by the Cooperative Movement. This move was designed more to tighten state control over the vital groundnut sector than to strengthen the Cooperative Movement vis-à-vis the private sector. With ONCAD in place, the state's tutelage over the Cooperative Movement actually increased.

During the late 1960s, ONCAD and the Cooperative Movement became increasingly unpopular. Frequent shifts in state policies, late distribution of agricultural inputs and payment for groundnut crops, sharp cutbacks in food loans, corruption, and heavy-handed debt collection methods caused widespread peasant discontent. Lower producer prices, three years of drought, and rising indebtedness added fuel to the fire. Peasants began to complain that they had become 'captives' of the Cooperative Movement. The 'malaise paysanne' of the late 1960s (A.M. Diop, 1971; Dumont, 1970; Fougeyrollas, 1970; D.C. O'Brien, 1979; Gellar, 1980) was characterized by (1) a decline in the volume of fertilizer and agricultural equipment ordered through the Programme Agricole; (2) a growing reluctance and inability to repay debts contracted through ONCAD and the cooperatives; (3) disenchantment with government pricing policies and regulations, ONCAD, and the Cooperative Movement; (4) declining peasant interest and participation in cooperative activities; and (5) the development of vigorous parallel markets (Gellar, September 1983a: 38-41).

The late 1960s and early 1970s witnessed a period in which Senegalese development policy was furthest removed from the communitarian socialist vision of the early independence years. In 1970, the Senegalese government decided to expand the role of the RDAs by giving them the main responsibility for coordinating all development activities taking place in their zone of operations. The Animation Rurale service vigorously opposed this policy on the grounds that the RDAs would neglect cooperative education and rural community organizing because of their narrow 'productionist' orientation. The decision to build up the RDAs as multifunctional extension services prevailed while Animation Rurale saw its own role and influence drastically reduced. The Cooperative Service became even more of a 'poor relation' within ONCAD than it had been within the CRADs and received inadequate funds to carry out its cooperative education mission (Thiam, 1972: 70).

During the 1970s, older RDAs like the Société d'Aménagement et d'Exploitation des Terres de Delta et des Vallées du Fleuve Sénégal et de la Falemé (SAED) and SODEVA which replaced SATEC in the groundnut basin in 1968 expanded rapidly in size and scope while the government created new RDAs to provide extension services and agricultural inputs for peasants in the Casamance, Eastern Senegal, and the Sylvo-Pastoral Zone.

Foreign donors encouraged and financed the expansion of the RDAs. The severe Sahelian droughts of the late 1960s and early 1970s spurred the Senegalese government to promote food self-sufficiency as a major national goal and donors to shift more resources into the rural sectors during the mid and late 1970s. The RDAs promoting cotton, rice, and other crops outside the ground-nut basin set up village-based *groupements de producteurs*. A *groupement* comprised a small number of farmers, usually from the same village or *quartier*, who registered as a group under the tutelage of an RDA in order to have access to credit for seeds, fertilizers, and other inputs.

The authoritarian style of the RDAs left little room for peasant participation in decision making. Goals, priorities, and techno-logical packages were set by the RDAs without consulting the farmers. While the RDAs showed little interest in promoting the Cooperative Movement under the tutelage of ONCAD, many cadres thought that the RDAs should assume full responsibility for organizing the peasants. This attitude placed the RDAs in competition and conflict with ONCAD and the Cooperative Ser-vice and sparked bitter interservice rivalries between the RDAs and the Cooperative Service.

The late 1970s were marked by the deterioration of peasant purchasing power, record levels of peasant indebtedness, and grow-ing disaffection of the rural populations with ONCAD, the Cooperative Movement, and the rural credit system in place. The 'second' *malaise paysanne* was also accompanied by a growing crisis in public finances, donor dissatisfaction with the effectiveness of the RDAs and state rural credit system, and increasingly vocal demands for rural reform by the Senegalese intellectual elite and opposition leaders.

E. The Rural Development Debate and the Last Days of ONCAD

The major actors in the rural development debate which began in 1979 – i.e., the national government, the RDAs, the Cooperative Service, donors, and Senegalese intellectuals and cadres committed to the official socialist ideology of the regime – agreed on four important points: (1) that the Cooperative Movement was in serious trouble; (2) that ONCAD had to be drastically reformed;

(3) that the RDAs had to become both more efficient and more responsive to the rural populations they served; and (4) that the rural populations had to be given greater responsibility in managing their own affairs.

Three different perspectives dominated the debate. The first perspective, essentially a technocratic one, stressed economic rationality and efficiency as the main criteria for reform. Hence, the priority was to be given to rationalizing the groundnut marketing and credit system, reducing state spending on the RDAs, improving ONCAD's accounting procedures, and regrouping the existing cooperatives into larger, more economically viable entities. This perspective was held by those primarily concerned with the financial crisis facing the state and the Senegalese economy. From this perspective, reform of the Cooperative Movement was needed to maintain the solvency of the state's rural credit and groundnut marketing systems that generated state revenues, employment opportunities, and the foreign exchange needed to finance imports.

A second major perspective stressed the need to reform the existing rural credit system by establishing village sections as the basic unit for distributing credit and decentralizing the RDAs to make them more responsive to the local populations. SODEVA, the World Bank, and the Caisse Centrale (Pince, 1979) shared this perspective and regarded the village section as more credit-worthy than the existing inter-village cooperatives where there was little or no control over the 'bad payers.' SODEVA wished to work more closely with the peasants and assume responsibility for managing the *Programme Agricole*, organizing village sections and providing management advice and training to village section officers (SODEVA, 1979b).

The third perspective had the most in common with the development strategy of the early 1960s and regarded the revitalization of the moribund Cooperative Movement and the evolution of cooperatives into self-governing bodies as the heart of rural reform (Sy, 1979; Belloncle, 1980b; and Gentil, 1980). Partisans of this perspective had much in common with SODEVA in supporting the creation of village sections, the establishment of sound village coop accounts as a precondition for restoring peasant confidence in the rural credit system, and functional literacy and numeracy training programs to enable peasants to run their own affairs. However, supporters of the third perspective which included officials from the *Ecole Nationale d'Economie Appliquée* (ENEA) and the Cooperative Service were committed to strengthening the

Cooperative Movement as a national movement and creating a strong, autonomous National Cooperative Office which would collaborate with representatives of the Cooperative Movement to promote and defend the cooperative cause. They also opposed the effort of SODEVA and other RDAs to usurp the role of the CS in organizing peasants at the grassroots level and favored using the CERs as the principal state agency for providing extension services and technical assistance to the peasantry.

Not everyone in Senegal favored major changes in the co-operative system. Prominent local politicians, rural notables, and state officials working for ONCAD opposed major reforms which would reduce their control over the Cooperative Movement and patronage opportunities. At its height, ONCAD had more than 4,000 employees and saw more than a 100 billion CFA pass through its hands annually. Despite frequent criticism of its chaotic accounting procedures and charges of widespread corruption and mismanagement, ONCAD failed to crack down on crooked and incompetent officials. It also did little to promote cooperative education and training or to produce simplified cooperative documents and forms in the local languages.

The national commission charged with studying the reform of ONCAD in February 1980 recommended the following in its report to the Senegalese government: (1) the transfer of the Cooperative Service from ONCAD to the Ministry of Rural Development and the elevation of the Cooperative Service into an autonomous direction responsible for overseeing national cooperative policy; (2) giving the RDAs the job of executing coop policy and providing cooperative training and assistance to village sections; (3) the maintenance of ONCAD's role in financing and executing the Programme Agricole; and the establishment of more elaborate and rigorous control procedures to insure greater accountability; and (4) permitting some cooperatives to sell directly to the groundnut crushing factories without going through ONCAD.

In addition to incorporating the recommendations of the ONCAD reform commission, the Rural Development Minister's report (D. Sene, 1980a) to the National Council of the Socialist Party called for an expanded role for the CERs in supporting local community development projects, which had become an increasingly important component of the government's rural development policy.[5] The Rural Development Minister also insisted that the rural populations must assume more responsibility to ensure that the reforms work. This theme reflected both ideological considerations

– the withering away of the state embodied in the regime's official ideology – and practical concerns – the need to reduce the state's expenditures in a period of financial crisis.

The National Council of the Socialist Party approved the report which became the main reference point for Senegalese rural development policy during the early 1980s. A few months later, the government decided to completely eliminate ONCAD which had become a political as well as economic liability. In August 1980, the National Assembly voted to dissolve ONCAD. The fall of ONCAD was accompanied by a revival of the principles contained in *Circulaire 32* as the basis for reforming and revitalizing the Cooperative Movement in the 1980s.

II. THE EVOLUTION OF THE SENEGALESE COOPERATIVE MOVEMENT IN THE 1980s

During the 1980s Cooperative Reform revolved around three sets of issues: (1) the role to be played by the Cooperative Movement as an instrument of national economic policy; (2) the respective roles to be played by the Cooperative Service, the RDAs, and other state agencies vis-à-vis the Cooperative Movement; and (3) the cooperative structures best suited to ensure greater popular participation and control over the Cooperative Movement.

National policymakers, the various state agencies vying to provide support and technical assistance to the Cooperative Movement, and rural notables, herdsmen, and fishermen organized within the Cooperative Movement often had different perspectives on these issues as well as different priorities and interests. The government's efforts to reconcile and mediate different and often conflicting perspectives, priorities, and interests made it difficult to pursue a consistent and coherent cooperative policy during the early 1980s despite the general consensus concerning the need for cooperative reform.

A. National Economic Policy and the Cooperative Movement

Donor pressure to reduce the size of the state bureaucracy, chronic state deficits resulting from the groundnut marketing system inherited from the ONCAD era, the disintegration of the rural credit system at the end of the 1970s, and the desire to reactivate the moribund rural economy were all factors affecting the evolution of state policy towards the Cooperative Movement during the early 1980s.

1. Restructuring the Cooperative Movement
and the Groundnut Marketing System

In 1980 the groundnut production and marketing system was in deep crisis. ONCAD had left a liability of over 75 billion CFA. Groundnut production had plummeted to 400,000 tons and only 200,000 tons were marketed through the cooperatives and official channels during the 1980-81 season. The peasants had suffered from two consecutive drought years and were in no position to pay back their debts. In April 1981 the government cancelled previous debts for seed and fertilizer and declared a moratorium on the repayment of debts for agricultural implements. To stimulate groundnut production, the government raised official groundnut prices from 50 to 70CFA for the 1981–82 season.

The near collapse of the groundnut marketing system coupled with a deep crisis in public finances moved the government to press forward with plans to restructure the Cooperative Movement to make groundnut marketing operations more efficient. This was to be achieved by reducing the number of cooperatives and reorganizing them into a smaller number of larger and more economically viable cooperative units. The main impetus for reducing the number of cooperatives came from the state which justified consolidation in the name of economic efficiency. During the mid-1960s, when groundnut production and marketing were close to peak levels, the general average for cooperative collecting stations was less than 350 tons (Diarrasouba, 1968: 206). However, to be economically viable, it was estimated that groundnut collection centers had to market at least 1500 tons of groundnuts during the season in order to cover all the costs entailed in the marketing process. Despite the elimination of the *Organismes Stockeurs* in 1967 and the establishment of a cooperative groundnut marketing monopoly, the average tonnage marketed through rural cooperatives had not increased significantly.

Since the mid-1970s, the *Bureau d'Organisation et de Méthodes* situated in the General Secretariat to the Presidency has sought to reduce the number of cooperatives in order to cut state transportation and administrative costs and give the cooperatives an adequate financial base to enable them to become economically viable. The government and Rural Development Ministry supported this policy and began efforts to implement it in the regions of Thiès and Diourbel which were chosen as test zones in 1978. Resistance

TABLE 2

Senegal's Groundnut Cooperatives (1981)

Region	No. of Coops	Membership	Social Equity (CFA)
Cap-Vert	24	3,359	2,218,875
Casamance	469	66,090	34,951,387
Diourbel	198	41,784	25,547,204
Flueve	123	23,120	2,336,150
Thiès	181	45,584	28,969,720
Sine-Saloum	510	128,500	89,628,381
Senegal Oriental	215	41,153	12,102,691
Total	1,887	391,298	219,816,278

Source: COPAC, 1983: 61.

to change was particularly strong in Diourbel, the fief of the Murids, where nearly three-quarters of the cooperatives rejected consolidation (Direction de la Coopération, 1981b: 93). Groundnut farmers opposed this proposal for several reasons: (1) the additional transportation costs entailed in bringing their groundnuts to the cooperative collective station (*secco*) in the event that their village was not chosen to be the seat of the new cooperative; (2) the loss of time waiting in longer lines to handle one's groundnut marketing transactions; (3) the loss of prestige and economic advantages for those villages losing their status as cooperative seats; and (4) the added difficulty of grassroots control over cooperative transactions and fraud, a major issue for peasants already dissatisfied with their lack of control over existing cooperative transactions.

The debate over consolidation was not so much over the size and form of cooperatives as it was over the allocation of the benefits deriving from the groundnut economy and the costs of modifying the present system. Thus, those primarily concerned with reducing state deficits and minimizing the operating costs of the *Société Nationale de Commercialisation des Oléaginaux du Sénégal* (SONOCOS) promoted cooperative consolidation while groundnut farmers and those primarily concerned with retaining the support of groundnut farmers by keeping down their costs of marketing their crops generally opposed it.

During the second half of 1983, the government moved ahead with its plans to reduce the total number of Senegalese cooperatives by establishing a 'development cooperative' in each *Communauté Rurale*. By mid-October, the Cooperative Service had established 314 'development cooperatives,' one for each *Communauté Rurale*.

About 10 percent of these communities were also allowed to retain a second cooperative. For the 1983–84 season, however, the government decided to retain the same number of cooperative crop collection stations existing before the new system went into place, therefore delaying the moment of truth until the 1984–85 season.[6]

Many proponents of cooperative reform have regarded the creation of village sections as the heart of any serious effort to reform the Cooperative Movement and regain the peasants' flagging confidence in the system (Belloncle, 1980b; Gentil, 1980; Pince, 1979; and Sy, 1979). One of the main causes of the disintegration of the Cooperative Movement was the collapse of the system of collective debt responsibility (*caution solidaire*), which broke down when the good payers in one village no longer felt obliged to cover the debts of the bad payers in other villages within the same cooperative (Belloncle, 1980b). This sentiment was further reinforced when the government periodically cancelled all debts without making distinctions between good and bad payers, thus penalizing the honest payers and rewarding the bad payers for their delinquency.

The system set up in the early 1960s had been built around cooperatives encompassing several villages. The collective solidarity which existed in individual villages, however, did not extend to other villages in the same cooperative. Moreover, since villages were unable to exercise much control over cooperative transactions taking place outside their village, it was not uncommon for villages to withdraw or sharply curtail their participation in cooperative activities when in conflict with other villages. Those promoting the establishment of the village section as the basic unit of the Cooperative Movement argue that this reform would give villagers greater control over cooperative activities directly affecting their village and the state greater assurance that loans would be repaid because the principle of collective responsibility for debts was more likely to work at the village level.

The resistance of rural notables and local party leaders dominating the Cooperative Movement to cooperative reform was a major factor in delaying the establishment of village sections. The rural notables and their political allies wanted to maintain as much control as possible over the resources channelled through the cooperatives. Hence, it was not surprising that they expressed strong reservations about according too much autonomy to village sections, especially in financial matters. On the other hand, peasants dissatisfied with their own village's lack of control over cooperative decisions in the past supported the creation of village sections able to exercise direct control over financial transactions related to its cooperative activities (Guèye and Ndiaye, 1981; Sagna and Cissé, 1981; P. Sene, 1980).

External donors like the World Bank and Caisse Centrale also entered the debate. Donors have argued in favor of village section autonomy in credit matters because of their belief that village sections would be more creditworthy than the older cooperatives. Although some village sections had been organized on an experimental basis in the groundnut basin and the Casamance during the early 1980s, village sections had no legal status until the passage of the new Cooperative Statutes in January 1983.[7] The 1983 Cooperative Statutes referred to the village section as the basic constituent unit of rural cooperatives (Article 64). Village sections were granted the right to handle directly a wide range of activities including the distribution of credit, seed management, the production and marketing of agricultural products, and collective equipment programs. They were also designated as the basic unit for cooperative education and agricultural extension.

The status of the village section was apparently clarified in the new Rural Development Minister's *Lettre-Circulaire 069* of September 5, 1983 which ordered the Cooperative Service to organize village sections throughout the country and implicitly gave the sections a great deal of autonomy vis-à-vis the 'mother' cooperative by not mentioning the latter in discussing the section's financial arrangements. During September and October 1983, the Senegalese Cooperative Service organized more than 4,200 sections. *Circulaire 069* set the minimum size of a village section to be 200 inhabitants for Louga, Eastern Senegal, and the Casamance and 300 inhabitants for Thiès, Diourbel, and Sine-Saloum. This meant that smaller villages had to regroup or attach themselves to a larger village in order to form a section. Since small villages and sub-village groups could not form their own autonomous sections, the principle of collective responsibility was undermined in some areas.

2. The Cooperative Movement and Rural Diversification: The Specialized Cooperatives

With the groundnut basin in decline and the future of groundnut exports bleak, national development policy during the 1980s placed much greater emphasis on encouraging the diversification of the primary sector. This meant a larger role for the so-called specialized

– i.e. non-groundnut oriented – cooperatives which had been neglected during the ONCAD era.

TABLE 3

Senegal's Specialized Rural Cooperatives (1981)

Type of Cooperative	No. of Coops	Membership	Social Equity (CFA)
Vegetable	53	38,100	3,715,000
Millet and Rice	113	16,950	21,900,000
Banana	5	232	NA
Maritime Fish	80	8,429	8,157,000
Continental Fish	21	1,697	1,696,500
Forestry Products	37	3,289	10,005,250
Herders	165	8,000	25,625,366
Totals	474	76,697	71,099,116

Source: COPAC, 1983: 60.

Issued by the Rural Development Minister on July 17, 1982, *Circulaire 2680* reasserted the government's strong interest in promoting specialized cooperatives. *Circulaire 2680* noted the growing willingness of the international donor community to provide more aid to the specialized cooperative sectors to promote national food self-sufficiency and urged the Cooperative Service to expend as much effort in organizing specialized cooperatives as it had expended for the groundnut sector which accounted for nearly 85 percent of the Cooperative Movement's total membership. To help finance the marketing activities of specialized coop unions, the government used part of the funds in a special Intercooperation Cooperative Fund to provide interest-free loans for the specialized cooperatives.[8] These funds came from resources usually reserved for the groundnut marketing cooperatives.

Although they received little financial support and credit from the Banque Nationale de Développement du Sénégal which was primarily concerned with extending credit to the groundnut sector, the specialized cooperatives involved in non-agricultural activities were generally more dynamic and better managed than most groundnut marketing cooperatives. Unlike the groundnut marketing cooperatives where all male household heads were generally expected to join, most members of the specialized cooperatives were there because they wanted to join.

The specialized cooperatives were more actively involved in the free market than the groundnut cooperatives where the distribution of seed, fertilizer, and other inputs and sale of groundnuts were carefully regulated by the state. Coop agents have often demonstrated considerable entrepreneurial skills in organizing and promoting the expansion of the specialized cooperative sectors. However, these same agents frequently expect the state to provide their clientele with an edge over their private sector competitors by offering subsidized inputs to coop members – e.g., subsidized cattle feed for herders, motors for the boats of fishermen, seed for potato and onion farmers. In some instances, people join the specialized coops to get access to subsidized inputs or easy credit with no real commitment to cooperative principles.[9]

Limited access to credit hindered the development of the specialized cooperatives in the past. Senegalese banks today are still reluctant to extend credit, thus placing greater pressure on the state to provide more credit. While credit subsidies provide some fortunate producers with inexpensive inputs and stimulate production, they also place heavy financial burdens on the state, foster corruption and favoritism, and promote distortions in the market. Hence, the government must exercise considerable discipline and proceed cautiously in offering credit and input subsidies in order to discourage the specialized cooperatives from falling into bad habits and their demise once the flow of easy credit and subsidies stops.

B. The Cooperative Service and the Rise of the Cooperative Unions

The dissolution of ONCAD in 1980 gave a new lease on life to the Cooperative Service and offered new opportunities for the Cooperative Movement to take over some of the economic middleman functions involved in distributing inputs and marketing groundnuts. It also marked an important step towards reducing the state's tutelage over the Cooperative Movement which had been one of the major objectives of *Circulaire 32*. It envisaged the vertical integration of the Cooperative Movement through cooperative unions which were eventually to take over the tasks performed by various state agencies. While local, departmental, and regional cooperative unions existed during the 1960s and 1970s, they had remained largely inactive. State agencies like ONCAD owned and managed nearly all of the Cooperative Movement's infrastructure and equipment and provided most of the services. The economic initiative of the unions had been stifled by the blocking of funds in the Cooperative Movement's BNDS account which had been originally set aside for the Cooperative Development Fund (Beaudry-Somcynsky, 1981).

On May 13, 1978, the Senegalese government approved the creation of Senegal's first national cooperative union, the *Union Nationale des Coopératives Agricoles du Sénégal* (UNCAS). UNCAS and the cooperative unions became more vocal in their criticism of ONCAD and the state's rural credit policy. Besides giving a greater role to the existing cooperative unions following the demise of ONCAD in 1980, the government also promoted the establishment of other national cooperative unions such as the *Union Nationale des Coopératives d'Eleveurs* and the creation of a National Cooperative Federation to represent the entire Cooperative Movement.

The decision of the government to transfer certain tasks previously carried out by ONCAD to the cooperative unions meant a greater role for the Cooperative Service. The Cooperative Service, now an autonomous division within the Ministry of Rural Development, welcomed this new development for several reasons. First, the expansion of the role of the cooperative unions gave the Cooperative Service the opportunity to expand its own activities in an area which was not contested by the RDAs or other state agencies. Second, the fact that UNCAS and the regional unions assumed part of the costs of supporting personnel from the Cooperative Service assigned to the cooperative unions meant less pressure on its own budget and greater logistical support for coop agents working in the field. Third, the assignment of coop agents to the unions and the assumption of some of their support costs by the unions offered tangible evidence the Cooperative Movement was at last moving in the direction called for in *Circulaire 32*. For its part, the Cooperative Service provided the regional unions with office space, office furniture and materials, and vehicles inherited from ONCAD.

Cooperative officials hope that the cooperative unions will eventually become strong enough financially to pay the salaries of coop agents working directly for the Cooperative Movement. This would be made possible from profits generated by the cooperative sector in a wide range of economic activities – marketing, transport, consumer goods distribution, etc. – previously dominated by the state and the private sector. The absorption of the Cooperative Service by the cooperative unions ideally would be beneficial for both the Cooperative Service and the state. It would be good for the Cooperative Service because coop agents could work directly for the Cooperative Movement and not have to worry about interservice rivalries, jurisdictional disputes, and competing for scarce state funds. It would be good for the state because the state would no longer have to bear the costs of supporting the Cooperative Service. However, such an evolution is unlikely to take place in the near future for several reasons: (1) given its current financial situation, the state is not about to transfer more resources to the cooperative unions; (2) control over most middleman functions previously handled by ONCAD has been turned over to the groundnut oil factories, thus depriving the Cooperative Movement of potential profits generated by the groundnut trade; and (3) given their current mode of operations and scale of activities, the cooperative unions will not be able to generate the resources needed to sustain large numbers of cooperative agents.

Because they are obliged to work closely with the notables now controlling the cooperative unions, Cooperative Service officials have to be sensitive to the leadership's concerns and choices about the allocation of resources. Officials attached to the UNCAS and the cooperative unions often find themselves in a delicate position. On the one hand, they are there to insure the smooth functioning of the unions and to prevent the misuse of cooperative resources. On the other hand, they have little authority to overrule questionable decisions made by the powerful notables dominating the national and regional unions.

C. The Cooperative Service and the Devolution of Middleman Functions to the Cooperative Movement

Although the cooperatives were authorized to sell groundnuts directly to the crushing industries, relatively few of the other middleman functions in the groundnut *filière* have devolved to the Cooperative Movement since the demise of ONCAD. Government plans to give the village sections the major responsibility in the area of groundnut seed management have not yet materialized. During the early 1980s, this task of collecting and storing groundnut seed was carried out by the *Société Nationale d'Approvisionnement du Monde Rural* (SONAR) which was established in 1980 to replace ONCAD. In 1984 the government announced plans to phase out SONAR in 1985 and turn over distribution of the seed stock to the crushing industries (A.B. Diop: 1984). It is possible, in the future, that village sections will assume more responsibility for storing and managing groundnut seeds.[10]

While the Cooperative Service has devoted much of its energies towards promoting the cooperative unions and specialized coop sectors since the abolition of ONCAD, it still remains actively involved in the affairs of the groundnut marketing cooperatives. Each year coop agents organize seminars for officers, weighers, officials from the *Contrôle Economique*, and representatives from the crushing industry to explain the rules of the game for the coming marketing season. The Cooperative Service also intervenes frequently to provide technical advice to the cooperatives and crushing firms in drawing up contracts and in arbitrating disputes between the cooperatives and the various actors involved in groundnut trade. Disputes usually revolve around the relative responsibility of different actors in bearing the costs of losses in storage, weighing, and transportation. Coop members have complained about the alleged collusion of groundnut oil factory officials and the transporters in cheating the cooperatives by making them pay for weight losses incurred en route to the factories. Cheating on weight had been one of the major causes of the loss of peasant confidence in cooperatives and the groundnut marketing system during the ONCAD era (Belloncle, 1980c). In 1983, the government defused the issue by turning over full responsibility for paying, training, and supervising the weighers to the factories, which had to absorb the losses if the weighers did not do their job properly and control for impurities.

D. Political Decentralization and the Development Cooperative

The original blueprint for a decentralized communitarian socialist society formulated during the early 1960s called for the establishment of *Communautés Rurales* as the basic unit of government in the countryside. Each *Communauté Rurale* was to have its own multifunctional 'development cooperative,' which would be a federation of all its smaller cooperative units. The seat of the *Communauté Rurale* would be the main center for providing social services for the villages within the boundaries of the *Communauté Rurale* and contain the economic infrastructure – scales, trucks, seed and equipment storage facilities, wholesale consumer goods outlets, etc. – needed to support the development cooperative's multifunctional activities.

The *Réforme Administrative* of July 1972 set the legal stage for establishing *Communautés Rurales* throughout rural Senegal (Gellar, 1982: 38–42). Between 1974 and 1982, the Senegalese government set up 314 *Communautés Rurales* in the country, about three to four *Communautés Rurales* for each of Senegal's 85 *arrondissements*. Each *Communauté Rurale* had a Rural Council which was granted broad powers to regulate local markets, allocate uncultivated land, and revise existing land tenure systems. One third of the members of the Rural Council were chosen by the cooperatives in the *Communauté Rurale* and the other two-thirds by universal suffrage. The important cooperative representation in the Rural Council was intended to reflect their key role in the rural economy. Although a step in the direction towards political decentralization, the *Communautés Rurales* during the early 1980s still remained very much under the tutelage of the sous-préfêt who maintained tight control over the budget.

The 1983 Cooperative Statutes provided the legal basis for establishing development cooperatives at the *Communauté Rurale* level. Although designated as the central economic institution of the *Communauté Rurale*, it is still not clear what new economic functions the development cooperatives will be carrying out in the near future. In addition to serving as the primary marketing stations for the village sections in their area, they might also set up local savings and credit unions and become important centers for cooperative training and education, seed management, distribution of consumer goods, repair of agricultural equipment, and other cooperative services. During the early 1980s, the local cooperative unions organized at the *arrondissement* level aspired to carry out many of the multisectoral and multifunctional activities now being earmarked for the development cooperatives. The future division of labor between the development cooperatives and other echelons of the Cooperative Movement still has to be worked out.

E. Role of the Cooperative Service and the RDAs in Servicing the Cooperative Movement

Despite the fact that the reform of the Cooperative Movement was to be built around village sections, the Cooperative Service had little to do with organizing village sections until the second half of 1983. During the early 1980s, SODEVA was responsible for organizing village sections in the groundnut basin. The Cooperative Service opposed SODEVA's growing involvement since this raised the fear that many coop agents would be assigned to SODEVA, a larger and more powerful agency, while the Cooperative Service itself would again lack the means to fully assume its responsibilities. Most Cooperative Service officials did not see SODEVA as a populist reformist agency; instead, they saw SODEVA as usurping the role of the Cooperative Service in order to use the village sections to achieve its own productionist objectives.

Outside the groundnut basin, other RDAs organized *Groupements de Producteurs* to implement their extension programs (Gellar, 1983: 51–53). The Cooperative Service had little contact with the *groupements* since they had no formal links to the Cooperative Movement and were not regulated by its statutes. While granting legal status and financial autonomy to village sections, the 1983 statutes did not give similar privileges to the *groupements* under the tutelage of the RDAs or to independent village-based peasant associations because these groups were not part of the Cooperative Movement. With the creation of some 4,200 sections throughout the country, the Cooperative Service now has a presence in most of the villages serviced by the RDAs and organized into *groupements*. The Cooperative Service would like to see the *groupements* become part of the cooperative structure by joining village sections while the RDAs want to retain the *groupement* structure which is more conducive to promoting their more production-oriented goals. As to the peasants, it is in their interest for their village-based associations whether formally linked to the Cooperative Movement or not to have financial autonomy and direct access to credit without having to go through a higher cooperative unit or an RDA.[11]

F. The Cooperative Service and Cooperative Education and Training

During the ONCAD era, cooperative education and training had been limited primarily to the presidents and weighers of the groundnut marketing cooperatives, with little attention paid to providing the rank and file with the skills they needed to control and manage cooperative affairs without constant supervision. In 1981 the Cooperative Service announced a new cooperative training policy which articulated a strategy for preparing the Cooperative Movement to assume greater responsibility in managing its own affairs (Direction de la Coopération: 1981a). The creation of village sections as the grassroots unit of the Cooperative Movement meant that the section would become an important focus for cooperative training. During a first phase, cooperative training would be directed toward the secretary of the section and section officers. Later, efforts would be made to reach the rank and file through functional literacy programs in regional languages. In addition to promoting literacy, these programs would also develop simple accounting documents in local languages to enable the peasants to understand and monitor individual and cooperative transactions.

During the early 1980s, the Cooperative Service could do little to implement this policy because of the hold of SODEVA and other RDAs over functional literacy programs at the village level. As a result, the Cooperative Service concentrated its educational and training programs on three other target groups: (1) officers and managers of the rural cooperatives; (2) officers of the cooperative unions and managers of different cooperative union activities; and (3) officials from the Cooperative Service. To date, the Co-operative Service has probably given its greatest attention to up-grading the training of its own officials to prepare them for their expanded educational and training role. The Cooperative Service conducted several seminars throughout the country in 1982 and 1983 for coop agents to explain the new cooperative education policy and to provide them with guidelines and methodological training to carry out their new duties. Plans are now being made to provide advanced specialized training for coop agents in market-ing, transport, and other skills needed to manage larger-scale cooperative enterprises and to upgrade the management skills of higher coop officials, thanks to improvements in ENEA's Co-operative College curriculum.

One of the main issues to be resolved is the content of functional literacy programs to be provided for the village sections. While the Cooperative Service and the RDAs agree on the necessity for such programs, inter-service rivalries have prevented them from work-ing out a collaborative program. The RDAs developed their own functional literacy programs independently of the Cooperative Service. SODEVA, for example, in organizing village sections in the groundnut basin developed its own 'auto encadrement' strategy. This entailed setting up functional literacy centers and providing literacy and numeracy training to the *paysans relais* named by the sections to serve as intermediaries between SODEVA and the villages. The *paysans relais* were an updated version of the village *animateurs* promoted by *Animation Rurale* during the 1960s (Gellar, 1980). In principle, the *paysans relais* expressed the section's felt needs and development priorities to SODEVA which in turn used them to transmit information and technical advice back to the villages. Other RDAs have set up their own functional literacy programs in the areas under their jurisdiction. Perhaps the most effective one has been that run by SODEFITEX in Eastern Senegal and the Upper Casamance which emulated successful functional literacy programs undertaken in cotton producing areas in Mali. There is clearly a need to integrate the functional literacy strategy of the RDAs which promotes the diffusion of technological innovations with that of the Cooperative Service which is geared more towards providing peasant skills in cooperative governance and management.

III. INCREASING GRASSROOTS PARTICIPATION AND CONTROL OVER THE COOPERATIVES

Two major issues confronting Cooperatives in the 1980s concern the extent to which the reforms recently initiated by the Senegalese government will: (1) restore peasant confidence and promote greater rural participation; and (2) put more political and economic power in the hands of the peasantry by giving them greater control over cooperative institutions.

During the ONCAD era, Cooperatives were largely an instrument of state economic policy. Unpopular economic policies alienated the peasantry and discouraged active participation. Moreover, participation was generally limited to male heads of households while major decisions within the cooperatives were usually made by a small number of rural notables, religious leaders, and local politicians. Most functions usually associated with cooperatives were, in fact, carried out by state officials.

During the 1980s, it became increasingly clear that the Senegalese government could not implement a successful rural development program without greater support and participation from the rural populations. It became equally clear that the government had to put more political and economic power in their hands if it were to carry out its official political and ideological commitment to building a decentralized communitarian socialist society around the Cooperative Movement.

A. Leadership and Participation in the Cooperative Movement: Old Wine in New Bottles?

Before the cooperative reforms of the 1980s, leadership and participation came largely from the groundnut marketing cooperatives. Nearly 85 percent of the total membership were members of groundnut cooperatives and more than 70 percent of the groundnut cooperative membership was concentrated in the four regions constituting the groundnut basin – Sine-Saloum, Thiès, Diourbel, and Louga. Given these numbers, it is not surprising that the main leadership of the Cooperative Movement has come from the groundnut cooperatives. Mbole N'Diaye, the first president of the *Fédération Nationale des Coopératives du Sénégal*, which was established in early 1983 to represent all cooperative sectors, was a Wolof groundnut farmer from the Sine-Saloum.[12]

The predominance of the groundnut cooperatives, the predominance of the groundnut basin cooperatives among the groundnut marketing cooperatives, and the preeminence of the Wolof within the groundnut basin groundnut cooperative leadership affected the style and character of the Cooperative Movement in several ways: (1) governance and relationships with the state tended to be highly politicized and built on patron-client relationships paralleling those in the political arena; (2) the cooperatives tended to be dominated by rural notables and religious leaders; (3) the Cooperative Movement was more concerned with issues related to the functioning of the groundnut ' *traite*' – e.g., groundnut prices, the number and location of collection centers – than with broader development issues.

The dominance of the groundnut basin and the Wolof in the Cooperative Movement has meant that the populations of the so-called peripheral regions – Casamance, Eastern Senegal, and the Fleuve – have remained largely outside its mainstream. Until recently, the RDAs working in these regions in organizing irrigated perimeter and village-based producer groups have kept these groups outside the formal cooperative structures. However, the passage of the 1983 Cooperative Statutes and the recent establishment of village sections throughout the country may change past patterns of participation by bringing the populations of the peripheral regions into the system. In time, this could eventually reduce the now predominant influence of the groundnut cooperatives.

It is interesting to note that the Senegalese government promoted the revitalization of the local and regional cooperative unions and the establishment of a National Cooperative Federation *before* establishing the village sections and development cooperatives at the community level. As a result, the top leadership of the Cooperative Movement during the early 1980s was closely identified with the discredited cooperative system of the past. The *Fédération Nationale des Coopératives du Sénégal* held its first congress in Thiès on January 29 and 30, 1983, less than a month before Senegal's national presidential and legislative elections. Although purporting to represent the entire Cooperative Movement, the Congress was hastily prepared and largely the affair of the notables dominating their respective cooperative sectors rather than an emanation from the grassroots. In addressing the Congress, the Rural Development Minister expressed the wish that 'conflicts of interest would give way to the will to promote the most capable' in choosing the Federation's officers (S. Diop, 1983). Because of the highly charged political atmosphere, the Federation did not name a president until several months later.

While the higher echelons of the Cooperative Movement are still dominated by the old-line rural notables, the establishment of village sections and development cooperatives at the *Communautés Rurales* level may be laying the foundation for greater grassroots control over the leadership. Village sections were thus established before the *Communauté Rurale*-based development cooperatives in order to give the sections the opportunity to choose their representatives in the General Assembly of the development cooperative.

B. Broadening Participation: The Role of Women and Youth

Cooperatives in Senegal have traditionally been male-dominated and membership largely restricted to established male heads of households. Although a vital part of the production process, women and unmarried youth have been left out because social organization within the cooperatives reflected traditional decision-making structures. Rather than integrating women and youth into the Cooperative Movement, the government has organized parallel women's and youth groups which are serviced by neither the RDAs nor the Cooperative Service but by other state agencies – e.g., GOPEC, *Animation Féminine*, etc. – most of which are under the jurisdiction of the Ministry of Social Affairs.

While having the legal right to join and participate fully in cooperative affairs, women and unmarried males over twenty-one have rarely exercised these rights.[13] Even in the Casamance where women have been far more 'liberated,' they constitute only 5 percent of the membership. Because unmarried men and adult women rarely joined the cooperatives, they had no direct access to state rural credit and had to depend upon the male household head to which they belonged to furnish them with seed, fertilizer, and other inputs. Since the interests, needs, and obligations of the male household heads, on the one hand, and those of the unmarried males and women often did not coincide, the lack of participation of the latter in cooperative decision-making undermined household solidarity and fostered widely diverging individual economic strategies, changes in the division of labor between the sexes, and a growing generation gap. The creation of new cooperative units – the village sections – could broaden popular participation in the CM and make it more responsive to the needs of women and youth.

It is still too early to determine the extent to which the traditional gerontocratic male village leadership will accept a more active role in cooperative affairs and governance for women, unmarried males, and youth. However, it seems clear that failure to move in this direction will stifle the revitalization of the Cooperative Movement.

C. Independent Peasant-Based Associations: Alternative to the Cooperative Movement?

During the 1970s and early 1980s, a number of independent peasant-based organizations emerged throughout Senegal that wished to organize their own development programs without submitting to the tutelage of the RDAs or affiliating with the Cooperative Movement.[14] Many of these were youth-oriented groups having the blessing and support of their elders. These associations provided outlets for the energies of youth which had little representation in the Cooperative Movement. Women's groups have also increased in numbers and have been involved in a wide range of economic activities – e.g. sheep fattening, vegetable gardens, tie-dying, etc.

The independent peasant associations often had much more in common with the self-governing multifunctional cooperatives envisaged by Senegal's communitarian socialist theorists than either the *groupements* organized by the RDAs or the cooperatives in the groundnut basin. First of all, these groups emerged as a result of grassroots rather than state initiatives. Second, they were not dominated by powerful notables and religious leaders. Third, they were more attuned to the needs and wishes of youth and women who were given a larger voice in decision-making. Fourth, they were concerned with more than just increasing production and marketing crops; they also promoted social projects to improve the quality of life in their villages. Fifth, these peasant associations raised their own capital by collecting dues from their members, reinvesting profits from group projects, and soliciting money from friends and relatives working in Dakar or in France. Sixth, rather than passively accepting the tutelage of the state, they actively negotiated the terms of their relationships with state agencies and vigorously solicited non-governmental organizations to provide financial and technical assistance.

It will be interesting to see whether the independent associations will affiliate with the Cooperative Movement or continue their present status. Their affiliation with the Cooperative Movement could broaden participation, stimulate the further democratization of the Cooperative Movement, and provide new sources of leadership to challenge the old guard Cooperative Movement leadership.

D. Preconditions for Autogestion and Grassroots Control over the Cooperative Movement

Although the Cooperative Movement in Senegal today still bears little resemblance to the system described in *Circulaire 32*, there are promising signs that one may soon see significant progress towards greater grassroots control. The 1983 Cooperative Statutes, the establishment of village sections, and government policies to reduce the tutelage of the state over rural institutions have set the stage for cooperative reform. If these reforms are to succeed, then four important preconditions must be met: (1) the base – i.e., the village sections – must control the higher echelons of the Cooperative Movement; (2) the Cooperative Service, RDAs, CERs and other state agencies working with the rural populations must permit the local populations to take more initiative in setting rural development and cooperative priorities; (3) functional literacy and numeracy programs must be generalized as quickly as possible to give peasants the tools they need to control and manage cooperative affairs; and (4) the Cooperative Movement must reduce its financial dependency on the state by generating more capital through its own economic activities.

The establishment of sections having their own legal status and financial autonomy provides smaller units of population far more control over their own affairs than in the past. The sections send representatives to the General Assembly of the development cooperatives at the Rural Community level. In principle, this promotes grassroots control over the development cooperatives which in turn send representatives to the higher echelons of the Cooperative Movement. It is still too early to determine whether the sections will change the current leadership structure emanating from the older, highly politicized intervillage cooperatives.

While the government, RDAs, the Cooperative Service, and other state development agencies have clearly moved to become more responsive to the wishes of the local populations, the fact still remains that the state services generally expect the 'dialogue' to lead to popular acceptance of state initiated policies rather than revisions in policy to more accurately reflect the priorities of the people.

Government policy has recently obliged the Cooperative Service with its limited resources to organize more than 4,200 sections in a two month period throughout the country during a period of intense agricultural activity. This massive mobilization could hardly have left much time for a 'dialogue' between coop agents and villagers concerning all the ramifications of the cooperative reforms. The entire country is now organized into sections not because of any massive demand from below to establish them but because of a government decision to create sections and development co-operatives before the beginning of the 1983–84 marketing season. It might have been more prudent for the Cooperative Service to establish a limited number of sections on an experimental basis. To provide training for the officers and managers for sections is a monumental task. Moreover, the existence of 4,200 sections on paper does not mean that all these sections will function as they are supposed, or that the entire countryside is now firmly committed to the Cooperative Movement, since it is not clear whether villages had the option not to belong to a section.

Effective functional literacy and numeracy programs are vital ingredients needed to insure greater grassroots control over cooperative transactions and self-management. Cooperative specialists have already formulated effective methodologies for organizing functional literacy progams and developed materials in Senegal's national languages which simplify existing cooperative documents and accounting records to make them more accessible to the people (Belloncle, 1980a; P. Sene, 1982). Given the current financial situation of the state, the most likely source for development of functional literacy programs in the near future will come from external donors. A good test of the level of peasant commitment to the literacy programs will be reflected in the extent to which the Cooperative and local communities will be willing to make some contribution in cash or kind to support them.

To reduce its financial dependency upon the state, the Cooperative Movement will need to generate more internal resources. At present, the Cooperative Movement's main source of revenue is the one CFA per kilo marketing levy on the groundnut crop.[15] In

1982–83 the levy was approximately 800 million CFA; for 1983–84 the revenue was substantially lower because of a mediocre groundnut crop. At any rate, the revenues derived from groundnut marketing fall far short of meeting the Cooperative Movement's growing needs. As private traders once again legally compete in the marketing process, the levy may drop even further.

There are several ways in which the Cooperative Movement could raise capital to finance cooperative projects: (1) raise the marketing levy on the groundnut crop; (2) increase the rebates by withholding a larger percentage of the producer's price at marketing time and using the rebates for collective projects; (3) profits earned from buying and storing food crops which can be resold or lent out to coop members in the form of food loans; (4) profits generated from the sale of consumer goods by the coop consumer stores; (5) profits earned from cooperative seed management; (6) profits from processing agricultural products; and, (7) revenues generated from collective fields and the earnings of collective work groups.[16]

Most of the methods cited above for raising capital call upon the Cooperative Movement to generate resources from activities whose benefits previously went to the state or to the private sector. Without its own independent sources of capital, the Cooperative Movement will continue to remain heavily dependent upon the state.

An important issue that is likely to become more acute in the future concerns the relative weight of the different echelons of the cooperative system in generating, controlling, and allocating cooperative resources. Partisans of a grassroots-oriented cooperative development strategy want most cooperative projects to take place at the village level and the village sections to have more autonomy vis-à-vis the higher echelons of the Cooperative Movement in making resource allocation decisions affecting their villages.[17] Concentrating most resources at the village section level could, however, limit the Cooperative Movement to small scale projects and block the vertical integration needed to build a strong national cooperative sector. On the other hand, concentrating too much control over cooperative resources in the cooperative unions risks losing grassroots support and participation, especially if the rural notables now heading the cooperative unions mismanage funds and divert them to their own personal use.

IV. CONCLUSIONS: PROSPECTS FOR REVITALIZING THE COOPERATIVE MOVEMENT

Since 1980, there have been several signs of a serious commitment on the part of the Senegalese government to rural reform and revitalization of the Cooperative Movement along the lines recommended in *Circulaire 32*. These include the passage of the 1983 Cooperative Statutes, stepped up efforts to organize and provide funding for local, regional, and national cooperative unions, the creation of village sections and development cooperatives at the Rural Community level, the expansion of functional literacy programs, a greater emphasis on developing the non-groundnut cooperatives, and a less paternalistic attitude of the Cooperative Service, the RDAs, and other state rural development agencies towards the peasantry.

Despite these positive signs, efforts to implement a coherent cooperative policy have been hindered by several factors: (1) past delays in passing legislation and implementation decrees needed to clarify the legal status of the Cooperative Movement and its constituent elements, a problem which now seems to be in the process of resolution since the establishment of the village sections and development cooperatives; (2) insufficient financial and logistical resources to implement programs properly. Because of government austerity measures which have cut operating budgets to the bone, the Cooperative Service, RDAs, and other state agencies lack the means to carry out their missions; (3) inconsistencies and frequent changes in state agricultural, pricing, and rural credit policies. Electoral promises, interest group politics, battles within government over policy, and donor pressures provide much of the explanation for these inconsistencies. Unkept promises and sudden changes in policy detrimental to the interests of the peasantry run the risk of undermining popular confidence in the government's rural reform programs;[18] and, (4) donor pressures that have pushed the government to take unpopular measures and change policies designed to win popular support for government reform programs.

In some areas, the government may be moving too rapidly in its efforts to revitalize the Cooperative Movement. More than 4,200 sections and 345 development cooperatives were organized in great haste in 1983 by the Cooperative Service according to overly mechanical guidelines laid down by the Rural Development Ministry which did not necessarily fit local conditions everywhere.

This kind of top-down approach could lead to a repeat of the situation during the 1960s and 1970s when there were hundreds of '*coopératives sans coopérateurs.*'

Further progress towards revitalization of the Cooperative Movement will depend largely on the following key factors: (1) restoration of the peasantry's confidence in the cooperative system by demonstrating that participation will provide tangible material benefits and improvements in living standards and giving the rural populations direct control over cooperative institutions; (2) consistent and coherent state rural credit, pricing, and marketing policies providing greater incentives for peasants to increase production and market more of their production through formal channels; (3) stepped up financial, logistical, and pedagogical support to carry out the functional literacy and cooperative management programs needed to provide peasants and coop managers with the skills they need to make the cooperatives work; (4) expansion of the capacity of the Cooperative Movement to generate its own capital for financing its cooperative activities; and, (5) greater donor comprehension of political, social, and economic constraints on Senegalese policy-makers and willingness to provide more financial aid to support the kinds of policies and programs they have encouraged the Senegalese government to adopt.

NOTES

1. For a detailed history of the cooperative movement in the West and attempts to establish them in the Third World, see (Desroches: 1976).
2. This formulation was by no means unique to Senegal. Other Francophone states – Mali, Niger, and Upper Volta – also promoted cooperative movements on this basis (Belloncle and Gentil: 1983) as did Tanzania (Nyerere: 1968).
3. During the mid-1930s, there were approximately 175 collecting stations in Senegal for the peanut crop. One of the most pressing peasant demands during the post-war period were requests for more peanut collecting stations to reduce the transportation costs for peasants having to bring their crops to distant *seccos*. By independence the number had climbed to 300. Merchants operating out of small urban peanut trading centers (*escales*) opposed the proliferation of collecting stations because it sharply reduced their volume of business. On the other hand, many peasants gained an extra .3 to .5 CFA per kilo (Vanhaeverbeke: 1970, 204) thanks to the establishment of hundreds of new peanut collecting centers created by the expansion of the CM.
4. For a detailed discussion of Senegal's development strategy and the formulation of Senegal's First Plan, see (Gellar, 1967: 229–262).
5. One of the main reasons underlying this policy was the desire of the regime to regain some of the popular support that it had lost during the late 1970s. With the increase in competitive party politics, the regime stepped up its efforts to woo the support of the rural populations.
6. SONAR was eliminated in 1985. In reaction to the small volume of peanuts marketed through official channels during the 1984–85 season – less then 200,000 tons – the

government decided to end its practice of distributing all the groundnut seed in advance. For the 1985–86 season, the government declared that it would distribute only 60,000 tons of seeds in advance and only to those producers who marketed their crops through regular channels at the official price during the 1984–85 season. Another 40,000 tons would be sold on a cash basis.

7. For a more detailed discussion of the 1983 Cooperative Statutes, see (Gellar, October 1983: 7–12).

8. These funds were disbursed rather loosely during the 1982–83 season, a period of intense electoral campaign activity in the country.

9. For example, maritime fishing cooperatives are extremely popular in Senegal because members can buy motors at highly subsidized prices less than half the retail price. In 1983 the government offered Yamaha motors to the coops at less than cost. The demand for the motors of course quickly outstripped the supply.

10. Since independence, Senegalese groundnut farmers have become more dependent on groundnut seed loans from the government than they were during the colonial era. Instead of being used for planting, the groundnuts are often resold in the so-called *petite traite*. Non collection of groundnut seed debts has also been one of the major causes of state deficits in its involvement in the *filière arachidière* during the late 1970s and early 1980s.

11. In April 1984, the National Assembly passed a law permitting small groups to organize themselves as financially autonomous legal entities (*groupements d'intérêt économique*). This means that small peasant-based groups (three or more members) can have direct access to credit without having to pass through either the Cooperative Movement or the RDAs.

12. In 1984 the government removed Mbole N'diaye from the presidency of the National Cooperative Federation because he appeared to be linked to the disappearance of large amounts of cooperative funds for which he was responsible. Another prominent peanut farmer from the peanut basin was chosen to take his place. Throughout its history, the Senegalese CM has been plagued by embezzlement and misuse of funds by cooperative officers who often went unpunished or received light punishment because of their political connections. The capture of rural notables and local politicians of course is a widespread phenomenon throughout Africa. For example, see (Hyden: 1973; Young, Sherman, and Rose: 1981; UNRISD: 1975; and Heyer, Roberts, and Williams: 1981).

13. Provisions in the 1983 Cooperative Statutes permitted young men and women under 21 to join and participate in the life of the cooperative. Although not given voting privileges, young people could attend the deliberations of the General Assembly and internal committee. They also had the possibility of setting up their own sub-groups and committees within the section.

14. For example, two of the best known independent peasant associations in Senegal are the *Foyer des Jeunes de Ronkh* headed by a dynamic former school teacher who patiently organized groups in the Senegal River Delta (A. Diop, 1982) and the Federation of Bakel which for many years opposed SAED's irrigation programs in the Senegal River Valley (Adams, Adrian, 1977; and Aprin, 1980). Independent peasant-based associations have also been proliferating in the Casamance.

15. One problem with the *marge de commercialisation* or marketing levy is its instability because of fluctuations in weather and the size of the peanut crop. During a poor harvest year, cooperative receipts can drop drastically and play havoc with cooperative union budgets and local cooperative projects. The other problem is that the *marge* has often been blocked in the past by the government and more recently by SONOCOS.

16. For an excellent and detailed discussion of different ways of financing cooperatives, see (Belloncle and Diarra, 1983).

17. While it is true that village sections are more likely to be responsive to the wishes of their membership than the higher echelons of the Cooperative Movement, the village is not always the model of peasant democracy, unity, and probity often depicted by supporters of bottom-up cooperative development. Villages can also suffer from factionalism,

poor leadership, corruption, and other problems that have plagued big intra-village cooperatives in the past.

18. The 1983 shift in seed policy is a case in point. After first encouraging groundnut producers to keep part of their crops for seed and promising to pay 80 CFA a kilo to those that did, the government suddenly reversed its decision a few months later and urged farmers to sell all their groundnuts at 60 CFA per kilo. Many groundnut farmers who complied with the government's policies found themselves short of seed for the 1983–84 season while non-groundnut producers were often able to obtain seed at distribution time even though not farmers. Shifts like this do not build peasant confidence in the government's promises.

CHAPTER FIVE

Financial Markets in Rural Senegal

Laura Tuck

I. INTRODUCTION

Various types of financial services have always been available to farmers in Senegal from local, informal sources. Policy-makers, however, have commonly charged that these services are not consistent with those which farmers need if they are to undertake intensive agricultural development. As a consequence, the Senegalese government has implemented formal credit programs in an attempt to provide more appropriate services.

These formal programs, however, have not been without their own deficiencies and problems, and after 20 years of extensive government intervention in the financial markets, the flow of credit through public programs has almost completely ceased. While several small programs remain in operation, the informal market has again become the primary source of financial services for farmers. As before, these informal services are accused of being inadequate and there are new plans for formal intervention.

It may be true that informal markets do not currently provide all financial services of potential benefit to Senegalese farmers. It may also be true that informal markets are unlikely to ever provide adequate services for accelerated agricultural development. The formal programs implemented in Senegal, however, have not been entirely adequate either. Moreover, the government has not been able to sustain viable programs for the services that it has provided.

This chapter evaluates the success of government intervention in providing financial services to the agricultural sector. Both the ability of the programs to meet farmers' needs and the operational efficiency of the programs will be considered.

II. DESCRIPTION OF THE GOVERNMENT CREDIT
PROGRAMS

The French colonial government in Senegal engaged in various types of financial arrangements with Senegalese farmers; however, most important public programs were introduced after Independence. At that time, the new Administration began a serious campaign to increase agricultural production. One major component of this effort was the creation of Regional Development Agencies (RDAs) to provide agricultural extension services in virtually every region of the country. Another important initiative was the establishment of programs to make inputs such as seeds, pesticides, fertilizers and farm equipment available to farmers on credit, and to provide marketing services for the cooperatives (on cooperatives see Gellar; and Tignor; in this volume).

To accomplish these objectives, the government created an institution called the *Office National pour la Coopération et l'Assistance au Développement* (ONCAD – when it was created in 1960, it was initially called the *Office de Commercialisation Agricole* and was transformed into ONCAD in 1966 with only minor functional changes) which was endowed with comprehensive authority. In advance of the growing season, ONCAD's responsibilities included the assessment of farmers' needs for inputs, the procurement of these inputs from local factories and seed multiplication farms, and the distribution of inputs to the farmers. Following the harvest, it was responsible for the collection of payment for the inputs, the purchase of the crop output from the farmers and the transportation of the production to the local processing factories. In most regions, the relevant RDA acted as an intermediary between ONCAD and the cooperatives for one or more of these functions, or assumed the responsibilities directly itself.

All of these packaged services provided by ONCAD and the RDAs were characterized by centralized decision-making pertaining to the selection of inputs, and the timing and pattern of input distribution. All of the programs supplied seeds and fertilizers of varying types. They all offered the farm equipment that had been deemed appropriate by the government for that particular crop and/or region. Until 1979, most of the programs distributed food, primarily cereal grains, on a credit basis during the *soudure*, or hungry season.

The items ONCAD and the RDAs selected for sale were distributed at the onset of the growing season. Payment for seeds, fertilizers, fungicides, and food was required at the end of each growing season, approximately six months later. Farmers could amortize equipment purchases over a five to seven year period, with equal installments due each year after harvest. ONCAD collected payment for the inputs, theoretically, by deducting their cost from the revenues due the farmers for their output after the harvest. Hence, credit was an integral element of the government programs; however, it was only available via these in-kind distributions of farm inputs. No credit could be obtained directly in the form of cash.

Credit was tied to the consumption of specific inputs because policy-makers assumed that farmers would not otherwise make appropriate purchases. This presumption prevailed despite the fact that advice and training were available to farmers from the extension agents operating throughout the regions. Policy-makers further assumed that farmers would make proper use of the inputs once they were distributed.

Interest rate policy varied across the different programs. The groundnut seeds distributed through the *Programme Agricole*[1] cost a flat 25 percent of the amount borrowed in interest. Since the duration of these loans was only six months, this corresponded to an annual interest rate of approximately 45 percent, calculated on the basis of continuous compounding. It is interesting to note that this is roughly equal to the average interest rate on informal loans in-kind which the government has generally called usurious (see Tuck's Appendix to Waterbury in this volume). Though high, this rate was subsidized since the revenues generated from the interest charges were still insufficient to cover the operating costs of the program.

Interest rates on other credit extended through the *Programme Agricole* (for fertilizers, food, and equipment) were based on a fixed markup over the preferential discount rate at the Central Bank. Programs such as SAED and SODEFITEX did not charge interest on their credit sales.

Farmers responded to the inducements offered by the programs and absorbed quantities of specified inputs at an unprecedented rate. For the *Programme Agricole* alone, the increase in annual input distributions for the years of the program relative to the years that had preceded it was striking (see Table 1). Similar increases in distributions by other programs were also recorded.

Despite the large increases in the amount of inputs obtained by the farmers, it is not clear whether crop production actually rose.

TABLE 1

Average Annual Distribution of Farm Inputs

	Fertilizer (tonnes)	Seeders (units)	Hoes (units)
Before the Program 1950–59	3,444	3,488	412
During the Program 1960–79	47,000	133,000	10,600

Source: DGPA.

However, an evaluation of the general agricultural packages is not intended here; the focus of this section is on the performance of the credit services integrated therein.

The credit components of the government programs never operated as policy-makers had intended. Inputs were frequently not used by the designated beneficiaries. When farmers became short of cash or food they would obtain credit in any form available. Often they would acquire more agricultural inputs than they wanted or needed. They would then sell them immediately for cash, at a discount, or post them as collateral to borrow cash or food from local merchants.

Furthermore, even when farmers kept the inputs they purchased, they would frequently use them for purposes other than those intended by the policy-makers. Horses and carts were often used as transportation for petty trade; and oxen, designated for animal traction, were often fattened and sold for meat. It was not uncommon to find farmers acquiring seeders through the program and dismantling them to use the handles to chase warthogs off their fields.

But the most important weakness of the credit program, the weakness that led to its ultimate demise, was that many farmers did not repay their debts. For the years between 1970 and 1980, the nationwide repayment rate for all inputs distributed under the auspices of the *Programme Agricole* averaged only 60 percent (see Table 2). Only for the credit extended by SODEFITEX did farmers consistently repay their loans.

As shown in Chart 1, repayment rates for the *Programme Agricole* generally varied with the level of groundnut production (the correlation between the two over the relevant period was 0.80). They rose in good years, although never enough to prevent a steady

TABLE 2

Repayment Rates
(percentage of amount due)

	BNDS	Seeds	Total
1970/71	48.6	34.5	37.3
1971/72	95.8	95.8	95.8
1972/73	50.5	44.3	45.7
1973/74	75.3	57.6	61.7
1974/75	80.0	92.7	90.2
1975/76	88.9	88.2	88.7
1976/77	82.5	72.3	75.2
1977/78	–	27.8	11.4
1978/79	54.7	62.1	63.1
1979/80	8.0	47.6	24.6
1980/81	–	–	–

Source: Debt and repayment data from BCEAO and BNDS; production data, DGPA.

CHART 1

Comparison of Repayment Rates and Groundnut Production
1970–1980

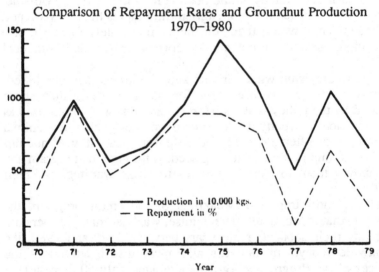

increase in arrears, and they fell in bad years. Even excluding the years of exceptionally poor production, however, the repayment rate was still declining over time, and the cumulative amount of debt past due rose at an average real growth rate of 10.7 percent per year over the decade of the 1970s.

For reasons which will be discussed in more detail below, the

TABLE 3
Debt Due as a Percentage of Groundnut Production

	BNDS Debt Due*	Seed Debt Due	Total Due
1970/71	7.1	28.6	35.7
1971/72	3.2	13.0	16.2
1972/73	7.7	25.2	32.9
1973/74	6.7	22.6	29.3
1974/75	3.5	14.8	18.3
1975/76	3.6	11.7	15.3
1976/77	6.4	16.3	22.7
1977/78	15.0	39.9	54.9
1978/79	10.1	20.7	30.9
1979/80	17.6	38.8	56.4
1980/81	28.5	75.7	104.2

Source: Debt data from BCEAO; production data, DGPA. Figures are cumulative, starting over with each annulment.
*BNDS debt included debt for fertilizer and equipment loans.

government not only tolerated these low repayment rates, but reduced or eliminated the amount of debt due after particularly bad years. 'Poor' harvests had become more common in the 1970s (in half of the years between 1970 and 1979 levels of groundnut production below 700,000 tons were recorded whereas none had been in the previous ten years), and on five occasions the government annulled some or all of the debt owed by the farmers.

In 1970/71 and 1972/73, two particularly bad years of drought, the government simply assumed all of the debt due that was left unpaid after the harvest (including arrears). In 1977/78, a different annulment technique was tried whereby the goverment reduced the debts of all farmers by a specified percentage equivalent to the percentage drop in crop production (a function of that year's deviation from some chosen mean) suffered by the entire region in which the farmers resided. In 1979/80 and 1980/81, the government returned to its previous policy of covering all of the post-harvest debt left unpaid.

Each annulment proved to be more expensive for the government than the one that preceded it. By late 1980, the amount of unpaid debt owed by the farmers for their agricultural inputs, excluding that which had been forgiven earlier, had climbed to approximately $30 billion CFA (over $100 million at the 1980 exchange rate). The government, suffering severe macroeconomic problems at the same time, could not sustain a program generating an increasing accounts receivable balance of that magnitude, particularly when the potential for ultimate collection appeared poor.

Therefore, in late 1980, the government again expunged the cooperative debts. But the cost of this annulment was so substantial, and the problems of the credit programs so intractable, that the entire credit program was cancelled along with the debts.

The 30 billion CFA of outstanding farm debt that was annulled was combined with the debts ONCAD itself owed to suppliers and other creditors. The bulk of this combined debt was rediscounted at preferential rates at the Central Bank with repayment spread over 15 years. By July 1982, the amount due had accumulated additional interest charges and was reported to total approximately 110 billion CFA (or almost $300 million dollars at 1982 exchange rates). This amount was equivalent to more than 13 percent of GDP in 1982 and almost 63 percent of the government's revenues from the preceding year. Clearly these circumstances have had serious consequences for Senegal's already precarious macroeconomic situation.

III. THE FARMERS' PERSPECTIVE: POTENTIAL BENEFITS FROM FINANCIAL MARKETS

To evaluate how well the formal programs in Senegal have met farmers' needs for financial services, the nature of the benefits that can be conferred by financial markets must be understood. This section, however, does not attempt to provide a complete discussion of the importance of financial intermediation (see, among others, McKinnon, 1973; and Ray, 1981). Nevertheless, this section

TABLE 4

Debt and Repayment Rates for Seed Loans
(tons of groundnut seed)

	Seed Distrib.	Principal + Interest	Arrears + Moratoria	Total Due	Repayment	Unpaid Due	Rmbt. Rate
1970/71	88,909	113,139	53,593	166,732	57,500	109,232	34.5
1971/72	101,350	128,296		128,296	122,970	5,326	95.8
1972/73	110,135	139,850	4,026	143,876	63,667	80,209	44.3
1973/74	117,119	148,760		148,760	85,700	63,060	57.6
1974/75	114,309	144,993		144,993	134,410	10,583	92.7
1975/76	134,486	168,107		168,107	148,353	19,754	88.2
1976/77	127,863	162,029	17,888	179,917	130,074	49,843	72.3
1977/78	124,751	157,803	44,916	202,719	31,858	170,861	27.8
1978/79	149,154	194,075	24,345	218,420	135,582	82,838	62.1
1979/80	125,160	156,450	132,027	288,477	43,989	244,488	47.6
1980/81	123,300	150,000	144,488	394,488	–	394,488	–

Source: BCEAO based on information from the BNDS and Ministry of Rural Development.

TABLE 5

Debt and Repayment Rates
(millions of CFA)

	Amount Due from this year	Amount Due from past years	Arrears	Total Due this year	Repayment	Unpaid Due	Rmbt. Rate
1970/71	327.7	366.6	107.1	801.5	389.8	411.7	48.6
1971/72	398.7	353.6	–(a)	752.3	721.8	305.0	95.8
1972/73	627.1	364.0	25.4	1,016.5	513.4	503.1	50.5
1973/74	860.7	444.0	–(b)	1,304.7	982.6	322.1	75.3
1974/75	580.9	500.9	360.0	1,441.8	1,153.5	288.3	80.0
1975/76	1,228.2	574.8	335.1	2,138.1	1,922.7	215.4	89.9
1976/77	2,088.5	663.6	176.1	2,928.2	2,417.0	511.0	82.5
1977/78	1,870.1	833.2	459.5	3,162.8	–	3,162.8	0
1978/79	2,720.7	1,190.8	541.7	4,453.1	2,491.0	2,024.0	54.7
1979/80	1,186.1	1,631.8	2,565.7	5,383.5	444.2	4,939.2	8.0
1980/81	2,500.0 (c)	–	4,939.2	7,439.2	–	–	–

Source: BCEAO

 (a) the amount left unpaid as of December 31, 1970 was covered by the GOS.

 (b) the amount outstanding as of December 31, 1972 was covered by the GOS.

 (c) fertilizer only.

does attempt to cover several aspects of financial markets that are particularly relevant for rural Senegal. Specifically, three inter-related uses of financial markets will be discussed very briefly: risk management, accumulation of wealth, and efficient allocation of resources. Each discussion will consider whether farmers in rural Senegal were able to use the formal services available to them for these purposes.

A. Risk Management

As suggested by Newbery and Stiglitz (1981), financial markets can reduce consumption risk as well as the risk of project failure. For a country such as Senegal, the following characteristics make consumption risk of particular concern.

(1) Rainfall varies widely and unpredictably from year to year; (2) the positive correlation between the amount of precipitation received and the yields for agricultural output in the same year is extremely high; (3) though declining as a share, agricultural production generates the major source of income for Senegal's rural sector inhabitants (70 percent of the national population); (4) these large fluctuations in rainfall induce large changes in rural income; (5) because insurance and financial markets are not available to

rural sector residents, these fluctuations in income can translate into sizable fluctuations in annual consumption.

Risk-averse farmers are more concerned with avoiding large fluctuations in their levels of consumption than in their total income flows. Since income equals consumption plus savings, farmers can reduce the variance in their consumption patterns by changing their year to year savings levels. Savings can even be negative, either through the depletion of reserves or borrowing.

This income averaging allows farmers to maintain a relatively stable pattern of consumption despite fluctuations in the amount of rainfall and consequent crop yields. If the resulting average level of consumption is too low (i.e., below subsistence), then some type of income transfer might be contemplated for periods of shortfall. This would raise the mean consumption level as well as reduce its variance. But the riskiness of consumption can be substantially mitigated through well developed financial markets without an income transfer.

For Senegalese farmers to shift adequate amounts of income intertemporally, however, assets of some kind (e.g., savings accounts) must be available for purchase during periods of liquidity. The assets must be relatively risk-free and preferably interest-bearing. It must be possible to liquidate them when cash is needed. Of course, the assets need not be strictly financial instruments such as savings accounts. However, holding financial assets is generally less costly and less risky than holding real assets, such as grain and livestock, unless the country is subject to high levels of inflation or radical changes in the price level.

While the ability to store wealth following years of good production is essential for the reduction of consumption risk, it must also be possible to borrow in order to supplement income when necessary. This is particularly important after several successive years of shortfall when individual farmers' reserves have been depleted.

The formal programs in Senegal did not make any savings opportunities available to farmers. Therefore, one of the two mechanisms for reducing consumption risk did not exist. To the extent that farmers could save on their own using instruments available on the informal market, this omission was not particularly important. However, most informal instruments are relatively risky. A 1983 study by Tuck, which examined informal saving in the rural sector, showed that farmers in Senegal tend to store their wealth in traditional assets such as seeds, cereal grains and/or livestock (see the Appendix to Chapter 2). The risk of fire, theft, deterioration, destruction by pests, or sickness and death in the case of livestock, is particularly high and the adjusted returns on these assets are often low and sometimes negative.

For credit, the services described in Section II were available every year including years after poor harvests. This meant that farmers could vary their borrowing between zero after a good year, and the total amount available through the programs after a bad year. However, they could not increase their borrowing beyond that. If they were already borrowing the maximum in good years, there were no means to smooth consumption using formal programs. Moreover, farmers who did not need the inputs which were available, or who could not resell them on the secondary market, could not benefit at all in this respect.

The Senegalese government, however, had a somewhat unique mechanism to help farmers deal with risk. As described in Section II, it tolerated, de facto, a repayment rate on farm loans that was positively correlated with the level of national production. In particularly bad years, the government went so far as to annul the outstanding debt (which varied inversely with the level of production). This scheme was not officially institutionalized, but throughout the 1970s it occurred with enough regularity that farmers expected and planned for it explicitly.

This annulment policy was, in essence, an insurance program paid for by the government which resulted in a transfer of income to the agricultural sector in bad years. As mentioned above, this is one method that can be used to reduce farmers' consumption risk. However, the manner in which it was accomplished in Senegal had several deleterious consequences.

First, it was necessary to borrow for agricultural inputs in order to obtain the insurance policy. Therefore, it encouraged borrowing over saving in a very capital scarce economy. This is not necessarily an adverse result if the relatively poor farmers borrow the most. In fact, as in many LDCs, this was not the case in Senegal. The largest producers had the closest relationships with government authorities and were better able to obtain both more and larger loans (Dumont and Mottin, 1982).

Second, except for the annulments in 1977, this policy did not reduce the debts of each farmer by some specified percentage, but instead simply allowed more farmers to default entirely. It is not clear that this is undesirable either, if it is the marginal farmers who default more the greater the shortfall. This could be the case, but there is no proof that it is.

Third, as a general policy, it clearly distorts incentives to repay. Those who default are rewarded at the expense of those who reimburse. Farmers in Senegal quickly learned that debts left unpaid in good years would be annulled in bad years.

Fourth, the use of capital markets to transfer income means that when macroeconomic constraints or waning political will inhibit continuation of the transfer, the functioning of the financial markets is affected. In the case of a complete termination of funds, the markets can totally collapse. These last two points will be discussed in more detail in the section dealing with institutional efficiency.

Developed financial markets also enable farmers to reduce the risk of investment failure, as well as consumption risk. When an investment is made with borrowed capital, project risk can be shared with the lender. Failure of the project may lead to debt rescheduling or complete default. As a consequence, a farmer who borrows is likely to incur a lower financial cost if his project fails than if he finances his investment himself.

In Senegal, the expected quality of inputs delivered through the government programs was dubious. Seeds were frequently poor, farm equipment often arrived broken or inoperable, and it was common that inputs would be delivered too late to be of use. As a consequence of these events, farmers' investments in these inputs often resulted in net losses. If they had bought the inputs on credit, the farmers could then exercise their de facto option to postpone repayment or default. The fact that such delays and defaults were tolerated allowed farmers to mitigate the risk involved in using the inputs distributed by the programs.

B. Profit

It is commonly assumed that farmers can raise the net returns on their agricultural activity if they use credit. This is often, but not always, true. Under certain circumstances, if a farmer has funds of his own higher profits can be realized by self-financing input purchases.

Policy-makers tend to dismiss this possibility, believing that 'farmers are too poor to make investments out of their own savings.' For the typical Senegalese farmer, this argument is particularly tenable with respect to large-scale investments. Access to credit for these expenditures may allow farmers to raise their profits. However, it is common practice for farmers to hold assets, particularly livestock, of value greater than their expenditures for growing season inputs such as seeds and fertilizers.

For an individual farmer, the relative profitability between using his own funds or borrowing for investment purposes depends on the relationship between the risk-adjusted opportunity cost of capital and the interest rate on credit for inputs. This latter must also be adjusted to account for the probability of partial or total default on the loan.

If a farmer knows with complete certainty that he will have to repay his loan (e.g., when debts are automatically deducted from revenues earned on production), the calculation of relative profitability is straightforward. When the risk-adjusted opportunity cost of capital is higher than the interest rate on borrowing, the farmer may be able to increase his profit by borrowing the maximum permissible amount.

The above situation is common when interest rates are held artificially low as a result of government policy. It prevails in many western economies, including the U.S. and Europe, where highly subsidized agricultural loans and the numerous opportunities to make high-yielding, low-risk investments mean that farmers can borrow cheaply for inputs while keeping their own capital in money-market funds or other high return assets. In the Senegalese context, the analogous situation would involve borrowing for inputs at low or negative real interest rates while investing in peripheral rural activities such as petty trade.

In rural Senegal, however, the opportunities to earn risk-adjusted returns which are higher than the cost of borrowing are extremely limited. As mentioned above, farmers tend to invest their wealth in fairly risky, traditional assets. When the returns are adjusted to take this risk into account, they are frequently low and sometimes negative. Since the risk-adjusted returns on traditional assets are frequently less than the real interest costs of borrowing in Senegal, the provision of improved savings services can often raise farmers' financial standing more than the provision of short term credit services.

In Senegal there was a government policy that tipped the profitability calculation in favor of using credit. Farmers that borrowed from the formal lending programs were never completely convinced that they would have to repay their loans. Their belief was derived from the frequent annulments of farm debt during the 1970s which significantly decreased their expected financial cost of borrowing.

171

In fact, because of the annulments, a farmer could potentially raise his financial standing by borrowing for inputs, even if the real, risk-adjusted return on his own funds was negative. The annulments made it more profitable for farmers to borrow than to self-finance their inputs. However, if they had been required to repay their loans, many of them would have found that using credit was the less profitable option.

Senegal's credit programs did make many different types of inputs available over their twenty years of operation. Frequently these inputs were entirely appropriate and farmers were able to earn higher profits than would have been possible had the credit not been available. Even when inputs were not appropriate, farmers were often able to resell them on the secondary market and purchase the items they preferred, still raising the overall wealth of their households.

There were, however, farmers that did not have access to the formal programs at all. Some were deemed 'uncreditworthy,' some were isolated geographically, some were not targets of the programs. Examples of the latter would include women and *sourgas*. Credit programs usually benefit only a selected portion of the population. The programs in Senegal, despite their massive scale, were no exception.

Savings services, which are usually less exclusive, were not available through Senegal's formal programs. One result of this omission was that those who were not able to borrow, usually the very poorest, were disproportionately hurt. It also had a deleterious impact on many of the average farmers who *were* permitted to borrow. These farmers often expected to repay their loans and frequently did. Many of them also faced opportunity costs on their capital which were less than the cost of borrowing. It is this segment of the rural population which has the greatest potential to raise its financial standing by saving funds between the harvest and the growing season, and self-financing inputs. However, without savings services provided through the formal programs, these farmers often found storing wealth for agricultural investments to be extremely difficult. Cash budgeting, a difficult process for anyone who receives an entire year's income at one time, is particularly problematic in rural Senegal.

C. Allocation of Resources

Since wealth and investment opportunities are usually not comparably distributed, and current income rarely coincides exactly with current consumption, there will almost always be a demand for and supply of borrowed funds. Since there are also real transactions costs to matching borrowers and lenders, economic efficiency can usually be improved by the exchange of funds through a broker, or intermediary. The more accurately the price of borrowing and the return to lending reflect the scarcity (or availability) of funds, the more efficient the allocation of those funds will be.

The formal financial programs in rural Senegal did not provide the signals for the efficient allocation of resources among individuals, across time or among competing activities. No saving services were offered, with the crucial result that farmers' behavior was biased toward spending or borrowing.

Some of the programs charged no interest on their loans, reinforcing the tendency to spend. The real interest rate on groundnut seeds, while positive, did not vary over time, offering no guidance whatsoever for efficient changes in borrowing and saving patterns. Interest rates on fertilizers, fungicides, farm equipment and food did vary as a function of the discount rate at the Central Bank, and hence probably did reflect changes in the availability or scarcity of capital in the economy. However, these rates were never announced before the growing season began and hence could not be used by farmers in their decisions to allocate their funds.

Furthermore, farmers that needed credit could only obtain it in the form of specific agricultural inputs, narrowly limited to specific quantities and specific times. The quantities were usually determined on the basis of technical specifications rather than on the basis of economic efficiency.

When the inputs provided by the system were technically appropriate and economically profitable for an individual farmer, the system worked relatively well. Often, however, the inputs were not appropriate and a farmer would realize a marginal cost for inputs far different from the marginal revenues they could generate.

IV. INSTITUTIONAL PERSPECTIVE

Conventional economic theory suggests that there are substantial benefits to be reaped by the rural sector from efforts to develop efficiently operating financial markets. This is particularly relevant for farmers with regard to risk management and increased profits. It is also relevant for the economy as a whole in terms of a more efficient allocation of resources across individuals, time, and activities. However, the cost of providing such services may be unacceptable in a country such as Senegal.

The Senegalese institutions that offered credit services in the past experienced major problems with program implementation. This poor performance of credit programs is not unique to Senegal. In fact, the general experience across Africa with agricultural banks has been poor. As Marvin Miracle writes in his analysis of 30 agricultural credit programs in Africa:

The record of attempts to build new agricultural credit institutions in Africa shows that failure is more common than success – defining failure as the inability to provide small farmers with a lasting source of credit ... default rates have been so high that most have either had to abandon their programs or greatly restrict their operations. (Miracle, 1972)

Some of the reasons for these 'failures' are discussed below.

A frequent source of problems for institutions offering financial services to the rural sector in LDCs is that they concentrate their efforts exclusively on agriculturally related activities. This overly focused strategy usually has several negative consequences.

In an agricultural economy where most farmers cultivate the same crop, or where the planting and harvesting calendars for different crops are very similar, there will be seasonality in the supply of and demand for capital. Most depositors will want to withdraw their funds at the beginning of the growing season, the same time most borrowers will want to borrow. Deposits and repayments will coincide in a similar manner after harvest.

Furthermore, when there is a correlation in the expected yield on all crops, there will be covariance in the income of those whose revenues are derived from crop production. This will generate a covariance in the supply of and the demand for funds across years as well as across seasons. In years of good production, most everyone will have deposits to make but few will want to borrow. In years of poor production, most everyone will want to withdraw their deposits or borrow (Binswanger and Rosensweig, 1982).

As a consequence, an institution lending to a sector comprised of individuals engaged in similar activity can provide little effective intermediation. For depositors, it can hold their funds and then simply return them. This is a service which, theoretically, depositors could perform themselves. For borrowers, it can only lend from its own reserves, something it could do without accepting deposits.

Thus the design of programs offering financial services in LDC's rarely includes the provision of savings services, inhibiting farmers' ability to reduce risk and raise profit. Furthermore, this inability to act as an effective intermediary also implies that the institution will always be dependent on an external credit line from commercial, government, or donor sources.

As mentioned above, when the potential clients of the financial institution are all involved in rainfed agriculture or related activities, the expected yields on clients' investments are highly correlated. In addition to causing covariance in the demand for and supply of funds, this also means that the portfolio of loans held by the lending institution will be poorly diversified. When there is a bad crop year, most clients' investments will fail simultaneously, with disastrous consequences for the intermediating financial institution.

If the institution is extending a large amount of credit on an annual basis, it can be expected to incur major losses in years of poor production. In countries where droughts are common, this means that repayment rates will be low and the institution will have difficulty re-establishing its credit line. Unless it is the beneficiary of continual budgetary or donor assistance, it will not be able to sustain its programs on a long-term basis.

The credit that has been supplied to the Senegalese rural sector through the formal government programs has been targeted exclusively, albeit indirectly in the case of food, for agricultural activity. Senegal's agricultural economy is dominated by a small number of rainfed crops, for which the expected yield and the crop calendars are highly correlated. As a consequence of the resulting covariance in income (both seasonally and annually), none of the lending programs have functioned in an intermediary capacity. All of them have relied on external financing for the loans they have extended.

Furthermore, all of the programs have held a portfolio of loans with highly correlated returns. In years of poor rainfall, borrowers have suffered reduced income and defaulted on the bulk of their loans simultaneously. Major crop shortfalls occurred in Senegal in five of the ten years between 1970 and 1980. As was shown above, repayment rates dropped substantially during these years, requiring large infusions of government capital to maintain the solvency of the lending programs.

Loans to Senegalese farmers were also particularly risky, not only because of the frequent droughts and resulting shortfalls in production, but because individual investments requiring agricultural inputs had a high probability of failure. Often the inputs that farmers acquired on credit could not be profitably employed. In some instances, the technical feasibility studies to determine the return on the inputs were undertaken in an optimal research environment rather than under more realistic local conditions. As a result, farmers did not achieve the increases in returns necessary to finance the input. Sometimes the advice given to farmers by extension agents was simply not appropriate for their particular circumstances. Sometimes the inputs arrived too late, in unusable condition or not at all. Thus the profit farmers expected their inputs to generate was reduced or eliminated and they would default.

Production shortfalls, resulting either from a lack of rain or from inefficient use of inputs, represent only one of the several determinants of low repayment rates. 'Moral' risk, or the risk of default by the borrower when he is able to repay, is also common. Even in years of good production, farmers in Senegal still did not completely repay their debts.

Generally, borrowers feel little, if any, moral compulsion to repay an impersonal credit program. This is especially true if the overall system of which the credit program is a component, is treating them unfairly in other ways. Under such circumstances, motivations for reimbursement will come primarily from the threat of sufficiently severe sanctions for default, or sufficiently compelling economic gains from repayment. However, in a country such as Senegal, establishing an effective set of sanctions and incentives can be extremely difficult.

Sanctions are defined here as actions that would impose financial or other costs on the farmer at least as great as the costs of reimbursement. These sanctions might include the seizure of assets or the attachment of income.

The typical Senegalese farmer perceives little threat of punishment for non-repayment of loans provided through formal programs. While it is theoretically possible to take a farmer who defaults to court, the legal process is slow and time-consuming. Farmers never go to prison for unpaid debts and they know that formal sector lenders are unlikely to attempt collection of delinquent loans through legal action.

Most Senegalese farmers have little collateral that they fear losing. The lack of valuable assets that can be seized in the event of default is probably the most serious impediment to the implementation of a viable formal credit system in Senegal. There is almost no land tenure in the rural areas. Instead, the government legally owns all of the land and allocates 'rights of usage' to households according to certain criteria. These conditions include the 'development potential' and work capacity of the beneficiaries and their families. The law expressly forbids property transactions, including sales, rentals, or the use of landholdings as collateral.

The significance of this form of tenure is that private lending institutions are effectively deprived of the best possible tool for ensuring the repayment of the loans they disburse. Technically, the government, or programs run under government auspices, could seize and redistribute the land being used by farmers who default on loans. In reality, this has proved to be politically and socially infeasible. The tenure systems that exist de facto within a village are often the consequence of distributions based on criteria other than those applied by the government; an official reallocation might not change the actual pattern of holdings, and/or might result in severe social malaise.

The land tenure situation is slightly different for SAED, the RDA that works with farmers engaged in irrigated agriculture in the Fleuve region. SAED is responsible for assigning rights to plots on new irrigated perimeters. These are lands which were not previously worked by village members and are not assigned by social criteria to any particular household. SAED has, in fact, evicted some families that have not reimbursed the loans they received through SAED's credit program. The reclaimed plots were subsequently allocated to other families. This practice, however, has not been applied consistently. Some households have avoided repayment for many consecutive seasons; some households repay in certain seasons and not others. Some households simply skip repayment in one season, but dutifully repay thereafter. In most of these cases there have been no repercussions.

It is not clear how effective the threat to seize land has been under these conditions. The repayment rates on SAED loans, while too low to enable the program to be self-sustaining, have been higher than the repayment rates for the *Programme Agricole* in general. Moreover, repayment rates to SAED have been rising over time. This may result from the cumulative experience of farmers in the Fleuve region witnessing, or incurring, the eviction consequence of default.

Local housing cannot be considered as effective collateral either. Aside from the political difficulties associated with the seizure of a poor farmer's house, the fact remains that the typical farmer's house is generally constructed from mud and may be virtually worthless as a financial asset. Moreover, the communal traditions of the rural countryside would make it nearly impossible to seize a house from a farmer and his family and resell it to someone else in the village. Neither can it be expected that a family from outside the village could simply buy the house and move in without serious consequences of social alienation.

The implications of the above are that the two assets, land and housing, which are generally considered acceptable collateral by formal institutions, are not available in rural Senegal. Other assets farmers might possess, such as livestock and farm equipment, are subject to collateral-specific risk. This means that they may be lost, sick, stolen, or broken at the time of seizure. Thus their risky nature reduces their value as effective collateral against default.

It is also extremely difficult to attach farmers' incomes when they do not receive a formal salary. To the extent that a farmer markets his crop for cash, it should be possible to deduct his debts from his revenues. In reality, however, there are many ways for the farmer to avoid such an occurrence. The easiest strategy is for the borrower to simply market the output in some other name.

Seizing income has proved to be particularly difficult in Senegal. This is partially attributable to flaws in the design of the credit programs. The most common of these flaws was that the laws allowed farmers to sell their output through a different cooperative from the one where they acquired their inputs on credit. Since effective communication between cooperatives was lacking, farmers could avoid repayment fairly easily. Even with better program design, however, farmers could still escape having their income attached. It is always possible for a farmer to have a wife or cousin who is not indebted to the system market his crop.

Furthermore, when loans are made for food crops where virtually all of the output is consumed within the household, farmers do not earn cash revenue that can be tapped. In the rice growing regions of the Casamance, the repayment rates were the lowest of those for any part of the country. This situation is beginning to change in the delta area of the Fleuve where households have begun to generate a surplus of rice. However, the time is still far in the future when the majority of food crop production will pass through marketed channels, as is the case with groundnuts.

When there is a dearth of effective sanctions that can be employed to assure levels of repayment sufficient to maintain the viability of the credit programs, it may be possible to establish a system of positive incentives instead. Incentives are defined here as options that could make farmers better off in financial or other terms but which are available to them only if they repay their debts. One example is continued access to specific services. Incentives can encourage repayment, but in general they have proven to be less effective than a credible threat of sanctions.

Confronted by a set of incentives, a farmer will make a determination of the costs and benefits surrounding both the repayment and default options. Loan repayment will allow him continued access to certain benefits that would not be available if he defaulted. These benefits might include the present discounted value of all returns he can generate from the future use of additional credit. They might also include the maintenance of his reputation with the formal sector, which may increase his ability to receive future extension assistance. Defaulting on his loans, on the other hand, enables the farmer to keep the loan principal plus any interest he owes. Clearly, the larger his debt, the more his financial situation can be improved by defaulting on his debts.

Obviously, the more services provided in conjunction with the lending program, the more attractive the repayment option will be. The most common incentive for repayment is the availability of additional credit only to those not delinquent on previous debts. However, the low repayment rates recorded by formal institutions that rely primarily on this incentive show that it is not entirely effective. It has become clear that certain conditions must prevail for this policy to have a positive impact on repayment.

First, the threat of curtailed credit from the original lender in the case of default must be credible. This has rarely been the case in Senegal because the government programs continued to make disbursements even when farmers had unpaid loans outstanding. It is not completely clear why this was allowed. Some argue that the government had incentives to be permissive. One possibility was that the government needed the foreign exchange generated by the groundnut production and believed that the credit programs were sustaining, if not increasing, the level of output. Another possibility is that government officials tolerated default as an easy means to transfer resources to the rural sector.

Second, other potential sources of credit for the borrower must have access to information about default to the original lender. Furthermore, these potential creditors must be motivated to include a farmer's default to another lender as a criterion in making their own lending decisions. It is not clear that, in Senegal, a local merchant would care if a farmer had defaulted on a loan from a government program or from a formal bank when deciding whether or not to extend credit. If either of these conditions do not hold, a farmer may still be able to borrow from other formal and/or informal sources, even if he defaults on a loan to a formal program. Thus, forgoing a future credit line from the original lending institution may not involve a significant welfare loss.

Third, there must be a demand for future credit. A farmer must perceive potential gains from additional borrowing. It is not clear that this will always be true. The farmer may find that he would be better off if, in the future, he financed the acquisition of certain inputs himself, as explained above. Alternatively, he may reach a point where his equipment needs are satisfied for the foreseeable future. In fact, research has shown that repayment rates fall as credit programs for farm equipment mature (Long, 1973). As farmers' needs for additional implements decline, so does their need for borrowing, and thus their incentive to repay.

Fourth, there must be a supply of future credit. This means that the funds demanded by farmers must be available. This may not always be the case. For instance, many programs stipulate that once a farmer has a certain amount of equipment, he cannot borrow for more. Another example might be that farmers value access to loans for food during the hungry season but such credit might not be available from the lending institution.

If either the demand for or the supply of future credit is below a critical level, the incentive to repay simply to be eligible for additional borrowing will be low.

In Senegal, curtailed future credit in the case of default has been official policy of all the lending programs. However, judging from their poor repayment records, the willingness of the program administrators to employ this sanction can be seriously questioned. All of the formal lending programs except that of SODEFITEX continued to lend despite high default rates. As a consequence, most farmers were never convinced that their ability to obtain loans in the future was seriously impaired. The threat to farmers working under the SODEFITEX program, however, was real, and they repaid their debts with relative consistency. This outcome was probably the result of several factors – some of which will be described below – and not just the threat of curtailed credit. Nonetheless, this policy made an important contribution to the impressive repayment rates that SODEFITEX has been able to achieve with its lending program.

All of the credit systems in Senegal were designed with what policy-makers termed 'guarantees.' These so-called guarantees were nothing more than policies that increased the incentive to repay outstanding loans. The first of these was the 'guarantee of collective solidarity.' This policy required that loans be extended to groups rather than to individuals. All members of the group would not actually use the credit at the same time, but the entire group would lose access to future borrowing if the previous debts were not repaid. The purpose of such a policy is to ensure a continuing interest by the group in maintaining a good relationship with the lender. The rationale for group lending is that even if the initial borrowers have all the equipment they need, there will be others that do not. Thus peer pressure might encourage the earlier beneficiaries to repay so their successors can have similar opportunities.

This policy can only be effective, however, if there are social ties of 'solidarity' between the members of the group. In Senegal there is considerable controversy over whether or not this solidarity actually exists, and if it does, at what level of organization. The designers of the past credit programs expected it to develop at the cooperative level (or producer group level in the Fleuve and the Casamance). Cooperatives eventually proved to possess little or no cohesiveness among members, although the willingness of the government to continue lending, even after the cooperatives had not repaid their debts, never required them to actually exert social pressure in this context.

Current thinking among some government officials and many donors is that group solidarity actually exists at the village level and that loans should be made to *sections villageoises* (village groups). Others, particularly those working at the local level, disagree that the village inhabitants necessarily manifest such solidarity. They cite examples of villages with internal feuding among families or villages composed of different castes and ethnic groups which, while tolerant of each other, exhibit little solidarity. Whether or not this village level solidarity exists, *sections villageoises* currently have no legal jurisdiction to borrow.

Collective guarantees may create an effective incentive system if there is truly some form of solidarity among members of borrowing groups. The solidarity concept would not, however, be expected to raise the incentive for repayment when a loan is made to the entire group for one large piece of equipment, such as an irrigation pump or a cold storage unit for fish, if this is all the group will be eligible or willing to borrow for. The same incentives for default in the case of the individual borrower, as discussed above, would apply to this group loan situation.

The second so-called guarantee required by the government programs was the *ristourne*, or rebate system. *Ristournes* were cash distributions made during the hungry season to groups that had attained a designated repayment rate. This was actually another policy designed to increase the benefits from repaying an outstanding loan. When a cooperative marketed its crop, 1.5 CFA per kilogram were automatically deducted from its revenues. The funds generated from this deduction were blocked in bank accounts until the cooperative had reimbursed a certain percentage of its debt due. Once this designated repayment rate was attained, 25 percent of the funds were set aside in the cooperative's name. This money could then be used by the cooperative to make collective investments. During the hungry season, the remaining funds, less storage and transport losses, were distributed in cash, to individual farmers via the cooperatives. Since the farmers are lowest on cash at that time, they greatly appreciated these distributions. The government believed that this promise of cash would encourage repayment. The rebate that any farmer could potentially receive, however, was always less than what he owed in debt. Hence as an incentive, the rebate was not very successful.

There were two aspects to this rebate system that the government assumed would make it effective. The first was the fact that the distributions came in cash during the hungry season. It was thought that these distributions would be valued by the farmers more than the amount of their debt repayments which, though larger, were made when the farmer had cash after harvest. Assuming that the rebate would encourage repayment by farmers who would otherwise have defaulted was tantamount to assuming that farmers were willing to pay a very large fee for a cash management service.

The second way in which this rebate system was thought to motivate repayment was through the social pressure associated with group lending. Farmers who had repaid their debts would presumably put pressure on the other members of their cooperative to reimburse as well so they could all receive the transfer. In fact, this social pressure did not prove to be very significant.

This rebate policy was essentially a production tax on marketed output. Farmers who produced food crops which they consumed themselves were exempt. Those who sold their production simply viewed the producer price on which they based their planting decisions as 1.5 CFA below the posted price. The tax collected in this manner contributed only marginally to defray the losses incurred by the programs from default.

One last incentive to motivate repayment can be implemented when credit programs are components of larger packages of services. A farmer who defaults can be excluded from future training, extension assistance, or the subsidized or free inputs available under the overall program. Again, for this incentive to be effective, the fundamental condition must hold that the present discounted value of the returns which the farmer can generate from these services and/or inputs is greater than the value of the debt he owes.

For the SODEFITEX program, the services contingent on repayment included free distribution of seeds and fertilizers for all of a farmer's cotton fields. Under the *Programme Agricole*, the only services available, other than credit, were distribution of inputs and extension. However, a farmer's eligibility to receive either of these services was never jeopardized by non-repayment of loans. Access to *free* inputs in future years is clearly of more value than access to *credit* for inputs, and the high repayment rates observed for the SODEFITEX program are partially due to the effects of this incentive.

There are other reasons why formal lending institutions experienced difficulties in Senegal. Agricultural operations are spatially disparate, making the collection and transmission of information extremely costly. This problem is exacerbated by the lack of good transportation and communication networks in the rural regions of Senegal.

As just mentioned, borrowers are physically dispersed. Centralization of the banking services decreases the ability of the bank to collect adequate and reliable information at a reasonable cost. But decentralization requires bankers to remain in the field. Management problems are often the binding constraint in the development of viable agricultural banking services. Finding agents who are honest, trained and competent enough to run branches, and are also willing to remain in the rural areas, is extremely difficult when such skills are in high demand in the national or regional capital cities. Bank employees who have undergone such training will generally migrate toward urban centers.

V. CONCLUSIONS

● Savings services available to rural sector residents can enhance farmers' abilities to increase their wealth, allow them to reduce their consumption risk and to allocate their resources more efficiently. Incorporation of savings mechanisms in public sector programs allow the poorest and most uncreditworthy farmers, who generally do not have access to credit, to enjoy some of the benefits that financial markets can offer. None of the programs in Senegal have provided savings services.

• Efficiency of resource allocation is increased when farmers are allowed to select inputs themselves, and when they can borrow the necessary cash to make these purchases. In any case, as indicated by the vitality of the resale market in Senegal, making the acceptance of prescribed inputs the only means to obtain credit does not ensure the desired use of those inputs.

• The most efficient allocation of resources is not achieved in rural Senegal when the interest rate on lending, or its base, is fixed at some arbitrary level rather than having it fluctuate as a function of the discount rate at the Central Bank. This is a separate issue from the question of whether or not the interest rate should be subsidized.

• Farmers in rural Senegal do not have enough trust in financial institutions, nor enough basic literacy and numeracy training to use them well.

• The credit institutions operating in Senegal's rural sector limit themselves solely to lending for agriculturally related activities. Financial institutions in a country such as Senegal, however, need a clientele derived from each of the primary, secondary and tertiary sectors as well as from both urban and rural settings in order to develop an adequately diversified loan portfolio. This is necessary to avoid a high correlation in the yields of its loan portfolio and, subsequently to reduce risk.

Furthermore, a diversified clientele provides a greater inter-temporal variance in the demand for and supply of funds. This allows the financial institution to act as an effective intermediary, reducing its dependence on the government budget or donor sources for an external line of credit.

• Senegal's financial institutions do not offer the savings services necessary to function as effective intermediaries and reduce their dependence on external capital. This lack of savings facilities prevents farmers from reducing risk and raising profits at a much lower cost and with less risk for the financial institution.

• One important reason why Senegal's government credit programs experience low repayment rates was because they did not enforce sanctions against default nor offer adequate incentives for repayment. This situation might have been avoided had the programs incorporated one or more of the following policies.

– The lending institutions could have required some form of collateral, even if it was not considered satisfactory by financial standards. Lending institutions frequently cannot use the assets possessed by most farmers as effective guarantees on their loans. However, the assets are valuable to their owners, and seizing them in the event of default may impose a cost sufficiently serious to induce the farmer, or other borrowers, to repay future loans. The most obvious choice would be the items the farmer purchases on credit, although for growing season inputs, livestock or farm equipment might be possible.

– New loan disbursements could have been halted to farmers who were delinquent on their loan repayments. For a credit system with few sanctions, the promise of additional credit may be the most powerful tool available to encourage repayment. To be effective, this policy must be employed consistently so all who participate in the program are motivated to seriously consider the consequences of default.

– Access to additional services, such as input distribution or extension, could have been made contingent on meeting designated repayment schedules. Offering credit for a variety of purposes will increase the general demand for credit. This will in turn increase farmers' interest in maintaining a relationship with the lender and therefore increase their incentive to repay.

• In Senegal, borrowing groups were not always organized at a level where there was a social solidarity among members. The current shift in emphasis from cooperatives toward village sections will probably increase the cohesiveness of producer groups. However, it will not be a complete solution. Groups organized to perform similar functions do not all possess the same degree of solidarity. Some of the old cooperatives may have been socially cohesive though most were not. Village sections will be the solution for many other producer groups, but will still not be sufficient for others. Ideally, credit programs would be flexible enough to accept groups of varying organizational levels whenever they exhibit adequate social solidarity.

• Government regulations have allowed farmers membership in more than one cooperative, producer group or village section for the purpose of obtaining inputs and marketing output. This has complicated the problem of attaching income, and reduced farmers' accountability.

• The lack of flexibility in repayment schedules during years of poor rainfall contributed significantly to the failure of the formal credit system. Had some flexibility been institutionalized, the drought years of the early 1980s might not have led to the demise of the entire rural financial system. This collapse could also have been avoided had there existed a system that transferred income to farmers during years of poor rainfall enabling them to repay their debts. This parallel system could involve some combination of the following mechanisms.

– Voluntary savings services which are designed explicitly to enable farmers to store wealth after years of good production for use after bad years.

– An insurance program into which farmers pay after years of good production and from which they receive benefits after bad years. This would essentially be a forced savings program due to the correlation in expected inflows and outflows of funds to the insurance program.

– Simple transfers to farmers from general government revenues or donor funds during years of poor rainfall. This policy would be similar to the implicit policies of the last decade, except that the transfers would go to all farmers (or to all 'poor' farmers) rather than just those who borrow for particular reasons and/or those who default once they have borrowed.

All of the problems listed above could be eliminated or substantially mitigated with careful design of a new financial system in rural Senegal. Even if this were to occur, however, certain problems would remain.

• As long as the land tenure system in Senegal forbids land transactions, it will be difficult for private lending institutions to find collateral which can guarantee their loans. Government programs are unlikely to have an advantage in this regard since political and social obstacles seem to impair their abilities to seize and redistribute the land worked by farmers who default.

• Debt recovery through income deductions will also remain extremely difficult until a level of development is reached where the majority of farmers' revenues pass through formal institutional channels. Furthermore, loans for the production of food crops which are consumed primarily within the household will remain risky until the cereals sector begins to produce a surplus and farmers market output of value in excess of their debts.

● Deficiencies in the production and distribution of inputs are beyond farmers' control. However, such deficiencies can cause farmers to suffer reduced crop yields and income. Until improvements are made in these processes, farmers' abilities to pay for their inputs will be impaired and they will frequently default.

● A lending program which can mobilize few effective sanctions against farmers who default, and which depends primarily on voluntary compliance will always have relatively poor rates of repayment. Financial institutions will have perpetual difficulties sustaining programs and will always be in need of external support. However, the provision of financial services may be an acceptable social investment if the benefits to the entire rural sector outweigh the costs of the programs. The losses from default do not constitute a social cost, *per se*, since they merely represent a transfer of income within the economy. However, the distribution consequences may be regressive and undesirable. Moreover, from the point of view of the lending institution, default does impose a cost, and if the prospects of perpetual external funding are poor, the institution is not likely to be sustainable over the long term.

In conclusion, financial services for the rural sector should be as independent and self-sustaining as possible. Savings programs, either voluntary or forced, should be strongly emphasized. If credit is provided, concentration should be on larger-scale and longer-term investments, and timely loan repayment should be consistently and vigorously enforced. Income transfers, if deemed appropriate, should be given to farmers in an explicit manner, rather than through the mechanism of implicitly forgiven default. The riskiness of farm activities and the lack of effective sanctions in a country such as Senegal should be recognized and adequately considered by planners of financial systems. These conditions imply that a formal lending institution will probably require external financial support for the indefinite future and it is unrealistic for government and donor organization budget planners to expect it to be totally independent.

CHAPTER SIX

Dimensions of State Intervention in the Groundnut Basin

John Waterbury

The groundnut basin has been a testing ground for public agricultural policy since the 1920s, rivaled only by the delta of the Senegal river. The delta, however, has never remotely approached the groundnut basin in agricultural or social importance. As the following summary statistics indicate, the groundnut basin has been the center of gravity of the entire Senegalese economy and polity:

Total area	69,000 km² (34 percent of Senegal's surface)
Cultivated area	1,920,000 ha (75 percent of national total)
Total pop. (1976)	2,564,250 (50 percent of national total)
Total pop. (1981)	2,902,610 (49 percent of national total)
Rural pop. (1976)	2,138,090 (60 percent of total rural population)
Rural pop. (1981)	2,278,024 (58 percent of total rural population)
Cereals production	ca. 65 percent of national total on average
Groundnut production	ca. 75 percent of national total on average
Cattle population	ca. 46 percent of national total on average

Most of the groundnut basin is currently cultivated. There is room for some expansion, but probably only onto marginal lands and at the expense of the cattle transhumant zones of the Ferlo (see Table 1). There are some 175-215,000 farming units (*exploitations*) in the basin with an average size of about 7.5 ha. It is important to keep in mind that the basin can be roughly divided into two ecological zones; a north-central zone with low irregular rainfall, and a southern zone comprising the Sine-Saloum and part of Sénégal Oriental with higher, more regular rainfall. Under careful management, the south may have a promising agricultural future. The same cannot be said for the north.

Under existing forms of social organization, cultivator practices, and levels of agricultural technology, the groundnut basin may have attained maximum yields per hectare for major crops and a long term process of soil depletion and ecological degradation has set in. This process may evolve more slowly than one would suppose, given the elimination of fallows and increasing animal and human population pressure upon the land, but it is indisputably underway.

TABLE 1

Agricultural Land Resources, Groundnut Basin

	Tot. Pop.	Cultivated hectares	Cultivable hectares	Difference	Percent of cultivable surface
Louga	463,870	390,000	500,000	110,000	22
Diourbel	465,160	310,000	350,000	40,000	11
Thiès	809,980	360,000	370,000	10,000	3
Sine-Saloum	1,163,600	860,000	1,150,000	290,000	25
Total	2,902,610	1,920,000	2,370,000	450,000	23

Source: GOS, Sixth Plan.

What can or should the Senegalese state do to deal with the situation? First, it can draw on the lessons of more than two decades of intense public involvement in agricultural production in the groundnut basin. In the following pages we shall seek to assess various aspects of that involvement. Second, it can approach what at best must be a *holding operation* through policies either of *mise en valeur* or policies of benign neglect. The latter would entail a reduction in the investment of state resources and personnel, along with foreign assistance, to a bare minimum. It might entail heavy emphasis on developing Sine-Saloum at the expense of Diourbel and Louga. It would also entail a kind of *triage* among the cultivating population in which only the most efficient or well-endowed would survive. The rest would migrate to other regions (Fleuve, Terres Neuves), to the cities, or remain as a rural proletariat upon whom successful peasants could draw for a cheap source of labor. In this scenario only the best lands and the best cultivators would benefit from state programs in extension, credit, and infrastructural development (roads, markets, deep wells, etc.).

In terms of 'efficient' resource allocation, an argument can be made for benign neglect, but in terms of servicing major politico-religious constituencies concentrated in the north-central region, such a policy would be risk-laden.

I. THE STATE CONNECTION

Senegalese peasants are experienced participants in the market system. They are, as well, experienced participants in the state system. The relationship of cultivators to state agencies has been, in both directions, manipulative or adversarial, but seldom co-operative. As Goran Hyden has argued with respect to Tanzania, there are not the same morally binding constraints prevailing between administrators and peasants as prevail among the peasants themselves. The lack of such moral obligations may lead to a kind of ransacking for the benefit of private individuals or groups of publicly-supplied collective goods. As we shall be focusing upon parastatal intervention in agricultural production and in the pro-vision of collective goods, it is important to understand this adver-sarial relationship.

One of the crucial providers of collective goods in the Senegalese countryside has been the network of cooperatives. Other con-tributors to this volume (Gellar, Tignor, and Tuck) treat the subject in detail. They are referred to here only to illustrate a few general points on cultivator-state relations. The coop can be seen as part of that realm to be plundered rather than sustained. To the extent such mistrust exists, the result is widespread debt default, misuse of loans in kind, attempts to 'cheat' marketing agents, and so forth. Guy Belloncle echoes Goran Hyden's argument in his discussion of collective responsibility for debts (1980b: 4):

If it is the village that is responsible for credit, we were told repeatedly, then many things are going to change, because *jom* (sense of honor) will force each person to pay back [his debts]. Could you betray the confidence that has been placed in you? We should note in passing this astonishing reversal of values, one that is not peculiar to Senegal. What would be valued in the former system – deceive the state by failing to repay one's debts – suddenly becomes shameful in relation to the village community that has 'placed its trust in you.'

In a far broader sense, the peasant knows that the state has large sunk costs in agricultural production in the form of infrastructure, marketing boards, and administrative personnel. He is aware that the state and its agencies want to perform well (as measured by production, successful extension programs, sales of equipment, etc.) and that the state has, therefore, little incentive to act toward the peasant in an openly punitive manner. The peasant learns how to extract free or subsidized services from the state by foot-dragging, by obliging the state to assume more functions, to deliver more services, all the while failing to pay for those for which he is legally debited. Private money lenders may take over assets from or deny credit to delinquent borrowers, but probably not the State. In the wake of the *malaise paysan* and the beginning of the Sahelian drought in 1971, the state forgave peasants 2.6 billion CFA in debt arrears, paid out 1.3 billion as 'exceptional' rebates, and offered 2 billion CFA as a planting incentive (*prime de l'ensemencement*). Peasant expectations vis-à-vis the state were formed or confirmed at that time and will be hard to change.

When the peasant hears of *responsabilisation*, he may see it as a State gambit to divest itself of obligations to provide goods and services; in this sense, returning power and responsibility to the peasant may appear highly threatening. Assumptions made by experts such as Guy Belloncle that peasants cherish autonomy and will use it profitably may be seriously off-target. On the other hand, Gérard Pince (1981) assumes that the state or its local agents will have the will and the incentives to deny credit to delinquent peasants. That too is not at all clear.

The 'amoralism' of the peasant is rendered in kind by the State. What we find is that despite the peasant's wily dealings with the 'authorities', he nonetheless in large measure pays for them. Throughout the 1960s, but especially during the *malaise paysan* and the drought, the cultivators' share in the proceeds of groundnut sales fell from about 65 percent to 43 percent by 1972-73, while the state acquired the residual (IBRD, 1974:12 and FAO, 1976:18). Throughout this period groundnut production was maintained; the peasants and the state simply traded forgiven debts for greater indirect taxation through the price mechanism.

The situation has changed little in the last decade. Three times between 1972 and 1980 the government assumed some or all of peasant debt to the cooperatives (see Tuck in this volume). By contrast, despite the proclaimed goal of lightening the administrative grip on the countryside after the dissolution of ONCAD in 1980, we find that the RDAs still fielded 5500 employees, and SONAR, the new groundnut seed distributing agency, employed another 1500. It was estimated that 10-20 percent of the gross value of agricultural production was needed to support this load (Association Sud-Ouest, 1981). Handling costs (row 2 in Table 2) remained between a quarter and half of the value received by the peasants for their groundnuts. In an important sense, peasants continued to pay for bureaucrats.

We come up then with the following dialectic. The urban and public sector bourgeoisie wants to appropriate privately-generated rural surplus for collective ends. The peasant wants to appropriate collective, state-generated goods for private ends. The game is played out through coops, credit banks, marketing boards, and the RDAs. It would be illusory to design policy that assumes the established expectations on either side will change.

TABLE 2

Costs of Groundnut Harvests: 1980/81–1981/82

	1980/81	1981/82
Quantity Groundnuts Marketed (Tons)	189,256	690,350
Value Groundnuts Marketed (CFA)	8,854,000	41,686,000
Handling Costs (*barème*)	4,348,000	10,795,000
Refining Costs	7,049,000	10,866,000
Product Marketing Costs (with taxes)	5,107,000	11,231,000

Source: Thénevin, 1982: 105–109.

For the first three or four years following independence, Senegal's declared policy was to transform social relations in the countryside by building new, egalitarian institutions that would be the instruments of broad-based (or what Kilby and Johnston call 'unimodal') agricultural development. The organization of coops and the nationalization of the groundnut trade on the one hand, coupled with the training of peasant extension workers through programs of *animation rurale* on the other, constituted an approach that emphasized social and political factors in the production process more than the technical and agronomic. The effort was short-lived and its successes and set-backs are too well-documented to bear summary here (see Schumacher, 1975; Gellar, 1980 and in this volume; and Camboulives, 1967).

The emphasis on the building of 'popular' rural institutions gave way in the mid-1960s to a much more technicist approach aimed above all at production increases, and in the early 1970s to an elitist approach, centered on the best-endowed peasants, that was, again in the Kilby–Johnston lexicon, bi-modal.

In all these phases one theme remained constant: the need for the state to organize production and guide the peasantry – to agrarian socialism in the vision of Mamadou Dia or to material prosperity in the eyes of the young technocrats who picked up the baton in the middle 1960s. This paternalism was echoed by most international donors who only in recent years have decried the harmful effects of over-involvement of state agencies in the agrarian sector (IBRD, 1974:23).

Senegalese farmers, because of their very traditional mentality, limited training, insufficient information, and lack of resources, develop little initiative without outside help.

The counterpart of course is that Senegalese farmers have left initiatives to the state, especially when they bear high financial or physical costs, and have developed what is commonly called a 'mentalité d'assisté.'

II. THE SATEC EXPERIENCE

In June 1963 at Yaoundé, a convention by the same name was drawn up defining economic relations between the members of the EEC and their former African colonies and protectorates. The Convention provided for the gradual phasing out of all price supports and guaranteed quotas for the exports of African states to the EEC. The former colonies of Britain and France in West Africa were particularly affected. With respect to Senegal, Yaoundé meant that by 1968 the guaranteed price above world market levels offered by France to Senegal for groundnut products would be terminated. In anticipation of this, Senegal, with support from the CCCE and the IBRD, contracted in March 1964 with a semi-public French consulting firm, the Société d'Aide Technique et Coopération (SATEC) to launch a program aimed at increasing groundnut production by 25 percent between 1965 and 1969 so as to offset the revenue losses incurred by lower producer prices. The program also aimed at increasing millet production (Pélissier, 1970; Gatin, 1968; Brochier, 1968; Hopkins, 1975).

SATEC's approach was reflective of efforts undertaken in several other LDCs in the 1960s. It emphasized production gains through technical packages, especially the propagation of 'miracle' seed varieties. No such high yielding varieties existed either for groundnuts or millet, but it was nonetheless clear that production could be increased through a package whose major components were:

1. much greater use of chemical fertilizers

2. improved cultivator techniques in sowing, thinning and weeding
3. rational rotations, known as JAMA (jachère, arachide, mil, arachide)
4. use of certified, regionally-adapted seed
5. much greater use of equipment; seeders, tool bars, ploughs, groundnut lifters (*souleveuses*), and, where possible, oxen teams. The seeder would permit uniform early sowing, and the plough (*houe*) would facilitate weeding of groundnuts and free labor for thinning (*démariage*) and weeding of the millet crop. The lifter would permit late harvest.

The target group was the entire cultivating population of the groundnut basin, covering three regions (there are now five), fifteen *arrondissements*, and employing 250 extension agents. Toward this some 5 billion CFA, over a third of which came in foreign assistance, was mobilized. SATEC's stated strategy was unimodal, or *vulgarisation de masse*; distinctions among cultivators were made only in terms of the kind of technical package (*thèmes*) urged upon them.

These packages or *thèmes* were of three kinds and represented a kind of hierarchy through which all cultivators could hope to climb.

1. *Traction bovine, fumure forte* (TBFF). This aimed at those peasants who could afford (with *exploitations* of over 12 ha) to acquire on credit a team of oxen and could thus undertake deep-plowing soil preparation involving the plowing in of tricalcium phosphate, or of green manure on fallow lands, etc. These peasants would also use the recommended amounts of groundnut fertilizer (150-200 kg/ha of NPK 7-21-21).

2. *Traction bovine*. This package emphasized animal traction but assumed modest resort to chemical fertilizers. It also took into account peasants who could not afford oxen but did have access to donkeys or horses that could pull most equipment (seeders, tool bars, lifters) but not heavy plows.

3. *Thèmes Légers*. These were designed for peasants unable to acquire equipment and fertilizers on credit on the same scale as the previous two groups. Emphasis here was upon certified, high quality groundnut seed and improved techniques: early sowing, early thinning of millet, careful weeding, avoidance of premature groundnut harvesting, strategic use of limited amounts of fertilizers.

SATEC, in one way or another, probably did reach most of the population of the groundnut basin. The distribution of equipment on credit was spectacular.

TABLE 3

Spread of Equipment and Oxen Teams into the Groundnut Basin under Auspices of SATEC 1963/64–1969/70

	1963/64	1969/70
Total stock of seeders	33,307	117,969
Total stock of plows	21,029	118,120
Total stock of lifters	3,147	18,152
Total stock of oxen teams	4,228	737

Source: Pélissier, 1970.

The objective of a 25 percent increase in groundnut production was not achieved, but total production and average yields were maintained despite below average rainfall and declining producer prices (see Chart 1). It is likely that by the end of the decade, most peasants in the groundnut basin were at least familiar with the various *thèmes* propagated by SATEC, even if many were unable or unwilling to apply them faithfully.

The shortcomings of the SATEC program were numerous and in various ways have plagued its organizational successor, SODEVA. It was noted in Chapter 2 that Hopkins, Pélissier and others felt that SATEC had focused too much on the *chefs de carré* rather than on the *chefs de ménage* whom they see as the main actors in production decisions. The result was that despite slogans like *vulgarisation de masse*, the *chefs de carré* were relatively favored – they could absorb the most equipment thereby enhancing the image of SATEC's ability to promote technological change, and they could bring about the most rapid increases in production, thereby enhancing the image of the extension workers. An implicit bi-modal strategy emerged that was made formal by SODEVA in the early 1970s.

A second failing consisted in the fact that equipment was misused in at least two ways. First, equipment and above all the seeder, served mainly to increase the area cultivated, not primarily to encourage early sowing and to intensify production on existing acreage. Total production was maintained through this expansion but at the expense of the JAMA rotation. Fallows were sacrificed thus entailing a reduction in fodder crops, green manure, and soil fertility. SATEC built its own prison. Its program was premised on increasing groundnut production so that any reduction in ground-

CHART 1

Levels of Rainfall and Groundnut Production 1959/60–1979/80

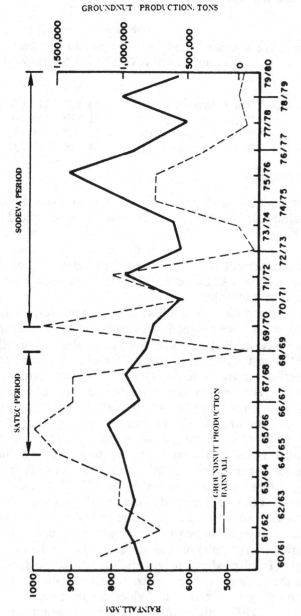

Source: Ministry of Rural Development, annual reports in Bilan de la Campagne Agricole.

nut acreage was unthinkable. If we take an 'average' *exploitation* of 7.5 ha, the ideal, from this point of view, might be 4 ha under groundnuts, 2 ha under millet and 1.5 ha fallow. However without major increases in millet yields, this *exploitation* could not meet its members' food needs. Fertilizer was the key to increased millet yields, but to buy it, even on credit, the peasants would have to grow even more groundnuts. For SATEC, there really was no way out of the prison (Gatin, 1968). For the peasant, invasion of fallows was his only safety net.

Equipment was misused in a second way. As producer prices and the climate deteriorated, peasants, heavily indebted to the coops, turned to private lenders and put up equipment as collateral. Or they simply sold it to large peasants at bargain prices. Further, it was far more profitable for peasants to obtain pairs of oxen, fatten them and then sell them for beef than to retain them for traction. This practice explains the absolute reduction of such teams in the groundnut basin over the period of SATEC's involvement (see Table 3). Experienced observers of the society of the groundnut basin attribute to this period the emergence of a new 'class' of middlemen, especially in non-Murid areas, replacing the Lebanese as merchants, money-lenders, etc. and who became known as the *borom barke* (in an ironic sense 'owners of blessedness'; see Klein, 1979:86; and Van Chi-Bonnardel, 1978).

With the emphasis on groundnut production, SATEC paid little more than lip service to goals of production diversification. Indeed, with the elimination of fallows, animal husbandry suffered badly from lack of fodder and grazing. Encouragement of other crops, like millet, maize, *niebe*, vegetables, etc. was not accompanied by attention to storage facilities and marketing networks.

Institutionally, SATEC effectively skirted, and in so doing subverted, the Centres d'Expansion Rurale Polyvalents (CERPs) that had been set up in the early 1960s. These operated at the level of the *arrondissement* and periodically brought together all officials of government agencies (forestry, animal husbandry/veterinary, agricultural extension, rural credit, seed services, and so on) to enable them to concert policy and not trip over one another's shoelaces. Under SATEC, the extension services became the major official actor alongside OCA (Office de Commercialisation Agricole and the forerunner of ONCAD) and the coops, while other agencies, under the aegis of the Ministry of Rural Development, atrophied (in general, see Schumacher, 1975: 86-229).

SATEC's relative failure, however, was in large part due to

factors beyond its control. First, the beginning of *Opération arachide-mil* corresponded to a major change in land tenure legislation. Second, the drop in groundnut production prices was foreseen and inspired the entire program. A third factor, the deterioration of the quality of certified seed could have been avoided by more careful management through the seed service (*service semencier*); the fourth, rainfall, was an act of God.

The National Domain Law (Law n. 64-46, 6/17/64 'relative au domaine national') stipulated that the State had succeeded to the 'masters of the soil' (*maîtres de la terre*) as sole proprietor of peasant lands and, in turn, delegated the responsibility for the management and allocation of agricultural land to the rural communities, represented by rural councils. Land became inalienable and designated for use by those rural dwellers in the *communauté rurale* who had established claims to it through previous, proven usage. The law was to be applied gradually, through the setting up of *conseils ruraux* department by department and settling claims as they arose. Full application of the law has now been achieved.

Léopold Senghor was almost lyrical in his description of the Law (*Dakar Matin*, May 2, 1964):

Equidistant from individualist, egotistical private property and from leveling collectivism, this new teneurial system, founded basically on personal cultivation and *mise en valeur*, will well represent the original path of African Socialism.

The Law did put an effective end to the market in rural real estate and attendant speculation in land values. However, it had a number of less positive effects. Foremost among them was that inasmuch as rights of land use (*droits d'usage*) were established on the basis of previous, proven use, peasants reacted by reducing or eliminating fallows so as to bolster their claims to land. They also reduced the practice of land-lending that had provided a mechanism for providing access to land for the poorest peasants. Such loans, it was believed, could provide the borrowers legal claims to the land (see Dore, 1981).

It would be wrong to suppose that this Law had much of an impact on SATEC's performance but it did accelerate the trend toward the elimination of fallows and by extension undermined the practicality of SATEC's JAMA rotation. On a broader scale, the new legislation provided an added element of uncertainty and litigiousness in an atmosphere already troubled by impending producer price declines.

After 1966/67 the groundnut basin and SATEC's program went into a period of decline. In 1967/68 the producer price dropped from 21.6 CFA/kg to 17 CFA/kg. Between 1965 and 1967 the price of chemical fertilizers rose from 12 CFA/kg to 16 CFA/kg. Despite that peasants acquired 63,000 tons on credit in 1967/68. Finally in 1968 rainfall declined to its lowest level in a decade. The upshot was that peasants tried to maintain production (along with a large amount of fertilizer, 89,000 tons of groundnut seed were distributed in 1967/68 on credit, the highest level of the decade) and revenues. They were defeated by drought on the first count and falling producer prices on the second. After 1968 they were faced with massive debts for fertilizer, seed, and equipment. Poorer peasants sold or placed the equipment in hock. Draught animals were sold or slaughtered along with traditional herds. Even the richest peasants could turn no profits. By and large rural revenues dropped by about half: they totaled 22 billion CFA in 1965 and fell to 10 billion in 1970 (IBRD, 1974: 145).

One of the most telling effects for SATEC of the *malaise paysan* was the subsequent flight from fertilizers; distributions on credit dropped in 1968/69 to 37,000 tons and to 14,000 tons in 1970/71 – that despite a sharp drop in the price per kg from 16 to 12 CFA. Fertilizer acquisitions, Gatin (1968) argues, represent the peasants' only variable input cost: annuities on equipment and the amounts of seed and fungicides needed for post and pre-harvest storage of groundnuts are stable and the costs fixed. Production costs could be reduced only by decreasing fertilizer applications and by default on equipment and seed loans from the coops. The state responded in 1971, as mentioned, by forgiving short-term debt, raising the groundnut price to 23 CFA/kg, and by holding fertilizer prices steady at 12 CFA/kg. Some resurgence in production resulted, but in many ways Senegal is still trying to find its way out of the crisis of the late 1960s and early 1970s. SATEC's mission expired in the midst of all of this, and it fell to SODEVA to pick it up.

III. SODEVA

In 1968 SODEVA (Société de développement et de mise en valeur agricole) was created as a *société anonyme mixte*, in which the Senegalese state held a 55 percent interest while other state enterprises (ONCAD, the BNDS, the CPSP) and SATEC itself held smaller shares. SODEVA was given entire responsibility for all agricultural activities in the groundnut basin. Its mandate was to:

1. increase overall production
2. double per worker productivity between 1970 and 1980
3. promote diversification
4. increase cultivator income.

Its strategy initially represented no change from the SATEC formula – a combination of *vulgarisation de masse* and promotion of the TBFF (animal traction, chemical fertilizer) *thème* through well-endowed cultivators or *paysans de pointe*. They could readily absorb the package and then through example and the weight of their local prestige attract others to it.

External financing from the IBRD, CCCE, and EDF, begun under the SATEC program, tapered off by 1970, but was resumed once again in 1973. Table 4 shows the growth of SODEVA's budgetary resources and the share of the national government in them. With the exception of the interlude from 1971 to 1973, SODEVA has been heavily dependent upon external assistance to carry out its program and to meet its recurrent costs. After a decade of activity, however, its principal foreign benefactors questioned the utility of the organization and began, as we shall see, to cut back their financing of it. It is well to remember that Senegal's emphasis upon SODEVA and other RDAs came with the urging of these funding sources. E.J. Schumacher (1975: 213) summarized the initial plunge, taken by the then-Prime Minister Abdou Diouf and the then-Minister of Rural Development, Habib Thiam, in these terms:

a fierce debate also raged among the central echelons of Senegalese development services over the measures to be taken in response to the 'malaise' and the advent of SODEVA. In a speech to a UPS National Council meeting in April 1970, Prime Minister Abdou Diouf indicated what was to become the guiding principle of the latest reorganization of rural development structures. He declared that just as the World Bank had insisted on the reorganization of ONCAD as a condition for its loan, so the European Development Fund was pushing for the initiation of 'vast integrated projects organized on a regional basis, each placed under the control of a single structure capable of coordinating all activities in a given zone and responsible for its development.'

It is a sad irony that a decade later the IBRD and the CCCE were to deny their progeny.

The contraction of revenues in the first years of the 1970s forced SODEVA to adopt an elitist approach to extension that made the most of limited numbers of *encadreurs de base* (extension agents).

TABLE 4

Growth of SODEVA Resources and Contribution of the National
Budget to them 1968/69–1978/79
(Millions of CFA)

Fiscal Year	Total Resources	Nat'l Budget Contribution	% of Total
1968/69	508	107	21
1969/70	435	173	39.7
1970/71	423	242	37.2
1971/72	360	301	83.6
1972/73	353	168	47.6
1973/74	566	241	42.6
1974/75	797	292	36.6
1975/76	1775	462	26
1976/77	2211	399	18
1977/78	2574	428	16.6
1978/79	2414	436	18.1

Source: SODEVA, *Rapport présenté aux journées d'étude*, May 1979, p.12.

This focus was encouraged by the IBRD and CCE which supported
the diffusion of the TBFF *thème* in the relatively well-watered Sine-
Saloum. It centered on the well-endowed *paysan de pointe* who
could readily absorb new *thèmes* and by example attract others to
them. In 1982 I visited one of these farmers, near Mbacke, who had
worked closely with SODEVA agents for over a decade. He had 54
ha in his *exploitation*. His *carré* included 12 men, 6 women, 17
children some of whom were *taalibe*. The cultivated surface was
allocated among groundnuts (25 ha), millet (20 ha), manioc (4 ha)
and vegetables (5 ha). The *carré* had at its disposal 2 pairs of oxen, 2
pairs of brood cows, 4 horses, 4 donkeys, 6 carts (used to haul
water), 12 seeders, 12 plows, and 3 *polycultivateurs*. The *carré*
stored 2.3 tons of shelled groundnut seed or enough to plant 18 ha.
Its buildings had corrugated iron roofs to catch rainwater for
vegetables and for the compost pit. There is no question that this
farm and SODEVA's agents had done well by each other. It is
unlikely that this *carré* would demonstrate anything much of direct
relevance to smaller cultivators. By the end of the 1970s it was
estimated that the TB *thèmes* had reached at most 5 percent of the
farm units in the groundnut basin.

Throughout the 1970s SODEVA's personnel list grew prodigiously and recurrent outlays for personnel grew from 28 percent

TABLE 5

Growth of SODEVA Personnel

	1969/70	70/1	71/2	72/3	73/4	74/5	75/6	76/7	77/8	78/9	82/3
National Cadres	50	74	79	139	164	183	252	320	456	428	
Foreign Cadres	36	13	11	14	13	12	11	13	13	8	637
Administrative Personnel	3	40	34	86	103	125	149	204	243	288	
Extension Agents	669	444	442	586	712	742	926	959	1089	1158	661
Total	758	571	566	825	992	1062	1338	1496	1701	1882	1298

Source: SODEVA, Annual Reports, various issues.

of the budget in 1968/69 to 60 percent in 1978/79. Growth was most rapid in the upper echelons of the administration and in administrative personnel, while the corps of field agents grew far less rapidly. At least in this instance, however, because of the magnitude of external assistance, the peasant was not called upon to finance SODEVA's bureaucratic expansion.

By the middle 1970s, SODEVA began to stress agricultural diversification, increased millet production (USAID launched its Souna III millet project in these years) and diffusion of new groundnut seed varieties. In 1977, there was a formal move away from the *paysan de pointe* strategy and a return to the idea of *vulgarisation de masse*. This time the object was to create base units (*groupements de base*), probably the equivalent of a village, with which the extension agents would interact as a group. To some extent, the spirit of the approach of Mamadou Dia and Ben Madhy Cissé 17 years earlier had been revived.

All of this programmatic tinkering took place, as with SATEC, against a backdrop of below average rainfall. Between 1960 and the beginning of the Sahelian drought in 1968, rainfall for all the groundnut basin averaged 686 mm. per year. Between 1970 and 1980 it averaged 461 mm. As significantly the average number of days of rain in the *hivernage* dropped from 47 in the first period to 36 in the second. Another round of production decline and debt default ensued. While the groundnut producer price did not decline, it was held steady at 41.5 CFA/kg between 1974 and 1979. Fertilizer prices increased from 12 CFA/kg in 1973 to 20 CFA/kg in 1977. Despite these apparently adverse price shifts, peasants still tried to grow groundnuts and achieved a record harvest in 1975/76 of 1.4 million tons (see Figure 1). In the first half of the decade fertilizer distributions on credit averaged about 45,000 tons per annum and then surged to 116,000 tons in 1976/77, representing a debt of 2.3 billion CFA. Even as production declined, and unlike the SATEC experience, peasants continued to acquire fertilizers in annual allotments ranging from 50,000 to 110,000 tons. Between 1974/75 and 1980/81, peasants ran up, nation-wide, more than 12 billion CFA in fertilizer debts. When the second *malaise paysan* struck in full force in 1979/80 debts on seed and fertilizers were once again forgiven. The peasants must have expected such an outcome, for otherwise their high-risk assumption of heavy fertilizer debts in the face of adverse prices and poor rainfall would be hard to explain.

The second cumulative production failure called into question nearly all of Senegal's economic strategy, pushed the country toward the *plan de redressement*, and led to a far-reaching shake-up of all forms of state intervention in the agrarian sector. ONCAD, responsible both for groundnut marketing and supervising the coops, was abolished, presumably because of high cost, inefficiency, and corruption. The *Direction des Coopératives* was returned to the Ministry of Rural Development. Management of the national seed-stock, on the order of 120,000 tons each year, was turned over to SONAR. The major groundnut crushers and refiners, SONOCOS and SEIB, became directly responsible for purchasing and transporting groundnuts from the coops to the factories. The object, in part, was to lower administrative costs, but, as we have noted, the overhead charges on the producer price for groundnuts (the so-called *barème*) actually increased, and this despite a simultaneous increase in the producer price from 45.5 CFA/kg in 1979/80 to 60 CFA/kg in 1980/81.

The scope of state intervention in the groundnut basin was reduced to a minimum: provision of seed, and reduced amounts of fertilizers and fungicides on the one hand, and purchase of the groundnut crop on the other. Because of the size of the cumulative cultivator debt – perhaps 20 billion CFA in short term loans and 10 billion in equipment loans – it was decided to suspend all further sales of equipment on credit (see Table 5 and Tuck in this volume), to terminate the food loan program (*prêts de soudure*), and to replace sale of seed on credit with a new system. This consisted in distributing seed at no charge to bona fide cultivators on the basis of 100 kg for each adult male and 50 kg for each adult woman. Lists of those eligible were established on the basis of those subject to the rural head tax, and it was up to village headmen to prepare the lists. Beginning in 1981/82, the producer price was set at 70 CFA/kg. When the peasant brought his groundnuts to the coop for sale, he would receive 60 CFA/kg while 10 CFA/kg were withheld to cover seed costs (9 CFA/kg) and fertilizers (1 CFA/kg). In 1983 the amount withheld at the time of marketing was raised to 20 CFA/kg thereby reducing the real producer price to 50 CFA/kg.

In all this SODEVA found itself severely handicapped at the same time it was given new responsibilities. The suspension of equipment sales cut to the heart of its *programme agricole* and of the mission of its extension service. The reduction in fertilizer distribution was equally crippling. By contrast SODEVA was mandated to play a central role in what was hoped to be a thorough, detailed investigation of the accounts of all coops in the groundnut basin. It was argued by outside advisors and by Senegalese officials that this *assainissement des comptes des coopératives* was a necessary precondition to reorganizing the cooperative system and to launching a new rural credit program. SODEVA personnel, in cooperation with ENEA and with funding from the IBRD and the CCCE, were to begin the *assainissement* process in Sine-Saloum and gradually extend it to the entire groundnut basin.

TABLE 6

Cumulative Equipment Stock in the Groundnut Basin
1970/71–1980/81

	1970/71	*1974/75*	*1979/80*	*1980/81*
seeders	120,595	159,780	209,853	193,133
plows	124,090	174,014	191,185	176,138
lifters	16,892	14,541	34,684	29,002
oxen teams	2,316	3,507	12,809	9,269

Source: Touré, 1982. Thénevin and Yung (1982: 169) point out that cumulative oxen training between 1969 and 1979 involved 55,000 teams. One must conclude that over 45,000 were simply sold off by 1981.

Well before this nearly systemic crisis had set in, SODEVA had begun to rethink its entire role and to contemplate new kinds of intervention in the future. Three interrelated innovations grew out of this rethinking:

1. SODEVA would reduce its personnel and at the same time define with the Government and in a contractual manner its goals and tasks.

2. In anticipation of its own 'withering away' (*dépérissement*) it would help to organize *sections villageoises* that would become the basic building blocks in new structures of rural credit and cooperative organization. A reduced extension service would work with the *sections villageoises* to define credit needs, promote new *thèmes*, and set up collective village endeavors in seed storage, fuelwood production, vegetable production and so forth.

3. Redeploy personnel to undertake basic literacy courses for *paysans de relais* from the *sections villageoises* who would then become responsible in the village for diffusing *thèmes*, keeping accounts, and acting as liaison with SODEVA's field personnel.

The policy wheel had come nearly full circle. In its auto-critique of May 1979, SODEVA reflected in this manner:

From a development point of view, the pre-SATEC experience was more satisfactory. In effect, it better addressed itself to the total promotion of the peasant than does the present effort of SODEVA which is interested only in the producer. Thus henceforth we must move beyond this notion of extension strongly linked to such a conception of economic growth in order to encompass in the program of intervention all aspects of development. Production must of course be increased, but so too must a better quality of life for the peasants be assured (SODEVA, 1979: 99-100).

It was recognized that since 1965 the bulk of the groundnut cultivating population had been exposed to and understood the various technical packages proposed by SODEVA. If they did not apply them, it was not out of ignorance but rather because they were too expensive or competed for labor time that had higher returns in other activities (see Chapter 2).

If the extension message had been learned, then SODEVA's role should be to help peasants, collectively, to make use of it. SODEVA's two principal sources of outside support, the IBRD and the CCCE, urged as early as 1979 that SODEVA focus upon the *sections villageoises* which were envisaged as units of 20-30 adult members. Subsequently, as the default problem grew in magnitude, the IBRD/CCCE tandem came to see the *section villageoise* as the crucial unit in defining collective responsibility for debt (*caution solidaire*). It was proposed that in the process of *assainissement* itself, the *sections villageoises* would be identified and granted legal recognition (*personnalité juridique*) enabling them to borrow in their own name. This represents something of a flip-flop, for the

IBRD had advocated, in its agricultural sector survey of 1975, individual peasant accounts in the coops and the abolition of collective responsibility for debt.

It was in large measure the difficulties of reorganizing the rural credit system and creating the appropriate units of accountability that disrupted SODEVA's attempt to establish a contractual relationship with the Senegalese government – primarily with the Prime Minister's office (*la Primature*). In this respect Senegal borrowed directly from French experience of the late 1960s in drawing up *contrats plans* and *lettres de mission* that were to set performance targets for a variety of parastatal organizations and to define the obligations of all public parties in achieving them.

The objective was to reduce ministerial supervision of parastatal activity by agreeing upon a broad set of targets and objectives and checking on progress toward them *a posteriori*. With respect to SODEVA the rationale for entering into a *contrat plan* bore contradictory elements. As early as 1975, in its budget statement, SODEVA appeared to be groping for a 'productionist' standard to measure its performance and even to pay for its operations (SONED, 1977a: III, 63–64):

It will be soon a question of determining if an apparatus of this scale could pay for itself by surplus values levied on tons of production ... SODEVA could have its services paid for by such production levies. These revenues would then constitute the base of its operating resources.

SONED warned that such an approach would tend to emphasize groundnut production and reliance upon the *paysan de pointe*. At any rate, the deterioration of growing conditions in the ensuing five years left this proposition still-born.

Instead, in the wake of the dissolution of ONCAD, SODEVA and the *Primature* began to work on the terms of a *lettre de mission* that would set both quantitative production targets and social reform goals. In production terms, SODEVA undertook to increase groundnut production from 676,000 tons in 1981/82 to 806,000 in 1983/84. Millet production was to increase from 483,000 to 654,000 tons. Maize production was to increase ten-fold and *niebe* production to double. In addition SODEVA set targets in reforestation, village firewood projects (*bois du village*), animal husbandry in general, and animal fattening at the level of the *carré* (*embouche bovine*).

On the social side SODEVA committed itself to reconstitute 'la solidarité de groupe par la section villageoise.' It would undertake a unimodal strategy of *vulgarisation de masse* aimed at 'tous les agro-pasteurs du village.' Between 1981 and 1984, 671 *paysans de relais* were to be trained, and 3455 secretaries of *sections villageoises*. This latter effort would depend on converting the *encadreurs de base* into functional literacy instructors. SODEVA had already dismissed some 350 *encadreurs de base* in March 1981 (see Table 5) and in the *lettre de mission* pledged to drop another 60 by 1985.

SODEVA would be bound to these goals so long as four conditions beyond its direct control were met (see Diena, 1981; and SODEVA, Lettre de Mission):

1. That rainfall was between a minimum of 440 mm and 32 days and a maximum of 568 mm and 35 days.
2. That good quality seed, adequate supply of groundnut and millet fertilizers, and adequate supplies of fungicides were all available.
3. That the state pursued pricing policies conducive to increased production.
4. That the state met its financial obligations to SODEVA's budget.

Neither party, as it turned out, could meet its obligations. SODEVA estimated its budget needs over the four-year period at 8.5 billion CFA, 5.3 billion of which was 'committed' at the beginning of the period. Of that, 3.3 billion was to come from external sources and about 2 billion in counter-part financing from the GOS. Half the external financing had been pledged by the IBRD and the CCCE. The other half was to come primarily from USAID and IFAD. By early 1982, however, the World Bank and the CCCE judged that their participation in the *assainissement* process in Sine-Saloum, worth 800 million CFA or about 25 percent of SODEVA's projected external resources, was no longer warranted. Perhaps in anticipation of the presidential elections of February 1983, the GOS had quietly ended the *assainissement* program, tacitly forgiven about 10 billion CFA in equipment debt arrears, and pursued an 'inner-circle' debate as to the desirability of using *sections villageoises* as the building blocks of a new cooperative and rural credit system. The IBRD and the CCE made SODEVA pay the price of what they regarded as the dilatory behavior of the GOS.

SODEVA thus found itself with inadequate financial resources to carry on its old programs. Even the GOS was in arrears in committed budgetary support. Simultaneously the government decided, for balance of payments reasons, to hold down fertilizer distributions to 30,000 tons. Thus two of the four conditions governing the *contrat plan* were not met. Rainfall and seed quality and supply were sufficient to maintain production in 1981/82 and 1982/83. Still, with its finances drastically reduced, SODEVA had little choice but to consider very seriously its withering away. It made plans to eliminate another 700 employees by 1985. In the publication of *La Nouvelle Politique Agricole* in June 1984, the Ministry of Rural Development announced that SODEVA, along with other RDAs (SAED excepted), would be phased out over a five year period. While a skeletal organization may remain, mass targeted extension will come to an end.

Since independence, two approaches had been tried by the GOS and found wanting. The experiment in institution- and group-focused African socialism of Mamadou Dia was given its moment from 1960 to 1964 and then was replaced by the SATEC–SODEVA efforts to promote technological innovation and improved cultivator practices. By 1980 it was clear that new policies were in order, but it was not clear if they would be policies of benign neglect or *mise en valeur*.

IV. ELEMENTS FOR THE *MISE EN VALEUR* OF THE GROUNDNUT BASIN

In looking at the development of the groundnut basin over the next decade, one must be very clear about the contextual assumptions that define the argument. *First*, it is assumed that SODEVA will not experience a dramatic turn around in its finances and have to reduce its personnel and its level of activities. *Second*, it is assumed that the ratio of the world price of groundnuts to the real cost of nitrogenous fertilizers will not improve on a continuous basis and may continue to decline. The GOS will continue to confront severe foreign exchange constraints and will limit the amounts of fertilizer made available to the peasants at subsidized prices (in 1983, 25 CFA/kg). There is, however, the hope that with the opening in 1984 of a large fertilizer complex, from which most production is destined for export, the price of domestic fertilizer will be significantly reduced. *Third*, and concomitantly, while equipment will once again be distributed it will be on a more limited scale and with substantial down payments required. *Fourth*, there will be no major change in rainfall patterns nor will new, yield-increasing seed varieties become available. *Finally*, if current extensive techniques of groundnut and millet cultivation are maintained in the absence of off-setting fertilizer applications, a long term secular decline in soil quality and crop yields will be the inevitable result. The argument that follows could be invalidated if some or all of the assumptions prove incorrect. The country's new fertilizer complex, inaugurated in 1984 and designed to produce largely for export, could lead to some reduction in the domestic cost of fertilizer. A substantial rise in world prices for groundnut products or a genetic break-through in drought-resistant or nitrogen-fixing plant varieties could favourably alter the rather gloomy picture presented below.

To deal with the present situation, and to turn it to the advantage of both the cultivators and the state, will require a complex set of policies with far-reaching social implications. The policies would center on three dimensions of rural production systems:

1. The appropriate production and management units
2. Rural asset management
3. Production diversification

A. *Appropriate Production and Management Units*

The Cooperative Law of January 1983 is not entirely clear about the legal rights granted the *sections villageoises*. They are clearly sub-ordinate to the local agricultural cooperatives but do have the right, subject to the approval of the cooperative, to borrow in their own names (Article 37; and see Chapter 4). Whatever their formal powers, a number of crucial tasks in production diversification and asset management will fall to them. By 1985, with some 300 *encadreurs de base*, each of SODEVA's field agents will be responsible for about 400 farm units or perhaps 13 *sections villageoises* at a norm of thirty farm units in each *section*. The literacy instruction and basic agronomic training of the *paysans de relais* will be essential to the diffusion of new *thèmes*. It is proposed that these peasants receive no remuneration for accepting these time-consuming liaison functions. Perhaps it is expected that the honor and prestige attached to these functions will be sufficient to gain their commitment. This image of the *paysan de relais* complements that of the *section villageoise* and the kind of social solidarity that is hoped to reign in its midst. If there are peasant leaders willing to serve their villages for enhanced prestige, and if the villages themselves are conscious of and willing to pursue

209

collective ends, then the *mise en valeur* to be described below might work. The converse is equally true.

The argument over the existence of collective solidarity has given rise to two general types of analysis. For some, like Guy Belloncle and all the spiritual descendants of Père Lebret, it is not so much a question of the existence of peasant solidarity but rather of the level at which it exists (1980a and b). The old cooperative system was plagued by the 'free-rider' problem; peasants who paid off their debts had to pay the price for delinquent coop members. This came in the form of withheld rebates or postponement of the opening of the marketing season until each coop had collected 80 percent of its outstanding debts. Belloncle argued that 'free-riders' existed because coop membership was too large, often involving several villages, and that because the members had no moral leverage over most other members, the reaction over time was for good payers to become free-riders. For Belloncle the intimacy of the *section villageoise* would eliminate delinquent payments.

Moreover, he indirectly rejected the arguments of the World Bank and CILSS (CILSS, 1977) among others to the effect that only individual peasant accounts would solve the delinquency problem. These sources alleged that peasants would actually prefer individual accounts to *caution solidaire* (ITALCONSULT, 1970: Annex I). Belloncle countered that in all his discussions with Senegalese peasants they immediately saw the dangers of a system in which each peasant would have to be fully acquitted of his debts before any new credit was advanced to him. Marginal producers in a bad year would lose access to credit. Those in the *carré* who did receive credit would be under enormous pressure to share it with those not so fortunate. Finally solvent borrowers would be tempted to relend their credit to the less privileged at high interest rates. The only way out for Belloncle was and is the *section villageoise* as the basic borrowing unit and among whose members *caution solidaire* would be a reality.

Many equally qualified observers have voiced skepticism that the village would be more successful in handling collective obligations than any other unit. Pélissier (1966:132) warned against a kind of myth of village-based agrarian collectivism. Albenque (1974) posited that collective solidarity exists below or well above the village: one would expect to find it within the *carré* or perhaps at the level of the networks of Murid or even Tidjani brotherhoods, but certainly not at the level of the coop or the village.

For a number of practical policy reasons it probably makes sense for the government and for SODEVA to pin future programs to this unit. But no one should harbor any illusions that these units can easily be made responsible for their own welfare. SODEVA can and should test the nature of these units through systematic implementation of its goals to promote village-level storage of groundnut seed.

B. Rural Asset Management

1. Seed Stocks

In its *lettre de mission*, SODEVA pledged to develop storage capacity at the village level of about 42,000 tons of groundnut seed by 1984, and to see to it that that capacity was fully utilized. To reach this target would have required the construction of about 600 storage houses of 15 ton capacity each year. In this manner SONAR would have been called upon to constitute a national seed stock of only 75,000 tons. The time frame for this program has not been met and both SODEVA and SONAR are slated to disappear. Still the goal should be maintained. Ultimately the objective would be for peasants to store at the village level up to 80,000 tons while the state maintained a supplementary stock, of good varietal quality, of 40,000 tons. This would yield enough seed to sow nearly one million hectares. *At the household level* something like 20,000 tons of seed is already being stored annually throughout the groundnut basin.

The Gambia has had 25 years of experience in village-level storage of groundnut seed (see Ministry of Rural Development, 1980). Close to 80 percent of the country's annual seed requirements are so stored. The five-ton capacity storage facilities are jointly managed by village leaders and representatives of the groundnut marketing agency. During the dry season, January through April, the storehouses are locked and double-keyed. It is only under highly exceptional circumstances that seed could be withdrawn for purposes other than shelling and sowing.

By 1982 SODEVA had helped in the construction of 8 village store houses in southern Sine-Saloum (average cost per storehouse: $1500). The principles of management of the facilities are similar to those practiced in the Gambia, although it appeared in the field that villagers, or at least village headmen, could have unilateral access to the seed after it had been treated, sacked, and locked up.

The potential advantages of this system are numerous (Frahan, 1981). The slogan 'You shall reap what you store' captures the basic principle. Rather than depending upon an anonymous and inefficient bureaucracy to distribute seed each year, the peasant will depend upon himself. He will hold back from his marketed production good quality seed in order to ensure maximum yields in the following year. This seed will be sacked, marked with his name and locked away between December and May when he can withdraw it for shelling prior to sowing in late June. He will pay an annual subscription fee for the maintenance of the facility.

In this way the peasant minimizes incurring seed debts, and he has his seed when he wants it, not when the state delivers it. Moreover, from the point of view of the state, handling charges will be greatly reduced. The storehouses themselves, made of cement, will reduce the risk of fire, theft, exposure to the atmosphere and pest attacks. Initial tests of seed quality in the first villages to experiment with the system showed very satisfactory results; quality of locally-stored seed was in fact higher than that of the national seed stock. In a survey of over 4000 *chefs de ménage*, A. Dione (1982) found uniform enthusiasm for the principle of collective storage, and about 45 percent of the respondents thought the storehouses should be controlled by peasant delegates rather than village headmen (32 percent). If the system works, it would greatly reduce the scope for peasant indebtedness and might well increase production. The storehouses could serve as models for other collective village undertakings (*bois du village*, millet mills, vegetable plots, etc.).

But there are potential drawbacks. Some experts argue that the one major variable affecting groundnut production over which the state has some control is seed quality. Local storage of seed will make it very difficult to maintain quality or to introduce new varieties (I. Sene, 1981a; and Ministry of Rural Development, 1982).

More important, however, is how we might expect the peasants to hedge their new responsibilities. Among those with whom I talked there was a general sense that the state should not reduce its storage responsibilities at their expense. What, they asked, would happen after a bad year or years when peasants would simply not have enough seed to store? The state has to be there with a very large seed stock to bail them out. Second, the effort could be a disaster if the state is unable to distribute the fungicides necessary to protect the stored seed. In brief, the peasants were not eager for too much responsibility and clearly would like to have both village and national storage systems. They will not, however, want to pay for the latter. A major risk therefore is that Senegal will wind up with both systems and the heavy costs of maintaining the personnel, storage and transportation facilities of the old system while financing the construction and management of the new system.

Peasants may well hedge their local bets as well. A number of them, in widely differing locales, indicated a common strategy. They did not like the idea of *all* their personal seed being in the village warehouse. Most would hold some seed at home to meet cash needs in the dry season. It is precisely this 'improvident' practice that collective storage is designed to counter. Second, the *chefs de carré* and *chefs de ménage* envisaged storing their personal seed in the village storehouse while procuring seed for women and *sourgas* from SONAR's national stock. Almost surely they would continue the established practice of inflating the number of males in the *carré* to maximize their 'drawing rights' on the national stock. It also seems quite possible that collective storage would exacerbate intra-village cleavages. The *chef de ménages* and *chefs de carré*, with more land and somewhat higher yields than those of women or *sourgas*, will produce more groundnuts and have more good seed to store. In bad years or even average years they will be under pressure to lend seed to less fortunate villagers. Under the old system where the seed was held by SONAR such demands were kept to a minimum. At the local level the risk then is that storage capacity will be under utilized, those that pay maintenance dues will not want to pay for sporadic users, and that the physical structures and eventually the system itself may die of disuse. It is worth a major supervisory effort on the part of SODEVA or any successor agency to see that this is avoided.

To date, state policy on local seed storage has been highly inconsistent. Prior to the national elections of February 1983, the Ministry of Agriculture urged peasants to store locally as much seed as possible, promising them 80 CFA for each kilogram stored. Then in April, after the elections, the new Minister of Agriculture announced that the scheme had been dropped, that there would be no bonuses for local storage and that those peasants who had stored their own seed would still be charged at the time of marketing the 10 CFA/kg designed to defray the costs of maintaining the national seed stock. Once again the peasant was educated in the state's commitment to its own promises, and once again SODEVA's credibility was run down through no fault of its own.

Once again, in 1985, the State reversed direction. On the heels of a disastrous marketing campaign, the GOS announced that in 1985/86 only 60,000 tons of seed would be available, to be offered only to farmers who had marketed their harvest through official

213

channels. If the government holds fast to this policy, local storage programs will have to be implemented.

2. *Fertilizers and Fallows*

Inorganic fertilizers will not be available, at an acceptable cost, at anything remotely like the quantities ISRA's norms indicate: at a *minimum* of 75 kg/ha the groundnut basin alone would require 145,000 tons per annum. To sell fertilizers at full cost to peasants would raise groundnut production costs so high as to price Senegalese exports out of an international market in which their position is already precarious.[1] This being the case, and assuming that the state will not follow policies of benign neglect, there is only one way out. Fallows must be reintroduced to protect soil fertility, strategic applications of organic fertilizers must be promoted, and a careful policy for distributing limited amounts of inorganic fertilizers implemented.

Let us begin by a brief consideration of the record of inorganic fertilizer use in the groundnut basin. It was SATEC that made the first big push to encourage the use of inorganic fertilizers throughout the groundnut basin. Even in the late 1950s no more than 5000 tons per annum were being used. Although there was a surge in distribution under SATEC, per hectare use remained far below ISRA norms with great variations even within the *carré* and also from year to year. It became clear that peasants used fertilizer to maintain the fertility of heavily cultivated soils but not to increase productivity.

There have been intense debates in Senegal over the usefulness of inorganic fertilizers. There are major ecological variables. The northern, low rainfall zone of the groundnut basin shows the poorest response to fertilizers while southern Sine-Saloum shows the best. Thus both doses and the proportions of active NPK elements should be, but seldom are, regionally adjusted. In an earlier study in Sine-Saloum (SODEVA, 1971) it was found that when less than 90 kg/ha were applied, groundnut yields were actually below those when *no* fertilizers were applied mainly because of increased weed growth. Only after doses of 130 kg/ha were yields positively affected. It is often the case that with direct applications of fertilizer, groundnuts tend to put out more leaf and fewer nut clusters. It was also found that millet responded better to direct fertilization in the first year, and groundnuts in the second due to residual fertilizer in the soil.

Most tests have shown that the SATEC–SODEVA *thèmes*

légers, that involve no tillage or plowing-in of green manure and phosphates, remove more nutrients from the soils than can be compensated by doses even of 150 kg/ha. In view of this, if inorganic fertilizers are to be part of the extension package they must be accompanied by the animal traction and TBFF (animal traction, chemical fertilizer) *thèmes* as well as maximum doses per ha (ISRA, 1980). Even then there will be large net losses of magnesium, calcium, and potassium (J.P. Ndiaye, 1978). The implications of this should be clear. The *thèmes lourds*, after 15 years, had reached only about 5 percent of the *exploitations* of the groundnut basin. Even if the equipment program is relaunched, it appears inconceivable that a majority of peasants will have access to ox-drawn implements. It appears equally inconceivable that norms of 130–150 kg/ha of inorganic fertilizer can ever be achieved (See Ministry of Rural Development, 1981). Only a minority of privileged peasants – cotton producers, *mulitiplicateurs* of certified groundnut and millet seed, maize producers, etc. – will obtain the 30–50,000 tons of fertilizers that the GOS will mobilize, nation-wide, in the years to come.

Even if one could dismiss the formidable organizational challenges of turning to organic fertilizers, it would be unrealistic to see such nutrients as a solution to production problems in the groundnut basin. Even if there were no competing demands for crop residues and animal manure as fodder and fuel, the amounts that could be gathered and absorbed into the soil would not come close to compensating for the removal of nutrients through normal cultivation.

It will only be through a systematic and rationalized return to fallows that a holding operation against long-term soil depletion and declining yields can be maintained.[2] In 1976 the FAO was sufficiently alarmed by soil depletion in the groundnut basin that it recommended a decrease in the cropping intensity in the older areas of 25 percent and massive population transfers to the east and south. In general FAO saw the need to fallow 5 ha for every ha sown using traditional methods in the low rainfall zone, to one hectare fallow for each hectare sown with 'modern' techniques in wetter zones (1976: I, 97). This makes good sense except that it is impossible.

What is needed is a revised version of what might be called the Serer model. Traditionally, the Serer followed highly integrated practices of cattle raising, rotating fallows, and millet production. Land was systematically rotated into fallows by *chefs de carré*, cattle herds were kept on the fallow lands and their droppings were

215

absorbed into the soil. Scattered across the landscape were the famous *kad* trees (Acacia albida) that fix nitrogen in the soil, and drop their leaves in the dry season when fodder is scarce enabling cattle to feed on them (Pélissier, 1966: 190–300).

If the *sections villageoises* become a reality, one of their asset and production management tasks could be to plan fallows *at the village level*, grouping (*parcage*) the animals of all the *carrés* on the fallows for grazing. SODEVA would have a key role in designing the rotation for each *section villageoise*. The *paysans de relais* would be responsible for supervising the rotations. Not only would this contribute to the safeguarding of soil fertility, but would also maximize fodder production and facilitate the gathering of manure. It would promote animal fattening (*embouche bovine*) which is, as we shall see, an integral part of diversification projects. Assuming that most animals are owned by *chefs de ménage* and *chefs de carré*, they would be called upon to use their animals to improve the soil patrimony of the *section villageoise*.

Scale of fallows may be very important. If fallows were introduced at the level of the household, the move could be partially self-defeating. It was observed in in Upper Volta (Poulain, 1980: 66) that a holding of 8.5 ha with 2 ha fallow, produced about 9 tons of crop residues and green manure. The pair of oxen needed to plow in the green manure (*enfouissement*) on the fallow consumed about 8.2 tons of fodder. The net gain in organic material was thus very small.

In the absence of a fallow system, resort to organic fertilizers will bring very little return to the substantial effort needed to make use of them. Organic materials in this instance would consist in widely scattered animal droppings and crop residues. SODEVA has encouraged strategic applications of such materials according to a norm of 2 tons per ha. One must be skeptical, that at the level of the *carré*, there will be many peasants willing to put in the time and effort required to amass such quantities. Moreover their nutritive impact is reduced unless they are decomposed through composting, a process that demands about 45 days of wetting and the application of a mulching agent. Village water supplies, especially in the dry season, are severely limited. Households would have to have the carts and draught animals to haul water from wells to compost pits. Again, a village-run compost pit might make better sense; the game would be in finding a formula for distributing the compost.

3. Water Supply, Wells, and Pumps

Improving village water supply will be essential to any *mise en valeur* in the groundnut basin. There are today some 40,000 wells, serving all of Senegal's 12,000 villages. Their capacity is in a very modest range of 12,000–100,000 M^3 per day, depending on the season. Most are shallow and many have been unusable because of more than a decade of low rainfall (Ministère de l'Hydraulique, 1982 and *Le Soleil*, 6/22/83). Villages or clusters of villages could be put in charge of deep wells and pump sets to provide water for stock, compost, off-season vegetables, and *bois du village*. An installation and annual users' fee could be charged to the *sections villageoises*.

4. Herd Management

The most important facet of agricultural diversification to be pursued at the village level is herd management and animal fattening. There is tremendous scope here to improve peasant incomes, to provide draught animals, and to rationalize grazing in conjunction with fallow rotations.

It is estimated that between 1960 and 1977 the share of animal husbandry in gross agricultural product (including fishing) rose from 19 to 27 percent. Cattle stock in 1980 was valued at 100 billion CFA or about 8 percent of GDP (*Le Soleil*, 2/5/82). Despite losses during the Sahelian drought, herds were rapidly reconstituted and expanded. In 1981 sales of cattle were valued at 3.4 billion CFA or over 10 percent of revenues generated by groundnut sales. At the time of writing, another cycle of severe drought may have decimated once again Senegal's herds.

TABLE 7

Expansion of Animal Stock 1960–1980 (1000s)

	1960	1980
cattle/oxen	1,746	2,238
sheep & goats	1,022	3,103
horses	76	200
donkeys	54	236
camels	3	6
pigs	19	141
Total	2,920	5,924

Source: Ministry of Rural Development figures as published in *Le Soleil*, 6/22/82.

For some years SODEVA has been promoting beef fattening (*embouche bovine*) at the level of the *carré* and of the household. Even though cattle for fattening are no longer available on credit, the program has spread rapidly. One stratagem for the peasant is to buy a sheep during the *soudure* relatively cheaply, fatten it over the *hivernage* and sell it dear for the Tabaski (feast of the sacrifice of Abraham). With the profits he may be able to buy a steer for 30–40,000 CFA, fatten it for three months, and sell it for a profit averaging about 25,000 CFA (SODEVA, March 1982). This profit is the equivalent of earnings from the marketing of nearly half a ton of groundnuts. As Laura Tuck's data show, however, real profits may in many instances be negligible and SODEVA's estimates taken as the outer limits. Profits can be partially plowed back into purchases of more animals, perhaps a brood cow or draught animals. SODEVA advises peasants on the use of crop residues (millet stalks, groundnut leaves and stalks, groundnut skins) for fodder during the dry season. The reintroduction of fallows would provide wet fodder during the *hivernage*.

Improving animal husbandry may lead to a situation in which *carrés* or perhaps even villages can breed and train their own oxen for traction. There are some doubts that Senegalese oxen could ever be heavy enough to undertake deep plowing (Association Sud-Ouest: 1981), but as René Dumont (1980) has argued, the value of such animals may lie mostly in their ability to drive pumps, pull water carts, haul produce, or pull tool bars. The case for village ownership of some draught animals is derived from the fact of the high cost of animals and equipment. A Michigan State University study (1981) estimated that it would take the equivalent of one and a half to three years of the gross output of a 6 ha farm in the Sine-Saloum to pay for a team of oxen, a tool bar, a seeder, a cart, and a groundnut lifter.

5. Village Woods and Village Vegetable Plots

Two other activities that might best be undertaken by the *sections villageoises* would be the management of village woods (*bois du village*), primarily for the production of fuelwood and charcoal (fast-growing eucalyptus is the best-suited), and vegetable gardens to generate working capital for other village activities (purchase of pumps or millet mills). Both activities require predictable water supply and entail significant amounts of labor in the dry season.

To recapitulate, the *sections villageoises* might find themselves in charge of:

—village seed storehouses
—deep wells and pumps
—compost pits
—small fleet of carts and some draught animals
—management of village fallows
—village woods
—village vegetable gardens
—gathering manure and crop residues for composting and animal feed
—tending village woods
—tending and marketing the produce of village vegetable gardens
—maintenance of pumps, equipment, millet mills and storehouses.

As matters now stand, such a strategy would face great difficulties in attracting off-season adult male labor that is typically drawn off into seasonal migration and petty trade (cf. Levi, 1979; and see Chapter 2).

C. *Diversification*

One point should be very clear. The strategy suggested does not disrupt existing authority patterns in the *ménage* and the *carré* except insofar as some of the autonomy of these units would be ceded to leadership at the level of the *section villageoise*. Otherwise, the *chefs de carré* and *chefs de ménage* will not see their positions eroded. The major changes proposed are to compete for male, off-farm labor in the dry season and to free women of some of their existing tasks so that they can become actively involved in *mise en valeur*. There exist already vehicles by which this could be done: village level *associations des femmes* and *groupements des jeunes* (for examples, see Raulin, 1976; and A. Diop, 1982).

Members of these groups now have access to land on an individual basis. If they spontaneously and formally agree to farm land jointly or to undertake some other collective goal such as purchase of a millet mill, a truck to haul produce, a pump set, etc., a national fund could be established to *match* whatever working capital they are able to master. Such a fund could usefully be financed by bi-lateral or multi-lateral donors. The essential points are that the groups organize spontaneously, that they mobilize and commit some capital, and that their projects have the possibility of paying for themselves through sale of produce or users' fees and service charges. Participants in these groups and endeavors must see their personal stake in them as well as the tangible benefits they stand to draw from them.

If such groups turned profits, it might mean that the *chefs de carré* and *chefs de ménage* would no longer be able to rely upon *sourga* and female labor on their millet fields and private groundnut fields. It is a risk, but the process of fragmentation of the *carré* into small productive units is already well underway. One would hope that all the members of the village would recognize a collective interest in safeguarding their control over an essential food staple and would commit the labor necessary to assure that control. But there is no escaping the fact that for diversification to work, it must be profitable and it must involve women and young males.

There can be no minimizing the difficulties in managing and sustaining collective assets and undertakings. The growing rational choice literature has amply documented the dynamics by which groups run down their collective assets because of suspicions that some members are drawing disproportionate benefits, or are shirking obligations, or not paying their fair share (inter alia, see Russell and Nicholson, 1981). The free-rider problem in many ways did in Senegal's old cooperative and rural credit system. It is hoped that the intimacy of the *section villageoise* will prevent, through peer and kin pressure, a recurrence of the phenomenon. However, that may be a rather forlorn hope, and SODEVA personnel must be prepared to bolster flagging spirits and help resolve disputes. It may, in addition, be advisable for the *communautés rurales* to take on a real coordinating role, drawing up resource inventories at the level of the *commune*, reviewing land use schemes, designing pastorage allocations and the utilization of wells, improving local markets, and helping cope with the annual scourge of brush fires. Central state agencies, however, should not assume direct responsibility for any village projects.

There is a very real question whether in terms of its economic future the groundnut basin is worth this kind of effort. The effort would aim *maximally* at a holding operation, trying to arrest further degradation of the soils and productivity of the basin. There seem to be no production breakthroughs, no agricultural miracles hovering on the horizon. The strategy is hinged on the peasants, grouped in villages, taking responsibility for improving their patrimony and devoting off-season labor to collective tasks. It is conceptually a unimodal strategy but one which in practice will be very uneven (cf. Acharya and Johnston, 1978: 71; and, USAID, 1983a: 4). It will involve thousands of villages with unequal resource endowments, access to markets, and access to services. All of them will have weak financial bases; indeed, some so weak that they may be unable to muster any working capital at all. To compensate for this weakness activities undertaken must generate new revenues or reduce existing outlays. In short, *responsabilisation* would become much more than a slogan. At the same time the state would not deny its responsibility for the welfare of the cultivators.

The strategy is realistic to the extent that it could meet political demands for improvement in the welfare of the bulk of the nation's rural population. It is also realistic in that it assumes no improvement in Senegal's terms of trade and therefore no major increases in groundnut prices nor massive distributions of high-priced fertilizers. The strategy would mesh with a situation in which seed credit is greatly reduced, fertilizer credit nearly non-existent, and equipment sold for cash.

The strategy would certainly provide a new *raison d'être* for SODEVA or its successor, but a formidable challenge as well. It would become more concerned with monitoring highly dispersed rural institutions rather than with monitoring agricultural production *per se*. It would require from the EBs and ATCRs sensitivity to individual village politics and a grasp of the difficulties inherent in managing collective goods. Administratively, SODEVA personnel would have to interact closely with other public agents – from forestry, seed service, veterinary services, rural water supply, and so forth – and perhaps with the CERPs. Finally coordination with ISRA, which presumably would undertake the technical design of new programs of *mise en valeur* (*embouche*, composting, fallowing, fodder enrichment, diversification, etc.) would be crucial to the success of the strategy.

Mise en valeur is a package. It cannot be done piecemeal. It will require a sustained, consistent effort and set of policies. It should not be attempted if the first two conditions cannot be met. If they cannot, benign neglect is the better course. If they cannot, external donors should be clear about what they are doing: helping the GOS put bandaids on a politically important region.

There are real choices to be made here. If the social, administrative, and physical environment of the groundnut basin is such that this strategy could not be implemented with solid hopes for success, it might be best not to try at all. Scarce resources in that case might best be reallocated to areas where pay-offs are likely to be higher. Still, there are a couple of million peasants in the groundnut basin with vast experience and considerable skills in extracting a living from that environment. It might well be a major mistake not to invest in those human resources and in that place.

NOTES

1. This judgement is born out in a number of studies, including Thénevin and Yung, 1982: p. v of Conclusions. A USAID document justifying fertilizer imports notes, however, that fertilizer use on groundnuts will be attractive to peasants *only* if sold at current levels of subsidization, but would not be attractive to the state even if 75 percent of the subsidy were lifted. Fertilizer use on millet would be attractive to the state even if 75 percent of the subsidy were lifted. Fertilizer use on millet would be attractive to the peasant only if subsidies were maintained and the effective farm gate price for millet were 75 CFA/kg (USAID, 1983b: Annex F).
2. Despite the widespread use since 1965 of inorganic fertilizers, improved techniques such as early seeding and weeding, and the introduction of improved groundnut seed, yields are no higher today than in the 1940s and 50s when none of the above were widely available. SATEC and SODEVA can thus be seen as having mounted a high-cost holding operation in the face of declining soil fertility. F. Ganry (1980: 63) put the matter in aggregate terms. Assume groundnut production of one million tons and millet production of 750,000 tons. Assume, *very optimistically*, that 50 percent of all crop residues are returned to the soil. The annual loss would still be 200,000 tons of nutrients and 25,000 tons of lime.

CHAPTER SEVEN

Politics of Agricultural Price Decision-Making in Senegal

Sidi C. Jammeh

I. INTRODUCTION

This study is intended to contribute to the ongoing policy debate on price intervention policies, focusing more on the political basis of such policies. Specifically, it seeks to explain policy action in Senegalese agriculture. Who decides? Why and on what basis? Such a focus will facilitate critical evaluation of the role which political considerations have played in the process of agricultural price decision-making. The study examines the evolution of state intervention in agriculture, with special reference to pricing and commercialization policies. Senior government officials and others involved and/or concerned about pricing policies have been interviewed, and the responses analyzed in terms of their relevance to our understanding of which factors influence policy choice. State and parastatal institutions concerned with pricing, marketing and processing of agricultural commodities have been visited and relevant documents have been consulted as well. In addition, some farmers in parts of the peanut basin, particularly in Touba Mbacke, have been interviewed.

II. INSTITUTIONAL FRAMEWORK

Control of the price mechanism is considered by the administration as crucial to its revenue objectives as well as to rural incomes security and equity goals. To these must be added another equally important price policy goal which senior officials have constantly stressed, namely, the objective of maintaining social peace (la paix sociale). It is for these reasons that the President himself (and before the constitutional changes of 1984, the Prime Minister) takes the final price decision. He is assisted in this task by a team of technical advisers drawn mainly from public and parapublic institutions as well as local bankers and representatives of industry.

The underlying objective of pricing decisions has clearly evolved around growth in agro-industrial output; increased groundnut production, and to a lesser extent cotton production, through the diffusion of modern farming practices have been considered the key to industrial growth. In addition, the goal of self-sufficiency in sugar cane has also been emphasized, especially since the mid-seventies. This was to be achieved through production subsidies to the private sugar monopoly (CSS). Given this overriding objective, pricing policies have been determined after consideration of the following principal constituencies, in descending order of importance: industrialists, consumers and producers. As will be demonstrated later on, the interests of industry, mainly the peanut crushing firms, have been paramount partly because groundnut industrial activities generate scarce foreign exchange earnings as well as provide stimulus to the rest of domestic industry. The concern with consumers has tended to focus largely on industrial workers, bureaucrats and the urban working population in general. This concern stems from the notion that food prices should be used to shape wage and income policy, whereby lower urban food prices afforded by cheap imports and/or consumer subsidies, can forestall wage increases, which in turn will enhance the profitability of Senegalese industries as well as stabilize or reduce the financial costs of running an overmanned public bureaucracy. Concern for producer interests has centered on the vast majority of the smaller farmers who derive a substantial part of their incomes from crop production, notably groundnuts. Income security through stable producer prices has been the centerpiece of policy for this group of farmers.

As shown in the diagram below, price policy-making is centralized in three key ministries – Commerce, Economy and Finance and Agriculture and Rural Development. There is at present little institutional coordination between these ministries other than the interministerial council which is essentially an organ for debate and oversight. Ad-hoc committees have sometimes been set up in council in order to resolve the important differences in views among ministerial colleagues in the event such differences arise. The technical quality of pricing discussions has in general been low, partly because of differences in view or ignorance about what constitutes an economic price. Sometimes, technical considerations might not matter after all, since important pressures for short-term

DIAGRAM 1

Institutions and Other Actors Relevant to Agriculture Price Formation

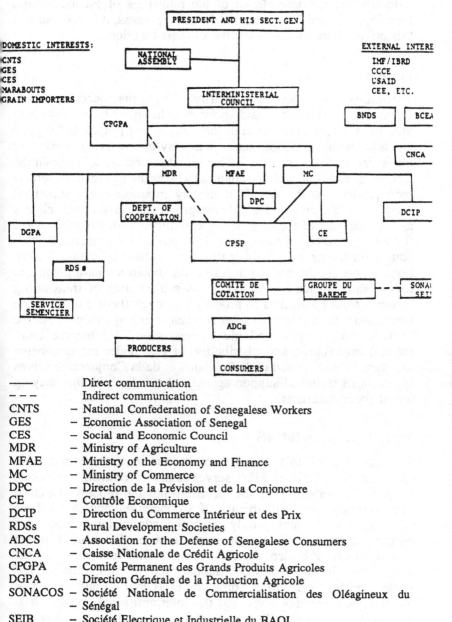

———		Direct communication
– – –		Indirect communication
CNTS	–	National Confederation of Senegalese Workers
GES	–	Economic Association of Senegal
CES	–	Social and Economic Council
MDR	–	Ministry of Agriculture
MFAE	–	Ministry of the Economy and Finance
MC	–	Ministry of Commerce
DPC	–	Direction de la Prévision et de la Conjoncture
CE	–	Contrôle Economique
DCIP	–	Direction du Commerce Intérieur et des Prix
RDSs	–	Rural Development Societies
ADCS	–	Association for the Defense of Senegalese Consumers
CNCA	–	Caisse Nationale de Crédit Agricole
CPGPA	–	Comité Permanent des Grands Produits Agricoles
DGPA	–	Direction Générale de la Production Agricole
SONACOS	–	Société Nationale de Commercialisation des Oléagineux du
	–	Sénégal
SEIB	–	Société Electrique et Industrielle du BAOL

objectives, from within and from without the administration, would call for a political rather than an economic price.

In light of the importance of the ministries of Finance, Rural Development and Commerce in the price process, it is necessary at this point to briefly discuss some of their functions.

Finance

This ministry is concerned primarily with the macroeconomic consequences of price and subsidy policies. It has often been drawn in to join the other two ministries in the initiation of proposals for price levels but it has been more active in the day-to-day fixing of prices of industrial products, notably edible oil, cake and crude, through the Comité de Cotation which it chairs as well as the financial operations (péréquation) of the CPSP. It closely monitors the commercial activities of the agro-industrial enterprises and actively participates in the meetings of the negotiating committee which is responsible for setting marketing margins and for voting a commercialization budget for the peanut crushing firms. Apart from the above institutional interests, the finance ministry has shown increasing concern for consumer price levels and opposes the notion of transferring incomes from consumers to producers through the use of the price mechanism. It has now completely taken over responsibility for the CPSP's price support activities (péréquation), leaving the commercial importation and distribution of rice under the commerce ministry. The Direction de la Prévision et de la Conjoncture serves as one of its technical-support agencies that helps with the carrying out of these functions.

Rural Development (MDR)

The interests of this ministry center on agriculture and rural environment in general. MDR serves as the government's advocate of producer interests in the decision-making process which it does through the Departments of Cooperation and Agriculture (DGPA). Its minister jointly proposes administered input and output price levels with the commerce minister. These are then sent directly to the President for final decision and ratification. In the past, it has played the key coordinating role in the interministerial committee for agricultural commodities (CPGPA) and served as the link between this body and the interministerial council. It is equipped with an excellent team of well-trained agronomists and agriculturalists in key decision-making positions while its reservoir of agricultural economists, found in middle-level positions, have seldom been used in the price formation process. As indicated in the diagram, all the rural development agencies fall under the responsibility of this ministry. It participates in all pricing discussions as well as in negotiations with the peanut crushing firms on the modality of groundnut commercialization. The minister has often come out strongly in support of remunerative production policies, including a continuation of input subsidy and/or tax exoneration programs for the agricultural sector.

Commerce

Relatively new (created in 1980), this ministry is involved in both the initiation and application of price policies in general. However, it is more suitably equipped to perform execution, regulation and surveillance roles than originating pricing decisions. It participates in meetings of all agencies and committees on price-related issues and co-sponsors pricing proposals with the rural development ministry. The Direction du Commerce Intérieur and the Contrôle Economique are its principal organs for the overall administration of price policies. In addition, the commerce ministry oversees domestic marketing and distribution of all products, including imported rice and local cereals. It is for the proper execution of these roles that it shares responsibility for the CPSP with the ministry of finance. Its most important clients in the past have been rice importers and presently, rice distribution quota holders, domestic traders and retailers as well.

Although the Interministerial Technical Committee for Major Agricultural Products (CPGPA) has in the past played a key role in pricing decisions, its future seems uncertain. It has not been convened since mid-1983 and most of its work now increasingly is turned over to the Interministerial Council and associated technical study groups. It was in the past the primary agricultural problem-solving institution dealing with oversight over all technical aspects of production, marketing organization, crop-specific studies, pricing and so forth. Its membership, variously put at between 25 and 40, consists of representatives from the different governmental agencies listed above in the institutional chart as well as the BCEAO, BNDS, SONACOS, SEIB and, sometimes, the National Confederation of Agricultural Cooperatives. Pricing discussions have been severely handicapped by lack of the necessary data.

This committee has been rendered ineffective for a few important reasons. First, a large part of its members rarely show up for meetings. Second, heads of departments and concerned agencies, with the exception of SONACOS and SEIB, seldom attend meetings in person; instead, they send junior officers with neither the technical expertise nor the decision-making power to participate in pricing discussions. Third, the work of the committee lacked effective coordination. This last has been attributed to the failure of the MDR (DGPA) to provide its assigned leadership role after the CPGPA's chairman, Medoune Diene, took over full-time responsibility for SODEFITEX. Fourth, most of the members have lost interest in serving on the committee, partly because they soon discovered that the final choice of a price regime was increasingly diverging from their recommendations and partly because matters related to prices slipped out of their hands without any official reasons being given. According to senior administration officials, the CPGPA existed and probably still exists as a technical advisory group, but it had to be relieved of its pricing functions largely because it lacks both the technical competence and political insight to deal with all the complex issues involved.

Some of these issues tend to be more political than economic. They derive in large part from pressure exerted directly or indirectly by important non-governmental actors, particularly the international donors (listed under external interests in the chart above). This interest group plays an increasingly important role in the Senegalese economy. They have consistently pressed for agricultural reform measures, including, in particular, changes in both consumer and producer price levels. The domestic interest groups listed in the left of the institutional chart also have tried to influence policy outcome. However, the interests of the marabouts have tended to be given more weight.

The first three groups (CNTS, GES, CES) have, in general, closely identified with the government and many of their leaders can be found in important political positions within the ruling party, in the national assembly and in the parapublic sector. They have in the past been invited to serve on different problem-solving commissions and have been consulted on matters related to consumer price policies. The scope of their activities seems at present limited to the urban areas.

The marabouts, on the other hand, do not possess a formal institutional organization for interest articulation, but there is always that traditional understanding between state and religion which ensures that their important interests form part of the agricultural policy agenda. Their most potent leverage is their reservoir of rural support, particularly in the groundnut basin, as well as their dominant influence over producer responses to government policy. In addition, the religious leaders of the leading Sufi orders have their special envoys to the state capital and a cluster of marabouts and faithful disciples, who have often enjoyed relative ease of access to the presidency and government ministries for purposes of bureaucratic intermediation or for one kind of state intervention or another, or simply for making a courtesy call. Some of these informal actors permanently reside in Dakar while some come and go. The interests of these spokesmen may not always be price-related. In fact, except in the case of the large producers ('gros producteurs') among them, agricultural prices seldom matter. They have increasingly become interested in obtaining access to donor-financed commercial projects and various institutional support services.

However, the finance ministry, in whose leadership the donors have reposed some confidence, clearly has emerged as the key actor in the pricing process, outside the presidency. In spite of this, the finance minister holds entirely different views on matters related to price and cereals policy. While he agrees with the donors' diagnosis of the country's economic problems, particularly as regards to the negative balance of payments effects of increasing rice importation, he disagrees with the prescription that price policy should be used to cut down on these imports or to promote production of domestic substitutes. He insists, instead, that the food sector's problems are structural ones and as such bear little relationship to pricing. The minister shares this view on cereals pricing policy with the President but for different reasons. In the opinion of informed sources, while the head of state supports the need for a coherent cereals policy as do the donors, he opposes the idea of using price policy for either production or consumption reasons on the grounds that the necessary empirical evidence on supply or demand responsiveness to relative grain price changes is still not available to back up such a policy. Other cabinet ministers, notably of Planning and Cooperation and Rural Development, have tended to hold the opposite viewpoint, and have consistently argued for a price policy that is more favorable to the food sector. However, as noted earlier on, the views of the finance minister in pricing discussions have been very determinant as evidenced by the rejection of the proposal to increase groundnut producer price levels in 1984–85 based mainly on his strong opposition to it. This decision was reversed with an executive decree raising nominal producer prices from 70FCFA/kg to 90FCFA/kg in the middle of the groundnut procurement campaign. It is instructive to note that this unprecedented move has been intended to induce farmers to refrain from trading their groundnuts in the parallel market and sell, instead, to the official collectors.[1]

In sum, the process of agricultural price policy-making has been dominated by bureaucratic actors and representatives of the peanut crushing firms. While there has been no effective organized consumer interest group participation in this process, urban consumer interests have not been completely left out. These have tended to be protected by public officials who themselves constitute an important segment of the urban population.

Marginal farmers, on the other hand, have been virtually excluded from the process and their interests have been inadequately represented in spite of the role played on their behalf by the Rural Development Ministry (MDR). Although the opposition press and certain influential social brokers, such as the marabouts, have in the past provided relevant price policy information and an outlet for expression of peasant reactions to policy outputs, these alternative communication channels seem inappropriate substitutes for a genuine producer-based interest group.

Once pricing decisions have been handed down, it then becomes the responsibility of the CPSP to execute them. In general, the Caisse carries out this task in conjunction with its marketing functions, as the price mechanism constitutes an integral part of the marketing system.

By far the most important agricultural pricing institution, the CPSP, enjoys the status of 'economic institution of privileged standing' but it has very little decision-making power on pricing or on its other important functions, such as péréquation, commercialization or distribution. It was intended to provide the government with what officials refer to as the institutional capability to insulate the agro-industrial economy from the effects of the confluence of unfavorable events in the world economy – recession in the market for groundnut products, price instability, inflationary pressures – and adverse weather conditions, through the use of pricing and marketing policies.

The price intervention functions of the CPSP have helped increase and reinforce the stakes of both governmental and non-governmental actors in the resource flows afforded by state manipulation of the price mechanism. In addition, the evidence shows that institutional price determination policies through the CPSP have revolved around two primary commodities – groundnuts and rice. Furthermore, there is reason to believe that the CPSP actually came into being partly as a result of the administration's failure to develop a rational and consistent price policy program for all crops, officially attributed to lack of the necessary technical knowledge, and in part to lack of a more politically expedient alternative and dependable system for allocating and distributing resources for development programs and/or patronage.

III. EVALUATION OF PRICING DECISIONS

The analysis in the remainder of this chapter will attempt to determine to what extent political considerations have influenced the primary decision-maker's choice of producer and consumer price levels of agricultural commodities. It is based on an examination of interview and other relevant data on major pricing decisions from 1961 to 1984.

Numerous studies have been done on decision-making behavior. Yet the issue of why policymakers choose one policy as opposed to another is still puzzling and largely unresolved. Appreciation of the social context of decision-making, particularly in contemporary Africa, is important because

the social environment in which public servants are enmeshed demands commitment to other reference groups and the fulfillment of obligations to other, competing role-sets. Obtaining social approval and esteem necessitates the isolation of the norms and requirements of the organizational role-set, so that precedence can be given to the obligations of some other personal role-set or tradition-oriented mode of social behavior. (Price, 1975, p. 206)

This is especially the situation of the western-educated Senegalese Muslim bureaucrat, who seems to be constantly pulled by different kinds of environmental forces from one direction to the other. On the one hand, this bureaucratic actor tries to operate in terms of the secular norms of the formal administration structures. On the other hand, there is his traditional background – allegiance to the Sufi establishment, kinship ties, ties to regional groups, friendship and other patron–client alliances – with all the primordial sentiments and internalized sacred values usually associated with it, dictating an entirely different behavior.

Without minimizing the significance of these approaches, it is important to note that they carry a certain deterministic logic against which ongoing efforts for administrative reform by new African nations, particularly Senegal, have poor prospects. The issue of hard choices arises from the inherent difficulty of reconciling short-run economic and political interests with long-run objectives. Obtaining the proper balance can be an extremely problematic decision-making task especially when political survival – remaining in political office – more or less depends on the economic policies pursued. Thus, the policy-maker's anticipation and/or perception of political constraints may be an important guide to policy choice.

Senegal's producer price policies have tended to revolve around groundnuts. The official price for this crop has consistently been adopted as the reference price for all other domestic crops. Foodgrain prices have been largely irrelevant in pricing discussions prior to the mid-seventies and have only recently received serious attention. Contrary to the official view, groundnut producer prices have seldom reflected prices in the world market prior to the early eighties. They have stayed above international prices during much of the colonial period through the latter half of the sixties largely because of the producer price support and other marketing privileges provided by France. In spite of this support, however, peanut producer prices represented about 50 percent or less of the export price of its by-products, with the exception of the price of groundnut cake. They remained unchanged at 22FCFA/kg for seven consecutive years.

The first important pricing decision was handed down by the President's office when the groundnut producer price decreased in 1967/68 by about 21 percent. This policy action was precipitated by an external event, namely, the withdrawal of France's price support and a general decline in international price levels. The magnitude of the fall in the producer price level was higher than the decline in international price relatives, in part due to pressure exerted by the Syndicat des Fabricants d'Huile et de Tourteaux du Sénégal. Perhaps another important contributing factor might have been the policy intent of lowering the producer price without significantly affecting the budgetary contributions of the industry.

Although this decision was resented by smaller farmers, little was done to mobilize producer response for understandable reasons. For one thing, traditional allies in the countryside, the 'gros producteurs,' have been more concerned with getting their regular supplies of subsidized inputs and other forms of patronage, which in general have been provided. For another, the producer price accorded them by the state was in all cases a superior price relative to the price paid to small producers.

After staying at the same levels from 1967/68 to 1968/69, producer prices suddenly went through a series of increases. First, by 6.4 percent from 1969/70 to 1970/71, then by 24.7 percent between 1970/71 and 1971/72 and finally by 27.7 percent between 1972/73 and 1973/74. Members of the CPGPA, which by now had emerged as an important advisory organ to the Prime Minister's office on all matters related to agriculture, argued that externally-induced shocks had been most determinant in these pricing decisions. It is true that world-wide recession, international price movements, transmission of inflation and so forth have been important contributing factors. But as conversations with certain close advisors to the primary decision-maker, the Prime Minister, have revealed, political considerations have been uppermost in the minds of the President and his team of advisors. Other sources seem to confirm this explanation as illustrated in the brief recall of relevant events below.

To begin with, while the decrease in producer prices has adversely affected rural incomes, especially after 1967/68, a series of droughts between 1966 and 1969 and then from 1970/71 through 1972/73 seem to have quickened the deterioration in rural living standards. But the most important issue, which provoked deep-seated peasant resentment and disaffection, had little to do with the escalation of petroleum prices or the rate of inflation which may have been transmitted to Senegal as a result of this. Rather, it was the unfair treatment which the majority of farmers suffered at the hands of the state marketing monopolies since the mid-sixties or before that, which in their cumulative effects precipitated general unrest in the farming community.[2] Confronted by statutory marketing institutions from a relatively weak bargaining position, the Senegalese farmer was subjected to different kinds of deductions in order to finance marketing losses and high interest payments, in-kind, on seed loans. In response, farmers not only refused to pay their input loans or receive further input supplies, they turned increasingly to trading their groundnuts in the parallel market. This event posed a veritable threat to the government's inflexible peanut production—security objectives and to its domestic industrialization programs as well.

This period of rural discontent could not be held in check

through maraboutic intervention as has been the practice since the colonial days, primarily because of the important changes which had taken place in the leadership of the Mouride order. President Senghor's long-term friend and ally had passed away in 1968. He was succeeded by his junior brother, Khalif General Abdou Lahatte Mbacke. This new leader has preferred to stay clear from direct involvement with political matters, thereby signalling a shift in the policies of his predecessor. He served notice to the administration that relations with the state, while remaining the same, structurally, could be expected to be confrontational especially when the interests of the Mouride family were at stake. With this declaration in 1973 at the Magal in Touba, the Khalif General actually increased the costs of his intervention in support of state objectives. According to Cruise O'Brien (1977) the Mouride leader even went so far as to command all loyal disciples to withdraw from groundnut cultivation since growing this crop had come to mean increasing indebtedness to the state.

Thus, the series of producer price increases which occurred between 1970/71 through 1973/74 had been motivated by the desire on the part of the final decision-maker to calm the uncertain political and social environment in much of the countryside during this period. External events have been important but only to the extent of their aggravation of the deterioration in the living standards of the agricultural population. Under circumstances of political uncertainty, such as the one above, the Prime Minister or the President himself takes the responsibility of publicly proclaiming price increases or decreases, as occurred in 1971 when Prime Minister Diouf made such an announcement at the Magal in Touba.[3]

Unlike the producer price for groundnuts and foodcrops, cotton producer prices have in general tended to be increased primarily for income-support objectives. This policy seems consistent with recent administration commitment to promoting increased cotton production through various incentive measures.

The prices of most foodgrains were for the first time raised in the early seventies (from 1973) largely because the administration had decided around that period to diversify away from groundnuts and the uncertainties which surround the management of its production. It was believed by certain officials that, by reducing reliance on peanuts, Mouride power would be substantially reduced (economic and political considerations). However, foodgrains production has traditionally been a supplementary activity for largely subsistence purposes. Partly for this reason and partly for the lack of an organized grains market, these price measures have tended to have little effect on the food sector.

In general, the government has been reluctant to raise consumer prices, especially for edible oil and rice, mainly because of the fear that such increases may lead to spiralling demands for wage and salary increases and to social and political unrest, particularly in urban industrial centers. Policymakers have often referred to the inflammation of social unrest via higher food prices in places such as Liberia, Morocco and Tunisia as cases in point. But the argument at the presidency has been that the administration's commitment to equity objectives – by protecting both urban and rural purchasing power – has been the overriding reason for maintaining consumer prices at acceptable levels. This argument is, however, weak as the analysis of the transactions in the CPSP's various accounts has revealed.

Consumer prices have changed only a few times since 1960. The first increase occurred in 1969 when the import price of rice was modestly raised by about 29 percent. This came one year after the student–labor unrest of the summer of 1968. However, these disturbances, originally thought to be foreign instigated, had little to do with food prices. Rather, they were part of the spontaneous outburst of student radicalism which began in France, later spreading to other parts of the former French Empire. Senegalese workers took advantage of this display of student consciousness to press for increases in wages.

Nevertheless, uncertainty about the likely behavior of urban political constituencies has continued to inhibit consumer pricing decisions. This uncertainty tends to increase more in years of sharp production shortfalls and less during good crop years. Until recently, there has been no consumer interest group. The Association pour la Défense du Consommateur Sénégalaise (ADCS) which came into being barely a year ago now remains peripheral to the price determination process. Thus, domestic political pressure for lower food prices probably exists only to the extent of the policy-maker's perception. This is not the same as saying that if food prices were left to move along with international prices and inflation, urban consumers would remain indifferent. It is simply emphasizing the point made earlier that, with or without such groups, consumer interests will be protected. This is so because the government has now become synonymous with industry, in theory as in practice. To the extent that this remains the case, the irresistible demands for higher wages and salaries which rising food prices trigger would affect the government more in terms of increased salaries for public and parapublic-sector employees and higher wages for state-owned agro-industrial workers if these demands were to be met. It is partly for these reasons, certain informants observe, that the government would be opposed to food price increases. On the other hand, however, it will be unreasonable to expect any Third World government to show indifference to escalation of the international prices of the basic food commodities in which it is not self-sufficient, and to allow domestic prices to keep pace with these price movements. This point has been strongly argued by administration officials. In their view, government action to protect domestic consumers from erratic international price changes for imported grains has been justifiable on economic and welfare grounds to protect consumers, particularly low-income urban workers and farmers in food-deficit areas.

In the great majority of cases, the outcomes of consumer pricing discussions have been influenced by the IMF. The Fund's and the World Bank's interventions which have generally been tied to the performance criteria of Structural Adjustment Loan agreements (SAL), have usually aimed at bailing out the CPSP, as a short-term adjustment measure; to be followed up with long-term policy reforms designed to effectively cure the causes of the original disequilibria. Hence rice prices, for instance, went up in 1982 in order to reduce the 4.7 billion FCFA deficit in the rice account in 1981. The Administration has also raised rice prices before, without IMF intervention, for the same purpose. This was true for the 1974 price increase which resulted in reducing the deficit from 5.3 billion FCFA that year to only 485 million FCFA in 1975. For understandable political reasons, probably attributable to uncertainty about likely behavior of urban constituencies, wage increases have almost automatically followed most increases in rice prices. For instance, when the consumer price was raised by 50 percent in 1974, wages were increased by about 84 percent. The corresponding figures for the increases in 1982 were 31.25 percent and 8.2 percent.

These cases present an illustration of how political considerations have influenced price decision-making. The uncertainties which have led to the choice of nonoptimal price policies are known by some decision-makers and there have been systematic efforts on the part of the administration to reduce the uncertainties in the policy environment in order to facilitate better informed and more flexible policy responses on pricing and agricultural policy issues. This is being done through debate at the cabinet and interministerial council levels, in committees, through continuing research and in discussions with donors.

APPENDIX A

Supporting Tables

TABLE 1

Special Treatment of 'Gros Producteurs' – Marabout in the Public Input Subsidy Program

Groundnut Price Stabilization Fund

Period	Amount (FCFA)	Recipient of Subsidy
1966/67	36,253,075	FMDR (PA)
1966/67	140,000,000	ONCAD[2]
1967/68	400,000,000	OCS[2]
1968/69	NONE	
1969/70	431,020,000	SIES (FERTILIZERS)
1970/71	332,344,000	SIES (FERTILIZERS)
1970/71	219,714,381	'GROS PRODUCTEURS'
1970/71	87,792,236	(Indemnity for decorticating plants put out of commission)
1971/72	305,922,000	SIES (FERTILIZERS)
1971/72	200,000,000	'GROS PRODUCTEURS'
1971/72	44,152,086	(Indemnity for decorticating plant closures)
1972/73 (1972)	300,000,000	'GROS PRODUCTEURS'
1972/73 (Jan. 1973)	60,000,000	'GROS PRODUCTEURS'
1972/73 (Feb. 1973)	60,000,000	'GROS PRODUCTEURS'
1972/73 (June 1973)	200,000,000	'GROS PRODUCTEURS'
1972/73 (June 1973)	200,000,000	BNDS

Cereals Price Stabilization Fund

1966/67	447,000,000	FMDR (PA)
1966/67	100,000,000	BNDS[3]
1971/72	206,000,000	FMDR (PA, 1970/71)
1971/72	117,382,123	BNDS[3] 1972/73 542,535,000 FMDR (PA, 1971/72)

Source: CPSP/FMDR

1. All the 6 stabilization funds, particularly groundnuts, have been in surplus. The state treasury has appropriated a substantial proportion of the surpluses for non-agricultural uses. It maintained a 'revolving loans fund' with the BNDS – Le compte K-2 – for financing priority agricultural production activities. The compte ended up being used largely for dispensation of political patronage and for financing certain undertakings of questionable economic merit.
2. Capital stocks.
3. Subsidies to the fund for clearing and ploughing of new land.

TABLE 2

Senegal: CPSP Consumer Price Stabilization Operations:
Refined Oil Account

Period	Quantity Consumed (1000 Mt)	Unit Value of Price Supp. (FCFA/kg)	Total Value of Intervention (Millions FCFA)	Comment
1970	35.066	−19.21	−673.62	Subsidy paid to firms.
1971	40.448	−45.22	−1829.10	Subsidy paid to firms.
1972	47.097	−32.08	−1510.87	Subsidy paid to firms.
1973	50.121	−50.61	−2536.62	Subsidy paid to firms.
1974	40.868	−107.62	−4398.21	Subsidy paid to firms.
1975	38.459	−2.03	−78.07	Subsidy paid to firms.
1976	41.191	+7.10	+297.56	Profits to CPSP.
1977	51.030	−40.59	−2071.31	Subsidy to firms.
1978	58.018	−81.18	−4709.90	Subsidy to firms.
1979	66.037	−68.86	−4547.31	Subsidy to firms.
1980	52.886	−22.68	−1176.78	Subsidy to firms.
1981[1]	63.769	n.a.	−6054.00	Subsidy to firms.
1982	65.536	n.a.	+110.00	Profit to CPSP.
1983	63.364	n.a.	+1697.00	Profit to CPSP.
1984	70.094	n.a.	−4900.00	Subsidy to firms.

Source: CPSP: Documentation Center and Direction Etude.

1. Importation of soya and sunflower oil for domestic refining started this year. Since then, price support applied also to imported oil. Approximately 87% of total subsidies for 1981 was absorbed by the price support on vegetable oil (see Arthur Andersen: CPSP Study, Vol. 3, 1982, p.8).

TABLE 3

Senegal: Price Formation in the Rice Distribution Circuit

	I	II	III	IV	V	VI
Period	Import Price of Rice (FCFA/kg)	CPSP's Selling Price (FCFA/kg)	Whole-saler's Price (FCFA/kg)	Retailer's Price FCFA/kg)	II − I (FCFA/kg)	IV as % of I
1971	24.7	37.0	38.4	40	12.3	1.62
1972	25.1	37.0	38.4	40	11.9	1.59
1973	49.6	57.0	58.4	60	7.4	1.21
1974[1]	87.0	57.0	58.4	60	−30.0	.69
1975	59.2	94.5	97.1	100	35.3	1.69
1976	43.7	74.5	77.1	80	30.8	1.83
1977	45.4	74.5	77.1	80	29.1	1.76
1978	52.8	74.5	77.1	80	21.7	1.52
1979	42.1	74.6	77.1	80	32.5	1.90
1980	59.8	74.6	77.1	80	14.8	1.34
1981	90.5	74.6	77.1	80	−5.9	.99
1982	82.3	97.0	100.8	105	14.7	1.28
1983	91.4	120.1	124.8	130	28.7	1.42
1984		120.1	124.8	130		
1985		147.9	153.7	160		

1. The rice consumer price was raised in November 1974 to 100 FCFA/kg in response to the increase in international prices. This increase is reflected in the 1975 figures because it affected only two months of the preceding year, 1974.

TABLE 4

Senegal: CPSP Consumer Price Stabilization Operations:
Imported Rice Account – 1973–1984

Period	Quantity (1000 Mt)	Unit Value of Price Support (FCFA/kg)	Total Value of Intervention (Million FCFA)	Comments
1973	206.978	−11.34	−2,347.131	ONCAD gains
1974	216.000	−24.54	−5,300.640	ONCAD gains
1975	115.000	−4.22	− 485.300	ONCAD gains
1976	199.000	+34.75	+6,915.250	CPSP gains
1977	254.896	+26.06	+6,642.600	CPSP gains
1978	213.516	+15.68	+3,347.931	CPSP gains
1979	230.000	+18.26	+4,199.800	CPSP gains
1980*	245.981	−10.25	−2,521.305	Importers gain
1981	340.000	−13.79	−4,688.600	Importers gain
1982	385.585	+6.756	+2,605.012	CPSP gains
1983[1]	374.329	+5.500	+2,058.810	CPSP gains
1984[2]	360.000	+1.843	+663.643	CPSP gains

Source: CPSP

*The figures for 1980 through 1984 are official estimates.
1. The official estimates for this year have now been revised as follows: Quantity imported = 379,889 tons; value of intervention = +2,089.390 million FCFA.
2. Quantity imported has been revised to 351,741 tons. The revised intervention value, based on the assumption of unchanged unit price support as in (11), amounts to +648.259 million FCFA.

TABLE 5

Senegal: CPSP Consumer Price Stabilization Operations:
Sugar Account

Period	Quantity (1000 Mt)	Unit Value of Price Support (FCFA/kg)	Total Value of Intervention (Million FCFA)	Comments
1973	78.098	−23.28	−1,825.931	Sugar monopoly CSS gains
1974	64.218	−16.43	−1,055.096	CSS gains
1975	59.613	+22.91	+1,465.734	CPSP gains
1976	63.410	+28.19	+1,787.528	CPSP gains
1977	73.639	+16.23	+1,195.161	CPSP gains
1978	63.700	+34.90	+2,223.130	CPSP gains
1979	70.693	+15.42	+1,090.086	CPSP gains
1980	75.709	−39.22	−2,969.615	CSS gains
1981	69.36	−24.33	−1,674.996	CSS gains
1982	73.014	−12.48	−912.404	CSS gains
1983*				

*The contract (Protocole) on the commercialization of sugar between the State and the sugar monopoly has not been ratified as of the writing of this paper.

TABLE 6

Senegal: CPSP Consumer Price Stabilization Operations:
Wheat/Flour Account

Period	Quantity of Flour (1000 mt)	Unit Value of Price Support (FCFA/kg)	Total Value of Intervention (Million FCFA)	Comments
1974[1]	23.675	−26.405	−625.139	Processing firms gain
1975	75.309	−25.372	−1,901.740	Processing firms gain
1976	91.260	−24.012	−2,191.335	Processing firms gain
1977	72.203	+7.301	+526.154	CPSP gains
1978	83.982	+8.827	+741.309	CPSP gains
1979	84.360	+12.150	+1,024.974	CPSP gains
1980	75.000	−4.011	+300.805	CPSP gains
1981	63.771	−7.005	−446.726	Processing firms gain
1982	87.881	+2.981	+261.948	CPSP gains
1983	79.650	+6.719	+535.146	CPSP gains

Source: CPSP
1. This concerns the period August–December 1974.

TABLE 7

Senegal: Consumer Prices of Major Foodstuffs, 1960–1984

Period	Broken Rice FCFA/kg	Sugar (Cubes) in FCFA/Pkt	Groundnut Oil (Bottled) in FCFA/Liter	Vegetable Oil (Bottled) in FCFA[1]/Liter
1960	32	60	98	–
1961	32	60	98	–
1962	32	60	98	–
1963	32	60	98	–
1964	32	70	98	–
1965	30	70	98	–
1966	35	70	98	–
1967	35	70	98	–
1968	35	70	98	–
1969	45	70	98	–
1970	45	70	98	–
1971	40	70	98	–
1972	40	70	98	–
1973	60	90	98	–
1974	100	150	140	–
1975	100	250	200	–
1976	100	225	200	–
1977	80	225	200	–
1978	80	225	200	–
1979	80	225	200	–
1980	80	250	240	–
1981	80	250	330	240
1982	105	250	330	240
1983	130	375	393	297
1984	130	375	500	452

Source: CPSP
1. Senegal started importing soya and refining sunflower oil at the Diourbel plants of SEIB in order to fill the increasing gap between demand and domestic oil production.

APPENDIX B
Institutions and Other Places Visited
During One Year of Field Work and Writing of Report

The Presidency (2 interviews with senior advisor to the President)

Ministère de l'Economie et des Finances (several visits to the Direction de la Prévision et de la Conjoncture and to the Direction de la Statistique

Ministère du Développement Rural (interviews with the General Secretary to the Ministry and three technical advisers)
   Direction de la Production Agricole; Service Semencier
   Projet Maïs
   Direction de la Coopération
   FMDR
   Commissariat à la Sécurité Alimentaire

Ministère du Commerce (several interviews with the Directeur de Cabinet)
   DCIP (interviews with the Director and technical advisers)
   Contrôle Economique (interviews with the Director)
   CPSP (interviewed the Director General, all department heads, and several working meetings with senior officials). Also interviewed all the former Directors of the Caisse.

Ministère du Plan (interviews with Director of Planning and other officials)

SODEFITEX (interviews with Président-Directeur Général)
SODEVA (interviews with technicians)
SAED (interviews with technical advisers)
SOMIVAC (interviews with technical advisers)
SODAGRI (interviews with the Director General and technical advisers)
SONACOS (several visits and interviews with senior officials)
SEIB (interviews with senior officials)
Grands Moulins de Dakar (interview with technical adviser)
Moulins Sentenac (interview with senior official)
Institut de Technologie Alimentaire (ITA) (interviews with technicians)
BCEAO (interview with researchers and several working meetings)
ISRA (met with Dr. Bingham, head of the MSU research team)
CNRA (visited the Bambey Research Center)
EEC (Dakar office – interviewed agricultural adviser)
FAO (interviewed the Representative and technical adviser)
CIDA (interviewed some officials)
USAID (regular consultations with senior officials)
FAC (meeting with technical advisers)
CCCE (meeting with technical adviser)

Several individuals, who would prefer to be anonymous, have also been interviewed from: Université de Dakar; Assemblée Nationale; Chambre de Commerce; BNDS; Le Soleil; Rice Distributors; CGPA; SONAR; ENAM.

Farmers Visited

Approximately 227 farmers, including 25 'gros producteurs' have been interviewed mainly in the Touba Mbacke area, and from the following locations as well: Touba Betel, Fattick, Nioro de Rip, Kaolack, Darou Mousty, Diourbel, Louga, Thiès, Cap-Vert (3 villages).

NOTES

1. Parallel market groundnut sales have officially been estimated at more than 100,000 tons in the 1984/85 procurement season. An undetermined proportion of this quantity has reportedly been artisanally processed into edible oil and cake for domestic sale.
2. See Schumacher (1975, pp.183–185) on the causes of the 'peasant malaise.'
3. Coulon (1981, p.286) argues that political considerations influenced the price increases of 1971, 1975 and 1979.

CHAPTER EIGHT

Small Countries in Monetary Unions: The Choice of Senegal

Jorge Braga de Macedo

I. INTRODUCTION

Senegal belongs since independence to the West African Monetary Union (known by its French acronym UMOA). The country has therefore chosen to fix its exchange rate against the other partners in the union. More importantly, all partners have agreed that the union currency – the CFA franc – will be kept at a fixed rate of 0.02 against the French franc. This fixed rate, enforced by the union-wide central bank, is guaranteed by France. Maintained since October 1948, the CFA–French franc rate is probably the oldest pegged parity.[1]

The type of interaction between Senegal, other UMOA members and France which follows from this unusual choice of exchange rate regime is the subject of this chapter. The consequences of the choice for macro-economic policy are illustrated in Section II by means of a theoretical model.

The set-up is such that one of two large countries establishes an exchange rate union with two small countries, which in turn form a full monetary union, with their own central bank. The effect of monetary and real disturbances originating inside and outside the union is analyzed. It is shown that even when an exchange rate union with the large partner only affects the price of output in the small countries, a full monetary union with an exogenous monetary allocation rule requires a transfer which may have real effects. This transfer is precisely provided by the large country, as guarantor of the fixed exchange rate arrangement.

Drawing on the implications of the theoretical model, Section III describes the interaction between Senegal, France and UMOA. First, the element of choice in Senegal's exchange rate policy is assessed and compared to the choice of neighboring Mali. Then, monetary allocations in UMOA are analyzed quantitatively, along the lines of Macedo (1985a).

Next, indexes of the real effective exchange rate of Senegal are constructed and compared to similar indexes in France and other African countries, especially Ivory Coast. Further evidence on these indexes is contained in the Appendices to a longer version of the present work, Macedo (1985b). Here, rather than drawing strong implications about the competitiveness of Senegal's exports from these indexes, the trade-off between nominal stability and real variability is addressed. Section IV brings together the theoretical model and the experience of Senegal, offering some concluding remarks.

We attempted to make the Section on Senegal, France and UMOA self-contained, so that reading Section II – especially after the overview of subsection A – is not required in order to follow the discussion in Section III. Moreover, Section II only reports selected results in loglinear form. Their full derivation can be found in Macedo (1985c), together with the detailed description of the model and references to the considerable analytical literature on monetary unions.

II. MONETARY UNIONS IN A WORLD OF FLEXIBLE EXCHANGE RATES

A. *Overview of a two-tier model*

The key factors on which the impact of a monetary union depends are, first, the sources and types of economic disturbances giving rise to exchange rate fluctuations, second, the trade patterns of the country joining the union, and, third, wage and price behavior at home and abroad. As Marston (1984) states, the conditions under which a fixed exchange rate regime is superior to flexible exchange rates usually involve a complicated weighting of these key factors.

The relative size of the partners is generally reflected in the source and types of disturbances as well as in the trade pattern. In our analysis, however, size is the major structural characteristic of a country. Specifically, large countries are not affected by disturbances originating in small countries but small countries are affected by large countries' domestic disturbances. To sharpen the analysis, small countries are assumed not to trade with each other. There are two pairs of identical economies, large and small.

The bilateral exchange rate between the large economies is fully flexible. The choice of the small economies is whether or not to fix their exchange rate with one of the large countries. If they choose to fix, they can also choose to allow a common central bank to determine the allocation of the union-wide money stock between its two small members. In the terminology of Corden (1972), there is a pseudo-exchange rate union between one of the large countries (France, labelled country star) and the small countries (Senegal and Ivory Coast, labelled countries one and two) but full monetary integration between the two small countries. There is also a large country outside the union (the United States, labelled country double-star) whose currency is chosen as the numeraire.

The difference in size between the partners in the exchange rate union has a crucial implication for monetary policy. In fact, even though the money stock of Senegal and Ivory Coast is endogenously determined under price flexibility, its distribution can be modified by the common central bank, thereby inducing changes in their real exchange rates.

The national economies are described by conventional aggregate relationships, with all variables expressed as logarithmic deviations from steady-state equilibrium.

Demand for domestic output (the IS curve) is a function of foreign outputs, relative prices or the real exchange rate, and the real interest rate and it can also be changed by an exogenous demand disturbance, denoted by u_A. Demand for real balances (the LM curve) is a function of domestic output and the nominal interest rate, as a measure of the return differential. By eliminating the nominal interest rate, we obtain an aggregate demand curve that relates domestic output to the real exchange rate, to foreign output, and to the exogenous demand and monetary disturbances (the latter being denoted by u_m). A real depreciation increases the demand for domestic output along conventional foreign trade multiplier lines.

The supply of domestic output is derived from labor market equilibrium, where the supply of labor by workers responds to the wage deflated by a consumer price index and the demand for labor by firms responds to the wage deflated by price of the domestic good. Eliminating the nominal wage, we obtain an aggregate supply curve relating domestic output to the real exchange rate and an exogenous supply disturbance, denoted by u_π, which can be interpreted as an increase in productivity or (if negative) as a harvest failure. A real depreciation lowers the supply of domestic output because it raises the product wage. While the assumption of labor market equilibrium is particularly strong, the introduction of elastic labor supply does capture one relevant feature of developing countries.

The model is closed by the assumption that domestic and foreign assets are perfect substitutes, so that interest rates are equalized in the steady-state. This determines recursively the real exchange rate and the price of domestic output, in terms of the exogenous real and monetary disturbances respectively. Then, under flexible exchange rates, the nominal exchange rate is given by monetary disturbances, whereas, under fixed rates, the nominal money stock is determined endogenously.

Since the exchange rate union rules out some special risks attached to small developing countries' assets, the perfect substitutability assumption becomes slightly more palatable. On the other side, the comparison with a perfectly flexible exchange rate regime is biased against the exchange rate union, because pure flexibility may not even be a viable – let alone desirable – option for a small developing country, as argued by Corden (1972), Lewis (1977), Kenen (1978) and many others. The comparison provides therefore an 'acid test' for the existing arrangement.

Size does not affect the interest-rate elasticities of money demand and aggregate demand, which are common to all four countries, and the other parameters are identical between the pairs of large and small countries. These assumptions could be somewhat relaxed but an analytical solution does require a strong symmetry between economic structures.

In particular, within-tier symmetry allows variables to be expressed as average sums and differences, as proposed by Aoki (1981). Thus for any variable or disturbance x in the upper tier, we define:

$$^*x^s = (x^* + x^{**})/2$$
$$^*x^d = (x^* - x^{**})/2$$

Since the two small countries do not trade with each other, in the lower tier we can express a national variable as a difference from the average sum in the upper tier:

$$^ix^d = {^i}x - {^*}x^s \qquad i = 1,2$$

The model is used to assess the effect of fixing the bilateral exchange rates of the two small countries with one of the large countries. Under price flexibility, the choice of an exchange rate regime has no effect on the real exchange rate, since the effect on the nominal exchange rate and the price level offset each other. That being said, a monetary union between one of the large countries and the two small countries may require a monetary transfer from the large partner, whose money stock continues to be exogenous. Furthermore, since the union allows the small countries' central bank to choose an asymmetric monetary allocation rule, the choice of exchange rate regime can have real effects. As a consequence, nominal stability may be achieved at the expense of real variability.

B. *Effective exchange rates*

We refer to the small country as Senegal for expository convenience. The analysis could also be applied to Ivory Coast because there is no trade within the lower tier.

We begin by defining the nominal effective exchange rate of Senegal as an average of the exchange rates relative to France and the United States, using as weights the shares of their goods in the consumer price index of Senegal:

(1) $\quad {}^E e = \bar{\alpha} e^* + (1 - \bar{\alpha}) e^{**}$

where $\quad \bar{\alpha} = \alpha_* / (1 - \alpha)$, $\alpha_* (\alpha_{**})$ being the share of goods from France (U.S.) in the price index of Senegal so that $\alpha + \alpha_* + \alpha_{**} = 1$;

and $\quad e^* (e^{**}) =$ the price of the French franc (the US dollar) in units of the currency of Senegal.

By triangular arbitrage, $e^{**} = e^* + e$ is the franc-dollar rate, so that we can rewrite (1) as:

(1') $\quad {}^E e = e^{**} - \bar{\alpha} e$

It is clear from equation (1') that, if the franc depreciates relative to the dollar, the only way to avoid the appreciation of the CFA relative to the dollar is through a rise in e^{**} by $\bar{\alpha} e$. If consumption shares are the same, $\bar{\alpha} = \frac{1}{2}$, whereas if there is no trade with the U.S., $\bar{\alpha} = 1$. Note that the effective exchange rate of the large countries is assumed to be the same as the bilateral rate (e).

The real effective exchange rate of Senegal can be defined in the same way as in equation (1) above:

(2) $\quad {}^E \theta = \bar{\alpha}(e^* + p^*) + (1 - \bar{\alpha})(e^{**} + p^{**}) - p = \theta - \bar{\alpha}\theta^*$

where $\quad \theta = e^{**} + p^{**} - p$ the real exchange rate of Senegal;
$\quad \theta^* = e + p^{**} - p^*$ the real exchange rate of France;
$\quad p^*(p^{**}) =$ the price of output in France (U.S)

and   p = the price of output in Senegal.

Solving the model and substituting into (2), we can write the real effective exchange rate of Senegal in terms of foreign and domestic disturbances:

$$(2') \quad E\theta = \frac{1}{H} [A^*\theta^* - (v^* - v^{**}) \tilde{U}^d_* - u^d_A + \bar{u}^d_\pi]$$

where $H = \tilde{a}^* + \tilde{a}^{**}$;

$\tilde{a}^* = a^* + h\alpha_*$ ($\tilde{a}^{**}$) the sum of the real exchange rate elasticity of aggregate demand in Senegal with respect to France (U.S.), $a^*(a^{**})$, and of the real exchange rate elasticity of aggregate supply in Senegal, h, weighted by α_* (α_{**});

$A^* = (a^*\alpha_{**} - a^{**}\alpha_*)/(1 - \alpha)$ a measure of the 'imbalance' of trade sensitivities in Senegal;

v^* (v^{**}) Senegal's output multiplier with respect to France (U.S.);

$\tilde{U}^d_*$, a weighted average of relative real disturbances in the upper tier ($^*u^d_A$ and $^*u^d_\pi$);

and $\bar{u}^d_\pi = u^d_\pi + (v - v^* - v^{**})^*u^s_\pi$, v being the foreign-output multiplier in the upper tier.

The first term in (3) measures the relative sensitivity of the Senegalese economy to the French real exchange rate in terms of the trade elasticities with France and the U.S. (a^* and a^{**} and the share of French and U.S. goods in the consumer price index (α_* and α_{**}). The French real exchange rate will have a positive effect on Senegal's real effective exchange rate if trade with France is relatively more sensitive than reflected on the French share in the Senegalese consumer price index. Conversely, if the share is large relative to the trade elasticities, a real depreciation of the franc will imply a real appreciation of the CFA.

The second term captures the effect of trade patterns. If the trade multipliers with France and the U.S. are the same (v^* and v^{**}), relative real disturbances there have no effect. Global supply disturbances in the upper tier still have an effect, however, as long as Senegal's output multiplier ($2v^*$) differs from the output multiplier in the upper tier (v). This is captured in the fourth term, denoted $\bar{u}^d_\pi$. If $v/2 > v^*$, a favorable supply disturbance in France will lead to a real depreciation of the CFA and conversely. When trade patterns are strongly symmetric ($v/2 = v^* = v^{**}$), then $\bar{u}^d$ = u^d and $\tilde{U}_*^d$ drops out.

The effect of relative real disturbances is captured by the third and fourth terms, where the cyclical position of Senegal is measured relative to the world average. For example, if demand for Senegal's output increases ($u_A > {}^*u_A^*$) or, if there is a harvest failure in Senegal, such that $\bar{u}_\pi^d < 0$, then its real exchange rate appreciates by $1/H$.

Note that the choice of the numeraire continues to play a role unless the trade elasticities are proportional to the weights in the consumer price index, i.e. unless $A^* = 0$, which implies $\alpha = \tilde{a}^*/H$. Alternatively, the weighted sum of demand and supply elasticities with each trading partner, α^j/H, can be seen as an optimal weighting scheme to offset the effect of the choice of the numeraire. If $A^* > 0$, the consumption share of France is too low relative to the trade elasticities so that a real depreciation of the franc – say because of a shift in demand toward US goods – is positively transmitted to the lower tier. If the output multiplier with France is low relative to the one with the U.S., $v^* < v^{**}$, however, this asymmetry is weakened.

C. Flexible exchange rates

Solving the model for the price of domestic output and expressing it as a difference of the weighted average of foreign prices, we have the effective price ratio under flexible exchange rates:

$$(3) \qquad {}^E p = p - \alpha p^* - (1 - \alpha) p^{**} = \bar{u}_m^d - \bar{u}_\pi^d - h(1 - \alpha)\, {}^E\theta$$
$$- (1 - 2\alpha)\, \tilde{U}_*^d$$

where $\bar{u}_m^d = u_m - [\alpha\, u_m^* - (1 - \alpha)\, u_m^{**}]$

According to equation (3), the effect of the real effective exchange rate is weighted by the supply elasticity and the effect of the composite cyclical output disturbance is lower the closer α is to $\frac{1}{2}$. Indeed, when $\alpha = \frac{1}{2}$, $\bar{u}_m^d = u_m^d$, the usual measure of relative domestic disturbances. Adding (2') to (3), we obtain the nominal effective exchange rate of Senegal as:

$$(4) \qquad {}^E e = \bar{u}_m^d - U^d - A$$

where $U^d = \xi\, u_A^d + (1 - \xi)\, \bar{u}_\pi^d$

$$\xi = 1 + h(1 - \alpha)]/H \gtrless 1$$

and $\quad A = -\xi\, A^*\, \theta^* + [1 - 2\alpha + \xi\, (v^* - v^{**})]\tilde{U}_*^d$

When trade patterns are strongly symmetric, in the sense that $A^* = 0$, $v^* = v^{**}$ and $\alpha = \frac{1}{2}$, then $A = 0$ and $\bar{u}_m^d = u_m^d$. If in addition $2v^* = v$, then $\bar{u}_\pi^d = u_\pi^d$. In this special case, all disturbances enter as differences between the domestic and average foreign value. Equations (3) and (4) show that monetary disturbances have off-setting one-to-one effects on the nominal exchange rate, and the price level and (2') showed a zero effect on the real exchange rate. The real effects of the exchange rate regime will stem from distortions to the separation between nominal and real variables.

Real disturbances have less than one-to-one effects on the price level. The effect is smaller the lower the supply elasticity relative to the demand elasticity, as captured by $h(1 - \alpha)/H = \xi - 1/H$ in (3). The effect on the real exchange rate depends inversely on both elasticities, as captured by $1/H$. The effect of demand disturbances on the nominal exchange rate will be more than one-to-one if elasticities are low ($\xi > 1$), in which case a favorable supply shock will involve a depreciation.

These effects have to be modified in the presence of asymmetries. If $v^* > v^{**}$, the condition for a real appreciation to be associated with a demand expansion in France is weaker than $A^* > 0$, because a larger output multiplier with France ($v^* > v^{**}$) reinforces the positive transmission between the French and Senegalese rates. In that case, furthermore, the real appreciation will be larger than the nominal.

D. Fixed exchange rates

Fixing a bilateral nominal exchange rate makes money supplies endogenous, with no consequences on real exchange rates. Under price flexibility, there is no trade-off between the level of output and its price in the two regimes. Prices will be higher (lower) under the exchange rate union of Senegal and France than under flexible exchange rates depending on whether the CFA–dollar rate is higher (lower) than the franc–dollar rate, or on whether domestic monetary expansion is higher (lower) than required by solving equation (4) for the money stock. The reason is that the French money stock continues to be exogenous, due to the size difference. Denoting variables under the union by a tilde, we can write:

(4') $\tilde{m} = {}^E\tilde{e} + \alpha u_m^* + (1 - \alpha) u_m^{**} + A + U^d$

where ${}^E\tilde{e} = (1 - \alpha)e$ the effective exchange rate under the union with France.

Equation (4') shows that if monetary policy under flexible exchange rates was used to stabilize $^E e$, so that $\bar{u}_{\overset{d}{m}} = U^d + A$ in (4), then there will be monetary expansion under the union, given by $^E \tilde{e}$. This required monetary expansion can be interpreted as a monetary transfer from France, which guarantees the fixed exchange rate agreement. It is associated with a higher price level under the union:

(5) $\quad e - e^{**} = \tilde{m} - u_m = \tilde{p} - p$

Conversely, if the fixed exchange rate is lower than the one prevailing before the agreement, the money stock and the price of domestic output will fall by the same amount. The fall in the money stock is brought about by a capital outflow which would increase in magnitude if the government of Senegal attempted to increase the supply of domestic assets to the public. Since real output does not change, the real money stock remains fixed and the fall in money balances is transmitted to prices. Only by increasing demand for real output could the government enforce a different nominal income.

Thus the exchange rate union with the large country eliminates the possibility of monetary accommodation which would otherwise stabilize the nominal effective exchange rate. Since the money stock is now endogenous, an expansion of domestic credit will lead to a loss of reserves if the franc–dollar rate appreciates and conversely. Once again, size allows us to neglect the endogeneity of the French money stock under the exchange rate union with Senegal.

If, instead, Senegal fixes its exchange rate with the Ivory Coast, we will have $e_1^* = e_2^*$ (introducing subscripts in the equations above). Furthermore, any exogenous increase in the union-wide money stock, denoted by t, will be allocated between the two partners in proportion to their steady-state shares, assumed to be equal, so that $\tilde{m}_1$ and $\tilde{m}_2 = 2t$. Noting the new definition of U^d implied by the existence of country subscripts, we can write the solution as

(6) $\quad \tilde{m}_1 = t + U^d$

(6') $\quad \tilde{m}_2 = t - U^d$

(6'') $\quad ^E e = t - [\alpha\, u_m^* + (1 - \alpha) u_m^{**}] - A - U^s$

where $\quad U^d = \dfrac{_1 U^d - _2 U^d}{2}$

and $\quad U^s = \dfrac{_1 U^d + _2 U^d}{2}$

When $t = 0$ and demand and supply disturbances in the two small countries are perfectly correlated ($U^d = 0$), the money stocks are unchanged: $\tilde{m}_i = 0$, $i = 1, 2$. In that case, if there are no asymmetries ($A = 0$) and money stocks are also given in the upper tier, the franc–CFA appreciates by $U^s = \xi\ ^1u_A^d + (1 - \xi)\ ^1u_\pi^d$.

Finally, if both countries fix the exchange rate with France they are making $^E e = {}^E\tilde{e}$ in (6''). As before, this requires a change in the union-wide money stock, denoted by a tilde:

(7) $\qquad \tilde{t} = {}^E\tilde{e} + [\tilde{\alpha}\ u_m^* + (1 - \tilde{\alpha})\ u_m^{**}] + A + U^s$

We interpret again the endogenous increase in the union-wide money stock as a transfer from France: while t could be zero in equations (6), $\tilde{t}$ will only be zero in (7) if there are no disturbances, or if $e = u_m^* = u_m^{**} = A = U^s = 0$. Indeed, a depreciation of the franc against the dollar requires an increase in $\tilde{t}$ which is larger the higher the consumption share of U.S. relative to French goods (the lower $\tilde{\alpha}$). On the other hand, a union-wide demand expansion (increase in U^s) requires an increase in $\tilde{t}$ which is larger the larger the consumption share of non-union relative to union goods (the lower α). Alternatively, a large ξ may derive from low trade elasticities. Note also that in the previous example where $U^s = {}^1U^d$, the required transfer would be exactly the same as in (4') above and it still would have no effect on the French money stock.

Clearly, if the union-wide central bank allocates this transfer according to equations (6), the full monetary union will exactly replicate a three-country pseudo-exchange rate union. This is easy to verify by eliminating $t = \tilde{t}$.

If, instead, there is a monetary allocation rule, such that money increases in each country – denoted by u_i^T – are based on a share ω of the sum of the equilibrium money stock increases, we write:

(8) $\qquad u_1^T = 2\omega\tilde{t}$

(8') $\qquad u_2^T = 2(1 - \omega)\tilde{t}$

Substituting into (5), we obtain the price gap in the small countries:

(9) $\qquad \tilde{p}_1 - p_1^T = (1 - 2\omega)\ \tilde{t} + U^d = -(\tilde{p}_2 - p_2^T)$

where p_i^T is the price level associated with u_i^T, $i = 1, 2$.

If $\omega = \frac{1}{2}$, the gap is entirely determined by the relative cyclical positions of Senegal and Ivory Coast, as captured by U^d. Otherwise, a demand expansion in Senegal will raise $\tilde{p}_1 - p_1^T$ by $2 (1 -$

$\omega)\xi 2u_A^1$, so that the effect is larger the smaller the share of Senegal in the transfer. Conversely, a demand expansion in Ivory Coast will raise $\tilde{p}_1 - p_1^T$ by $-2\omega\xi u_A^2$. The effect of a harvest failure in Senegal will be in the same direction as a demand expansion if $\xi > 1$, and a world positive supply shock may also raise $\tilde{p}_1 - p_1^T$. The effect is given by $(v - v^* - v^{**})(1 - \xi)*u_\pi^s$; it will be positive if the two expressions are of the same sign.

E. Real effects of the monetary union

In general, the price of domestic output has to be different from its equilibrium level for the real exchange rate to be different under the union.

Consider a rigid price level p_1^R which, under the union, gives a real exchange rate θ_1^R. Since the nominal exchange rate is the same, the difference in real exchange rates equals minus the difference in the price levels, which in turn can be decomposed further into the difference in money stocks and in real outputs:

$$(10) \quad \theta_1^R - \theta_1 = \tilde{p}_1 - p_1^R = \tilde{m}_1 - m_1^R - y_1 + y_1^R$$

$$= \tfrac{1}{H}(u_A^1 - {}^R u_A^1) < 0$$

where m_1^R is the money stock associated with price p_1^R.

The price rigidity induces a fiscal expansion ${}^R u_A^1$, which raises prices and appreciates the real exchange rate by $1/H$. When account is taken of the induced real appreciation, the demand expansion increases output by a factor less than one. Given monetary policy, this expansion would reduce prices by the same amount it expands output so that the nominal appreciation equals the sum of the two effects, which is ξ. As shown in (4) above, ξ will be less than one if trade elasticities are high enough. Since now neither the nominal exchange rate nor prices can change, the money stock has to increase by the same factor ξ. In other words, demand expansion consistent with the increase in the money stock is ${}^R u_A^1 = m_1^R/\xi$.

To combine the monetary allocation rule in (8) with a price rigidity, simply substitute into (10) having set ${}^R u_A^1$ to zero and express the real exchange rate gap in the small countries in a form like (9). The previous discussion applies exactly to $\theta_1^T - \theta_1$ and to $\theta_2 - \theta_2^T$. In particular the effect of domestic disturbances on the real exchange rate between Senegal and Ivory Coast can be analyzed in this way.

For example, the real depreciation of Senegal's real exchange rate relative to France and Ivory Coast (documented in Section III) can be explained both by larger fiscal expansion and negative supply shocks in the face of low trade elasticities. It would have been larger if Senegal's monetary share in UMOA had not risen during the period.

In sum, the effects of a fixed exchange rate regime are confined to nominal variables unless there is a price rigidity or an induced demand for domestic output, which may in turn be a consequence of fiscal expansion or of a transfer from abroad.

The results depend of course on the particular allocation rule postulated in equations (8). They illustrate, however, how a monetary allocation rule may induce a change in the real exchange rates of the members of a monetary union. The transfer of French real resources to UMOA modifies the automatic adjustment of the balance of payments of Senegal and Ivory Coast when the administrative monetary allocation rule does not reflect the assumed symmetric structure of their economies, including the domestic real disturbances facing each one of them.

III. SENEGAL, FRANCE AND UMOA

A. The Franc Zone: tradition or choice?

The CFA–French franc exchange rate goes back to the Franc Zone, established in the mid-forties between France and its colonies. Unlike their Asian counterparts, especially the Monetary Union of Indochina described by Bloomfield (1955), the African Monetary Unions have survived both the declarations of political independence in the early sixties and the move to generalized floating in the early seventies.

Upon independence, the Franc Zone was adapted through the creation of common central banks for the former French colonies of West, Central and East Africa. In particular, Benin (formerly Dahomey), Burkina–Faso (formerly Upper Volta), Ivory Coast, Mauritania, Niger, Senegal and Togo created UMOA, managed by the Central Bank of the West African States (known by its French acronym BCEAO), and signed an agreement of monetary cooperation with France. The agreement specified that the exchange rate between the franc and the CFA was fixed, foreign exchange reserves were pooled, exchange controls were common to the whole zone and an 'operations account' at the French Treasury guaranteed the convertibility of the CFA.

While Mali participated in the UMOA negotiations, it refused to sign the agreement and left the Franc Zone in 1962. Monetary sovereignty, Mali argued, was an essential instrument of development; monetary stability was a less pressing consideration.

Mali's justification is consistent with Mundell's summing up of the African monetary experience of the Bretton-Woods era:

The French and the English economic traditions in monetary theory and history are different. At the risk of gross oversimplification ... the French tradition has stressed the passive nature of monetary policy and the importance of exchange stability with convertibility (within the franc area); stability was achieved at the expense of institutional development and monetary experience. The British countries by opting for monetary independence have sacrificed stability, but gained experience and better developed monetary institutions. The simplest test of this is the extent of development of money substitutes. (1972, p. 93)

Indeed, his figures show that, in 1968, the median propensity to hold cash was 21 percent in OECD countries, 33 percent in the 'Sterling' category, 47 percent in the Franc category and 45 percent in the remaining two categories.

The criticism of the Franc Zone as a neo-colonial obstacle to 'self-reliance' is a manifestation of the fairly widespread view that the arrangement is more beneficial to France than to its peripheral members. Despite having allowed a substantial trade diversification away from France, monetary discipline did ensure a surplus on the balance of payments of the Zone, so that the guarantee of convertibility did not require UMOA members to draw on the 'operations account' until the late seventies. On the other side, France has remained a major aid donor to UMOA members, especially Senegal.[2] The net effect for the countries involved is difficult to ascertain but it certainly became relatively more favorable to Senegal in the seventies.

Since the repeated devaluation of the French franc after 1981 and the implementation of tighter area-wide exchange controls, however, the desirable trend toward diversification of trade away from France has probably been reversed. As a consequence, the 'English tradition' could almost provide an argument for leaving the Franc Zone: there will be no monetary stability in UMOA if there is none in France.

On the other side, the real depreciation of the franc against the dollar seems to have been transmitted to the real CFA-dollar, a possibility suggested by the analysis of the previous Section and documented below.

No serious attempt can be made to compute the costs and benefits of the Franc Zone. Rather, the controversy was mentioned to illustrate that the volatility of major exchange rates over the last ten years has changed the terms of the Mundellian trade-off between monetary stability and development. Stability relative to one currency means instability relative to other floating currencies, so that fixing 'the' exchange rate is no longer an option.

Figures on the development of money substitutes in the early eighties also suggest a blurring of the difference between the French and English monetary traditions. Certainly, the propensity to hold cash remains higher in the former French colonies than, say, in Kenya. But, except for Madagascar, the propensity to hold near-money increased much faster in the countries of Franc Africa than it did in Kenya or the Sudan.[3]

To the extent that both groups were subject to the global shocks of the seventies, the acceleration of financial development casts the agreements of monetary cooperation with France in a new light. The originality of their design has been emphasized in the work of the Guillaumonts (1980, 1981, 1984). Rather than a historic relic, the Franc Zone represents in their view a conscious choice of monetary and exchange rate policy by sovereign states. Similarly, for Vinay (1980), it is a 'unique organization' where 'the traditional legalism of French institutions was replaced by a fertile pragmatism.' The fact that some former French colonies, such as Madagascar and Mauritania, left the union in 1972 is of course consistent with the idea of choice.

Pragmatism and choice can also be found in the return of other former French colonies. While Bourdin (1980) reports the possibility of Mauritania finding it advantageous to return to the Franc Zone, Mali did return. Its choice thus provides an actual example, as well as a vivid illustration of the evolution of attitudes towards the French and British monetary traditions in Africa.

Three years after choosing monetary sovereignty, Mali began negotiations for a return to the Franc Zone, and a special arrangement was agreed upon in 1967, whereby the Malian franc was devalued by 50 percent relative to the CFA. Also, France was to convince UMOA members to vote for the accession of Mali. It was not a simple task. As Kasse (1984) remarks, full membership for Mali was not welcome by the other members. This is not surprising in light of its singular monetary underdevelopment (a propensity to hold cash of 62 percent versus 32 percent in Senegal) and a persistently negative operations account with France.

The 1967 agreement involved two preliminary phases. A one-year fiscal adjustment-cum-liberalization was followed by bilateral cooperation with France along BCEAO lines. While the duration of this phase was not specified, it certainly took much longer than anticipated. Serious negotiations only began in 1981 and were further delayed because of a border dispute with Burkina–Faso, as described in Crum (1984).

Nevertheless, Malian membership in UMOA was agreed upon at Niamey, Niger, in October 1983. The third phase was thus completed in 1984. Due to the increasing transfer of resources from France to UMOA, the reversal of Mali's choice might be explained by a desire to receive the transfer through UMOA, the previously accumulated credit of the operations account being written off by France. This may also be the reason why the CFA continued to be worth two Malian francs, despite the puzzling preference for a restoration of the one-to-one parity expressed by the Malian authorities.

If fixing is impossible in a floating world of flexible exchange rates and full flexibility is not a viable – let alone desirable – option for a developing country, an alternative to the institutions of the Franc Zone would be for UMOA to collectively peg to a basket of currencies. This choice was proposed by Nascimento (1981) on the basis of an econometric analysis of the costs and benefits of various exchange rate regimes for the union as a whole. He infers a trade-off between monetary sovereignty and 'liquidity' by comparing the loss in reserves associated with an excess supply of money (the offset coefficient) to the variances of departures from purchasing power parity (real exchange rate variability). According to this operationalization of the Mundellian trade-off, offset coefficients and real exchange rate variability in UMOA are smallest under a basket peg and largest under a crawling peg relative to the French franc.

Both the neglect of the French transfer – which allow the sterilization of the loss in reserves – and the assumption of purchasing power parity cast doubt on the applicability of Nascimento's analysis to UMOA, let alone to Senegal. The theoretical model presented in Section II showed clearly that a monetary transfer was implied by the choice of a fixed exchange rate regime. When several small countries collectively peg their rates to a single currency, furthermore, the allocation of the transfer becomes an important policy issue.

All the same, for a given transfer, pegging to a basket allows for the choice of optimal weights. Since it is unlikely for the optimal weight of a single currency to be one, such a regime would dominate the present arrangement. Similarly, it is unlikely that the rate of crawl be zero, so that a regime where indicators are optimally chosen will also dominate the basket peg.[4] Then UMOA would look like the European Monetary System (EMS) rather than like part of the 'traditional' Franc Zone. But without the operations account, Senegal would be unable to receive a transfer from its partners in UMOA of the magnitude allowed by past monetary allocations to the union. Especially because its monetary share has been rising, the economic consequences for Senegal would be serious indeed.

B. Monetary allocations in UMOA: the fall and rise of Senegal's share

During its first decade, UMOA followed the prudent course cited earlier as being characteristic of the French monetary tradition. From its Paris headquarters, BCEAO managed to keep the composition of the union's money stock (M2) virtually constant. The net foreign assets of the banking system (line 31n in *IFS*) grew almost without interruption and remained at about one third of the money stock, so that domestic assets accounted for (roughly) the other two thirds. As a share of the French money stock, UMOA's money remained at around one percent. Both trends are clear from Chart 1.

Senegal revealed the opposite pattern: it lost foreign assets virtually every year after independence but did not reduce credit creation, so that the foreign backing of its money stock tended to decline. As shown by the dotted line in Chart 2, foreign assets did increase more than the money stock in 1966 and 1970. In the first instance, this was due to the exceptional groundnut harvest of that year (the highest until 1976) and the high export price guaranteed by France (about 10 percent over the world price in 1965/67). The increase of 1970 was instead related to a boom in exports of manufactures and services (which increased by 50 percent). Despite the continued strength of tourism and the burst in exports of phosphates in 1974, the decline in foreign assets has not been reversed since that year.[5]

This is also what happened to the foreign assets of the union, but the reversal was obscured by drastic increases in the reserves of some of its members. At the same time, the institutional reforms allowed greater freedom for BCEAO to conduct monetary policy from its newly established Dakar headquarters.[6]

After 1977, the overall foreign asset position of UMOA began to deteriorate steadily. The dotted line in Chart 1 shows that the domestic assets of the banking system increased from 96 percent of the union money stock in 1978 to 143 percent in 1982.

The share of Senegal in UMOA's money stock dropped substantially after independence and then remained in the 20 percent range until 1977. Unlike foreign assets, though, it increased subsequently, and was over the 1973 share in 1982 (Chart 2).

Senegal's allocation has therefore been insulated from the decline of the total. On average the insulation was at the expense of the Ivory Coast, as suggested by a high negative correlation between the two monetary allocations. The strength of the inverse link between the balance of payments of the two major partners in UMOA was even higher in the sixties (for 1962–72 the correlation was perfect), largely because of the positive correlation implied by the deterioration of the Ivorian external position after 1980. Not surprisingly, the share of the Ivory Coast has been positively correlated with the

CHART 1

UMOA and France

(percent)

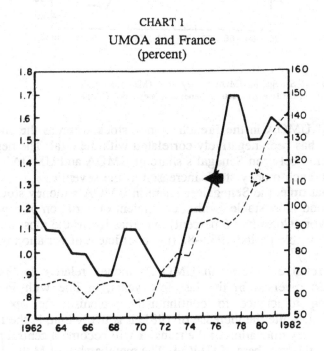

———— share of UMOA in French money stock (M2) – left scale
– – – share of domestic credit in UMOA money stock (M2) – right scale
Source: Table 2 in Macedo (1985a).

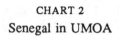

CHART 2

Senegal in UMOA

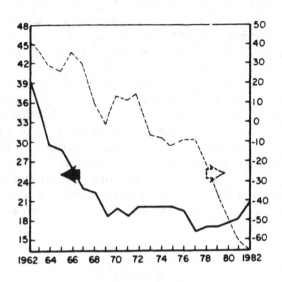

——— share of Senegal in UMOA money stock (M2) – left scale
– – – share of net foreign assets in Senegal money stock (M2) – right scale
Source: IFS.

share of UMOA in the French money stock whereas the share of
Senegal has been negatively correlated with the total. The negative
correlation between Senegal's share in UMOA and UMOA's share
in the French money stock increased in the seventies.

At that time, the Senegalese share in UMOA's money stock was
the second most stable (with a coefficient of variation of 8 percent
when Ivory Coast had 6 percent), whereas it was the most unstable
over the whole period 1962–82 (the coefficient of variation became
29 percent).[7]

The relative increase in UMOA's money relative to France's
has been reversed in the last few years, in line with France's
emerging reluctance to continuously replenish the operations
account. Despite the increase of 1981, it is likely that, in the future,
the monetary allocation of the transfer will become a central policy
issue for the members of UMOA. The membership of Mali, another
structural deficit country, also tightens the constraint on the shares
incorporated in the theoretical treatment of Section II.

262

C. Simplified Effective Exchange Rates

When the French franc devalued against the dollar under the Bretton-Woods system (1958 and 1969 during the sample period), it also devalued against most of the European currencies, and the same holds for the Smithsonian revaluation of 1971. Similarly, there were several devaluations of the French franc against the European Currency Unit (Ecu) since 1981. In the intervening ten years, as shown in Table 1, column 1, the French franc first appreciated against the dollar and depreciated with the oil crisis, to appreciate again during the 'weak dollar' period of 1977-79.

The simplified nominal exchange rates reported in Table 1 ignore the changes in the franc–Ecu rate, and simply weight the franc–dollar rate by rough trade shares. Then, the ratio of effective exchange rates in France and Senegal is 10 percent of the bilateral rate, with the two extreme values in 1980 (lowest at 98) and 1982 (highest at 103).

TABLE 1

Simplified Effective Exchange Rate Indexes (1965=100)

	(1) Franc-Dollar Rate	(2) Effective Exchange Rate of France	(3) Effective Exchange Rate of Senegal	(4) (2)/(3)
1968	100	100	100	100
1969	105	103	102	101
1970	113	106	105	101
1971	112	106	105	101
1972	102	101	101	100
1973	90	95	96	99
1974	97	99	99	100
1975	87	93	95	99
1976	97	98	99	100
1977	99	100	100	100
1978	91	96	96	99
1979	86	93	94	98
1981	110	105	104	101
1982	133	115	112	103

Source: (1) average annual exchange rate (French Francs per U.S. dollar) IMF, *International Financial Statistics.*
  (2) (1) raised to the power .5 (share of non-Ecu area trade in France).
  (3) (1) raised to the power .4 (share of non-Ecu area trade in Senegal).

This contrasts with the indexes presented in Table 2 below, where the ratio keeps increasing, to reach 140 in 1982 using 1980 import weights (Appendix Table 2, last column).

These results suggest care in interpreting the implications of the two-tier model presented in Section II. A more accurate procedure would be to specify a three- (rather than two-) tier structure. If the two large countries are the U.S. and Germany (as a proxy for the EMS), and France is treated as a small country, the recursiveness of the model is preserved. The structure of the monetary union between two (very) small countries would allow them to trade with France and the two large countries, or at least one of them (the U.S.), but not with each other. This would again preserve the recursiveness of the model but there would be two exogenous exchange rates, the franc–dollar rate and the franc–Ecu rate shocking the (very) small economies.

In order to analyze the interaction between France and Senegal in the UMOA framework, though, a three-tier model would be too cumbersome.

TABLE 2

Nominal Effective Exchange Rates of Senegal
(Indexes Base 1965=100)

| | Exports | | Imports | |
	1965	1980	1965	1980
1968	100	98	100	98
1969	100	100	101	101
1970	101	101	104	105
1971	101	101	104	106
1972	101	101	103	101
1973	101	99	102	96
1974	101	101	104	101
1975	100	97	101	93
1976	100	97	103	95
1977	101	97	104	95
1978	101	96	104	92
1979	101	96	103	90
1980	101	96	103	91
1981	102	101	106	98
1982	103	104	110	102
Memo 1982	105	112	113	104

Source: Average annual exchange rates from *IFS*, geometric average with weights from Appendix Table 1.
* 'Other' share in Appendix Table 1 added to U.S. share.

D. Trade Patterns: the fall and rise of France's share

France still accounts for about one third of the foreign trade of Senegal but its share has fallen considerably since the mid sixties, when it was 81 percent for exports and 54 percent for imports.

In 1965, twelve trading partners with shares higher than 1 percent accounted for over 70 percent of Senegalese imports. As shown in Appendix Table 1, in 1980 (the last year for which revised figures were available), there were twenty trading partners with import shares higher than 1 percent, and they accounted for over 90 percent of the total.[8] The 'oil crises' and the drought in the Sahel were partly responsible for this diversification: three of the new partners are oil-exporters; Argentina, another new partner, exports wheat; and the share of Thailand – a rice exporter – rose from 4 percent to 6 percent.

There has been an upward trend in 'South–South' trade: in 1965, only one other African country (Madagascar) accounted for more than 1 percent of Senegalese exports, but, in 1980, Ivory Coast, Mauritania, Mali, Guinea-Bissau and Nigeria accounted for 24 percent of Senegalese exports.

In any event, exports are much less diversified than imports.[9] An export-weighted effective exchange rate index will be less variable than an import-weighted index, as shown in Table 2, where the four sets of weights from Appendix Table 1 were used.

Similar data for France show the decreasing importance of the Franc Zone on the export and import sides, as well as the increase from 1 percent to 13 percent of the import share of oil-exporters. The Ivory Coast, Madagascar and Mali show a lower share for imports from the dollar-area (obtained residually) than Senegal. The share of imports from the U.S. is similar to that of Mauritania, Cameroon and Madagascar. The Franc Zone export share is highest in Senegal, followed by Mauritania, Mali and the Ivory Coast. On the import side, however, Senegal has the lowest share among Franc Zone countries.[10]

Thus trade diversification increased the dollar-area share in the trade of the Franc Zone countries, but Sene (1983) claims that the trend has been reversed by the franc devaluations of 1981/82 and the associated tightening of exchange controls, as seems plausible.

The use of export and import shares to measure the relative importance of trading partners' currencies neglects the growing weight of tourism on the credit side and of factor income on the debit side. In the case of Senegal, however, adjusting the shares for invisible transactions does not produce shares too different from the ones used in the computations of the indexes of the effective exchange rate.[11]

While 1965 export weights gave an effective exchange rate even closer to the franc–dollar rate than the simplified index reported in Table 1, there are sizable differences between the nominal effective exchange rate of France and Senegal (Appendix Table 2). Clearly, they are in part due to the different trade patterns, but the importance of changes in the effective exchange rate of the U.S. dollar is also relevant.

E. Nominal Stability and Real Volatility

After a decade of experience with flexible exchange rates, the failure of purchasing power parity is widely recognized.[12] The variability of the indexes of the import- and export-weighted real exchange rates of France and Senegal appearing in Charts 3 and 4 respectively is evident.

In Senegal, the adjustment of prices was opposite of purchasing power parity, so that the major source of a higher exchange rate is a lower domestic price level, as measured by the African consumer price index. The nominal devaluation of the French franc had virtually no effect.

The implications of these results for the external competitiveness of Senegalese products are limited by the nature of the price index used. If the terms of trade are roughly proxied by the ratio of export to import unit values, the correlation of the changes in this ratio with changes in the 1980 import-weighted real effective exchange rate is only 22% for the 1967-1980 period (28% using export weights).

A more careful comparison, carried out by Plane (1983a and b) relies on ratios of unit values for 36 manufactures at the 3-digit SITC level from ten West African economies. In Senegal, almost half of industrial output is accounted for by four products, namely fertilizers (16 percent), cotton fabrics (17 percent), machines for special industries (11 percent) and clothing (7 percent). With base 1970=100 and data through 1979 – except 1976 – Plane's indexes have as extreme observations 1971 and 1978 for fertilizers (133 and 433) and clothing (108 and 287), 1971 and 1979 for cotton (100 and 326) and 1971 (=1974) and 1977 for machines (166 and 246). The 'synthetic index,' on the other hand, increases to 139 in 1973, showing a gain in competitiveness, then falls to 95 in 1978. While this pattern is very different from the one shown in Chart 4, it also

CHART 3

Real Effective Exchange Rate
1980/81 Import Weights (1965=1)

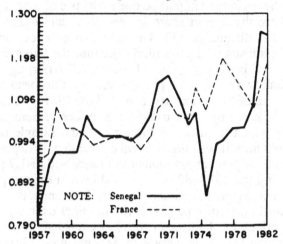

CHART 4

Real Effective Exchange Rates
1980/81 Export Weights (1965=1)

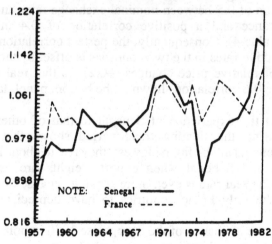

diverges substantially from the real effective exchange rates he computes, based on 1970 total trade weights.[13]

Independently of implications for Senegal's competitiveness in manufacturing, the difference in the behavior of relative prices in France and Senegal may in part be due to the use of a price index for Senegal where the import share is very small and many items are controlled. The difference with Senegal's European consumer price index can be substantial, particularly because the latter has a much higher share of imported goods. Thus, in 1977 (strong franc) the African inflation rate was 11 percent and the European 6 percent, whereas the rates were exactly reversed in 1981 (weak franc).[14] Nevertheless, it is important to note that prices in Senegal did not significantly adjust to prices in France over the sample period.

Using 1980 import weights, the real exchange rate depreciated by an average of 1.4 percent *per annum* in France and of 1.7 percent in Senegal during the 1973–82 period, as shown in the top panel, last row of Table 3. More interesting than this difference, though, is the relative contribution of changes in the nominal exchange rate and in relative prices to changes in the real exchange rate. The contribution of nominal depreciation in Senegal was 0.2 percent *per annum* while higher foreign inflation contributed the remainder. In France, nominal depreciation was about 2.5 percent *per annum*, which was offset by higher domestic inflation of one percent per annum.[15]

Moreover, real exchange rates and relative prices were twice as variable in Senegal as they were in France. This is due to a negative correlation of 0.5 between nominal exchange rates and relative prices in France and a positive correlation of 0.4 in Senegal (Appendix Table 4). Consequently, the perfect correlation between nominal effective rates in the two countries is offset by the negative correlation of relative price changes (–0.2), so that real exchange rates have the 0.6 correlation shown in the bottom panel, last row of Table 3.[16]

Comparing the experience of Senegal to that of other African countries during the floating trade period shows that nominal changes in Senegal are by far the lowest (they rise to about 1/3 for the Ivory Coast and Senegal when export weights are used). The evolution of the real rate is even more striking because Senegal and France are the only Franc countries to have depreciated in real terms.

The mean rate of change of the Senegalese 1980 import-weighted nominal effective exchange rate was only 0.7 percent *per annum*

TABLE 3

Exchange Rates and Prices in Senegal and France 1973–82

	Weights	Nominal Exchange Rate		Ratio of Foreign to Domestic CPI		Real Exchange Rate	
		Senegal	France	Senegal	France	Senegal	France
mean (% p.a.)	X65	.14	2.60	−.17	−1.97	−.01	.55
	M65	.63	2.31	−.42	−1.67	.25	.57
	X80	.36	1.70	.42	−.82	.84	.83
	M80	.16	2.54	1.40	−1.00	1.69	1.44
coefficient of variation	X65	3.64	1.85	42.44	.68	984.49	7.71
	M65	3.18	2.28	16.36	.75	31.45	8.09
	X80	7.02	3.07	13.09	1.88	8.28	5.42
	M80	29.06	2.40	5.10	3.02	5.90	3.74
coefficient of correlation	X65	.89		−.21		.47	
	M65	.99		−.17		.62	
	X80	.91		−.20		.62	
	M80	.96		−.20		.62	

Source: Same as Table 2.

over the 1958–1982 period, the lowest figure (except for a 0.4 percent *per annum* appreciation in Mauritania). But all African countries (not including Sudan) show a lower mean change than France, at 2.72 percent *per annum*. Given this low mean, it is not surprising that the variability of the nominal exchange rate of Senegal be highest after Mauritania. Accordingly, the correlation of these changes with Senegal's are one for Ivory Coast, 0.9 for Cameroon, Mali and Madagascar, 0.2 for Kenya, zero for Sudan, and −0.2 for Mauritania. For real rates, the correlation drops (to 0.2 for the Ivory Coast). The mean change in Senegal is generally lower than in other Franc Zone countries and higher than in countries outside, while the coefficient of variation is higher. The correlations are not substantially altered by the weighting scheme, except for the higher (0.20) positive correlation with Mauritania using 1965 shares.[17]

Nominal variability increased enormously in Senegal (28 versus 3 for the Ivory Coast). In terms of real variability, Senegal was close to France (6), Mauritania highest (8), and the Ivory Coast lowest (4). The mean changes are close in absolute values but the correlation between nominal and real changes is lower in the Ivory Coast. Also, the correlation between real rates in the two countries increased to .45 in the 1970s. Aside from the real depreciation of the franc since 1968, Chart 3 showed very substantial swings around the upward trend, most pronounced when the 1981 weights are used. Using export weights (as in Chart 4), the upward trend is less noticeable.

Chart 5 shows rates of change of the real exchange rates of Senegal and Ivory Coast. While the latter records negative values throughout the seventies, there is a real depreciation in Senegal after the dramatic increase in prices of late 1974.[18]

After 1976, Senegal moved opposite to France, whereas the Ivory Coast magnified the French movement. There is a substantial gap between the real rates of the two partners until 1980, as would be expected from the divergent performances of their balance of payments. This suggests that the monetary allocation rule did respond to the economies' external position, particularly when the total share of UMOA ceased to increase in relation to the French money stock.[19]

CHART 5

Changes in Real Effective Exchange Rate
(1980 import weights)
Ivory Coast and Senegal

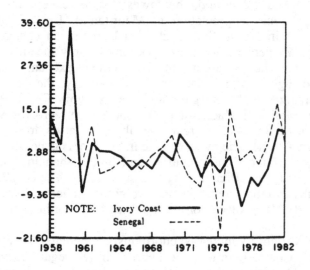

IV. CONCLUSION

Based on a theoretical model of a three-country monetary union in a four-country world of flexible exchange rates, this chapter analyzes the monetary and exchange rate experience of Senegal in the last twenty years in light of its membership, together with five other African countries, in the West African Monetary Union. UMOA is, in turn, linked, via an agreement with France, to the European Monetary System, whose currency floats against the U.S. dollar.

The model in Section II generated real effective exchange rates which, under complete symmetry, only depended on domestic real disturbances relative to the world average. Indeed, with passive monetary policy, the nominal fate is more variable than the real. Therefore, the trade-off between nominal stability and real volatility depended on domestic monetary accommodation rather than on the volatility of the international prices of Senegalese exports and imports. The major implication of the monetary union in the model was the elimination of this possibility. In fact, when the central bank allocates the transfer to the union, it will exacerbate the movements in the real exchange rate unless the allocation is neutral.

The model suggested an exogenous administrative procedure to determine the crucial monetary allocation parameter. Therefore, the effect of the recent threat of reduction in the transfer from France is likely to be increasing conflicts about the monetary allocation rule, making it endogenous. A set-up like the one presented in Section II can of course be extended to incorporate some of these conflicts.

At the beginning of Section III in this chapter, the process of monetary allocation in UMOA is analyzed quantitatively. The drastic deterioration of the net foreign asset position of UMOA in the last five years shows the importance of the French transfer. Over the last twenty years, however, monetary allocation within the union involved a very high negative correlation between the two major partners, Senegal and the Ivory Coast. To the extent that the transfer from France disappears, a fixed exchange rate with the French franc will require a restoration of this pattern rather than the growing union-wide deficit which has been observed since 1979.

The comparison of the interaction between exchange rate and relative price changes in Senegal and France confirmed the expected failure of purchasing power parity to stabilize the real exchange rate. More surprising – despite the presence in the price index used of non-traded goods and goods whose price is controlled – was the insulation of (African) consumer price inflation in Senegal from French consumer price inflation: relative prices in the two countries showed a negative correlation of about $\frac{1}{2}$ over the sample period. This finding explains that the strong positive correlations between nominal effective exchange rates in the two countries are associated with a weak correlation between real exchange rates. For the whole sample period, 1958–82, as well as for shorter periods (1963–72 and 1973–82), furthermore, Senegal's stable nominal effective rate was accompanied by an unstable real effective exchange rate. Since this relative price has a weak positive correlation with the terms of trade, it can be said that the monetary union achieved nominal stability at the expense of the real volatility. The unfortunate consequences of this pattern for resource allocation led Nascimento (1981) to propose a basket peg. But his argument ignores the increasing French transfer of the last four years.

The comparison of the real effective exchange rate of Senegal with six other African countries confirms the singularity of the country's experience. All depreciated in nominal terms, but Senegal achieved a real depreciation during the floating rate period whereas other former French colonies appreciated in real terms. Real exchange variability over the sample period was less pronounced in Madagascar, Mauritania, and the Sudan. In fact, neighboring Mauritania reveals a strong pattern of negative real exchange rate correlation with Senegal after leaving the Franc Zone in 1972 and a strong positive correlation before that.

This suggests that, if the loss of monetary autonomy did not induce a gold-standard type adjustment to external inflation in Senegal (as it did in other UMOA countries, such as the Ivory Coast before 1980), the reason is to be found in the increase of the union-wide money stock relative to the exogenously determined French money stock in the seventies. More importantly, from 1975 to 1980, if the monetary allocation rule had allowed the Ivory Coast to drain money from Senegal through the balance of payments it would have induced real appreciation in the former and real depreciation in the latter, as was indeed observed.

NOTES

*Earlier versions were presented at the Seminar of International Monetary Economics (SEMI, Paris, France), the University of Lausanne (Switzerland), the New University of Lisbon (Portugal), the School of Business Administration (ESGE, Dakar, Senegal), the University of Dakar- Fann (Senegal), the University of South Carolina, the University of Coimbra (Portugal), the United Nations Secretariat, Princeton, Columbia, the University of Paris IX (Dauphine), the Institute of Politics (SciencePo, Paris), and the African American Issues Center, Boston University. Comments from participants are gratefully acknowledged. Thanks are also due to C.T. Hu for help with the computations, and to J.-C. Nascimento for his comments in the Appendix to this chapter.

1. Before independence, CFA stood for French Colonies of Africa. After independence, the currency was renamed Franc of African Financial Cooperation, whose French acronym is also CFA.
2. Raffinot (1982) attempts to defend the 'self-reliance' view. On French aid to Senegal, see Lewis in this volume.
3. Chambas (1983) proposes comparing exchange rate policies in Senegal to the ones in the Sudan.
4. See the analysis of Branson and Katseli (1982) and, on the choice of indicators, Branson and Macedo (1982).
5. The 1965/66 episode can be deduced from the data gathered in IMF (1970, p. 507) and Chambas et al. (1981, p. 3). There is no similar source on the 1969/70 increase because WB (1979) begins the analysis in 1970. We used the *Balance of Payments Yearbook* figures reported in Guillaumonts (1981) and the output figures from Daniel (nd). On expected output, see Chapter 1.
6. Bhattia (1982) emphasizes the importance of the 1974 reform in his study of UMOA up to that date. The need for a more active interest rate policy in UMOA is clear from Leite (1982).
7. The coefficient of variation is obtained by dividing the standard deviation by the mean and multiplying by 100. Further evidence on monetary allocations is in Macedo (1985a).
8. Figures from other sources are sometimes widely different. Thus Kuhn et al. (1982, p. 28) has the 1980 French share as 38 percent of exports and 40 percent of imports, based on provisional BCEAO figures, but the 1964 figures reported by Guillaumonts (1981) are closer to the ones reported in Appendix Table 1 for 1965.
9. This is consistent with the so-called 'supermarket view of world trade,' whereby monopoly power is virtually absent from the import side, but not from the export side. See Dervis, de Melo and Robinson (1982).
10. Trade shares for France, Ivory Coast, Cameroon, Mali, Mauritania, Madagascar, Kenya and Sudan are reported in Macedo (1985b, Tables A-2 and A-6 through A-12).
11. According to provisional figures for 1981, tourism revenues were slightly higher than groundnut exports (about 8 percent of merchandise import payments, including insurance and freight). According to Senegal (1983, p. 231), the French share of tourists in 1980 was 39 percent and the share of tourists from other EMS countries was 20 percent. But according to Kuhn et al. (1982, p. 29, 31), the two adjustments go in the opposite direction. See the calculation of current account weights in Macedo (1982, Appendix A to Essay III).
12. See the general debate and evidence in Macedo (1985d). Nonetheless, Nascimento (1981) and Connolly (1983) assume that purchasing power parity holds between UMOA and EMS (or France).
13. Plane's index of average market share based on 27 manufactures is highest in 1975 at 191 and lowest in 1979 at 45. Note that Senegal is the country where his indicators diverge most from each other.

14. See Kuhn et al. (1982, p. 8). A comparison of the African index with the national output deflator appears in Plane (1983a).

15. Taking the weight of the last years before independence into account, in particular the reported 6 percent deflation of (African) consumer prices during 1962 evident from charts 3-5, increases the inflation gap with France. Results for alternative sample periods appear in Macedo (1985b, Tables A-3 through A-5).

16. Denoting the difference between the average foreign price and the price in Senegal by p, the three correlation coefficients are related by an hyperbola in the space of any two of them, with equation:

$$1 - \rho_{ep}^2 - \rho_{e\theta}^2 - \rho_{p\theta}^2 + 2\rho_{ep}\rho_{e\theta}\rho_{p\theta} = 0$$

The hyperbola collapses into a 45° line if one of the coefficients is one. Thus, in France $\rho_{e\theta} \cong 1$, so that $\rho_{ep} \cong \rho_{\theta p}$ whereas in Senegal $\rho_{p\theta} \cong 1$ so that $\rho_{ep} \cong \rho_{e\theta}$, the striking failure of purchasing power parity in both sample periods is evident. It would imply a correlation of −1 between nominal exchange rates and relative prices, and the correlation between real exchange rates and nominal exchange rates and relative prices would be equal and of opposite sign. But the coefficients in Appendix Table 4 whose absolute values are closer to each other, referring to 1980 export weights, are −.24 and .86 for France.

17. See Table 8 in Macedo (1985a). Charts A-1 through A-5 in Macedo (1985b) compare the real rates of Senegal to the others. No real rates were reported for Mali due to the absence of a price index in *IFS*. Plane (1983b) presents such an index and singles it out as showing a clear overvaluation, unlike the other 9 African currencies he studies.

18. They followed the freeze of July, 1974 which led to a depletion of the resources of the CPSP and involved substantial reduction in the subsidies on rice, sugar and edible oils. Wages and salaries were also substantially raised. Thus in December, 1974 food prices (share 56 percent) were 65 percent higher than in June.

19. The correlation of the relative shares in UMOA and the ratio of real effective exchange rates of the two countries was rather weak in the period 1965–82 (−0.25 using 1980 import shares) and basically disappeared in the 1970s (−0.05). This was also the case, but to a less extent, of the correlation between monetary shares and relative consumer prices, which dropped from −0.35 to −0.15 between the two sample periods.

APPENDIX TABLE 1

Trade Shares of Senegal (percent)

Partner	Exports		Imports	
	1965	1980	1965	1980
France	80.64	32.25	53.96	33.73
Germany	2.72	2.53	4.46	3.36
Italy	1.48	1.94	3.05	3.11
Ivory Coast	*	7.57	3.72	2.84
Netherlands	*	*	2.69	2.66
Belgium	*	*	1.95	1.53
Guinea-Bissau	*	3.29	*	*
Algeria	*	*	2.44	3.22
United Kingdom	1.40	5.70	1.34	5.37
Mauritania	*	5.96	*	*
Morocco	*	*	1.40	*
Nigeria	*	1.43	*	7.35
Thailand	*	*	4.03	6.01
Iraq	*	*	*	5.85
United States	*	*	4.09	4.32
Dominican Republic	*	*	*	1.90
China	*	*	1.83	1.85
Norway	*	*	*	1.81
Spain	*	*	*	1.42
Pakistan	*	*	*	1.39
Argentina	*	*	*	1.26
Saudi Arabia	*	*	*	1.17
Japan	1.87	2.30	*	1.12
Finland	*	2.48	*	*
Other	10.02	28.63	13.51	8.73
Total	100.00	100.00	100.00	100.00

Source: IMF, *Direction of Trade,* various issues.   *less than 1 per cent.
Countries were ranked by currency area and, within it, by their 1980 import share if greater than 1 percent, otherwise alphabetically.

APPENDIX TABLE 2

Ratio of the Nominal Effective Rates Indices of France to Senegal (Base 1965=100)*

Weights	Export		Import	
Year	1965	1980/81	1965	1980/81
1968	98	100	99	101
1969	104	104	103	103
1970	112	111	109	107
1971	115	112	110	109
1972	113	110	109	111
1973	111	109	108	113
1974	119	114	113	116
1975	112	109	107	115
1976	116	111	110	118
1977	122	116	114	124
1978	124	118	115	128
1979	125	117	115	130
1980	125	117	115	129
1981	131	119	120	132
1982	142	125	127	140

Source: IMF, *International Financial Statistics.*
*Effective exchange rates computed with the weights reported in Appendix Table 1 for Senegal and in Table A-2 in Macedo (1985b) for France, adjusted to add up to one.

APPENDIX TABLE 3

Real Effective Exchange Rates Indices for Senegal
(Base 1965=100)

	Exports		Imports	
	1965	1980	1965	1980
1968	103	101	103	101
1969	105	104	106	105
1970	110	109	111	114
1971	112	111	113	116
1972	111	109	111	111
1973	107	104	105	104
1974	105	105	105	106
1975	88	90	87	86
1976	96	97	95	99
1977	95	98	95	99
1978	100	101	99	103
1979	101	102	99	102
1980	105	106	103	108
1981	113	118	113	126
1982	108	115	110	125

Source: Same as Table 2, African Consumer price index used.

APPENDIX TABLE 4

Exchange Rates and Prices: Correlations

Weights	Senegal Nominal and Real Exchange Rates	France	Senegal Nominal Exchange Rates and Relative Prices	France	Senegal Real Exchange Rates and Relative Prices	France
1958–82						
X65	.52	.86	.46	−.68	.99	−.20
M65	.57	.86	.32	−.65	.96	−.17
X80	.64	.86	.31	−.69	.93	−.24
M80	.73	.84	.27	−.62	.86	−.09
1973–82						
X65	.68	.96	.64	−.48	1.00	−.20
M65	.61	.97	.42	−.57	.98	−.37
X80	.70	.96	.42	−.58	.95	−.33
M80	.77	.86	.42	−.47	.90	.04

Source: Same as Table 2.

Appendix

Jean-Claude Nascimento

INTRODUCTION

De Macedo sets up a theoretical framework allowing, not only an explanation of Senegal's singular monetary experience, but also an analysis of up-to-date issues important to African countries. For example, what are the monetary consequences for small countries envisioning South–South monetary cooperation (e.g., should Guinée follow the Malian example or join UMOA directly?)? In the latter case,[1] what currency regime should they adopt, assuming that a fixed single peg guarantees a transfer of real resources from the large country?

Its analytical results explain the opposite behavior of the bilateral real exchange rate of the two major partners with France – the Ivory Coast (an appreciation) and Senegal (a depreciation); furthermore, both happened owing to a transfer of real resources from France.

The most important result in the paper is that small countries' real exchange rate is modified by a monetary allocation rule when they choose to form a full monetary union among themselves and a pseudo-monetary union with a large country, while their rate is not modified when they join individually with a large country to form a pseudo-monetary union. One shortcoming of Section III of the paper is precisely not to examine also the Malian case within the Franc Zone in relation to the second part of the proposition.

The paper raises also some questions relative to the transfer of real resources: does the administered monetary allocation rule cease to apply with its disappearance? If the transfer is required, any price gap given an allocation rule should depend on the existence of the transfer: this may not be true for all rules. The assumption of one such rule explains de Macedo's assessment relative to a fixed trade-weighted basket peg proposed by Nascimento (1981) as an optimal exchange rate regime for UMOA countries.[2]

The monetary allocation rule

Recent proposals have suggested the introduction of national

277

currencies for the UMOA countries (e.g. the 'Senegalese franc') pegged to the CFA franc at a fixed but adjustable rate in order to adjust their real exchange rate to heterogeneous economic performances while preserving the institutions for UMOA and the Franc Zone. They are reported by Michalet and de Boissieu (1983).

In that context, the paper contains a major contribution since the same result can be achieved through the central bank's enforcement of a monetary allocation rule, without reverting to a pseudo-monetary union and the tensions it creates. As there are many possible monetary allocation rules, however, one point with significant implication for UMOA remains unexplained: what analytical criteria govern the choice of a given rule by the union's monetary authorities?

In the recent situation of UMOA and in the specific case of Senegal two issues arise. Analytically, the rule based on the small countries' equilibrium money stock shows that the price gap depends on a monetary allocation rule and on foreign and domestic real disturbances. The rule is compatible with $t = 0$. In this case, the transfer of real resources need not come from the large country because the balance of payments settlement mechanism operates through the redistribution of assets in a full monetary union. This mechanism allows the case for chronic deficit as well as for chronic surplus countries. As Allen (1976, p.18) states,

in such a situation the chronic deficit country over time will receive real net transfers from other members of the union

This rule reflects more adequately the conduct of monetary policy in UMOA countries based on the determination of an equilibrium money stock increase ($\tilde{m}$) compatible with the countries' rate of change in hoarding. The BCEAO allocates u^T_i according to the country's performance with respect to the objective of external balance. A real transfer from the large country then occurs only when both (identical) small countries turn into deficit.

In sum, the monetary allocation rule requires primarily the existence of a real transfer of resources within the full monetary union. To quote Allen (1976) again,

If countries wish to form a monetary union, they must be willing to endure the possibility of long-run net transfers within the union as some countries have tendencies to fall into payments deficits.

This is the meaning of the solidarity existing between UMOA members that does not preclude, when needed, the second 'solidarity' mechanism, the operations account, coming into play.

The 'required' transfer

Equation (7) and its interpretation constitute the cornerstone of the analysis. This transfer represents the balance of payment adjustment mechanism assuring goods and services market equilibrium in the two regions since de Macedo substitutes here Mundell's (1961) factor mobility criterion for an optimum currency area by a real transfer of resources from the large country.

In its application to the UMOA economies, this result needs to be qualified on two accounts related to the direction of the real transfer and the power of the monetary policy actions of the BCEAO in the Franc Zone.

The structure of these economies and the distributional patterns of rainfall in West Africa give more weight to the case of global disturbances being negatively rather than positively correlated. The duplication of economic activities in the manufacturing sector primarily tends to produce counter-cyclical economic performances in the presence of temporary aggregate supply shocks.[3] Moreover, the intensive exploitation of the forest in the southern part of West Africa (e.g. the Ivory Coast which exports wood) seems to be positively correlated with the process of desertification in the Sahel. Similar observations are made in the southern hemisphere of Africa between Gabon for example and states like Mozambique and Zimbabwe.

Thus, with $u^1 = -u^2$, the transfer can go *either way* depending on the competitiveness of the large country's traded goods relative to the rest of the world traded products. We now see a major argument of the critics of the Franc Zone supported by Yeates' (1978) empirical findings: a lack of competitiveness of French products relative to those of other major industrial countries induces a transfer of real resources *from UMOA to France!* It explains in addition the call for the promotion of South–South trade relations which decreases the magnitude of the real transfer. Although the recent real depreciation of the French franc supports de Macedo's result, his reference to the direction of the transfer is by no means a general analytical result.

Demand expansion in the presence of domestic monetary stability requires a continuous flow supply of money to maintain excess real expenditures over real output. The Franc Zone 'safeguards' are institutional mechanisms which, despite the reform of 1973, limit such actions on the part of the BCEAO. When the monetary implications are taken into account, this result shows the consequences of the BCEAO financing demand expansion (example: investment of small and medium sized businesses as mentioned in the statutes since 1973) on their external position. A chronic union deficit situation then requires a lasting real transfer of resources from France which it is doubtful will continue forever, as both de Macedo and Nascimento (1983) point out. This is a fundamental difference between a full and a pseudo monetary union.

In sum, de Macedo implies here that the BCEAO has the power to make lasting external seignorage gains from France. This would not explain the presence of two French representatives on the Board of Directors of the BCEAO. Moreover, it does not reflect the basic idea behind the functioning of the operation account mechanism, which is to prevent the discontinuity of foreign payments caused by *temporary factors* adversely affecting UMOA's external balance.

A fixed versus a flexible exchange rate regime

A major implication of the paper is that the automatic balance of payments adjustment mechanism is only partial since the real transfer foregoes the real balance effect. If small countries in a pseudo monetary union with a large country can forego this painful adjustment process, there is indeed no reason why they should adopt a currency regime other than the fixed single peg.

This is the fundamental difference with Nascimento's (1981) analysis supporting exchange rate flexibility relative to the large country's currency via the adoption of a fixed basket peg. Empirical results (up to 1978) support the functioning of the automatic balance of payments adjustment under all exchange regimes examined: the offset coefficient is statistically not different from minus one for the small monetary union (UMOA) as a whole. This runs opposite to the idea of a transfer of real resources equivalent to the sterilization of foreign reserves movements on the money supply (a positive coefficient smaller than one). Moreover, it abstracts from the recent experience of UMOA countries engaged in stabilization programs with the IMF, where credit tightening has been systematically applied although with a time lag.

These opposite assessments of the working of the automatic balance of payments adjustment reflect the emphasis each analysis puts on real (de Macedo) versus monetary (Nascimento) foreign disturbances, their real effects and transmission channels to the foreign sector.

However it is striking to notice that, although the transmission channels are different, Nascimento's empirical results support some analytical results of the paper under a fixed and a flexible exchange regime.

First, under a fixed exchange rate arrangement,[4] foreign disturbances (e.g.: a depreciation of the franc) have a positive effect on the bilateral real exchange rate between the union and the large partner, dampened by the relative sensitivity factor. These disturbances are transmitted to the foreign sector indirectly through the real exchange rate effect (a direct transmission of real disturbances in the large country to the union's foreign sector is not significant in Nascimento, 1981). The magnitude of the effect is smaller in Nascimento since it is offset by *a rise in the domestic price level* due to imported inflation which de Macedo acknowledges in Section III.[5]

Second, expansionary monetary policies in the small country produce no real effects: purchasing power parity holds between the large country and the full monetary union as anticipated because of optimal currency area considerations – under a flexible exchange rate regime, a more expansionary monetary policy is more inflationary than a fixed single peg but the causes of the price gap once again diverge.[6]

CONCLUSION

In general, a monetary allocation rule does not require a transfer of resources from the large country although this may happen when the two small countries of the monetary union move, simultaneously, into a deficit. This is more in accordance with the whole history and institutional arrangement of UMOA as part of the Franc Zone.

Second, de Macedo and Nascimento's results diverge essentially due to their emphasis on real versus monetary foreign disturbances respectively – and the channels through which they are transmitted to the real and the foreign sectors. These divergences reflect the use of a Keynesian and a monetary approach as methodological frameworks of analysis.

The similarity of some important results relative to the conduct of monetary policy under various exchange rate regimes for small countries calls for a convex combination of the two approaches, as de Macedo's analysis shows the importance that the transfer may have under specific circumstances, and Nascimento's emphasizes the importance of the monetary disturbances in the case of UMOA.

NOTES

1. See, for example, the project of a monetary union among the CEDEAO countries in McLenaghan, Nsouli and Riechel (1982), and in Wade (1975), among others.
2. His doubts are rather strange as regards his statement that the theoretical results hold in the case of a peg to the Ecu, a basket currency. Aside from their diverging methodological frameworks, the fundamental issue in the two analyses would be the choice of an optimal basket peg. This issue has been assessed in Williamson (1982).
3. The neglect of this point arises in the paper because of the assumption of the absence of trade within the full monetary union.
4. This discussion refers to the case of a fixed single peg between one large and one small country.
5. The results in Section III are based on import weights, whose limitations are noted in Williamson (1982).
6. Here again different explanations arise: in Nascimento, this results from the inability of domestic monetary authorities to produce a lasting differential inflation rate, through monetary policy, as the former rate is determined in the foreign country (law of one price).

CHAPTER NINE

Aid, Structural Adjustment, and Senegalese Agriculture

John P. Lewis

The focus of this chapter is on the adjustment crisis in which Senegal has been embroiled since 1978. The case is not only recent; it remains current. It involves a multiplicity of donors with a degree of interaction among them. And yet – unlike such multidonor–multirecipient cases as the Club du Sahel–CILSS venture or the on-going Senegal River Basin (OMVS) irrigation and power scheme – the Senegal structural adjustment story focuses at the recipient end on a single recipient government, the Senegalese.

The case encompasses the whole economy and yet it is sufficiently related to agriculture to conform to the purposes of this volume. Agriculture is so central to the Senegalese economy that the latter can scarcely prosper in the medium term unless agriculture prospers. Symmetrically, agriculture will be unable to hold its own until the whole economy achieves sustainable closures of its gaps in both external and internal financing. There is this further point: it was aspects of rural policy which became the sticking point in what turned out to be the key recipient–donor relationships – those with the World Bank and the International Monetary Fund (IMF) – in Senegal's current structural-adjustment experience.

Two preliminaries are needed before we turn to that experience. First, some matters of definition, identification, and scale must be gone through on the side of aid. Second, from the Senegalese side, one should set the stage historically for the macroeconomic and agricultural events of the later 1970s.

I. SENEGAL'S FOREIGN AID AND THOSE WHO SUPPLY IT

A. *The scope of 'aid' and aid policy issues*

Strictly construed, the term 'aid' should be confined to official development assistance (ODA), i.e., to concessional transfers with a grant element of at least 25 percent and not including military assistance. Much of our focus in the following will indeed be on ODA. As is so often the case, however, in Senegal, one's interest in aid (and in aid donors) carries over, as well, to official transfers of lesser concessionality – to what OECD nomenclature calls 'other official flows.' Moreover, particularly in the case of the current structural adjustment issue, one's interest certainly extends to a multilateral agency, the IMF, that often is not listed as a donor, not only because its credits (other than Trust Fund loans) are extended on harder than ODA terms, but because its mission is not concentrated on the Third World and is not primarily developmental. The Monetary Fund is one of the central institutional actors this chapter examines. As to the aspects and effects of foreign transfers, we are, of course, concerned with their immediate macro effects on Senegal's balance of payments, liquidity, and GDP aggregates. But, in principle, we are just as interested in the delayed macro effects of aid terms on the country's indebtedness and debt burden; in the effects of tying and other aid characteristics on prices, in the sectoral composition of aid, and in the effects of aid on the country's project choices. In general we are concerned about the impact of aid on the efficiency of resource use as well as on inequalities among Senegalese people and groups. We are curious about the scale, quality and impact of technical assistance. We are intrinsically interested in the mix between aid and such more flexible modes as sectoral, program, and non-project assistance; and this, of course, is a specifically important dimension of the adjustment crisis case. Finally, an aspect of the impact of aid is its effects on the recipient government's policies.

B. The scale of aid

Senegal received official development assistance averaging annually well over 50 U.S. dollars per capita in the three years, 1980–82. This was a high aid allocation. It was not far above the average for all the Sahelian countries which, partly thanks to the Club du Sahel[1] mechanism, have been greatly favored by donors during the past decade. But it was well over twice the level of ODA per capita received by other Sub-Saharan African countries during the same period, and four or five times per capita levels for Asian aid recipients. The per capita figures for Kenya, Tanzania, and Sudan in the same years were in the $25 to $35 range; Bangladesh's and

Pakistan's levels both were in the neighborhood of $10, and India's was less than $3. The ODA estimates are from OECD (1983), Annex Table G–2; population estimates are from World Bank (1983, Annex Table 1).

The scale of aid's role was clear in the economy's macro data. By definition, together with nonconcessional transfers from abroad, aid covered that part of Senegal's yawning current-account gap that was not handled by drawdowns on reserves. According to World Bank estimates the current account deficit in 1981 was $590 million or 25 percent of GDP. Aid, of both the project and 'exceptional' types, covered $300 million of the gap. Nonconcessional external funding including such private flows as there were, as well as IMF credits and other official longer-term flows, accounted for about $125 million. Senegal's reserve position, the World Bank estimated, was indented a further $165 million, winding up some $526 million in the red (see below, and Chapter 8).

Table 1, to which we shall be making repeated reference, is drawn from OECD estimates and arrays the record of official transfers to Senegal, both ODA and other official flows, for the seven years, 1976 through 1982. It provides a rather different picture of 1981. Perhaps reflecting fuller donor reporting, it puts ODA fully $100 million higher than the Bank estimates just quoted. If most of the differences between the Bank's estimate of nonconcessional flows and the OECD figure of other official flows is accounted for by the latter's exclusion of private flows and IMF credits, then it would appear that, if the level of aid was as large as the table reports, the reduction in reserves in 1981 must have been less than the Bank calculated.

Be that as it may, both sets of data highlight Senegal's dependence on aid and other transfers. Together official transfers paid for all the country's investment and 6 percent of its consumption in 1981 (World Bank, 1983, Annex Table 5). Moreover, although the reliance was extreme in 1981, elements of this pattern of counting on aid for investment funding as well as gap-closing were established shortly after independence in 1960.

C. *The cast of donors*

Table 1 makes clear by how wide a margin transfers from France have outstripped those from all other donors to Senegal – even though laterally France has not dominated the formulation and advocacy of donors' policy preferences. In the years the table

TABLE 1

Official net transfers to Senegal disbursed 1976–1982

(millions of US dollars)

	1976			1977			1978		
	ODA	OOF	TOTAL	ODA	OOF	TOTAL	ODA	OOF	TOTAL
Sources									
DAC bilateral									
France	58.3	20.1	78.4	54.7	14.7	69.4	76.7	48.7	125.4
Belgium	2.3	0.3	2.6	3.5	4.3	7.8	5.0	12.7	17.7
Canada	6.2	0	6.2	6.4	0	6.4	10.5	1.5	12.0
Germany	2.7	3.1	5.8	8.1	0.2	8.3	5.8	–5.1	0.7 .
Japan	0.2	0.7	0.9	1.2	–0.3	0.9	1.5	0.4	1.9
U.S.	7.0	0	7.0	10.0	0	10.0	14.0	1.0	15.0
Others	4.9	18.2	23.1	5.4	16.5	21.9	8.1	0.8	8.9
Total	81.6	42.4	124.0	89.3	35.4	124.7	121.6	60.0	181.6 .
Arab/OPEC	9.1	0.3	9.4	3.7	20.0	23.7	12.7	2.0	14.7
Multilateral									
AfDB	—	1.2	1.2	2.8	–0.2	2.6	2.0	6.6	8.6
EEC	17.7	0	17.7	10.7	–0.5	10.2	47.8	–0.6	47.2
IBRD/IDA/IFC	12.1	4.9	17.0	9.6	12.1	21.7	11.1	2.7	13.8
IMF Trust Fund	—	—	—	—	—	—	17.7	0	17.7
IFAD	—	—	—	—	—	—	—	—	—
UN agencies	6.3	0	6.3	6.7	0	6.7	13.0	0	13.0
Total	36.1	6.3	42.2	30.0	11.3	41.3	91.7	8.6	100.3
TOTAL	126.8	48.9	175.7	123.0	66.8	189.9	225.9	70.7	296.6

covers, the French always provided more than half the bilateral ODA Senegal received from members of DAC. France supplied an even larger fraction of total official flows. In the earlier years of Senegal's independence France's share of the official transfers to Senegal was still larger. During 1967–71, for example, France provided 68 percent of Senegal's ODA, compared with the 12 percent supplied by Germany, the second largest donor in that period (OECD, 1973, Annex Table 26, p.216). In focusing on Senegal's links with France, we shall be noting later that aid is only one dimension of the ties and, further, that the importance of French aid has been as much a function of timing and flexibility as of scale.

Compared with France's 37 percent of the total ODA received by Senegal during 1976–82, the bilateral programs of the other members of DAC provided one quarter of the total. Thirteen, i.e.,

TABLE 1 (cont'd)

1979			1980			1981			1982		
ODA	OOF	TOTAL	ODA	OOF	TOTAL	ODA	OOF	TOTAL	ODA	OOF	TOTAL
81.3	25.4	106.7	107.7	140.4	248.1	124.7	26.8	151.5	95.6	198.8	294.4
7.7	−5.2	2.5	6.4	3.5	9.9	5.5	−2.3	3.2	7.1	−0.5	6.6
9.2	5.1	14.3	6.8	−0.4	6.4	13.7	−0.4	13.3	15.3	−0.1	15.7
11.7	+0.1	11.8	11.9	−6.7	5.2	12.6	−2.6	10.0	16.6	2.4	19.0
3.4	−1.0	2.4	4.6	−1.4	3.2	8.2	−0.3	7.9	5.9	−0.5	5.4
27.0	2.0	29.0	36.0	−2.0	34.0	38.0	−3.0	35.0	33.0	0	33.0
8.5	2.1	10.6	8.5	25.6	34.1	11.9	41.1	53.0	15.5	−6.3	9.2
148.8	28.5	177.3	181.9	159.0	340.9	214.6	59.3	273.9	189.0	193.8	382.8
5.8	0	5.8	11.5	10.3	21.8	60.1	0.5	60.6	16.5	2.2	18.7
0.2	6.0	6.2	0.4	6.2	6.6	0.9	5.8	6.7	0.6	−1.1	−0.5
108.5	−0.2	108.3	24.2	−0.2	24.0	60.4	−0.2	60.2	39.6	4.8	44.4
19.4	5.1	24.5	18.6	9.8	28.4	49.3	17.5	66.8	21.0	4.3	25.3
13.3	0	13.3	11.3	0	11.3	0.1	0	0.1	—	—	—
—	—	—	—	—	—	0.2	0	0.2	—	—	—
11.2	0	11.2	15.1	0	15.1	14.9	0	14.9	13.9	0	13.9
152.7	10.9	163.6	69.7	15.8	85.5	125.6	23.1	148.7	74.9	8.0	82.9
307.3	39.4	346.7	263.0	185.1	448.1	400.4	82.2	483.2	280.5	204.0	484.5

Source: OECD

all but two of the other DAC members, contributed, but only the five individually listed in Table 1 did so in any large measure. Of these five, Belgium has had a fairly substantial program but with an essentially flat level of expenditures in recent years. Canada, with strong domestic reasons for keeping its aid to Francophone African countries in approximate balance with its programs in the continent's Anglophone countries, has had a quite buoyant program, especially recently. The German effort, substantial, as we have seen, in some earlier years, has been undergoing a resurgence. The numbers for Japan have been rising since the late 1970s as the result both of the expansion in its overall program and encouragement from its donor partners to do more in Africa. The United States, having taken a major upward step in 1979, has become the second largest bilateral donor.

The seven lesser DAC donors who are grouped together have about matched Canada's ODA. These are countries that have had their aid concentrated on other recipients. As their comparatively high nonconcessional transfers in some years suggest (these being in part export credits), the interests some of these countries have displayed in Senegal have been more commercial than developmental.

The line labeled Arab/OPEC in Table 1 reflects transfers from three sources: (1) direct bilateral transfers, some of it concessional, some not, from the treasuries of Arab States, mostly for emergency purposes, (2) ODA mostly in project form from Arab national development assistance funds (notably the Saudi and Kuwait Development Funds) and (3) such Arab and/or OPEC multilateral funds as the OPEC Fund and the Islamic Development Bank. Arab/OPEC aid became significant in Senegal after 1976, and has provided a substantial – albeit, with the exception of the unusual year, 1981, not a striking – supplement to Senegal's resources. Such aid, which accounted for a little over 7 percent of Senegal's ODA receipts during 1976–82, usually was well short of the U.S. figure and more on the order of Canada's.

In order to group all of the Arab–OPEC inputs together (which makes political sense), the 'multilateral' category in Table 1 consists of other than Arab–OPEC multilateral. So defined, the category accounted for almost exactly one-third of ODA disbursements to Senegal during 1976–82 and for a somewhat smaller fraction of total official flows. The largest as well as most variable multilateral flow was from the European Economic Commission – both characteristics resulting in part from intermittent groundnut-related compensatory contributions under the STABEX scheme. The melange of such UN agencies as UNDP, FAO, and UNICEF produced a steady series of aggregates whose nominal values from 1978 onward remained in the $10–15 million range. But this steadiness was swamped by the World Bank Group's record as well as the EEC's, making the fluctuations in collective multilateral ODA sharper than in bilateral. Questions involving the variance in different flows from year to year, and whether the fluctuations in flows on balance aggravated or smoothed changes in Senegal's own generation of resources, are engaged later in the paper.

Meanwhile, the most striking aspect of the numbers in the multilateral entries in Table 1 may be the average smallness of those for the World Bank Group – given the weight which that institution lately has been bringing to bear on Senegalese policy.

II. THE SENEGALESE ECONOMY 1960–78:
MOMENTUM WITHOUT GROWTH

There does not begin to be space for a full review of Senegal's economic history since Independence, but certain aspects of the experience deeply conditioned the country, its government, and it politics. They set the background against which the adjustment crisis of the late 70s and early 80s took shape.

A. *The legacy of a top-heavy bureaucracy*

Students of development unfamiliar with Senegal are likely to find the country is smaller, at least less populous, than they had thought. Their image of Senegal may still hark back to the time when Dakar was the headquarters of France's West African empire. What was left at Independence was a comparatively massive administrative head, along with the rest of a large tertiary sector that had grown up symbiotically around it, which together had been shorn of most of their hinterland. The phenomenon is reflected in two of the economy's quantitative characteristics in 1960. First, in terms of average income per capita, the new country showed up as one of the most advanced in Sub-Saharan Africa.[2]

Second, the economy was extraordinarily dualistic. Earnings in the agricultural sector, in which 84 percent of Senegalese workers worked in 1960, were over-towered by those in the small industrial, and, more particularly, in the large 'services,' i.e., tertiary, sector. The latter accounted for no less than 59 percent of GDP, compared with a population-weighted average for the rest of French West Africa at the time of 35 percent. Indeed, if one takes the *World Development Report* numbers literally, output per worker in the tertiary sector in 1960 was some 19 times that in agriculture.[3]

The remarkably high level of urban service workers' apparent productivity did not mean they had comparative advantages that could be translated into foreign exchange earnings or into internal growth in other sectors. Rather, the large, highly paid, tertiary sector burdened the economy more than it buoyed it. The core of the problem was and remains the country's failure to escape the bureaucratic bloat with which it started. Predominantly tertiary economies can, of course, be very dynamic, witness Singapore. But Dakar is no major entrepot. While some members of the continuing large expatriate population are engaged in manufacturing, foreign trade, and finance, many of them serve the sector of indigenous private services and commerce, which in turn partly serves expatriates. What tend to determine the scale of both are the size and especially, the remuneration of government employment. What one has in mind here is mainly general government (not government enterprises and parastatals) whose products are not marketed. As a propulsive industry, general government has some peculiar characteristics. One knows intuitively it does not generate genuine productivity gains much faster than do universities or barber shops. But one cannot prove this statistically, because there is no independent estimate of the output; the output is measured by the input, i.e., the public wage bill, which is subjected to little or no market test.

If, as will be suggested, the government services budget until recently also has been spared severe budgetary testing and has been rather elaborately cushioned against foreign exchange restraints, one sees an urban Senegalese economy being carried along by a self-perpetuating bureaucracy that, having started big, has found little reason during most of the intervening period greatly to moderate its relative claim on resources.

As late as 1980 in Senegal output per worker in services, including, of course, the informal sector, was still reported to be nine times that in agriculture.[4] Urban tastes helped divert food demand toward imported rice away from indigenous millet. Government wages set a pattern for the private organized sector that impaired the competitiveness of the country's manufactured exports. More generally, Senegal begins to emerge as a system that, from Independence onward, was more concerned to preserve the living standards of large, relatively advantaged, mostly urban, minorities, than to invest in self-augmenting and self-reliant growth.

B. Dependence on groundnut exports

At the margin, this bureaucracy-centered system with a weak agriculture depended critically for its foreign exchange earnings on a particular export – groundnut oil and feed cake. Senegal has tried persistently to diversify its exports. As we shall see, there has been a phosphates boomlet. Manufactures, with high labor costs and little market volume, have not done well. Currently fish exports and tourism are promising – and it is perfectly clear diversification must be pursued. But so far nothing else has greatly diminished the role of groundnuts as the swing factor, and it is hard to imagine a worse pivotal export.

The groundnut oil is marketed mostly in France. Substitutes are encroaching on its share of the French and other markets; its long-term prospects are fairly bleak. It also has proved to be a remarkably unstable generator of foreign exchange (a) because of the volatility of international prices (in 1982, for example, world prices for the commodity were less than 60 percent of their 1979 level and only about one-third what they had been in 1974) and (b) because of radical weather-related variations in Senegalese production. During the past 10 years yields per hectare have fluctuated from a high of 1174 kilograms per hectare in 1975 to lows of 447 in 1978 and of 491 in 1980. In the first of the four years, 1977 through 1980, which bracketed the onset of Senegal's adjustment crisis, the volume of the country's groundnut exports already was down substantially from its 1975 and the record 1976 levels. But then in the three years 1978-80 export volumes were successively only about 1/3, then 3/5, then barely 1/4 their 1977 level.

It can be safely asserted that no economy as dependent on imports as Senegal whose foreign exchange earnings were so heavily dependent on groundnuts, could have sustained reasonable continuity in its economic affairs during the 60s and most of the 70s if it had not had a powerful and accommodating patron.

C. French cushioning

Senegal had such a patron. Among former French colonies, Senegal's ties to France have been particularly strong – partly because of the carry-over from Dakar's headquarters days, partly, no doubt, because of Leopold Senghor's great eminence and special standing in France.

The binding ties partly took the form of trade linkages. It was France, for example, which put Senegal into groundnuts: French households preferred groundnut oil, and rice from French Indo-china could readily meet French West Africa's foodgrains deficits. More generally, France has been Senegal's chief customer and chief supplier. The French–Senegalese connection involved private commercial and financial institutions; the large French expatriate population, a pervasively Francophone culture reinforced even now by a small army of French school teachers; and, from the early 60s onwards, a steady flow of worker emigrants (mostly Soninké from the Senegal River valley) to France together with the reverse flow of their remittances and, after a time, their return.

The official financial ties, however, are of particular interest here. On the monetary side, France's connection was not uniquely to Senegal but to the whole collection of ex-French colonies, which, with the assistance and blessing of the former metropole, formed the West African Monetary Union (UMOA) in 1962. The members established a central bank (BCEAO) in which they pooled their foreign exchange reserves, and they adopted a common CFA franc currency whose free convertibility into French francs at the fixed rate (50:1) France guaranteed. Clearly, if this convertibility were not going to give UMOA members unbounded access to foreign exchange, their supplies of domestic CFA had to be restricted. Hence one basic characteristic of the UMOA arrangement has been the high measure of multilateral monetary discipline to which it has subjected all of its members, including Senegal. Member governments' borrowings from their shared central bank have been limited to a modest fraction of their projected current tax collections; their access to overdraft facilities at the French Treasury has been curtailed when their collective reserves have fallen below a stipulated fraction of their liabilities; and individual bank loans of larger than moderate size have required case-by-case BCEAO approval (for further information see de Macedo in this volume).

During the 60s and 70s these disciplining arrangements, centered in the French Treasury, gave the members of UMOA the image of belonging to an orderly financial subsystem that was almost guaranteed against inflationary or other excess. This reputation may have diverted attention from another characteristic of the subsystem: within its somewhat elastic outer limits, it nested an individual member such as Senegal in a set of devices cushioning the country against internal and external shocks.

In the first place reserves within UMOA were pooled so that when an individual member came up short on its export earnings, its own reserves could be run down not only to, but below, zero without interrupting its access to foreign exchange. Moreover, this pooling of reserves extended beyond the membership of UMOA proper to the franc zone more broadly, in particular to such oil exporters-to-be as Gabon and Cameroon, whose earnings during the mid-1970s helped sustain Senegal's access to French francs. Third, there was, as it turned out, a fair amount of de facto play in BCEAO constraints on the expansion of CFA credits. Finally when, under its rules, the French Treasury was called on to take a stand against excessive CFA–French franc conversions, the French found reasons to keep their sanctions comparatively mild.

As we have seen, France also was Senegal's chief supplier of concessional assistance. During the 1960s and early 1970s the former was by no means a flamboyant donor in terms of scale but was the classic 'residual' donor: France tended to meet shortfalls that cropped up elsewhere in Senegal's funding arrangements, and in so doing was quicker than other donors to provide transfers – both ODA and OOF – in quick-disbursing nonproject forms. Below we shall note a recurrence of this pattern in the 1976–82 period.

This cushioning by France diminished the risks inherent in groundnut dependency – and, particularly, the *perception* of said risks. If monetary cushioning plus aid permitted a steadier pace of internal activity than otherwise would have been possible, one asks what kinds of activities the French program supported. It helped steady the flow of domestic investment. The latter, with net transfers from abroad filling in some of the gullies, was less erratic than domestic saving.

However, one cannot say that, in macro terms, the external support was effective in raising the growth path of investment. On the contrary, whereas real Senegalese GDP is estimated to have grown at an annual rate of 2.5 percent during the decade of the 60s, the annual growth rate of gross domestic investment was only 1.1 percent. What French support shored up more was consumption. Real consumption during the 60s grew at an average annual rate of 2.6 percent, and the domestic saving rate, which had been some 15 percent at the time of Independence, was squeezed. This, it should be remembered, was in a period before the more serious Sahelian droughts and in a country that statistically was one of Africa's better-off. While the French Government of course did not deliberately encourage a self-indulgent pattern of resource use, it condoned one.[5]

E. Domestic politics

We often talk these days about whether developing-country regimes are driven more by the growth or the equity objective. The Government of Senegal in the 60s and most of the 70s seems to have been driven by neither. Its strongest urban and bureaucratic constituencies were not keen on rapid or radical redistribution and, having started independence in relatively decent economic shape, they were also not all that preoccupied with growth. They were very interested in sustaining their own living standards and, beyond that, in making enough work for government to keep bureaucrats well employed as well as in sustaining the institutional and other arrangements that protected the advantages of favored groups in the countryside. The Government, to preserve itself and keep the peace non-repressively, did its best to accommodate these interests; and France in turn, valuing the stability, grace, and good will of the Senghor Government, accommodated it.

F. The good luck factor

One hears about the luck of the Irish. By the mid-seventies Senegalese leaders had good reason to trust in the luck of independent Senegal. Their main guardian remained France, but, in addition, by mid-decade, a fairly striking assembly of other pieces of good fortune had accrued.

1. *Phosphates:* Consider what happened to the country, for example, at the time of the first oil shock. Like those of other oil-importing developing countries, Senegal's import bill jumped sharply. But between 1972 and 1975 the adverse impact of oil prices on its trade account was more than offset by the positive effects of the parallel, equally precipitous, surge in the price of phosphates, Senegal's chief minerals export, which previously had accounted for some five percent of total export earnings. In 1974 and 1975 that fraction jumped to successive levels of 17 and 15 percent, and it would have gone higher if these had not also been years of an upswing in receipts from groundnuts.

The phosphates windfall did not contribute as much to either growth or equity as it might have (much of it was devoted to transferring existing assets from foreign to domestic ownership rather than to funding new investment) and it did not last very long (having overshot, phosphate prices went into retreat during 1976 to 1978). But the episode had a lasting effect: the burgeoning of phosphate earnings opened up Senegal's access to commercial credit in the Eurocurrency market for the first time in a big way. Rising debt and rising debt service became increasingly central features of the Senegalese scene as the decade proceeded.

2. *STABEX*: The launching of the collective development co-operation and promotion program of the European Community – specifically, the inclusion of the STABEX scheme in Lomé I in early 1975 – formalized the type of compensatory relief for which the instability of Senegal's groundnut earnings cried out. The quantity of relief offered was limited, but at least a piece of the country's instability problem had been met.

3. *Club du Sahel*: Even the great Sahelian drought had a benign effect when, as footnoted earlier, it led a number of DAC donors who had been giving drought relief in the region to form themselves

into the Club du Sahel for purposes of development promotion. The response of the donors was swift and strong. DAC aid commitments to CILSS members doubled in six years.

It is true that, in Senegal and the rest of the Sahel, the incremental Club du Sahel input was all project aid; that its effectiveness depended upon the adequacy of project design and implementation as well as on the recipients' general human and other infrastructure; that the donors thus found themselves competing with one another for scarce indigenous capabilities to whose augmentation the donors were not systematically contributing; and that, in any event, nearly all the projects were long-gestation affairs which would have required considerable time before registering much effect on the recipient's macro variables. Still, it is easy to see how the scale of the Club du Sahel response could have fostered the impression, for the Sahelian countries in general and Senegal in particular, that aid no longer was a problem. The Sahelian countries were awash in aid (never mind the distinctions among types of aid); their problems concerned how to make better use of assistance – in particular how to get pressure groups to share the benefits of aid more constructively and widely – or they concerned various non-aid matters.

4. *Arab Aid*: Such sentiments would only have been reinforced by the emergence of Arab–OPEC aid. Senegal is a predominantly Muslim country. It had diplomatic and bureaucratic skills at the ready for soliciting balance-of-payments assistance from the (bilateral and multilateral) Arab donors who, from the mid-1970s onwards, were extending the reach and scale of their aid to sub-Saharan recipients; and Senegal also had some large new project schemes well enough thought through to appeal to Arab–OPEC donors interested in project lending. Before 1979 neither the coming second explosion of oil prices nor their ensuing subsidence was anticipated. It was a reasonable assumption that the exceptional capacity and willingness of the capital-surplus oil exporters to give aid would continue for an extended period. It appeared that Senegal would remain a country with good access to this newer kind of assistance, and that the latter, therefore, was supplying a quasi-permanent add-on, an extra degree of freedom, to the country's financial planning.

5. *Food aid*: As the 1970s wore on Senegal found itself requiring more and more food imports, partly because of sluggish domestic production, partly because of the increasing preference for rice and wheat. The growing threat this posed to the country's balance of

payments was softened and veiled by the comparatively ready and abundant availability of food aid, from both the United States and the European Community.

G. *The lessons learned*

We have pieced together a picture of a government that, by the time the 1978–83 adjustment crisis struck, had developed a style and set of priorities devoted more to the maintenance of agreeable levels of consumption and influence for its favorite urban and rural constituencies than to the promotion of growth and/or equity in the economy as a whole.

Development promoters, however, should be slow to judge the GOS harshly. The government had an orderly, relatively open, non-repressive, political agenda that many donors admired. Moreover, the donors had conditioned GOS perceptions in two ways. With France chronologically and quantitatively in the lead, but with the others joining, they had taught Senegal that her donors were prepared not only to acquiesce in a slow-growth performance, but to fund most of the country's investment, substituting aid for domestic saving. The donors had not made self-help a high priority. In the second place, they had conditioned a government exceptionally exposed to erratic fluctuations in its export earnings to expect always to be cushioned against short-run adversity.

As it turned out, the Senegalese sense of security was exaggerated. Only an odd string of circumstances had kept the economy as secure as it had appeared during the 1960s and most of the 1970s. But when the string broke it was not surprising that some of the early policy responses of the GOS were not ones that would have been expected of a resourceful, self-reliant government.

III. GROWING RECOGNITION OF THE NEED FOR STRUCTURAL ADJUSTMENT

By the late-1970s in Senegal, with the economy scarcely growing, doing little saving, misallocating revenues, and running a widening foreign exchange deficit, there should have been little doubt about the need for structural shifts in the country's internal and external accounts. Although the need was disguised for a time, an adjustment imperative was embedded in the underlying situation. Moreover, short-term problems accentuated the case for policy changes. Yet within the government leaders differed greatly in their perception of the seriousness of the situation and, accordingly, in their thinking about appropriate responses.

A. Aggravating circumstances

In the first and third of the three crop years beginning in 1977/78 Senegal was hit by droughts. That raised to six the number of designated drought years during the dozen years ending in 1979/80. But this time the economy was less favored with the sorts of offsets that had cushioned the earlier droughts. International groundnut prices and, indeed, Senegal's terms of trade generally languished below their mid-decade values. Phosphate prices had crashed after 1975 and did not recover. These reversals were greatly aggravated by the world's second oil-price shock in 1979–80. But it is important to note that the crisis already had arrived dramatically in 1978, the year preceding the new surge in oil prices, when real GNP per capita fell 26 percent. This exceptional year-to-year drop started a sequence that was to lower real GNP per capita at an annual rate of 5.3 percent from 1977 to 1982.

The country's fiscal discipline had been breaking down since the early 70s when the push on public and parastatal investment began and the government fell into the habit of canceling farmers' debts with each severe drought. These moves, coupled with the inefficiencies of some of the parastatals, brought a rapid expansion in government and government-guaranteed borrowing. Advances from the central bank to the Government of Senegal rose from 1.9 billion CFA at the end of 1975 to 13.6 billion CFA four years later. The quality of internal credit deteriorated, due to the cancellation of farmers' debts and extensions of uncovered credit to the ponderous groundnuts marketing and inputs-supplying parastatal, ONCAD. The efforts of the central bank to keep some rein on credit expansion were only partly successful – by the end of the decade Senegal's money supply was more than 30 percent of GDP, i.e., twice its pre-1973 level; moreover, the political momentum attaching to public and quasi-public borrowing meant that such restraint as there was concentrated mainly on the private sector.

The combination of declining export earnings and increasing outlays on imports made for a rapid escalation in external borrowing – until the country's creditworthiness started wearing thin in 1980. The cost of servicing the external debt, less than four percent of the value of the country's exports in 1972, claimed more than 15 percent of exports in 1978 and 1979 – and was headed higher. At the same time, as we have seen, the country's foreign exchange reserves were run down markedly.

B. Competing reactions

The unfolding of this scenario of compounded crisis prompted a mixture of reactions from Senegal's leaders. There were, in effect, two competing views. That identified with the Prime Minister then President, Abdou Diouf, progressively displaced the first.

The first view was the product of Senegal's conditioning. Experience had taught that when the country's economic environment, external or internal, turned sour, someone, usually the French, would come to the rescue. In this crisis model, when bad times struck, the appropriate thing for the Government of Senegal to do was to ease the pain of its constituents, in particular its politically influential constituents, and wait for the cyclical tilt to right itself.

There were elements of such behavior in the government's policy responses from 1978 onwards. In the face of the new drought, farmers' debts were cancelled once again in 1978, evidently without great thought to the impact on the credibility of borrowers' future obligations. In 1979 after two years of economic decline in which public sector wages had been held constant as a matter of fiscal austerity, a moderate recovery occurred: instead of trying to hang on to the reduced levels to which consumption had been squeezed and channel most of the income increments into savings, the authorities, responding to their public administration constituencies, allowed government wage increases averaging 36 percent. In the same vein, they increased the subsidy levels of the major urban consumer imports, rice and sugar.

The alternative perception was that Senegal's economic troubles of the late 70s were not transitory or self-reversing. They were cumulative and structural and required a battery of changed policies. To define the package broadly in terms of its desired results, the goals of structural adjustment were, (1) to bring the country's payments deficit back to manageable size, (2) to lower consumption and raise savings in order to maintain the volume of investment while the net inflow of foreign resources was settling down to a sustainable rate, (3) to increase the efficiency of capital use, thereby squeezing more growth out of the investment flow, (4) to grapple more effectively with intersectoral inequities, especially rural–urban, (5) to reduce the system's dependence on imported food, (6) specifically, to promote agricultural expansion along lines of comparative advantage as a needed contribution to all the preceding objectives, and (7) to align the economy's patterns of internal public and private financing with the foregoing objectives.

Successful structural adjustment required a set of developing country policies aimed at such objectives. In the eyes of some of the aid donors it invited the use and conditioning of transfers to encourage such policy changes. It also involved the supply of the transfers themselves to facilitate and stretch out the needed adjustments making them less painful and less likely to provoke social and political disruption.

The first of the foregoing perceptions dominated the Government of Senegal's initial reaction to the crisis in 1978. A number of the aid donors also seemed to operate on the assumption that the country's problems were transitory and/or cyclical. Such, of course, was the specific and intended rationale of the European Community's STABEX aid, designed to compensate its ACP beneficiaries for slumps in their export crop production and earnings. A number of DAC donors used all the resources they had earmarked for Senegal for pushing ahead on the lines of project assistance to which they were already committed.

Much of Senegal's ODA during the crisis period was labeled 'exceptional' or 'emergency' assistance. If this simply reflected an effort by other bilateral donors, in the manner of France during Senegal's first 15 years of independence, to help Senegal through a difficult period, then it clearly represented the first of the rival perceptions. On the other hand, flexible, nonproject assistance (whether it called itself sectoral or program aid or outright balance-of-payments support) that was accompanied by a policy diagnosis and conditioned on some degree of policy performance by the recipient government would fall into the second category. It was aid addressed to and in support of Senegal's need for structural adjustment.

As to whether nonproject aid should be categorized as transitory or structural along the lines just suggested, most of Senegal's major bilateral donors would characterize themselves in retrospect as mixed cases. They were not unaware, particularly as the crisis proceeded, of the need for structural (policy) changes. But they were inclined to let others, especially the IMF, the World Bank, France, and, more recently, the United States, play the active roles in promoting and encouraging such changes. The major Arab donors have been quite explicit in this regard: they see needs for structural adjustments, but they say it is against their principles to intrude on the policy autonomy of the recipient government.

The EEC is a special case. STABEX, as noted, is explicitly cyclical. However, the Community extends a good deal of project assistance that might in some measure be keyed to issues of policy reform. However, the whole multi-year contractual format of EEC assistance tends to resist the intrusion of policy performance or other 'self-help' considerations into inter-country aid allocations. On the other hand, with a larger in-country presence than most donors in Senegal, the EEC is potentially influential, and the EEC's present leadership in the development field insists it is indeed highly mindful of Senegal's structural adjustment needs and is concerned to encourage effective responses to them.

France bears much of the responsibility for promoting the Senegalese perception of the cyclical nature of the country's problems. Yet the French themselves – for example, the leading aid-related officials in the Ministry of Finance – have been fully attuned to the structural adjustment assessment since the middle 70s. France, however, is another government that is not a monolith. The Finance Ministry and the project lending agency (the Caisse Centrale) that reports to it have been much more preoccupied with efficiency-seeking reform than have the Ministries of External Affairs and of Cooperation, whose portfolios encompass all other facets – cultural, political, technical assistance, commercial, exchange of persons – of the special Senegalese–French relationship. The 'political' ministries have remained more indulgent of Senegalese policy delays and lapses than the Treasury and the Caisse Centrale. The latter have dominated the financial flows and they have understood and supported the needs for structural adjustment. They have preferred to let the IMF and the World Bank do most of the talking. The French financial agencies, however, have been essential partners in the structural adjustment strategy in two ways. First, they have typically backed the Fund and Bank. At times they have pressed the multilateral institutions to take more accommodating note of Senegal's political calendar. Yet they have conditioned much of their own aid on GOS implementation of its undertakings with the multilaterals. The latter would have negotiated with the government with far less authority had they lacked comparatively consistent backing by the country's chief and residual donor. Second, France has provided much of the needed financial underpinning for structural adjustment. Various policy changes were infeasible without timely resources to cushion the necessary adjustments. France, in short, stood in the background during the past five or six years as a quiet, but not as a weak or passive, promoter of Senegalese structural adjustment, the need for which earlier French policies had helped create.

Until the onset of the overt crisis in 1978, the U.S. was a small-scale, project-bound donor with little demonstrated interest in Senegal's macroeconomic affairs. Between 1978 and 1979, however, American bilateral transfers doubled. USAID undertook a joint review with the Senegalese of the Agency's country program. The process of that review, reinforced by Washington's commitment to dialogue with aid recipients about policies, led from 1980 onwards to an active American participation in structural adjustment issues.

Two comments can help place the U.S. role in context. First, the U.S. probably has exerted greater influence at the margin than the size of its aid would justify. It commits a higher percentage of its management and technical personnel to resident missions than is the case with almost any other donor. If its personnel are of good quality, AID enjoys an advantage in pursuing a policy dialogue in an on-going, effective fashion. Second, there is a sense in which (sketched below) some of AID's positive efforts to provide additional funding in support of needed adjustments in Senegalese policies have been designed to offset some of the U.S. Treasury's negative effects on the IMF's Senegal program.

This leaves the IMF and the IBRD as the most articulate external proponents of the structural-adjustment perception of Senegal's late-1970s problems. Both have had long histories of favoring the kinds of diagnosis and policy prescriptions involved in the structural adjustment assessment, but neither had been particularly active or vocal in Senegal until the late 70s. By the time Senegal's external and internal payments crisis became overt in 1978, however, both institutions were equipped or becoming equipped with new instruments for dealing with the structural adjustment problems. The Fund had a new External Funding Facility (EFF) aimed at some longer-term, somewhat more supply-side problems than those addressed under its conventional standbys. The Bank was in the process of devising its new (nonproject) 'structural adjustment loans' (SALs) aimed at inducing needed recipient policy changes. Hence Senegal became a testing ground for both new efforts; in Senegal the two institutions, resolved on closer than usual co-operation, were engaged in very active structural adjustment promotion from the beginning of 1979 onward.

Finally, one must return to the perceptions of policy needs by the Senegalese themselves. Policy 'dialoguing' is a contradiction in terms if the process is not fully shared by leading actors in the host government. The GOS started out 1978 mainly with Perception No. 1. Very quickly, however, the dominant official perception shifted. In September 1978 a high level delegation from Senegal discussed with Bank management prospects for program lending. Late that year Bank staff visited Senegal and began discussions of major economic objectives and policies. The Bank, moreover, encouraged the Government to seek EFF accommodation from the IMF. By the end of 1979 the government announced a *Plan de Redressement,* its Economic and Financial Recovery Program, committing itself to a thorough-going structural agenda. The turn-about was so swift and so complete that, almost certainly, it had to be authored in some measure, and not just ratified, by the government's top-most leadership. President Senghor went along with the new direction, but structural adjustment does not appear to have been his initiative. Rather, the turn, quite clearly, was the work of his Prime Minister Abdou Diouf, to whom Senghor was due to hand over the presidency at the start of 1981.

We may now focus on the three-cornered transactions that ensued between the Fund and Bank, on the side of the donors – with France and, to a lesser extent, the U.S. aiding and abetting, – and Diouf and his supporters on Senegal's side. We shall try to examine the detailed, complex structural-adjustment agreement the three parties struck in 1980, consider the reasons and the responsibilities for its alleged collapse less than three years later, and assess some of the lessons and prospects that emerge from the experience.

IV. THE BANK, THE FUND, AND STRUCTURAL ADJUSTMENT, 1979–84

The Extended Fund Facility, created in the latter 1970s, represented another step in the evolution of the IMF's instruments for meeting the changing needs of its developing country members. Credit was made available to members in three-year rather than single-year commitments, and it was repayable over periods of up to eight years. Thus the new facility was meant to support medium term adjustments and it was said to be addressed to supply-side as well as demand-management issues. Yet the EFF was not radically new. It and the Fund's established one year standby (to which, as we shall see, the IMF reverted in Senegal) were both highly conditioned. Both were nonconcessional. The two involved the same personnel and the institution's same main-line macroeconomic expertise.

Structural adjustment lending, on the other hand, was almost a new departure for the World Bank. Although the Bank had, under special circumstances, engaged in nonproject lending over the years, many of its constituents were adamant that it concentrate on its chartered function of project lending. Many of the Bank's staff and officers resented their constraints in this regard. In part this was because they often saw an advantage in being able to move resources in forms that were more flexible and quick-disbursing than project loans. But their regret mainly reflected a contradiction that had built up within the Bank itself.

The Bank had long been the world's largest and, on average, best assemblage of development economics talent. As development analysts, its staff grew to appreciate the overwhelming importance of host government policies; they developed elaborate assessments of the appropriateness of various policies; and many of them came to believe that providing developing countries with constructive policy advice could be at least as helpful as giving them concessional resources. Yet as an institution largely confined to project lending, the Bank was obstructed from playing this role, because project loans were usually not satisfactory vehicles for conveying macro and sectoral economic policy advice.

When in 1979 the second oil shock provoked a rash of balance of payments crises through the oil-importing third world, Bank management saw an opportunity. The Bank's concern was not simply to divert resources into payments support. Instead management used the prevailing situation to obtain approval for an experiment in which long-term nonproject loans would be used to induce policy reforms (i.e., structural adjustments designed to achieve lasting closures of payments gaps while avoiding excessive growth and equity costs) in that minority of countries where governments, needing foreign exchange, were genuinely willing and ready to press such reforms.

Given these origins, the new-model loan had certain characteristics (see Stern 1983; Please 1984a and 1984b). Its designers were eminently practical people, and they emphasized the need for country-by-country tailoring. But nearly all their SALs shared common features. First, they reflected a strong preference for comprehensive, interlinked arrays of policy reforms. Second, nearly every SAL sought to change quite a large number of policies.

Third, the new design was quite precise and rigorous. Each SAL outlined a set of agreed policy reform objectives, then spelled out a set of measures for achieving the objectives over the space of five years, and indicated a set of specific pass-or-fail steps that could be monitored before authorization of the loan and/or within the first 18 months of implementation. Most SALs were in two tranches, the second to be triggered by the government's meeting certain further conditions. Most structural adjustment countries were expected, if and as they performed up to expectations, to get a short series of such loans. All this precision suited the no-nonsense image the designers wished the new instrument to have, but procedural toughness also helped the innovation win acceptance by the Bank's pro-project Board.

Fourth, the SAL paid for comprehensiveness and precision by being comparatively lumpy and unyielding. A whole set of macro and sectoral conditions were interdependent. These levered each of the SAL's policy targets with the weight of the whole loan, but by the same token, nonperformance of any one undertaking could block the whole package. One either passed or failed the exercise; there was little allowance for graded performance.

Finally, given the scarcity of resources, the Bank had to find ways to encourage big policy changes with small inputs of nonproject money. This, in principle at least, could be done constructively by encouraging other donors to join the Bank in making some of their own aid contingent upon the meeting of SAL conditions. But the accommodation of resource scarcity was less wholesome if it tilted the Bank – and/or the Bank and the Fund together – toward unrealistically modest forecasts of the country's up-coming financial needs.

B. Senegal's Commitments

There is often an image of the Fund and the Bank brow-beating beleaguered developing countries into reform and other commitments that the host governments in their native political wisdom and compassion are deeply reluctant to accept. This was not the story line in Senegal. On the contrary, with the nation's leaders having changed their perceptions of the economy's problems and needs, it was the Government of Senegal that took the formal initiatives and in many respects genuinely led the way in 1979 and 1980.

In October 1979 the GOS requested an EFF and SAL from the Fund and Bank respectively. In December, as we have seen, it broadcast its comprehensive and ambitious *Plan de Redressement.*

The Government completed its EFF negotiations with the Fund in August 1980, and at the end of October, with the SAL negotiations well advanced, it presented the World Bank with a Declaration of Economic Policy spelling out five realms of needed economic reform (fiscal-monetary, the investment program, prices and incentives, parastatals, agricultural reform) that established most of the substance as well as the format of the SAL agreement on which the Bank was to sign off two months later.

Further, there was the case of ONCAD. Of all of Senegal's parastatals, by the end of the 1970s the inefficient and corrupt monopoly that supplied inputs and cooperative credit to groundnut growers and marketed their output was the *bête noire* of the Bank, the Fund and AID. In mid-1980 the Bank pressed the GOS to experiment with alternative modes of rural organization that were more decentralized and market-oriented than ONCAD. Suddenly in August, after some further disclosures of ONCAD corruption, the Government wound up the parastatal on the spot, transferring its groundnut marketing function to the oil-crushing firms and only part of its personnel and its remaining functions to an allegedly temporary, less monopolistic, successor parastatal, SONAR.

In the macroeconomic area, the Senegalese agreed with the Fund, and the Bank, to curb domestic credit expansion as well as commercial foreign borrowing and to move from a budget deficit to a surplus. They were to hold debt servicing to 15 percent of export earnings, find public savings to cover at least 15 percent of public investment and raise that ratio shortly to 25 percent. They were to start retiring government and parastatal arrears to commercial banks and others in the private sector. The goal was to cut the country's current account deficit in half in the next four years, to raise the investment/GDP ratio from 16 to 18 percent, to hold overall credit expansion to less than the inflation rate and the latter to less than 10 percent, and to achieve a growth rate of 4 percent in national output and real income, or of 1.2 percent per capita.

In the case of *the investment program* the GOS agreed to raise the share of directly productive investment in its total investment program from 45 to 55 percent, and it undertook, with the help of Bank technical assistance, to effect improvements in its project selection. With respect to *pricing and producer incentives*, the Senegalese agreed to complete a de facto devaluation of 15 percent (extra duties on imports, subsidies on nontraditional exports), to pay farmers rewarding prices, reduce the subsidization of their inputs, especially fertilizer, eliminate the remaining subsidies on consumer imports and raise the price of imported rice. In the case of *parastatals* the government indicated its intent to create no new ones, to divest or disestablish some it had, and, in particular, to encourage more efficient operations in those that continued via a scheme of performance contracts. Under the latter the CFAF counterpart of the SAL's program lending would be used to fund contracts between the government and particular parastatals. The parastatal would agree to specified performance targets and then be left comparatively free of bureaucratic interventions as it implemented the targets. Issues of *agricultural reform*, on which the SAL to Senegal eventually foundered, are examined in a separate subsection below.

Senegal's structural adjustment undertakings were sweeping. In the paper mentioned earlier, Ernest Stern enumerated 17 policy foci featured in the Bank's whole array of early SALs. The Senegal SAL included 11 of the 17. (It left out only formal exchange rate policy, where the UMOA blocks single-country devaluations; energy pricing, conservation, and indigenous development; institutional improvements and subsectoral programs in industry; and interest rate policy.) Given the inclinations of the innovators on both sides, the range of subjects was not more than might have been expected. The more interesting, and worrisome, matter was that of modalities.

The procedural tone or style of the undertakings was ambiguous. There was a good deal of breadth and flexibility in the text of the Bank's original loan paper for the Senegal SAL: appreciation of the degree and boldness of the policy changes that GOS was undertaking, of the possible need to accommodate adverse changes in the environment, and at various points a clear recognition of the need for experimentation, for learning by doing, on both sides.

The startling aspect, therefore, was the rigidity of the contractual commitment and operational calendar into which the reasonable preamble was translated. There is nothing new about such rigidity with respect to the Fund and, as we shall see, it reappeared in the Senegal case. But the Bank was still in its first year of drafting SALs, and therefore it was noteworthy that this one enumerated no less than 32 measures the GOS was obliged to undertake under the terms of the loan. Most of these were to be specifically monitored by the Bank, with the timely performance of each becoming a condition for the second tranche.

There was an annex to the loan laying out a chronology of key dates for monitoring the performance of the structural adjustment program. The procedural texture of the whole transaction may be suggested by the fact that this calendar specified no less than 13 actions ('general progress under the Program, reorganization of agricultural agencies, financial reorganization of the CPSP, methodology and calendar for auditing cooperatives' accounts, new fertilizer formulas and prices for the 1982/83 crop, reorganization of agricultural research') the government was supposed to enter and/or complete and the Bank was to monitor and/or discuss *within the first three months of the life of the loan.*

C. Implementation and non-implementation

It would over-dramatize the truth to claim that the Bank's and Fund's assessment of the Senegalese structural adjustment changed from euphoria to certified failure in less than three years. Indeed the Fund found reason to put Senegal's EFF on hold as early as three months from its signing, cancelled it within ten months, and had shifted to a simpler one-year standby by September of 1981. Moreover, as to the Bank, whatever the empathy between donor and recipient technocrats, it is hard to believe that, even at the beginning, the Bank could have perceived good feelings from the Senegalese side about the kind of procedure the SAL mandated. To over-program the timing, number, and precision of policy conditions, especially for a government with such short experience with self-reliance, was probably to build an expectation of under achievement into the transaction from the beginning.

Nevertheless the fact remains that a country that had been mooted as a structural adjustment showcase as recently as late 1980 saw both the second tranche of its SAL and its IMF standby canceled in the second quarter of 1983. At that point both multilaterals assigned Senegal flat failing grades. One must ask how this came about.

For one thing, it was the product of bad luck. Following a poor weather year in 1979/80, 1980/81's weather, groundnut exports, and internal food output were a combined disaster. Likewise, thanks mainly to a set of U.S. domestic policy choices, international interest rates remained at much higher levels than nearly anyone expected in 1979 or even in 1980 (see John P. Lewis, 1983).

Second, the structural adjustment exercise was haunted by bad information. Data coming to hand, in part as the result of Bank and Fund promoted studies, showed that government-guaranteed foreign debt was much higher than the multilaterals or part of the GOS itself had known; that the government's deficit would be higher than expected; and that the arrears the government had to cope with far exceeded mid-1980 estimates, due particularly to the debts left behind with the liquidation of ONCAD. It was in light of these revisions that the IMF tried to tighten the EFF's fiscal and monetary targets before the end of 1980. When, in view of the drought-induced recession, the GOS refused to accept as much further austerity as the Fund wanted, the latter canceled the EFF and, after an interval, shifted to a series of standbys.

The structural adjustment exercise was plagued by excessively optimistic forecasts. The GOS, for example, raised producers' prices of groundnuts 43 percent in 1981. This may have been fine for producers' incentives, but implicitly the action rested on an expectation of rising world groundnut prices that seemed to run counter to the long-term trend of those prices versus other vegetable oil substitutes. Certainly it ran counter to cyclical prospects: the bottom dropped out of international groundnut prices in 1982. As a result, having to cover the difference between its buying and selling prices for groundnuts became, from 1981 on, one of the worst hemorrhages in the government's budget.

Similarly, the Fund made wishful forecasts. In late 1982 it gave tentative blessing to the government's financial projections for the balance of the fiscal year only on the assumption that the GOS would be able to raise an extra $50 million of program money from its Arab donors – a most unlikely development in view of what had been happening to petroleum prices. The following August, when negotiating a standby to replace the one canceled in May, the Fund double-counted some prospective external resources in a way that set AID, and then the French, to scurrying about for extra pro-gram money to repair the Fund's forecast and make good the projected balance upon which its new standby would be premised. My impression is that these were less errors or miscalculations on the part of Fund technicians than efforts to hold down the financial claims of its programs in order to improve the latter's chances of surviving scrutiny by the Fund Board – on which one of the more dyspeptic voices usually was that of the U.S. Treasury.

The Fund did in fact contribute $170 million of adjustment finance to Senegal during the three and a half years beginning in late 1979. It was, however, mainly concessional and non-concessional assistance from some of the bilateral donors that kept the economy viable. It was not program money from the Bank itself that made the difference. The first SAL tranche, the only one Senegal received, was a modest $40 million. The SAL innovators expected the loan's policy baggage to be more important than the loan itself. In terms of resources, they expected much of its weight to lie in the leverage it would exert on other donors. Still, it can be argued that the scantiness of structural adjustment lending was, itself, another factor complicating loan implementation.

What of implementation? What was the performance under each of the reform program's main substantive headings? By mid-1983 fiscal and monetary policies were heading in the right direction, although not at the pace the Fund would have preferred. After their rise in 1979, modern sector wage increases were held below inflation. Import duties had been adjusted as desired. The government had come around cautiously, experimentally, on non-traditional export subsidies, but by April 1983 had adopted the agreed stance. Likewise, given the squeezes on welfare that had intervened, government had been reluctant before the presidential election of February 1983 to move as fast at reducing consumer subsidies on imported rice and on fertilizers as the multilaterals wanted. By the summer of 1983 it was taking substantive steps in these directions. The fraction of directly productive investment had increased, and significant gains were being made in the quality of project selection. Although the extension of performance contracts to key parastatals was proving more time-consuming than expected, there was considerable enthusiasm within the Bank for the quality and effectiveness of parastatal reform. Some were to be abolished altogether (SONAR, SODEVA, STN, etc). In general, the implementation of structural adjustment clearly would have been judged of passing caliber had it not been for the confrontation that developed in the realm of agricultural reform.

D. Stalemate over agricultural reform

The Bank had grown particularly weary of ONCAD. After a time it concluded that ONCAD, representing a top-heavy, corruption-prone alliance of the bureaucracy and the country's rural elites, was beyond redemption. The Bank found the government very sensitive on the subject. When and as it could in the Senegal program the Bank pressed its characteristic theme of getting the prices right. It expressed its well-known interest in agricultural research, and it assisted some of the regional rural development agencies, of which SODEVA in the groundnut basin was the largest.

Yet, while these were not peripheral matters, during most of the 70s the Bank felt cut off from what it regarded as the core of the agricultural problem. That core, it and other observers had come to believe, was organizational. Senegalese agriculture was dominated by a centralized bureaucracy (much of it gathered in and around ONCAD) that superseded the market and sequestered resources. Peasants both leaned on and distrusted the bureaucracy; they took few initiatives for themselves. The needs, it was thought, were to devolve more responsibility onto the farmers individually and/or in their own (localized) organizations; to let them link up more directly and commercially with input and credit suppliers and product processors; and to remove or short-circuit much of the bureaucratic buffering in between.

Most of the Bank's people who had been working on Senegalese agriculture supported the decentralization, anti-bureaucracy theme. The more perceptive were quite clear they did not know which specific institutional and policy models should be chosen to implement the decentralization approach. The mainly Washington-based Bank professionals simply did not have a sufficiently complete grasp of the cultural, ethnic, status, migratory and other sociological dimensions of Senegal's rural fabric, or of the politics and micro-economics, to be sure.[6] For example, nearly everyone (other than those running them) was for the replacement of ONCAD's centralized cooperatives by village-level cooperative societies or sections. There was great uncertainty, however, whether credit repayment obligations might better be lodged with these local cooperatives as collective legal entities, or with individual farmers or households.

Hence, to its great credit, the Bank, in the course of negotiating the SAL in mid-1980, while pressing for reform, opted for *experimentation* with various non-ONCAD organizational alternatives, to be financed by funds remaining after the restructuring of an existing extension project in the groundnut basin (the Sine-Saloum Agricultural Project). When auditors established evidence of a major theft in ONCAD, the GOS preempted the issue; it knocked out ONCAD entirely, and imposed across-the-board answers to questions the Bank's more careful experimenting would have illuminated. Moreover, one of these 'answers' included a new parastatal that, although it was billed as temporary and had fewer people and functions than ONCAD, looked suspiciously like it. SONAR provided a ready-made rallying point for the regime's still-active anti-reform interests. Meanwhile the Bank's agricultural promoters found themselves cut off from two fields of potentially constructive policy influence by other precipitate GOS actions: the latest cancellation of farmers' short-term debts, and the promulgation of high producers' prices for groundnuts.

What, then, was left for the Bank to work on under the agriculture reform rubric of the SAL regime? Two subjects, fertilizer distribution and groundnut seed storage and supply, seemed to be available. They were not trivial topics, but as symbols they became larger than life-size. In each of the two areas Bank operatives pressed a particular policy formulation on the Senegalese. The latter were slow to agree, but finally the GOS did assent. It announced its acceptance of the particular seed and fertilizer distribution solutions advocated by the Bank, and the Bank, in turn, made it plain that release of the SAL's second tranche was contingent on the adoption of these two measures.

The fertilizer reform, involving the transfer of fertilizer distribution to the company that did Senegal's in-country fertilizer manufacturing and mixing, nearly worked. But it was damaged when the government failed to supply the firm on time with the funds it needed for implementing the remaining fertilizer subsidy.

It was the seed question, however, that was the more upsetting. In groundnuts, the problem for seed policy is comparatively modest: it is to prevent cultivators from selling or consuming that fraction of the current crop needed to provide adequate seed for next season. The Bank felt the established answer, which had been for ONCAD to hold seed out of current marketings and later give it back to growers in accordance with an arbitrary formula, was too paternalistic. Farmers should be weaned away from such dependency; they should be induced to hold their own seed, or to hold it collectively at the village level; and as a once-and-for-all incentive for so doing, those in the current season who would deposit next year's seed in a cooperative marketing center would be paid by SONAR a bounty per kg that exceeded the high, government-supported producer's price – and then get their seed back to boot when the time came.

This rather remarkable offer was announced during the winter of 1982-83 as government policy. It was well received by many growers. But then in late March 1983, one month after President Diouf's successful presidential election, the GOS suddenly rescinded the whole scheme without any forewarning to the Bank (whose people had been doubting, however, that officials in the countryside were ready with the necessary funds and other preparations).

One can imagine the reaction in 1818 H Street at this cavalier abandonment of what, by default, had become for the Bank the bottom-line issue in Senegal's bottom-line sector. Tranche No. 2 of the SAL was cancelled with vigor – although with enough delay and restraint, says the Bank, not to jeopardize Senegal's chances with certain other program loan decisions then pending with other donors.

E. Net Assessment

Both the GOS and the World Bank had good reason to behave as they did, but in many respect their actions were ill-conceived. The GOS, for instance, was wrong, if it (a) was serious on balance about structural adjustment and (b) recognized the Bank-Fund as its most active external adjustment mentors (both seem to have been the case) not to have consulted with them, especially with the Bank, more carefully about its cancellations of farmers' debts, about the level at which it might safely peg the producers' groundnut price, and particularly about winding up ONCAD. The effect of these non-consultations was greatly to narrow the agricultural reform terrain within which the Bank could conduct an effective policy dialogue.

The Bank, on the other hand, was wrong to have put all its SAL agricultural reform eggs into a fertilizer and seed distribution basket. It was especially wrong to let the procedural imperatives press it into plumping for particular fine-grained policy models, such as a specific format for local cooperatives, or the rather odd seed policy solution it anointed, before its knowledge was full and reliable enough to warrant imposing such policy specifics on the client. This is a troubling aspect of the record, because it bespeaks a kind of Washington-centered analytical arrogance that over the years often has tainted this mainly admirable institution.

The case also suggests some broader conclusions. The SAL philosophy, emphasizing the pivotal importance of host government policy and trying to bring aid influence constructively to bear on it is powerful and correct. But the approach needs to be implemented with some statesmanship and flexibility. It does not need to be as procedurally brittle as it was during the Senegal episode. A livelier continuing appreciation of the boldness of the policy turn President Diouf was making would have been appropriate. At the same time, a somewhat more realistic expectation of backsliding and/or crab-wise progress could usefully have been built into donor implementation.

There is another conclusion that may be fatal to some versions of the theory of the SAL but certainly is not at odds with its spirit. The pattern of tying a variety of policy issues from different sectors together and then allowing the implementation of the whole structural adjustment loan to be blocked by unsatisfactory performance in any one of its sectoral components turns out to be extremely awkward and probably dysfunctional. The pieces should be detachable. One is not arguing that the Bank should have compromised with bad agricultural reform performance on the part of the Senegalese. But there was no reason why, with good performance under four of the SAL's five substantive rubrics, the whole loan should have been aborted because of malperformance in a fraction of the agricultural sector.

It is true the *total* second tranche of the Senegal SAL that was canceled was only $16 million. To have pro-rated a fraction of that as the portion deserving cancellation on failed agricultural reform grounds would not have made much of a statement. But this difficulty could be handled by committing adequate resources to program-loan-type lending in behalf of policy reform.

The principle I am invoking is reminiscent of the famous Tinbergen postulate about matching policy instruments and policy targets. Tinbergen talked about matching numbers, namely, one and only one instrument with one and only one target. Here we are concerned with matching sizes: Policy dialoguing can be most effective when the scope of the instrument (i.e, the radius of use, whether project-size or sectoral, or economy-wide, to which the proceeds of a grant or loan are dedicated) matches the span of the policy reforms on which the transfer is conditioned. If this is a useful generalization, it is one way of saying why using a project loan (a micro instrument) to exert sectoral or macro policy influence is usually ineffective. The reverse is our present point: using a macro instrument in behalf of a sectoral policy target is clumsy and, in some inherent sense, unfair.[7]

In its post-SAL period in Senegal the Bank has been moving toward the position just argued. Whether or not it is having second thoughts generally about the sectoral interdependencies built into its SALs, in Senegal the Bank has been interesting itself and trying to interest other donors in flexible, program-type funding, but on a sectoral or sub-sectoral basis, not on a total-economy basis where every pertinent policy reform intertwines with every other.

Despite Senegal's nominal 'failure' the Fund, like the Bank, remains very actively engaged in encouraging and financially assisting Senegalese adjustment. I would see less reason than in the case of the Bank for the Fund to modify the operational mode it followed in Senegal during the 1978–83 period – except to take greater care not to make excessively optimistic, i.e., modest, forecasts of the country's financial needs in order to appease hard-liners on its Board. It is clear the adjustment process will continue to need a multilateral agency that is prepared to play a 'tough cop' role. The Fund should continue to discharge this function, focussing mainly and simply on the issues of demand discipline that have been its traditional preoccupation.

Is there not a further lesson to be drawn about the appropriate relationship between the Bank and Fund? This is an issue on which I do not find the facts of the case compelling. Quite clearly, there is advantage in the closer consultation in which the two institutions have engaged during their joint structural adjustment ventures, and it is useful, not only to the Bank but to other major donors, to have the Fund outline standards of minimum macroeconomic performance that other donors can adopt, with or without modification, as a condition for their own financial releases. But if practiced as in the Senegal case, this pattern may give the Fund an excessively sweeping, unqualified veto over too much of the economy's external program funding. The Bank, working with a different time horizon and in different and broader policy dimensions than the Fund, will need at times to reflect a different set of priorities than the Fund in its program funding decisions. Or alternatively, there is the hope that Stanley Please, one of the original theorists of the SALs, has expressed: namely, that if Bank-Fund consensus remains the rule in the structural adjustment realm, there will be more instances of the Fund's deferring to the Bank, particularly under circumstances where the latter is defending the interests of the low-end poor more actively than has been its wont in the early (including Senegalese) SAL experiences (Stanley Please, 1984a).

A final pair of conclusions would be the following: (1) of the two Washington institutions, the Bank plays the more central, multifaceted role vis-à-vis Senegal's continuing effort to adjust to a viable path of growth and equity promotion, and (2) in this role, the Bank will need to coordinate, not just with the IMF, but with Senegal's whole array of donors.

V. THE FLOW OF EXTERNAL RESOURCES – AND DONOR COORDINATION

One cannot conclude a review of the role of foreign aid in Senegal's adjustment crisis without considering the impact of the transfers themselves – their volume, modes, and timing – on the course of the economy during the turbulent period beginning in 1978. Have aid and other transfers been part of the problem or part of the solution? Which transfers from which donors have tended to aggravate the ups and downs in Senegal's own generation of resources? What has been the experience with donor coordination in the recent Senegal record? What are the opportunities for improvement?

A. *Aid impacts*

The issue of whether a set of aid flows has supported and, in particular, smoothed the recipient's macroeconomic performance is more complex than it sounds. It invites some counterfactual hypothesizing (what would have happened in the absence of the transfers?) and entails attribution problems (how much responsibility for macroeconomic outcomes should one nondominant variable be assigned?) as well as likelihoods of feedback and covariance. Hence the following is a quite rudimentary treatment.

In order to give a clearer view than that in Table 1 of the real proportions of the flows from different donors over time, all the values in Tables 2 and 3 have been converted into constant U.S. dollars. It is clear that transfers have made a large quantitative contribution to the economy. Senegal already had a high degree of dependence on aid in the 1960s and early 1970s. Still (Table 2), official transfers came to account for about one-fifth of GDP in 1981 and 1982. In the short term there can be no doubt that in the aggregate such a net resource flow is helpful to an economy struggling to balance its external accounts. In a longer perspective, however, if such an aid flow, instead of accelerating investment, becomes a crutch for habituating an economy to unsustainable levels of consumption, it can retard development. It can be argued that this pattern, already familiar in Senegal, was highly visible in the years 1977 through 1981, when saving averaged little more than one percent of GNP. Such a judgment may be too harsh, however; it may not give sufficient weight to the fact that during these particular years Senegal's real GNP was declining at an annual rate of five

TABLE 2

Senegal: Macroeconomic variables, 1976 through 1982

(Values in millions of 1972 US dollars; percentages are percentages of GDP)

	1976		1977		1978		1979		1980		1981		1982	
	$	%	$	%	$	%	$	%	$	%	$	%	$	%
Gross national product	1503		1596		1221		1447		1438		1300		1421	
Gross domestic product							1518		1485		1194		1213	
Consumption	[1368]	91	[1596]	100	[1176]	89	1488	98	1515	102	1254	105	1140	94
Saving	[135]	9	[0]	0	[134]	11	30	2	−30	−2	−60	−5	73	6
Investment	[255]	15	[225]	16	[281]	23	319	21	223	15	203	17	243	20
Net imports	[90]	6	[255]	16	[147]	12	289	17	252	17	263	22	170	14
Official transfers	133	[9]	136	[9]	197	[17]	212	14	251	17	248	21	234	19

Note: In the absence of dollar estimates for GDP for 1976 through 1978, the values in square brackets are rough estimates in which the percent-of-GDP estimates have been applied to a GNP base, just as the bracketed percentage figures in the bottom line are percentages of GNP rather than GDP.

Source: World Bank and US Department of Commerce (for US GNP deflator)

percent. Real GNP per capita averaged an eight percent per annum drop.

A second observation is that there was a strong positive trend in real transfers during the period. There was a mild contracyclical pattern; that is, in two of the years (1978 and 1980) when GNP and/or GDP fell sharply, transfers made atypically large year-to-year gains. The dominant change, however, was simply the pronounced secular increase of transfers.

Third, the relative stability of official transfers was striking compared with the extreme year-to-year volatility of other modes of external financing. The latter, labeled 'net imports less official transfers' in Table 3, included private commercial credit and changes in reserves. Throughout the 1978–1982 period this aggregate moved in an intensive, self-reversing, two-year cycle. The combination of these flows with the official transfers gave net imports as a whole a very uneven path.

Fourth, harking back to Table 1, it may be noted that ODA flows in the aggregate during these years had less relative year-to-year variance than OOF. The average changes in the latter (disregarding the signs) were nearly four-fifths the average level of OOF during 1976-82, whereas the ODA changes, similarly measured, were only one-third the average ODA level.

A fifth point, not reflected in our tables, concerns effects that the modes or forms of official transfers had on crisis funding. Project aid can exacerbate a recipient's financial crisis – and did in the Senegal case. Aid projects sometimes commit the recipient to funding imports that are complementary to the formation and/or operation of the project facility; and in any event, most projects call for complementary local-currency outlays. These commitments may be painful to implement when the government is struggling to regain internal and external financial balance. In the Senegal case they motivated project donors to consider more external funding of project recurrent costs (thereby relieving some of the budgetary pressure on the GOS); similarly, some of the donors, urged on by the World Bank, shifted from funding new projects to accelerating the completion of projects already underway. In the same vein (noted in Section IA) as the pressures of the crisis built up, several donors including Saudi Arabia, the United States, Canada and the Federal Germany as well as the Bank and France, deliberately increased the share of nonproject aid in the Senegal portfolio.

The most striking point that can be gleaned from Table 3 is the extent to which France has been the balance wheel in the recent flow

TABLE 3

Senegal: Official and other transfers from France and other donors, 1976 through 1982

(values in millions of 1972 US dollars: absolutes and changes from preceding year)

line		1976		1977		1978	
		value	change	value	change	value	change
A.	Official transfers	132.8		135.5	+2.7	197.2	+61.7
B.	France	59.3		49.5	−9.8	83.4	+33.9
C.	Other of which:	73.5		86.0	+12.5	113.8	+27.3
D.	EEC	13.4		7.3	−6.1	31.4	+24.1
E.	Arabs	9.4		23.7	+14.3	14.7	−9.0
F.	Net imports less off. transfers	[−42.8]		[119.5]	[+162.3]	[−50.2]	[−169.7]
G.	Net imports (lines A+F)	[90]		[255]	[+165]	[147]	[−108]

Note: In the absence of dollar estimates for GNP for 1976 through 1978 square-bracketed figures are rough estimates based upon applying estimates of net imports as percentages of GNP rather than GDP data.

of official transfers to Senegal. During 1976–82 the total (plus and minus) year-to-year changes in French transfers and those from all other donors collectively were contrapuntal, making the variance in total transfers much less than that in either of these two components. Moreover, although the numbers cannot show it, it is clear the initiative in contriving this smoothing effect lay with the French. When transfers from other donors spurted because of a Club du Sahel push, or the EEC's STABEX, or Arab increases or whatever, the French eased off somewhat (except in 1978 when the need for an overall increase was urgent). Similarly, they filled the troughs on the other side of the other-donor peaks.

Table 3 indicates the considerable volatility in both EEC (principally STABEX) aid and Arab aid remarked earlier in the paper. But it does not illustrate one final point, for which one needs to revert to Table 1: In playing their flows-smoothing role, the French have not been able to throttle up and down on their ODA as nimbly as on their other official flows. Thus the latter, which in part occur semi-

318

TABLE 3 (cont'd)

1979		1980		1981		1982		Addendum: Sum of year-to-year changes, 1976–82,
value	change	value	change	value	change	value	change	disregarding signs
212.2	+15.0	251.2	+39.0	247.7	−3.5	234.2	13.5	135.4
65.3	−18.1	139.1	+73.8	77.7	−61.4	142.3	+64.6	261.6
146.9	+33.1	112.1	−34.8	170.0	+57.9	91.9	−78.1	243.7
66.3	+34.9	13.5	−52.8	30.9	+17.4	21.5	−9.4	154.3
5.8	−8.9	21.8	+16.0	60.6	+38.8	18.7	−41.9	128.9
76.8	[+127.0]	0.8	−76.0	15.3	+14.5	−64.2	−79.5	629.4
289	[+142]	252	−37	263	+9	170	−93	554

Source: World Bank and US Department of Commerce (for US GNP deflator)

automatically through the UMOA mechanism, have done a disproportionate amount of the cushioning of declines elsewhere in the composite flow. This was particularly notable in 1980 and 1982.

B. Donor coordination

During the past several years the need for improved coordination among aid donors has become a favorite issue for those writing and conferring about foreign aid, see John P. Lewis (OECD, 1981, Chap. 3) and Rutherford M. Poats (OECD, 1982, pp. 32-35). The gains in an aid recipient's development that can be had from feasible improvements in donor coordination can be formidable. Nonetheless, there has been a lack of passion for the cause among the actors: recipients are reluctant to be 'bossed' by a donor collective, and/or they try to play one donor off against another; and aid bureaucrats and their political masters often prefer pursuing their own priorities to joining in a multi-donor amalgam. Yet the resource squeeze in which recipients and donors jointly have found themselves during the past few years has put such a premium on improvements in the effectiveness of aid that sensible participants have been forced to give fresh thought to the potentialities for better coordination.

Those opportunities have been considerable in Senegal. The country has by no means been totally barren of coordination effort lately. Since mid-1981 the GOS has been talking about holding a variety of donors' meetings – and has held some. The World Bank put a good deal of effort into organizing a donors' conference in late 1981. As indicated, there has been generally good coordination laterally between the French government and the two Washington multilaterals; the former usually has supported the latter's structural adjustment counseling. Among the other bilaterals, USAID has been the most active in conferring with the Bank and Fund as well as the GOS about Senegal's general and sectoral development strategies; but others also have responded to the urgings of Bank, Fund, and GOS to divert resources from new projects into quicker flowing forms of aid.

Yet far more effective and extensive coordination would have been possible. For one thing, from what we have seen in Table 3, it is clear that with better consultation mechanisms the donors could achieve a composite aid flow better fitted to Senegal's macro-economic needs – and less heavily dependent on compensatory modulations by the residual donor. After considerable anticipatory discussion, a consultative group for Senegal has now been inaugurated (see below). Properly managed, such a piece of standing machinery can go far toward injecting more coherence of the needed kind into the collective flow.

The advantages of more effective multi-donor interactions, however, could be at least as great in the realms first, of policy dialoguing and conditioning and, second, of policy (including sectoral policy) analysis and human resources development. The assessment at the end of Section IV was that the Fund probably should be left to do its own thing in the area of demand management. Other donors, including the Bank, may at times influence the timing and temper of Fund decisions, and they may, as now, adopt acceptance of a Fund program as a condition for the release of their own transfers. But the amount of on-going interpenetration that one expects to see between the Fund and other donors is fairly limited.

The Bank, on the other hand, will and should be in the middle of the coordination network. Fortunately there already is close co-operation between the two most important aid donors, France and the Bank. However, one would like to see the French, like the other major bilaterals and the EEC, become somewhat more active, less reticent members of the partnership. It will be to the advantage of the Bank to get other donors co-dialoguing with it on the same side of key policy issues. It could be even more helpful to the government to have other donors engaging in the dialoguing and contributing to consensus positions. The latter could well be politically more sensitive and realistic, as well as simpler than those the Bank would press alone. Consensus positions would be stripped of much of the procedural clutter that got into the Senegal SAL. They might be more disposed to identify agreed directions of change, leaving the choice of detailed policy models to the host government.

The other activity that the major actors in behalf of Senegalese development need to share more fully is analysis. Logically, of course, this should precede the formulation of consensus positions. At present donors' analyses of key development issues, sectoral and otherwise, often are painfully parochial. Different donors are pressing different diagnoses and prescriptions for the same problem. To the extent possible, existing studies and, as needed, further studies should be sorted into reliable syntheses. Senegalese technicians and officials need to be in the middle of this process.

As the agricultural reform case illustrates, the Senegalese themselves, like the Bank, and like other donors, lack the answers to key problems. While the array of major donors (not just the Bank) is participating actively in joint investigations, the same donors should be coordinating their contributions of technical assistance to the development of Senegalese cadres of expertise. Technical assistance in its design and delivery is the most parochial of forms. There is great scope for raising its effectiveness by better recipient-led planning and a more rational and collaborative division of labor among the donors.

No invisible hand will serve up all these coordination benefits. Getting them will depend, for one thing, on a more engaged, interactive kind of participation on the part of several donors – one thinks not just of the French and Americans but also, in particular, of the EEC and the Canadians, the Germans, and one or both of the chief Arab donors. At the same time, better coordination will call for a further commitment of emotional energy in this direction on the part of the Bank. One senses that, although the Bank has been formally committed to a heavy investment of effort in interdonor coordination for several years, Bank staff have not always been keen to submit their analyses and positions to more consultations and compromising. One logistical obstacle for the Bank is the thinness of its resident representation in Dakar. Unless that can be augmented, the Bank will need to rely in part on having its coordinative impulses seconded and implemented by those who are better represented, namely, the French, the EEC, and the Americans.

The GOS long has testified to the value of donor coordination, but, compared with organizing pledging conferences, it has exhibited less abiding interest in exchanging policy views simultaneously with a multiplicity of donors. It has not sought particularly to encourage and/or lead multi-donor syntheses of sectoral and subsectoral issues. As was seen repeatedly in the agricultural reform case, the GOS seemed to guard against donor intrusions on its analytics by jumping to policy conclusions, sometimes prematurely.

Confronted with such comment, however, some of the best informed observers among the donors insist that whatever hesitancies the government has exhibited as to donor coordination, just as in the case of structural adjustment itself, have mainly reflected human resources constraints and/or needed political prudence.

VI. EPILOGUE

The data, documents, interviews, and correspondence on which this study is based were those available before the end of 1984. However, during the interval since then developments have occurred that reinforce certain general reflections emerging from the preceding pages.

The first of these is that there are no villains but also no unblemished heroes in the episode we have examined. There is much room for an upgrading of the collective effort. A second reflection is that there is quite a lot about which to be hopeful. On the side of the donors the first meeting of the Consultative Group for Senegal held in Paris in December 1984 projected official transfers of $500 million a year for the next seven years; there were also prospects of a new IMF standby and a further rescheduling of commercial debt. The size of the donor undertaking was not overwhelming, given a probable diminution in Arab aid and an end (in view of paybacks) to net transfers from the Fund. But the continuity of the collective commitment is heartening in view of the particular stubbornness of the Senegalese payments crisis. Moreover, the attitudes of key donors are encouraging – the greater realism of the Bank and the evident willingness of France to continue to provide needed compensatory finance, but only to assist adjustment toward greater self-reliance.

Part of the reason, certainly, for donor solidarity with Senegal is the continuing accrual of evidence of the Senegalese government's, more particularly of President Diouf's, determination to press ahead with politically difficult structural reforms. The government has raised gasoline and rice prices. It has reduced and now proposes to eliminate fertilizer subsidies. It continues to project fiscal and financial austerity. It has wound up SONAR – just, and almost as soon, as it promised in 1980. And most strikingly and recently: when the government in March 1985 was hit with the rude shock that groundnut growers (whose product once again had experienced a price rise on the world market) had opted not to sell to the state marketing system but instead to divert their crop illegally to the Gambia and elsewhere, the government's response was not to strengthen the controls intended to monopolize its earning of groundnuts foreign exchange; it was, instead, to announce a partial privatization of internal and external groundnuts marketing for next year.

Some might argue that the way the GOS has been pursuing hard reforms only proves that rigorous SAL implementation taught a valuable lesson. My own interpretation would be the reverse: recent behavior proves that Diouf and his government deserved alternative modalities that would have given them more benefit of the doubt earlier on.

I would note only one further reflection – one less optimistic but also fortified by latest developments, in this case the redoubled unreliability of groundnuts as a foreign exchange earner coupled with the continuing difficulties of domestic food production. The premise that economic success for Senegal depends on some kind of breakthrough in agriculture may be misguided. One should not downplay the importance of both the Senegalese and the outsiders doing everything they reasonably and imaginatively can to build agriculture. But, given the comparatively bleak experience and prospects in that sector, it may be wrong to hang the country's future on major near-term advances in farm production.

In part of their policy analysis and planning, at least, perhaps Senegal and its friends should focus more basically and broadly on human resources development and consider how to translate various new skills into the efficient production of a wider array of tradable goods and services. This is a disquieting proposition because it cannot yet be cast into concrete, actionable form. But its assumption that the economy's future could depend on the effectiveness with which the Senegalese and their aid donors collaborate in a new research and training agenda may be correct.

NOTES

1. In 1976, at the initiative of the then Chairman of the Development Assistance Committee and member of the OECD Secretariat, certain DAC member donor agencies (the group has since grown to some dozen donors including certain Arab/OPEC agencies) accepted the invitation of President Senghor of Senegal to meet with and institute a program of assistance to the member countries of the CILSS, which then consisted of the six Francophone Sahelian countries and since, with the addition of the Gambia and the Cape Verde Islands, has grown to a membership of eight. The (donor) Club des Amis du Sahel continues to be assisted by a small OECD staff in Paris.
2. Calculating GDPs per capita from data in the Annex Tables to World Bank (1982), they appear for the countries indicated, to have been the following in 1960 (all in 1960 U.S. dollars):

Senegal	$195
Ghana	$178
Ivory Coast	$161
Cameroon	$97
Kenya	$88
Nigeria	$61

   In terms of 1960 GNP per capita, calculated from the same source, Senegal was only third on the list, substantially outranked by the Ivory Coast, and slightly by Ghana. The GDP–GNP discrepancy presumably is explained by the very large number of expatriates, mostly French, who stayed on in Senegal – again, a post 'headquarters' phenomenon – and continued to stay on. Indigenous–expatriate participation and income disparities, especially at the skilled, professional, and executive levels of Senegal's urban labor market were treated in detail by Harold Lubell in vol. 4, on Human Resources, of the extensive report on the *Economics Trends and Prospects of Senegal* the World Bank completed in December 1979.
3. This very crude productivity comparison may be somewhat exaggerated because, as John Waterbury points out elsewhere in this volume, many workers counted as members of the agricultural labor force spend part of their time working elsewhere, especially in the tertiary sectors. Still, such is the case in many developing countries, especially with significant seasonal rural–urban migration. Many development economists would think of ratios of 3 or 4 to 1 as 'typical' of the relationships between nonagricultural and agricultural labor productivities, and so they are for a variety of Asian countries. Cases of extreme dualism seem to have been, and to remain, more common in Africa where, for example, the 1960 ratios of service output per worker to farm output per worker were 11 and 10 for the Ivory Coast and Kenya respectively. No doubt, like Senegal, these were cases reflecting a heavy presence of non-Africans, a point which is reinforced by the remarkably low 1960 ratio – only about 1.5 – for Nigeria, a country with relatively few Europeans.
4. Here, as in the previous case, the calculation is simply

$$\frac{\text{Services share of GDP}}{\text{services share of LF}} + \frac{\text{agricultural share of GDP}}{\text{agricultural share of LF}}$$

   with all the estimates being drawn from the statistical annex of the *World Development Report*.
5. The data in this paragraph are drawn from the World Bank's *World Development Reports*, Government of Senegal data provide only a slightly different picture for the 60s: investment rises 1.4 percent annually; otherwise there is agreement with the numbers in the text.

6. In its own retrospective assessments of the SAL the Bank has noted that, in contrast to the other major reform components of the SAL, in the agricultural reform component the Bank was not informed by Bank-financed technical assistance operations.
7. I am indebted for this formulation to a July 1984 seminar in Venice in which consultants to the Development Committee's Task Force on Concessional Flows were presenting some of their findings on aid effectiveness. The concept of matching the scale of policy instruments with the scale of policy targets emerged particularly in presentations by Dr. Alex Duncan of Oxford University and Professor Brian Van Arkedie of the Institute of Social Studies, the Hague.

Notes on Sources

This paper is overwhelmingly dependent on interviews with persons in official capacities whom I cannot identify and on official documentation not in the public domain. Thus it would be wholly misleading for me to provide a 'bibliography' of accessible sources that, in fact, have been only peripheral for my purposes. Accordingly, I am not attempting to list references beyond those cited in footnotes. But I shall be happy to respond to questions about sources insofar as I am at liberty to do so.

May 1985

The Authors

Sheldon Gellar, Visiting Associate Professor, Department of Political Science and Member, African Studies Center, Michigan State University, East Lansing.

Mark Gersovitz, Senior Research Economist and Public Policy Analyst, Woodrow Wilson School, Princeton University.

Sidi C. Jammeh, Doctoral Candidate, the Johns Hopkins University and SAIS, and consultant to the World Bank.

John P. Lewis, Professor of Economics and International Affairs and Director of the Research Program in Development Studies, Woodrow Wilson School and Department of Economics, Princeton University.

Jorge de Macedo, Assistant Professor of Economics and International Affairs, Woodrow Wilson School and Department of Economics, Princeton University, and Research Fellow, Center for Economic Policy Research (London) and National Bureau of Economic Research.

Jean Claude Nascimento, Professor of Economics, Ecole Supérieure de Gestion des Entreprises, Dakar.

Robert L. Tignor, Professor of History and Chairman, Department of History, Princeton University.

Laura Tuck, Economist/Senior Associate, International Science and Technology Institute, Washington, D.C.

John Waterbury, William Stewart Tod Professor of Politics and International Affairs, Woodrow Wilson School and Department of Politics, Princeton University.

Bibliography

Acharya, S. & B. Johnston. 1978. *Two Studies of Development in Sub-Sahara Africa.* World Bank Staff Working Paper, no. 30. October.

Adams, Adrian. 1977. *Le Long Voyage des Gens du Fleuve.* Paris: François Maspéro.

Adams, Dale. 1977. *Policy Issues in Rural Finance and Development.* Studies in Rural Finance. Ohio State University.

Albenque, D. 1974. *Organisation du Travail dans le Carré Ouolof.* CNRA. Bambey, Senegal.

Allen, P.R. 1976. *Organization and Administration of a Monetary Union.* Princeton Studies in International Finance. Princeton: International Finance Section.

Amin, Samir. 1973. *Neo-Colonialism in West Africa.* Harmondsworth: Penguin.

Anderson, Dennis and Mark Leiserson. 1980. 'Rural Nonfarm Employment in Developing Countries,' *Economic Development and Cultural Change,* 28, 2, January: 227-48.

AOF. 1909. *Journal Officiel de l'Afrique Occidentale Française.* May 1. SNA 1K61 (158).

————. 1928-33. *Bulletin Mensuel de l'Agence Economique.*

Aoki, Masanao. 1981. *Dynamic Analysis of Open Economies.* New York: Academic Press.

Aprin, Robert. 1980. *Développement et Résistance Paysanne: Le Cas des Soninkés de Bakel.* Mimeo, Paris.

Association Sud-Ouest d'Aide au Développement Internationale Agricole. 1981. *Propositions pour l'Organisation d'un Système de Crédit Agricole au Sénégal.* January.

Barlett, Peggy. 1980. 'Cost-Benefit Analysis: A Test of Alternative Methodologies,' in P.F. Barlett, ed., *Agricultural Decision Making: Anthropological Contributions to Rural Development.* New York: Academic Press.

Barnett, Douglas. 1979. *A Study of Farmers' Goals and Constraints: Their Effects on the Cultivation of Crops in Sine Saloum, Senegal.* M.A. Thesis, Purdue University. August.

Bates, Robert. 1981. *Market and States in Tropical Africa.* Berkeley: University of California Press.

Batude, Fernaud. 1941. *L'Arachide au Sénégal.* Paris: Recueil Sirey.

Bauer, P.T. 1954. *West African Trade: A Study of Competition, Oligopoly, and Monopoly in a Changing Economy.* London: Cambridge University Press.

BCEAO. 1965-1985. 'La Campagne Arachidière,' *Notes d'Information et Statistiques*. Dakar.

―――. 1976. 'Nouvelle Politique de la Monnaie et du Crédit de la Banque Centrale des Etats de l'Afrique de l'Ouest,' *Banques et Monnaies*, no. 236, February.

―――-a. 'Le Commerce Extérieur du Sénégal,' *Notes d'Information et Statistiques*. Dakar: various dates.

―――-b. 'Statistiques Economiques et Monétaires: Sénégal,' *Notes d'Information et Statistiques*. Dakar: various dates.

Beaudry-Somcynsky, Micheline. 1981. *Coopératives, Etat et Paysans. Rôle des Coopératives dans la Production Vivrière au Sénégal*. Sherbrooke: CEDEC.

Belloncle, Guy. 1964. *Le Mouvement Coopératif au Sénégal*, Ministère de l'Economie Rurale.

―――. 1978. *Coopératives et Développement en Afrique Noire Sahelienne*. Centre d'Etudes en Economie Coopérative, University of Quebec. Sherbrooke.

―――. 1980a. *Alphabétisation Fonctionnelle et Coopératives*. Mimeo, Dakar, May.

―――. 1980b. *L'Assainissement des Comptes: Mission Impossible?* Dakar, June.

―――. 1980c. *Peut-on Sauver les Coopératives Sénégalaises?* Paris, June.

Belloncle, Guy et al. 1982. *Alphabétisation et Gestion des Groupements Villageois en Afrique Sahelienne*. Paris: Editions Karthala.

Belloncle, Guy and Mamadou Diarra. 1983. 'Organisation et Gestion des Coopératives Agricoles en Afrique et Haiti,' *Archives de Sciences Sociales de la Coopération*, no. 63, January-March: 56-80.

Belloncle, Guy and Doménique Gentil. 1983. *Politiques et Structures de Promotion Coopérative Dans l'Afrique Sahelienne* (Haute-Volta, Mali, Sénégal). *Rapport de Synthèse*. COPAC. Paris, March.

Benoit-Cattin, Michel. 1982. *Recherche et Développement Agricole: Les Unités Expérimentales au Sine Saloum (1968-81)*. IRAT. Montpellier, March.

Berg, Elliot. 1980. *Reforming Grain Marketing Systems in West Africa: A Case Study of Mali*. ICRISAT: 147-72.

Berger, Suzanne. 1972. *Peasants Against Politics: Rural Organization in Brittany, 1911-1967*. Cambridge, Massachusetts: Harvard University Press.

Beurnier. 1935. *Rapport sur le Résultat des Ventes en Commun des Graines Déposées dans les Seccos des Sociétés de Prévoyance par les Adhérents*. SNA 2G 35-76, January.

Bhattia, R. 1982. *The West African Monetary Union - Experience with Monetary Arrangements, 1963-74*. IMF Departmental Memorandum. September.

Binswanger, Hans P. 1980. 'Attitudes Toward Risk: Experimental

Measurement in Rural India,' *American Journal of Agricultural Economics*, 62: 395-407.

Binswanger, Hans and Mark Rosenzweig. 1982. *Production Relations in Agriculture*. Discussion Paper no. 105. Woodrow Wilson School, Princeton University. June.

Bureau International de Travail, PECTA. 1980. *Revenus, Prix et Commerce International*, Mission sur l'Emploi au Sénégal. Dakar.

Blanchet, Gilles. 1983. *Elites et Changements en Afrique et au Sénégal*. Paris: Ed. Pedone.

Bloomfield, Arthur I. 1955.'National Economic Independence in Cambodia, Laos, and South Vietnam,' *Federal Reserve Bank of New York Monetary Review*, April: 40-43.

BNDS. 1977-78, 1978-79, 1979-80, 1980-81. *Rapport d'Activité*.

Boisson to Governor at Conakry. 1943. April 30. SNA 1R2(1).

Bourdin, Joel. 1980. *Monnaie et Politique Monétaire dans les Pays Africains de la Zone Franc*. Dakar: Les Nouvelles Editions Africaines.

Box, G.E.P. and D.A. Pierce. 1970. 'Distribution of Residual Autocorrelations in Autoregressive-Integrated Moving Average Time Series Models,' *Journal of the American Statistical Association*, 65: 1509-26.

Boyer, Marcel. 1935. *Les Sociétés Indigènes de Prévoyance de Secours et de Prêts Mutuels Agricoles en Afrique Occidentale Française*. Paris: Editions Domat-Montchrestien.

Branson, W. and L. Katseli. 1982. 'Currency Baskets and Real Effective Exchange Rates,' in M. Gersovitz, *et al.* eds. *The Theory and Experience of Economic Development*. London: Allen & Unwin: 194-214.

Branson, W. and J. Macedo. 1982. 'The Optimal Choice of Indicators for a Crawling Peg,' *Journal of International Money and Finance*, 2.

Brevie to Minister of Colonies. 1935. February 21. SNA 13G 6(17).

Brochier, Jacques. 1968. *La Diffusion du Progrès Technique en Milieu Rural Sénégalais*. Paris: Presses Universitaires de France.

Caisse Centrale de Crédit Agricole Mutuel. 1941. *Rapport Annuel*. SNA 2G 41-127.

Camboulives, Marguerite. 1967. *L'Organisation Coopérative au Sénégal*. Paris: A. Pedone.

Cavaille, M. 1937. *Rapport à la Commission Centrale de Surveillance des Comptes de Gestion de l'Exercice 1937 des Sociétés de Prévoyance du Sénégal*. SNA 2G 37-131.

Center for Research in Economic Development. 1982. *Consumption Effects of Agricultural Policies*. University of Michigan. Ann Arbor, February.

Cercle de Kaolack, Sud division de Kaffrine, Saloum Oriental. 1934. *Rapport Politique Annuel*. SNA 2G 34–89.

Chambas, G. 1980. *Financement Extérieur et Répartition des Revenus dans les Pays en Voie de Développement.* CERDI, Université de Clermont I. Clermont-Ferrand.

Chambas, G. *et al.* 1981. *Le Stabex au Sénégal.* CERDI Discussion Paper. Clermont Ferrand, July.

Chambas G. 1983. *The Effect of a Fixed Rate of Exchange in the Adjustment Process of Franc Area: the Case of Senegal.* Research proposal, CERDI. Clermont Ferrand, April.

Chambre de Commerce de Dakar. 1944. *Extrait du Procès-Verbal de la Séance du Novembre, 1944.* SNA IR 2(1).

Charbonneau, Jean and René. 1961. *Marchés et Marchands d'Afrique Noire.* Paris: La Colombe.

Christin, Ivan. 1982. *Les Flux Financiers au Sénégal.* The World Bank. Mimeo.

CILSS. 1977. *Marketing, Price Policy and Storage of Food Grains in the Sahel: Vol. 1 Synthesis.* CRED/USAID. August.

Cleave, John H. 1974. *African Farmers: Labor Use in the Development of Smallholder Agriculture.* New York: Praeger.

Cochemé, J. and P. Franquin. 1967. *An Agriclimatology Survey of a Semiarid Area in Africa South of the Sahara,* Technical Note no. 86. Geneva: World Meteorology Organization.

COGERAF. 1963. *Commercialisation des Arachides; Tome 1, Situation Actuelle.* Paris.

Cohen, William B. 1971. *Rulers of Empire: The French Colonial Service in Africa.* Stanford: Hoover Institution Press.

Colvin, Lucie, et al. 1981. *The Uprooted of the Western Sahel.* New York: Praeger.

CIEH. 1976. *République du Sénégal: Précipitations Journalières de l'Origine des Stations à 1965.* République Française, Ministère de la Coopération, Office de la Recherche Scientifique et Technique Outre-Mer. Paris.

Commission of the European Communities. 1981. *Comprehensive Report on the Export Earnings Stabilization System Established by the Lomé Convention for the Years 1975 to 1979.* Brussels.

Connolly, M. 1983. *Le Choix de Régimes de Change pour l'Afrique.* Mimeo, University of South Carolina, Columbia, S.C., July.

Conseil de la République. 1947. August 22. *Séance:* 1855-1856.

COPAC. 1983. *Le Système Coopératif Sénégalais.* Mimeo, Paris.

Copans, Jean. 1980. *Les Marabouts de l'Arachide: La Confrérie Mouride et les Paysans du Sénégal.* Paris: Le Sycomore.

Corden, M. 1972. *Monetary Integration.* Princeton Essay in International Finance no. 93. Princeton: International Finance Section.

Coulon, Christian. 1981. *Le Marabout et le Prince: Islam et Pouvoir au Sénégal.* Paris: Editions A. Pedone.

Crum, David L. 1984. 'Mali and UMOA: A Case-Study of Economic Integration,' *Journal of Modern African Studies,* September: 22, 469-486.

Daniel, J. n.d. *Grandeurs Caractéristiques de l'Economie Sénégalaise 1959-1979, Tableaux et Graphiques.* Mimeo, Ministère du Plan, Sénégal.

————. 1977. 'Le Tableau d'Echanges Interbranches de L'Economie Sénégalaise en 1974,' *Bulletin Semestriel d'Information sur l'Exécution du Plan*, 4: 65-73.

David, Philippe. 1980. *Les Navetanes: Histoire des Migrants Saisonniers de l'Arachide en Sénégambie: Des Origines à nos Jours.* Dakar: Les Nouvelles Editions Africaines.

De la Rocca. 1934. Reports of November 13 and December 16. SNA 13G 6(17).

Dervis, K., J. de Melo and S. Robinson. 1982. *General Equilibrium Models for Development Policy.* Cambridge: Cambridge University Press.

Desbordes, Jean-Gabriel. 1938. *L'Immigration Libano-Syrіène en Afrique Occidentale Française.* Poitiers: Imprimerie Moderne, Renault & Cie.

Desroches, Henri. 1976. *Le Projet Coopératif.* Paris: Editions Ouvrières.

Development Alternatives Inc. 1975. *Strategies for Small Farmer Development: an Empirical Study of Rural Development Projects.* Vol. 1, Final Report, prepared for USAID, Contract no. AID/CM/ta-c-73-41, May.

Dia, Mamadou. 1952. *Contribution à l'Etude du Mouvement Coopératif en Afrique Noire.* Paris: Présence Africaine.

————. 1976. *African Nations and World Solidarity.* New York: Praeger.

Diarasouba, Valy-Charles. 1968. *L'Evolution des Structures Agricoles du Sénégal.* Paris: Editions Cujas.

Diena, Cheikh Birago. 1981. *Les Effets Economiques Prévisibles du Contrat Plan sur le Développement du Bassin Arachidier.* SODEVA, Dakar, July.

Dione, A. 1980. *Essai d'Etude sur l'Equilibre Alimentaire dans les Exploitations du Suivi-Agronomie.* SODEVA. Sine-Saloum, August.

————. 1982. *Enquête sur la Dynamique de la Conservation des Semences Arachide dans la Région de Thiès.* SODEVA. Thiès, May.

Diop, Abdoulaye. 1982. 'Jeunesses en Développement, Memento d'une Périphérie: Une Expérience Associative du Foyer des Jeunes de Ronkh à l'Amicale Economique du Walo,' *Archives de Sciences Sociales de la Coopération et du Développement* 62, October-December: 108-127.

Diop, Amadou Bator. 1984. *Conseil Interministériel sur la Nouvelle Politique Agricole.* Ministère du Développement Rural. Dakar, March.

Diop, Assane Masson. 1971. 'Le Mouvement Coopératif Sénégalais.' *Revue Française d'Etudes Politiques Africaines*, no. 61, January: 49-61.

Diop, Serigne Lamine. 1983. *Discours Inaugural, Congrès Constitutif de la Féderation Nationale des Coopératives de Sénégal à Thiès 29 et 30 Janvier 1983.* Mimeo, Dakar.

Direction de la Coopération. 1981a. *Nouvelle Orientation de la Politique d'Education et de Formation Coopérative.* Mimeo, Dakar.

————. 1981b. *Rapport du Séminaire d'Orientation sur le Service de la Coopération.* Mimeo, Somone, June.

————. 1983a. *Rapport Final du Récyclage et d'Initiation des Formateurs des Services Régionaux de la Coopération et des Unions Régionales des Coopératives Agricoles – Thiès du 19 au 28 Avril 1983.* Mimeo, Dakar.

————. 1983b. *Rapport Final du Séminaire d'Evaluation des Opérations Consommation (Casamance, Sine-Saloum, Sénégal Oriental) du 10 au 16 Décembre 1982 à Kolda.* Mimeo, Dakar.

Direction de la Statistique. *Situation Economique du Sénégal.* Dakar: various dates.

Direction Générale de la Production Agricole. 1950-82. *Rapports Annuels.* Ministère de Développement Rural.

Dore, Emmanuel. 1981. *Commercialisation des Céréales au Sénégal en Relation avec un Projet de Création de Crédit Agricole.* Dakar, March.

Dreyfus to Lieutenant-Governor of Senegal. 1911. (September 1) SNA 1R61 (158).

Dumont, René. 1970. 'Le Mouvement Coopératif Africain: Plus d'Echecs que de Réussites,' *Revue Française d'Etudes Politiques Africaines,* 59, November: 37-53.

————. 1980. *L'Afrique Etranglée.* Paris: Seuil.

Dumont, René & M.F. Mottin. 1982. *Le Défi Sénégalais: Reconstruire les Terroirs, Libérer les Paysans.* ENDA, Série Etudes et Recherches, nos. 74-82. Dakar, June.

Fall, Moussa. 1979. 'Analyse Socio-Economique de l'Introduction de Techniques Nouvelles en Milieu Rural Sénégalais.' *Socio-Economic Constraints to Development of Semi-Arid Tropical Agriculture.* ICRISAT, International Workshop. Hyderabad, India: 298-404.

FAO. 1976. *Perspective Study on Agricultural Development in the Sahelian Countries.* Vol. I: The Main Report, Vol. II: Statistical Annex. Rome.

————. 1979, *Agrometeorological Crop Monitoring and Forecasting.* Rome: Food and Agriculture Organization.

Faye, Adama. 1983. *Techniques et Systèmes d'Amélioration de l'Alimentation du Bétail en Milieu Rural.* SIRA. February.

Faye, Jacques. 1981. 'Zonal Approach to Migration in the Senegalese Peanut Basin' in Lucie Colvin, et al.: 136-160.

Foltz, William. 1965. *From French West Africa to the Mali Federation.* New Haven: Yale University Press.

Fonds Commun des Sociétés de Prévoyance du Sénégal. 1937-38. *Compte de Gestion de l'Exercice, 1937-38, Extrait du Compte-Rendu sur la Situation Morale et Financière.* SNA 2G 38-126.

Fougeyrollas, Pierre. 1970. *Où Va le Sénégal?: Analyse Spectrale d'une Nation Africaine.* Paris: Editions Anthropos.

Founou-Tchuigoua, Bernard. 1981. *Fondements de l'Economie de Traite au Sénégal.* Paris: SILEX.

Fouquet, Joseph. 1958. *La Traite des Arachides dans le Pays de Kaolack et ses Conséquences Economiques, Sociales, et Juridiques.* St. Louis.

Frahan, Henri Bruno de. 1981. *Le Programme des Magasins Semenciers dans le Sine-Saloum.* ACOPAM–SODEVA, Kaolack, October 30.

France, Chambre des Députés. 1933. First Session, July 6: 3522-3561.

Frankel, S. Herbert. 1938. *Capital Investment in Africa: Its Course and Effects.* London: Oxford University Press.

Ganry, F. 1980. 'The Importance of Cultural Methods to Increase the Quantity of Nitrogen (N) Fixed by a Groundnut Crop in the Sudano-Sahelian Zone of Senegal,' *Organic Recycling in Africa.* FAO Soils Bulletin, no. 43. Rome: FAO: 168-75.

Garine de, I. 1960. *Budgets Familiaux et Alimentation dans la Région de Khombole.* Rome: FAO.

Gastellu, J.M. and B. Delpech. 1974. *Maintenance Sociale et Changement Economique au Sénégal, vol. 2. Pratique du Travail et Equilibres Sociaux en Milieu Serer.* Travaux et Documents de l'ORSTOM. Paris.

Gatin, A. 1968. *SATEC Sénégal: Bilan de Quatre Années de Vulgarisation et Thèmes Techniques au Sénégal.* Bambey, November: 26-28.

Gaye, Karim. 1963. 'Histoire du Mouvement Coopératif au Sénégal,' Banque Centrale des Etats de l'Afrique de l'Ouest: *Notes d'Information et Statistiques,* nos. 97-98, August and September: 1-8.

Geertz, Clifford. 1973. 'The Rotating Credit Association: A Middle Rung in Development.' *AID Spring Review of Small Farmer Credit. Special Papers, Informal Credit,* 15.

Geismar to Governor General. 1943. May 16. SNA 1R2(1).

Gellar, Sheldon. 1967. *The Politics of Development in Senegal.* Ph.D Dissertation, Columbia University.

———. 1982. *Senegal: An African Nation Between Islam and The West.* Boulder, Colorado: Westview Press.

———. 1983. *Circulaire 32 Revisited: Prospects for Revitalizing the Senegalese Cooperative Movement in the 1980s.* Mimeo, Princeton.

———. 1983a. *The Cooperative Movement and Senegalese Rural Development, 1960-1980.* Mimeo, Princeton.

———. 1984. *Rural Development Policy and Peasant Survival Strategies.* Manuscript, Princeton, February.

Gellar, Sheldon et al. 1980. *Animation Rurale and Rural Development: The Experience of Senegal.* Ithaca: Cornell University.

Gentil, Dominique. 1980. *Réforme Coopérative et Crédit Agricole dans le Sine-Saloum.* Mimeo, Dakar.

Gerry, Chris. 1979. 'Petty Production and Capitalist Production in Dakar: the Crisis of the Self-Employed,' *World Development,* 6, 9: 1147-60.

Gersovitz, Mark. 1986. 'Agro-Industrial Processing and Agricultural Pricing under Uncertainty,' *Review of Economic Studies,* 53: 153-69.

Giraud, Xavier. 1937. *L'Arachide Sénégalaise: Monographie d'Economie Coloniale.* Paris.

Goujon. 1951. Inspection des Coopératives Agricoles. *Rapport sur la Situation des Coopératives Agricoles à la Date du 31 Aout.* SNA 2G 51-147.

Guèye, Babacar and Mamadou Ndiaye. 1981. *Sections Villageoises et Développement Rural Intégré.* ENEA. Dakar.

Guillaumont, P. and S. 1980. *L'Evolution de la Zone Franc comme Système de Change,* CERDI Discussion Paper.

————. 1981. *Problèmes Posés par le Régime de Changes des Pays Africains ayant pour Monnaie les Francs CFA.* CERDI Discussion Paper. Clermont-Ferrand, February.

———— 1984. *Zone Franc et Développement Africain.* Paris: Economica.

Hart, Keith. 1982. *The Political Economy of West African Agriculture.* London: Cambridge University Press.

Hayward, J.E.S. 1959. 'Solidarity: The Social History of an Idea in Nineteenth-Century France,' *International Review of Social History,* 4, Part 2: 261-284.

————. 1961. 'The Official Social Philosophy of the French Third Republic: Léon Bourgeois and Solidarism,' *International Review of Social History,* 6, Part 1: 19-48.

————. 1963. 'Educational Pressure Groups and the Indoctrination of the Radical Ideology of Solidarism,' *International Review of Social History,* 8, Part 1: 1-17.

Helleiner, G.K. 1975. 'Smallholder Decision Making: Tropical African Evidence,' in L.G. Reynolds, ed., *Agriculture in Development Theory.* New Haven: Yale University Press: 27-52.

Hewitt, Adrian. 1983. 'Stabex: An Evaluation of the Economic Impact Over the First Five Years,' *World Development,* 11: 1005-27.

Heyer, Judith, Pepe Roberts and Gavin Williams (eds). 1981. *Rural Development in Tropical Africa.* London: Macmillan.

Hopkins, Elizabeth. 1975. *Wolof Farmers in Senegal: A Study of Responses to an Agricultural Extension Scheme.* Ph.D. Thesis, Sussex University, July.

House of Commons. 1937-38. Sessional Papers, *Report of the Commission on the Marketing of West African Cocoa.* Vol. 9, cmd 5854.

Hyden, Goran. 1973. *Efficiency Versus Distribution in East African Co-operatives: A Study in Organizational Conflicts.* Nairobi: East African Literature Bureau.

————. 1980. *Beyond Ujamaa in Tanzania.* Berkeley: University of California Press.

IBRD. 1974. *Senegal: Tradition, Diversification and Economic Development.* A World Bank Country Economic Report, Washington, D.C., November.

ICRISAT. 1979. *Socio-Economic Constraints to Development of Semi-Arid Tropical Agriculture.* (Proceedings of the International Workshop on Socioeconomic Constraints to Development of Semi-Arid Tropical Agriculture: February 19-23). Hyderabad, Andhra Pradesh, India.

International Monetary Fund. 1970. *Survey of African Economics,* vol. 3: Dahomey, Ivory Coast, Mauritania, Niger, Senegal, Togo and Upper Volta. Washington, D.C.

ISRA. 1980. *La Politique de Fertilisation du Mil et de l'Arachide dans le Nord, le Centre, et le Centre-sud du Sénégal.* CNRA, Bambey, April.

ITALCONSULT. 1970. *Réorganisation de l'ONCAD; Rapport Général sur la Coopération.* Rome.

Jalin, Inspection des Coopératives. 1951. *Rapport sur le Fonctionnement des Coopératives depuis leur Création.* June. SNA 2G:51-146.

Jones, David B. 1982. 'State Structures in New Nations: the Case of Primary Agricultural Marketing in Africa,' *Journal of Modern African Studies*, 20, 4: 553-69.

Kasse, M. 1984. 'Pour la Création d'un Système Monétaire Ouest-Africain.' Mimeo, University of Dakar, January.

Keita, Alioune. 1978. *Idéologie et Organisation du Mouvement Coopératif Sénégalais.* EHESS. Paris.

Kenen, P. 1978. 'The Role of Monetary Policy in Developing Countries in Central Bank of the Gambia,' in *The Role of Monetary Policy in Developing Countries.* Banjul.

Kleene, Paul. 1976. 'Notion d'Exploitation Agricole et Modernisation en Milieu Wolof Saloum,' *L'Agronomie Tropicale*, 31, 1, January-March: 63-82.

Klein, Martin. 1979. 'Colonial Rule and Structural Change: the Case of Sine-Saloum,' in Rita Cruise O'Brien, ed., *The Political Economy of Underdevelopment: Dependence in Senegal.* London: Sage: 75-69.

Kuhn Loeb Lehman Brothers, Lazard Frères, S.G. Warburg. 1982. *Senegal.* September.

Lamonde, P. and J.L. Tellier. 1982. *Le Développement Economique du Sénégal, 1961, 1981, 2001, Synthèse et Prospective.'* Draft, INRS (Canada), March.

Lebret, L.J. 1961. *Dynamique Concrète du Développement.* Paris: Economie et Humanisme, Editions Ouvrières.

Leite, S. 1982. 'Interest Rate Policies in West Africa,' *IMF Staff Papers*, 29, 1, March: 48-76.

LeMoigne, M. 1981. *Evaluation des Besoins en Intrants Agricoles.* CEEMAT, SODEVA, January.

Letiche, J. 1972. 'Conditions and Objectives of African Economic Development,' in L. Di Marco, ed. *International Economics and Development (Prebisch Festschrift).* New York: Academic Press.

Levi, John. 1979. 'Traditional Agricultural Capital Formation.' *World Development*, 7: 1053-62.

Levi, John and Michael Havinden. 1982. *Economics of African Agriculture.* London: Longman.

Lewis, John P. 1983. 'Can We Escape the Path of Mutual Injury?' in John P. Lewis and Valeriana Kallab, eds., *U.S. Foreign Policy and the Third World: Agenda 1983.* New York: Praeger.

Lewis, W.A. 1977. *The LDCs and Stable Exchange Rates*, Washington, D.C.: IMF.

Linacre, Edward T. 1977. 'A Simple Formula for Estimating Evaporation

Rates in Various Climates, Using Temperature Data Alone,' *Agricultural Meteorology*, 18: 409-24.

Lipton, Michael. 1977. *Why Poor People Stay Poor*. Cambridge: Harvard University Press.

Long, Millard F. 1973. *Conditions for Success of Public Credit Programs*. Background Paper for the Ford Foundation Seminar on Rural Development and Employment. Ibadan, Nigeria.

Ly, Abdoulaye. 1958. *L'Etat et la Production Paysanne; L'Etat et la Révolution au Sénégal, 1957-1958*. Paris: Présence Africain.

Macedo, J. 1982. *Portfolio Diversification and Currency Inconvertibility: Three Essays in International Monetary Economics*. Lisbon: New University of Lisbon.

————. 1985a. *Collective Pegging to a Single Currency: the West African Monetary Unions*. NBER Working Paper no. 1574, March.

————. 1985b. *Small Countries in Monetary Union: The Choice of Senegal*. RPDS Discussion Paper no. 117. Princeton University. March.

————. 1985c. *Small Countries in Monetary Unions: A Two-Tier Model*. NBER Working Paper no. 1634, June.

————. 1985d. 'Exchange Rate Volatility in an Interdependent World Economy,' Supplement to *World Economic Outlook 1984*, New York: United Nations.

Malley, François. 1969. *Esquisse pour un Portrait du Père Lebret*. Brussels: Pensée Catholique, Office Général du Livre.

Marston, R. 1984. 'Exchange-rate Unions as an Alternative to Flexible Exchange Rates: The Effects of Real and Monetary Disturbances,' in J. Bilson and R. Marston, eds., *Flexible Exchange Rates in Theory and Practice*. Chicago: University of Chicago Press.

Martens, George. 1983. 'Syndicats et Partis Politiques au Sénégal,' *Le Mois en Afrique*, 18: nos. 205-206: 72-113 and nos. 211-12: 54-68.

McKinnon, Ronald I. 1973. *Money and Capital in Economic Development*. Washington, D.C.: The Brookings Institution.

McLenaghan, J., S. Nsouli and K. Riechel. 1982. *Currency Convertibility in the Economic Community of West African States*, IMF Occasional Paper no. 13. Washington, D.C.

Michalet, C.A. and C. de Boissieu. 1983. *Le Défi du Développement Indépendant*. Paris: Ed. Rochevignes, ch. 4.

Michigan State University, African Rural Economy Program. 1981. *An Assessment of Animal Traction in Francophone West Africa*. Working Paper no. 34. East Lansing, March.

Miller, Leonard F. 1977. *Agricultural Credit and Finance in Africa*. The Rockefeller Foundation.

Minister of Colonies to Governor General, AOF. 1910. (February 24) SNA 1R6l (158).

Ministère d'Economie Rurale. 1965. *Programme de Développement Accéléré de la Productivité Arachidière*. Annual Report for 1964, SATEC. Dakar, March.

Ministère de l'Hydraulique. 1982. *Hydraulique Villageoise Nord-Sénégal: Rapport Final.* SONED-BRGM.

Ministère du Plan. 1968. *Trente Ans de Commercialisation Arachidière.* (1935/36–1966/67) June.

———. 1972. *Some Problems with Efforts to Provide Agricultural Credit to Small African Farmers.* Agricultural Development Council Research Training Network Workshop on 'Agricultural Credit to Small Farmers in LDCs.' Arlington, Virginia, April 6-7.

Ministry of Rural Development. 1980. *Comité de Réorganisation de la SODEVA.* January.

———. 1980. *Mission d'Etude du Système de Stockage Collectif des Semences d'Arachide au Niveau du Village en Gambie.* Dakar, February.

———. 1981. *Note sur la Fumure Minérale de l'Arachide.* (Robert Schilling) Dakar, November 12.

———1982. *La Production Semencière au Sénégal: Propositions d'Organisation.* SEMA-IRHO. January.

Miracle, D. & L. Cohen. 1980. 'Informal Savings Mobilization in Africa,' *Economic Development and Cultural Change*, 28, July: 701-24.

Miracle, Marvin. 1972. *Some Problems with Efforts To Provide Agricultural Credit to Small African Farmers.* Paper prepared for the Agricultural Development Council Research Training Network Workshop on Agricultural Credit to Small Farmers in DLCs. Hospitality House, Arlington, Virginia.

Mundell, R. 1961. 'A Theory of Optimum Currency Areas,' *American Economic Review*, 51, September: 657-65.

———. 1972. 'African Trade, Politics and Money,' in R. Tremblay, ed., *Africa and Monetary Integration, Afrique et Intégration Monétaire*, HRW.

Nascimento, J.C. 1981. *The Choice of an Optimum Exchange Currency Regime for Developing Economies – The Case of the West African Monetary Union.* Ph.D. Dissertation, State University of New York at Albany.

———. 1983. 'L'Appartenance de l'UMOA à la Zone Franc dans le Contexte Actual,' *Le Point Economique.* Dakar, October.

Ndiaye, J.P. 1978. *Enquête Fertilité en Milieu Paysan dans la Région du Sine-Saloum.* CNRA. Bambey, May.

Ndiaye, Madia. 1982. *L'Assainissement au Sine-Saloum.* SODEVA.

Newbery, David and Joseph Stiglitz. 1981. *The Theory of Commodity Price Stabilization: A Study in the Economics of Risk.* Oxford: Clarendon Press.

Nicholson, Sharon E. 1979. 'Revised Rainfall Series for the West African Subtropics,' *Monthly Weather Review*, 107: 620-4.

Nisbet, Charles. 1967. 'Interest Rates and Imperfect Competition in the Informal Credit Market of Rural Chile,' *Economic Development and Cultural Change*, 16, 1, October: 73-90.

Nyerere, Julius K. 1968. *Ujamaa Essays on Socialism*. New York: Oxford University Press.

O'Brien, Donal B. Cruise. 1971. *The Mourids of Senegal*. London: Faber and Faber.

———. 1975. *Saints and Politicians: Essays in the Organization of a Senegalese Peasant Society*. London: Cambridge University Press.

———. 1977. 'A Versatile Charisma. The Mouride Brotherhood 1968-75,' *Archives Européennes de Sociologie*, 18, 1.

———. 1979. 'Ruling Class and Peasantry in Senegal, 1960-1976,' in Rita Cruise O'Brien, ed., *The Political Economy of Underdevelopment: Dependence in Senegal*. Beverly Hills: Sage Publications.

OECD. 1973, 1981-1983. *Development Co-operation*. Paris: OECD.

Office des Affaires Economiques to Lieutenant-Governor of Senegal. 1907. (July 13) SNA 1R6l (158).

Ondo Ossa, A. and A. Tshibuabua Lapiquonne. 1982. 'Faut-il Réformer la Zone Franc?' *Etudes Politiques, Economiques et Sociologiques Africaines*. Libreville.

ONCAD. 1977. 'Le Crédit Agricole Sénégal,' *Salon Africain sur l'Agriculture et l'Hydraulique à Dakar*. December.

Ortiz, Sutti. 1980. 'Forecasts, Decisions and the Farmer's Response to Uncertain Environments' in Barlett.

Pani, P.K. 1966. 'Cultivator's Demand for Credit: A Cross Section Analysis,' *International Economic Review*, 7, 2, May: 176-203.

Pélissier, Paul. 1966. *Les Paysans du Sénégal: Les Civilisations Agraires du Cayor à la Casamance*. Saint-Yrieux: Imprimerie Fabrègue.

———. 1970. *Les Effets de l'Opération Arachide/Mil dans les Régions de Thiès, Diourbel et Kaolack: Rapport de Synthèse*. Dakar.

Pince, Gérard. 1979. *Rapport de Mission sur le Fonctionnement du Crédit Agricole dans la Région du Sine-Saloum*. Mimeo, Dakar.

———. 1981. *Notes d'Etudes du Groupe de Travail Chargé de la Réforme du Crédit Agricole au Sénégal*. Mimeo, Dakar.

Plane, P. 1983a. *Taux d'Echange en Economie Sous-développée; Essai de Détermination pour Dix Pays de l'Afrique de l'Ouest*. CERDI Discussion Paper no. 12. Clermont Ferrand.

———. 1983b. *Problèmes Posés par la Mesure de la Surévaluation ou Sous-évaluation des Monnaies Africaines*. CERDI Discussion paper. Clermont Ferrand, June.

Please, Stanley. 1984a. 'The World Bank: Lending for Structural Adjustment,' in Richard Feinberg and Valeriana Kallab, eds., *Adjustment Crisis in the Third World*. Overseas Development Council. Transaction Books.

———. 1984b. *The Hobbled Giant: Essays on the World Bank*. Boulder: Westview Press.

Portères, R. 1952. *Aménagement de l'Economie Agricole et Rurale au Sénégal*. Haut Commissariat de la République du Sénégal. vol. 3.

Poulain, J.F. 1980. 'Crop Residues in Traditional Cropping Systems,' in

Organic Recycling in Africa, FAO Soils Bulletin no. 3. Rome: 38-71.

Price, Robert. 1975. *Society and Bureaucracy: Contemporary Ghana.* Berkeley and Los Angeles: University of California Press.

Raffinot, M. 1982. 'Gestion Etatique de la Monnaie, Parités Fixés et Dépendance: le Cas de la Zone Franc,' *Tiers-Monde*, July.

Rapport de Présentation à la Commission Centrale de Surveillance des Comptes de Gestion de l'Exercice, 1937-38 des Sociétés de Prévoyance du Sénégal. SNA 2G 38-125.

Rapport Economique Annuel. 1974. SNA 2G47-26(1).

Rapport Economique Annuel. 1974. SNA 2G49-69.

Rapport Moral et Financier sur l'Activité des Sociétés Indigènes de Prévoyance du Sénégal pour l'Exercice, 1943-44. SNA 2G 44-159.

Rapport Moral et Financier sur l'Activité des Sociétés de Prévoyance du Sénégal au Cours de l'Exercice, 1950-51. SNA 2G 51-149.

Rapport sur l'Activité des Sociétés de Prévoyance au Cours de l'Exercice, 1940. SNA 2G 41-129.

Raulin, H. 1976. 'Organized Cooperation and Spontaneous Cooperation in Africa (Niger Republic),' in J. Nash & N. Hopkins, eds., *Popular Participation in Social Change.* Mouton: 35-43.

Ravenhill, John. 1984. 'What is to be Done for Third World Commodity Exporters? An Evaluation of the STABEX Scheme,' *International Organization*, 38: 537-74.

Ray, Edward. 1981. *The Role of Finance in Rural Development.* Background Paper No. 5. World Bank Colloquium on Rural Finance, September.

Reboul, Claude. 1972. *Structures Agraires et Problèmes du Développement au Sénégal, les Unités Expérimentales du Sine-Saloum.* INRA. Paris, June.

République Française, Ministère des Relations Extérieures, Coopération et Développement. 1982. 'Evaluations.' *Evaluation de la Filière Arachide au Sénégal*, November.

République de Sénégal, Ministère de l'Hydraulique. 1982. *Hydraulique Villageoise Nord-Sénégal Rapport Final.* SONED-BRGM. July.

Robinson, Kenneth. 1950. 'The Sociétés de Prévoyance in French West Africa,' *Journal of African Administration*, 2, 4:29-34.

Robson, P. 1983. *Integration, Development and Equity: Economic Integration in West Africa.* London: Allen & Unwin.

Roch, J. 1975. 'Les Migrations Economiques de Saison Sèche en Bassin Arachidier Sénégalais,' *Cahiers ORSTOM*, série Sci. Hum. 12, 1.

Rocheteau, G. 1972. 'The Modernization of Agriculture: Land Utilization and the Preference for Consumption Crops in the Groundnut Basin of Senegal,' in Pierre Cantrelle, ed., *Population in African Development.* Dolhain, Belgium: Ordina Editions: 461-68.

Ross, Clark. 1979. *A Village Level Study of Producer Grain Transactions in Rural Senegal.* Discussion Paper no. 81. University of Michigan, Center for Research on Economic Development. Ann Arbor, June.

Russell, C.S. and N.K. Nicholson, eds. 1981. *Public Choice and Rural Development*. Washington, D.C.: Resources for the Future.

Sackiness, Lutz. 1982. *Approche d'une Politique d'Education Coopérative en Méthodes et Actions*. Dakar: Fondation Frederick Ebert.

Sagna, Jean Baptiste and Abdourahmane Cissé. 1981. *Le Projet Rural de Sédhiou et Le Mouvement Coopératif, Son Expérience de Réorganisation dans la Zone-Test de Marsassoum*. Mimeo, Dakar.

Sarr, Désiré. 1980. *Contribution à la Connaissance Socio-économique de la Zone Ndiemane* (Dept of Bambey). SERST, ISRA. March.

Schulter, Michael G. and Gokul O. Parith. 1974. *The Interaction of Cooperative Credit and Uncertainty in Small Farmer Adoption of New Cereal Varieties*. Occasional Paper No. 61. Department of Agricultural Economics, Cornell University, Employment and Income Distribution Project. July.

Schumacher, Edward J. 1975. *Politics, Bureaucracy, and Rural Development in Senegal*. Berkeley: University of California Press.

Sene, C. 1983. *Etude sur les Pertes de Devises: Le Cas des Organismes de Gestion de Devises au Sénégal*. Draft, CODESRIA. Dakar, February.

Sene, Djibril. 1980. *Communication du Conseil de Cabinet sur les Conclusions des Travaux de la Commission Nationale Ad Hoc de Réstructuration et de Réforme de l'ONCAD*. Mimeo, Dakar, February 18.

———. 1980. *La Réforme et la Rédynamisation des Structures d'Encadrement Rural*. Mimeo, Dakar, April 12.

Sene, Ibrahima. 1981. *Eléments de Réflexion pour une Relance de la Production Arachidière au Sine-Saloum*. Inspection Régionale de la Production Agricole. Kaolack, May.

———. 1981a. *Quelques Remarques sur le Différend ISRA-IFDC sur la Fumure Minérale au Sénégal: l'Example du Sine-Saloum*. Inspection Régionale de la Production Agricole. Kaolack, May 30.

———. 1982. *Réflexion sur la Commercialisation du Mil au Sénégal*. Inspection Régionale de la Production Agricole. Kaolack, February.

Sene, Papa Mamadou. 1980. *Rapport sur la Première Phase de l'Expérience de Réorganisation dans le Département de Mbour (10-29 janvier 1980)*. ENEA. Dakar.

———. 1982. 'La Mise en Point d'un Système de Comptabilité en Langue Joola et Mandinka à l'Intention des Groupements Villageois du PIDAC,' in Guy Belloncle, et al., *Alphabétisation et Gestion des Groupements Villageois en Afrique Sahelienne*. Paris: Editions Karthala.

Sénégal en Chiffres. 1983. Société Africaine d'Edition.

Senghor, Léopold Sédar. 1961. *Nation et Voie Africaine du Socialisme*. Paris: Présence Africaine.

———. 1968. *Politique, Nation, et Développement Moderne*. Rufisque: Imprimerie Nationale.

Shearer, Eric. 1982. *An Evaluation of the PIDAC Credit Program*. USAID evaluation.

Singh, Ambika. 1975. 'Use of Organic Materials and Green Manures as Fertilizers in Developing Countries,' in *Organic Materials as Fertilizers*. Rome: FAO Soils Bulletin, no. 27: 19-30.

Société Indigène de Prévoyance. 1933. *Rapport Annuel*. Sine-Saloum, SNA 2G 34-74.

SODEVA. 1970. *Aperçu sur la Mise en Oeuvre des Facteurs de Production dans un Carré*. BEM. Dakar.

——. 1971. *Les Débouches et la Commercialisation des Céréales Locales (Mil-Sorgho-Mais) au Sénégal dan le Cadre des Projets de la SODEVA*. Dakar.

——. 1973. *Résultats des Enquêtes sur les Structures d'Exploitation dans la Région du Sine-Saloum: 1971*. Dakar, July.

——. 1979a. *Rapport Présenté aux Journées d'Etudes de la SODEVA*. Dakar, May.

——. 1979b. *Rapport Présenté aux Journées d'Etudes de la SODEVA, 11, 12, 13 Juin 1979*. Mimeo, Dakar.

—— (Paul Pélissier). 1979c. *Comité de Réorganisation de la SODEVA: Rapport Provisoire au 16/11/79*.

——. 1979d. *Réponse de l'Arachide et du Mil à NPK dans le Bassin Arachidier du Sénégal, Rapport Provisoire du Consultant*. International Fertilizer Development Center. November.

——. 1981/82. *Rapport de Suivi Embouche Bovine*.

——. *Lettre de Mission Confiée à la SODEVA par le Gouvernement du Sénégal*. 1981/82-1983/84.

——. 1982. *Programme Technique: Réalisations de la Campagne 1981/82, Objectifs de la Campagne 1982/86*. Dakar, March.

SONED. 1977. *Programme Agricole: Bilan Diagnostic; Analyse des Systèmes de Production Agricole et Prospectives*. Tome III, SODEVA. Dakar, July.

——. 1977a. *Synthèse Comparative des Structures de Devéloppement Rurale*. Dakar.

——. 1978. 'Etude de Réorganisation de la Campagne Arachidière.' Rapport Intermédiaire. *La Collecte*, vol. 1, Ministère du Plan et de la Coopération. October.

——. 1979. *Modelisation des Prix*. Dakar.

Sow, Abdoul. 1976-77. *Les Sociétés Indigènes de Prévoyance du Sénégal, 1909-1936*. Mémoire de Maitrise, Université de Dakar, Faculté des Lettres et Sciences Humaines, Département Histoire.

Stern, Ernest. 1983. 'World Bank Financing of Structural Adjustment,' in John Williamson, ed. *IMF Conditionality*. Washington, D.C.: Institute for International Economics. Distributed by MIT Press: 87-107.

Stormal-Weigal, Bozena. 1981. *Economies Rurales de la Région de Thiès et de Diourbel*. Department of Agricultural Economics, Purdue University. March.

Suret-Canale, Jean. 1971. *French Colonialism in Tropical Africa, 1900-1945*, trans. Till Gottheimer. London: Hurst.

Sy, Cheikh Tidiane. 1969. *La Confrèrie Sénégalaise des Mourides, Un Essai sur l'Islam au Sénégal.* Paris: Présence Africain.

Sy, Cheikh Tidiane. 1979. *L'ONCAD Est-il un Mal Nécessaire?* Mimeo, Dakar. (Two authors with identical names.)

Taylor, D. 1982. 'Official Intervention in the Foreign Exchange Market.' *Journal of Political Economy,* 90, 2, April: 356-68.

Thénevin, Pierre and J.M. Yung. 1982. *Evaluation de la Filière Arachide au Sénégal.* Paris: Ministère des Relations Extérieurs, Coopération et Développement.

Thiam, Habib. 1972. *Rapport sur la Réorganisation de l'ONCAD.* Mimeo, Dakar.

Touré, Aissatou. 1982. *Bilan Céréalier dans le Bassin Arachidier Depuis 1960 et Perspectives des Années 1980.* SODEVA. Dakar.

Touré, El Hadj Oumar. 1981. *Cadre d'Action et Mission de la Société: Politique Générale et Stratégie d'Intervention.* SODEVA, Journées de Synthèse. March.

United Nations Research Institute for Development (UNRISD). 1975. *Rural Cooperatives as Agents of Change: A Research Report and a Debate.* Geneva: UNRISD.

USAID, Africa Bureau: Office of Technical Resources. 1983a. *African Bureau Agricultural Research Strategy Paper.* April 4.

USAID-Senegal. 1983b. 'Economic, Technical and Financial Justification for Fertilizer Imports,' in *Program Assistance Approval Document.* Annex F. May: 685-0249.

Vakil, F. 1981. *Macro-economic Issues and Aid Assistance, Balance of Payments and Agricultural Pricing Reforms in Senegal: An Analysis.* Mimeo, Louis Berger, Inc., Dakar. December.

Van-Chi Bonnardel, Régine Nguyen. 1978. *Vie de Relations au Sénégal: La Circulation des Biens.* IFAN. Dakar.

Van Wijnbergen, S. 1981. *Interest Rate Management in LDCs: Theory and Some Simulation Results for S. Korea.* Development Research Center. The World Bank. May.

Vanhaeverbeke, André. 1970. *Rémunération du Travail et Commerce Extérieur: Essor d'une Economie Paysanne Exportatrice et Termes de l'Echange des Producteurs d'Arachides au Sénégal.* Louvain: Centre de Recherches des Pays en Développement.

Vercambre, Martine. 1974. *Unités Experimentales du Sine-Saloum: Revenus et Dépenses dans Deux Carrés Wolofs 1972-73.* Institut des Recherches Agronomiques Tropicales, January.

Vinay, B. 1980. *Zone Franc et Coopération Monétaire.* Paris: Ministry of Cooperation.

Vogel, Robert. 1982. *Savings Mobilization: The Forgotten Half of Rural Finance.* World Bank Colloquium on Rural Finance, Discussion Paper No. 6, Revised Version January.

Wade, A. 1975. 'Vers une Monnaie Africaine,' *Jeune Afrique,* no. 743, April.

Ware, Helen. 1977. 'Economic Strategy and the Number of Children,' in John C. Caldwell, ed., *The Persistence of High Fertility*. Family and Fertility Change series: 1, pt. 2, v. 2, Canberra.

Weigel, J.-Y. 1982. *Migration et Production Domestique des Soninké du Sénégal*. Paris: ORSTOM.

Weiner, J.S. 1980. 'Work and Well-being in Savanna Environments: Physiological Considerations,' in D.R. Harris, ed., *Human Ecology in Savanna Environments*. London: Academic Press.

Wibaux, Fernaud. 1953. *Le Mouvement Coopératif en Afrique Occidentale Française*. Thèse d'Etat.

Williamson, John. 1982. 'A Survey of the Literature of Optimal Peg,' *Journal of Development Economics*, 11, 1: 39-61.

Winstanley, Derek. 1976. 'Climatic Changes in the Future of the Sahel,' in M.H. Glantz, ed., *The Politics of Natural Disaster: The Case of the Sahel Drought*. New York: Praeger: 189-213.

World Bank. 1979. *The Economic Trends and Prospects of Senegal* (in four volumes), Report no. 1720a-SE, December.

———. 1982, 1983. *World Development Report*. Washington: World Bank.

Wright, Gordon. 1964. *Rural Revolution in France: The Peasantry in the Twentieth Century*. Stanford.

Yeates, A.J. 1978. 'Monopoly Power, Barriers to Competition and the Pattern of Price Differentials in International Trade,' *Journal of Development Economics*, 5, 2: 167-80.

Young, Crawford, Neal P. Sherman and Tim H. Rose. 1981. *Cooperatives and Development: Agricultural Politics in Ghana and Uganda*. Madison: The University of Wisconsin Press.

Index

Index

ACP (African, Caribbean, Pacific
   countries party to the Lomé
   agreement), 299
ADCS (Association pour la Défense du
   Consommateur Sénégalaise), 235
African Socialism, 7, 8, 124, 125, 198,
   208
Afrique Occidentale Française (AOF),
   101
agricultural policy in Senegal since
   1960,
   overview of, 5–14
   compared with other developing
      countries, 5
   description of, 7–14
   problems involved, 5–7
agricultural price decision-making *see*
   price decision-making, agricultural
agricultural reform, World Bank's view
   of, 309–12
Agriculture, Ministry of, 213 *see also*
   Ministry of Rural Development
aid in relation to structural adjustment,
   3, 283–325
   donor coordination, 319–22
   economic history of Senegal *1960–78*,
      289–96
   flow of external resources: aid
      impacts, 3, 315–19
   foreign aid and those who supply it,
      283–8
   cast of donors, 285–8
   scale of aid, 284–5
   scope of aid and aid policy issues,
      283–4
   growing recognition of need for
      structural adjustment, 296–302
   aggravating circumstances, 297–8
   competing reactions, 298–302
   IMF, World Bank and structural
      adjustment, 302–15
   assessment, 312–15
   characteristics of EFF and SAL,
      302–4
   commitments of Senegal, 304–7
   implementation and non-
      implementation, 307–9

(aid *contd.*)
   stalemate over agricultural reform,
      309–12
   recent developments (since 1984),
      322–4
   see also names of donors
Albenque, D., 210
Algeria, 93
Allen, P.R., 278
allocation of resources, 172–3, 184
Aménagement du Territoire, 74
Amin, Samir, 6
Angola, 100
animal fattening (*embouche bovine*),
   216, 217, 218
animal husbandry, 65, 87, 197
   see also animal fattening; cattle; herd
      management; livestock as a form
      of savings; oxen
animal population growth, 5
animal traction, *see* TBFF *thème;*
   traction bovine thème
Animation Féminine, 151
Animation Rurale, 8, 128, 132, 148, 192
annulment of debts, 9, 11, 13, 137, 139,
   165–6, 169–70, 171–2, 191, 203,
   207, 297, 298, 312
AOF (Afrique Occidentale Française),
   101
Aoki, Masanao, 248
Arab aid, 288, 295, 299–300, 308, 318,
   321, 322, 324 n1
Argentina, 265
Ariza-Nino, Edgar, 54
assainissement des comptes des
   coopératives, 204, 205, 207
assakas, 84
assets *see* collateral; rural asset
   management; savings/assets
Association pour la Défense du
   Consommateur Sénégalaise
   (ADCS), 235
associations des femmes, 219
Associations d'Intérêt Rural, 128
auto encadrement strategy, 148

Bakel region, 63

Printed in the United States
by Baker & Taylor Publisher Services

Printed in the United States
by Baker & Taylor Publisher Services